ST2

YO-AAI-743

G

# BLACK ENTERPRISE, INC.

BLACK ENTERPRISE, INC. *is the starting point for any competent analysis of where Black business is going in this country today.* In recent years, millions of dollars have been spent on programs designed to help Black Americans start businesses. Community Business Development Organizations (CBDO) have provided much of the management and financial support to Blacks who had ambitions of starting their own businesses, but who possessed limited experience and little capital. Public funds and CBDO resources are keeping these fledgling businesses alive, yet few studies have dealt with the CBDO's effectiveness and the experiences of Black businessmen.

These nine case studies provide a penetrating look at the role CBDOs have played and the Black businessmen they have assisted. Each case presents facts on each businessman, from his initial involvement with the CBDO through such recurring problems as

(*continued on back flap*)

(*continued from front flap*)

low initial financing, insufficient management skills, and inadequate CBDO support.

BLACK ENTERPRISE, INC. deserves the attention of all those concerned with the future of Black business development.

# BLACK ENTERPRISE, INC.

## CASE STUDIES OF A NEW EXPERIMENT IN BLACK BUSINESS DEVELOPMENT

ALVIN N. PURYEAR, Ph.D.

AND

CHARLES A. WEST

ANCHOR PRESS/DOUBLEDAY

GARDEN CITY, NEW YORK

1973

Published simultaneously in hard and paperback editions by Anchor Press/Doubleday & Company, Inc. in 1973.

The authors gratefully acknowledge permission to print a portion of *Getting It Together* by John Seder and Berkeley G. Burrell, published by Harcourt Brace Jovanovich, Inc. in 1971. Permission granted by the publisher.

TO OUR WIVES

1742191

# CONTENTS

# PREFACE

Three years ago the authors had an opportunity to observe firsthand one of the nation's largest community organizations designed to help American blacks enter business. Located in Brooklyn, New York, the Bedford-Stuyvesant Restoration Corporation was dedicated to the economic development of the nation's second largest black ghetto. During those early days as we watched the movement of Restoration's business development program, we became fascinated with the necessity of researching the initiation, development, and accomplishments of similar programs across the country.

The Bedford-Stuyvesant story was well-known. In 1966 the late Senator Robert Kennedy had taken a walking tour of Bedford-Stuyvesant and was shocked by the poverty of the community. By 1967 he had convinced white leaders of New York City's business community to create the Bedford-Stuyvesant Development and Services (D & S) Corporation as a technical assistance organization; he survived the revolt of one black organization and finally formed a second community-based organization—the Restoration Corporation; he recruited a white civil rights lawyer to serve as president of the D & S Corporation; he found a highly capable black to run the Restoration Corporation; and he co-sponsored legislation which subsequently has pumped over $30,000,000 of federal aid into the community.

As we conducted our investigations, we found that while the Bedford-Stuyvesant story was well-known and the stories of similar agencies were emerging, little was known about the types of persons being assisted by these community programs. Many knew the story of the few successful black businessmen, but no one was looking at the important relationship which was developing between the community business development organizations and the businessmen they were helping. We concluded that this emerging relationship should be investigated and analyzed, since it is these newly created community-based development corporations which are trying to fill the century-old entrepreneurial vacuum existing in the black community.

Having decided that this was a fertile area for investigation, we began gathering data from the nation's largest community-based business development programs. The emerging pattern was clear: no agency could guarantee success to the black entrepreneur—an agency could only minimize his chances for failure. Understanding this we then began to examine the problem-solving efforts of various agencies, the result of which are nine case studies showing the learning experiences resulting from these community efforts. We feel these learning experiences will enable such agencies to improve upon their services and eventually foster the development of an entrepreneurial base in the black community. It is through viewing the learning experiences of these organizations and entrepreneurs that the reader will improve his understanding of the problems involved in and efforts expended on behalf of black business development, in general, and the black businessman, in particular.

Though the emphasis of this book is on black business development as a learning experience, it also touches upon some of the theoretical notions surrounding the value of business for the development of depressed communities. It is only through a thorough understanding of the theoretical concepts that one is able to appreciate the *realities* of black business development and to determine to what degree reality coincides with theory. As the reader becomes aware of certain realities, he should begin to have implicit feelings about the important *and* correct techniques which must be employed to launch and operate successful black-owned ventures. So while this volume is not intended to be a "cookbook," it will, by necessity, become a guide to successful black business development.

We feel that our effort should be of interest to several groups. Its initial appeal should be to the students in business and economics, as well as the enrollees of Black Studies programs, who have certain preconceived notions about this phenomenon. Perhaps, for the first time, they will have the ingredients necessary really to understand, through case examples, the total implications of the subject.

A second group of interested readers will be public officials at the local, state, and national levels who are responsible for providing much of the support for these programs. Crucial to these officials are the answers provided by this analysis of the experiences of black businessmen and the groups assisting these entrepreneurs.

A third and equally important group of readers will be community-based groups who view business development as one mechanism for bringing their communities back into the mainstream of American society. This book will enable these community leaders to avoid many of the pitfalls inherent in such programs.

A fourth group will be businessmen whose corporations must exist in close proximity to the depressed communities of our cities. This corporate interest, as well as a desire to become involved in such rehabilitating efforts, will make the study required reading for all the industrial leaders of this country.

Finally, this book will appeal to the interested observer who wants to be informed about the events of his times. It will give to him the conclusive answer to the question: "Just how effective are programs that put blacks into business?"

As one might expect, there was a continuous temptation to judge the effectiveness of business development programs from a cost benefit view; from a political view; from an ideological view on the relevance of capitalism; and from many other perspectives. Despite many pressures, we were determined to focus this effort only on the economic contributions that the community-based group made to the black businessman. In later volumes we will look at these other issues, but let it suffice now to measure this first element.

This book has benefited from the direct and indirect support of several persons. Special attention must be paid to Franklin Thomas, president of the Restoration Corporation, and John Doar, president of the D & S Corporation, for it was only through our initial involvement with their organizations that we were able to get our first insight into black business development. Credit should also be signaled out for Benno Schmidt and Justice Thomas Jones, the respective chairmen of the D & S and Restoration boards, who best exemplify an emerging black/white partnership in economic development. Finally, we pay tribute to Robert F. Kennedy, who was gone before we entered upon the community business development scene, but whose inspiration filtered down through the Doars, Thomases, Joneses, and Schmidts, and convinced us that this investigation should be undertaken.

As in all such projects as this, we are indebted to many persons for their assistance. First, we must acknowledge the sound recommendations of those who read and commented on various sections of our manuscript. Thus, we extend a very special note of appreciation to Professors Thomas Gardner, Philip Harris, and Robert Parket of the Bernard M. Baruch College; Dr. Courtney Blackman, the governor of the Central Bank of Barbados; William Young III and David Boone of Boone, Young and Associates, Inc.; Dr. Robert Hearn of the New School for Social Research; Hassell McClellan of The Circle, Inc.; John Oxendine of Fry Consultants, Inc.; Maurice Emeka of the Black Economic Research Center; Charles J. Hawkins of Washington Shores Savings and Loan Association; Professor Isaiah of the University of Maryland; Professor William Davis, Jr., of the Massachusetts Institute of Technology; and E. B. Williams of Morehouse College.

Special words of thanks are due to Leon Wright of Inner City Merchandisers, Inc., an innovative black entrepreneur, whose practical guidance was instrumental in helping us to choose among the many data we had collected for the cases compiled for this volume. We also gratefully acknowledge the contributions of Ms. Anna Johnson, who provided critically needed secretarial assistance whenever it was necessary.

Last, but far from least, words of appreciation are due our wives: to Catherine W. Puryear and to Nadyne Jackson West for their patience in what must now appear to be a never-ending succession of research projects.

*December 1972*                                     ALVIN N. PURYEAR
                                                    CHARLES A. WEST

# BLACK ENTERPRISE, INC.

# I

# The Evolution
# of Black Business Development

This section presents the background to our presentation of nine case studies of black entrepreneurs. It describes briefly the parallel development of American and black business development in the United States.

# 1

# ONE ASPECT
# OF A COMPLEX PROBLEM

## THE COMMUNITY
## BUSINESS DEVELOPMENT ORGANIZATION
## (CBDO)

On December 2, 1969, Kenneth Alston, a Chicago real estate dealer, took over his deceased cousin's new plastics company. By the end of 1970 the business had failed and Alston lamented:

I should not have attempted to take over and run the company. I know now that it was not my cup of tea. I'm a real estate man. I guess I was so emotionally concerned about all the work that (cousin) Cliff had put into this thing that I did not want to see it go. You know I was very naïve about a lot of things. I had thought that by getting myself a good board of directors and advisers, that they would help me operate the company, but I never saw any of those people more than once or twice. Every time I looked around there was a problem: rent was due, salaries were due, material had to be paid for—and these things were high. I never realized that a business could eat up so much money.

I thought that I was having problems with . . . corporations being unresponsive (to my bids) and believed that if I went after government business, things would be better. Well, brother, let me tell you, the government has ninety different ways of jerking you around. And they can have that government business; the time and effort just ain't worth it . . .

Well, I've learned my lesson and . . . the manufacturing business you can have. People talk about business as though there is something romantic about it, but *business is a lot more than a notion—a hell of a lot more.*

In December 1971 Gilroy Black, a forty-two-year-old Watts

(Los Angeles) security guard service operator who was running into severe cash shortages, said:

I made several mistakes and had it not been for the CBDO . . . I would have been wiped out. I started off putting a lot of money in renovations and furniture. Later, when I needed money, I realized that I would have been much better off to put one-third of the [same] money into renovations and furniture and fixtures . . .
Another mistake I made was staffing up too soon. Here again I could have saved a lot of money that might have allowed me to take on additional work . . . And the biggest lesson of all was not to mess around with [paying] those taxes. They can get you in trouble . . . Those Internal Revenue boys will put you in jail for messing with Uncle Sam's money.

On May 28, 1970, Larry Holmes bought the San Francisco radio and television repair store where he had worked for thirteen years. One year later his shop was operating at a breakeven position and he said:

I dreamed that one day I would own a radio and TV store. In fact, I had gotten up in my thirties and it looked like I would be a TV repairman all my life. It's bad to say, but if old man Krescent hadn't gotten ill, I probably never would have attempted to start my own business.
But my problems were just beginning for I didn't know anything about running a business. I had never been allowed to see the books; all I knew about was fixing radio and TV sets.
If I had it to do all over again, I would still do it [start a business], because that is the only way we are going to have anything. *We must start businesses and then our children can take them over. That's what the whites do.*

Ken Alston, Gil Black, and Larry Holmes have three things in common: they are *black,* they received financial and management assistance from a *Community Business Development Organization* (*CBDO*), and they are similar to thousands of other blacks who are trying "to get a piece of the action" with the assistance of Community Business Development Organizations.
Alston, Black, and Holmes are but three of this book's case studies which detail the histories and operations of nine black-owned

4                                   BLACK ENTERPRISE, INC.

small businesses. In addition to relating the experiences of these black entrepreneurs, this book also begins to examine the thesis that integral to the development of black businesses in America is the presence of the CBDO as a catalytic agency.

It is generally known that blacks want to own businesses— that is consistent with the American way of life. But what is less familiar is the Community Business Development Organizations; their origins; and their functions. While there is probably some debate about which black community organization is most effective in helping black business to get started, there is less debate about the genesis of the CBDO as a recent effort to foster black business development in this country. Many agree that the CBDO concept was conceived on a cold day in February 1966 when the late Senator Robert F. Kennedy of New York took a walking tour of Bedford-Stuyvesant, a large depressed black community in the heart of Brooklyn. What he saw appalled him: rows of dilapidated houses, vacant lots heaped with debris, burned-out buildings where junkies and prostitutes congregated, abandoned cars rusting in streets— poverty and neglect everywhere. While Kennedy's planned tour got lots of publicity, it was not greeted enthusiastically by community residents. To Bedford-Stuyvesant residents, he was just one more in a long procession of politicians who walked through their misery into newspaper headlines. A community leader put it to him bluntly:

Senator, we've been studied, examined, sympathized with and planned for. What we need now is action.[1]

In December 1966 Kennedy returned to Bedford-Stuyvesant and announced that the area was to become the testing ground for an experiment in community rejuvenation—an experiment which was to be the catalyst for black communities across the country to sponsor black economic development programs. By May 1967 Kennedy's program was in operation as the Bedford-Stuyvesant Restoration Corporation, a community-based, non-profit organization, was organized to initiate and direct projects to revitalize the economy of Bedford-Stuyvesant. (See Appendix A for a brief history of the Restoration Corporation, the nation's largest CBDO.)

An important activity of the Restoration Corporation was to

[1] Bedford-Stuyvesant Restoration Corporation, *Annual Report 1968,* p. 6.

assist community residents to start business enterprises. By June 1969 Restoration had generated over $3 million to assist approximately forty black-owned businesses to get started in Bedford-Stuyvesant. Of equal importance, it became one of the chief models for dozens of other black communities as CBDOs sprang up in Boston, Rochester, Philadelphia, Baltimore, Durham, Atlanta, Memphis, Detroit, Chicago, Cleveland, St. Louis, Houston, San Francisco, Los Angeles, Seattle, and other American cities with large black populations. In the few years following Kennedy's walking tour of Bedford-Stuyvesant, these CBDOs would devote major portions of their resources to black business development. (See Chapter 3 and Appendix B for more detail on the locations, funding, and operations of Community Business Development Organizations.)

## CBDO BLACK BUSINESS DEVELOPMENT: AN INITIAL APPROACH TO ECONOMIC DEVELOPMENT

Given the fact that there are dozens of institutions in black communities across the country dedicated to helping blacks operate businesses, as well as to improving the economic life of the black community, an important question is what aspects of economic development we will cover in this book. The authors recognize that the economic development of America's black communities is a complex subject. For many blacks see economic development as not only including the ownership of businesses by blacks, but improved housing, better educational facilities, adequate municipal services, sufficient employment opportunities, and a host of other areas which are usually absent or at best substandard in black communities.

Though the authors appreciate that there is a need to discuss all of the issues of community economic development, this volume will not attempt to deal with all of these important aspects. For the breadth of the relationship between black business development and the CBDO alone raised numerous issues, all of which we finally decided could not be examined at the present time. The following partial listing of these issues illustrate the dilemma we faced in narrowing the focus of this book:

6                                                      BLACK ENTERPRISE, INC.

1. The roles of "non-community-based" organizations which are attempting to assist black businessmen. These include such organizations as the Interracial Council for Business Opportunity, the National Business League, the Presbyterian Church, the Ford Foundation, Motors Enterprise, Inc., a division of General Motors, and the Chase Manhattan Economic Development Program.

2. The influence of grantors on the operations of CBDOs. How are business development programs influenced by the requirements of such funding agencies as the Department of Commerce, the Small Business Administration, the Office of Economic Opportunity, and various private foundations?

3. The question of whether blacks should even be encouraged to start businesses. One might successfully argue that blacks should seek education and jobs rather than risk limited resources in marginal business enterprises.

4. The question of whether CBDOs have really contributed to bettering the economic conditions of blacks. Could these resources be better used by the black community?

5. The question of whether CBDOs should provide debt or equity capital or both. Are CBDOs lending agencies or venture capital operations?

6. The question of whether CBDO ownership improves a business' economic potential? Is CBDO ownership a form of socialism?

7. The role of the black bank in the economic development of the community. Is the black bank a community institution or an institution which happens to be in the black community?

8. The question of whether there should be black economic development. Should black communities be dispersed, resulting in a completely integrated society?

9. The question of whether economic development is important for the black community. Is political power a more realistic goal?

10. The question of whether other racial minorities—Mexican-Americans, American Indians, Puerto Ricans, etc.—should be lumped together with blacks in examining the role of the CBDO.

11. The question of whether America is too far advanced industrially for blacks ever to make significant inroads in capital intensive business enterprises. Should blacks stick to service and retail operations?

The above is but a partial list of issues which came to mind as we attempted to build a framework for presenting our nine case studies. Further compounding our dilemma was the fact that each time we discussed the scope of the book with our colleagues and CBDO officials they raised more issues to be resolved. Finally, it became clear that the whole area of black economic and black community development has been overlooked so long that no one book can even begin to do justice to all of these many areas. Therefore our task became a relatively simple one: *it was not a question (in this book) of what should happen with CBDOs and Business Development Programs but rather a question of what has happened. For only by showing clearly the situation today can we begin to evaluate its current status and think about ways to improve upon it. Thus, in this volume our* sole *objective is to give the reader case examples of how black business development is being fostered by community-based organizations formulated primarily for that purpose.*

Not surprisingly, we found that there was a great deal of interest in this subject, and that ironically very little had been written about:

- the experiences of blacks assisted by business development programs;
- the initiation of business development programs;
- the individuals working in business development programs;
- the blacks receiving assistance from business development programs; and
- the success of these new black entrepreneurs.

We felt that the best way to learn about these and other pertinent issues was to visit the major black communities of this country to research those community groups which had expressed interest in economic development, "black capitalism," local entrepreneurship, and similar areas concerned with helping blacks have the opportunity to participate in the ownership of profit-making ventures. (Appendix B is a listing of selected business development organizations in this country.) Thus, using the experiences of various Community Business Development Organizations (CBDOs), we will present nine case studies which will *begin* to deal with many of the issues listed above on the present course of CBDOs' black business development efforts.

Though these cases may often appear to be critical of the CBDO, the businessman, or the community leaders, this is not their objective. For CBDOs are trying to provide a service in a very critical area. What will become clear to the reader is that the area of business development is so complex that it is difficult for CBDOs to have a very high initial success ratio. Thus any implied criticism is only relative to the problems which CBDOs have to overcome in accomplishing their goals.

## THE APPROACH

Chapter 2 of Part I sets the stage for our presentation of the CBDO concept and operations and the nine case studies of black entrepreneurs. It traces *briefly* the development of capitalism in America and the parallel slower development of black business in this country. In this latter regard, it begins a discussion of the events which led to the creation of community-based organizations designed to assist the black man get his "piece of the action."

Chapter 3 deals with the creation of black community groups whose primary purpose is to assist local residents to start businesses. It shows that while these CBDOs also become involved in other types of projects, their emphasis is on helping black residents to become owners of business enterprises. This chapter begins with a discussion of the factors underlying the CBDOs' development and examines their policy formulation, staff selection, and procedure development. It is these variables that largely determine the extent to which CBDOs are able to deal with the demands of a black population desiring to own and operate profitable businesses.

Parts II, III, and IV are the heart of our effort for they contain nine case studies which represent typical experiences of black businessmen assisted by CBDOs. Part II relates the experiences of two franchise operations:

- *Bailey's ARC Transmissions* focuses on the problems of a black accountant who bought a transmission repair business in Detroit in 1970 after it had been abandoned by a white dealer.
- *Jeff's All-Star Ribs* is a study of a black Baltimore college counselor who tried to operate a rib franchise which was under the control of a *black franchisor*.

Part III relates the experiences of CBDO-assisted manufacturing businesses:

· *Merritt Plastics Manufacturing Corporation* is the case study of the previously mentioned misguided real estate salesman who tried to manage his cousin's Chicago plastics operations.
· *Albert's Originals* relates the experiences of a black handbag manufacturer who was helped by a New York CBDO to overcome his management deficiencies.
· *Clark's Creations* is a case study of a black dress designer who started an unsuccessful manufacturing operation in Atlanta with an insufficient $45,000 loan.

Part IV deals with the experiences of four black service and retail firms who were launched by CBDOs across the country:

· *Four Brothers Trucking Company* is the case study of four young men in Roxbury, Massachusetts, who expanded their moving company with a $100,000 loan, only almost to fail after receiving the capital.
· *Larry's Radio and TV Service* is the aforementioned study of the black repairman who fulfilled his dream of operating his own television shop in San Francisco.
· *ABC Shoe Store* is a case study of a black shoe salesman who purchased a profitable Harlem men's shoe store from his white employer and then proceeded to siphon off revenue to "invest" in other less successful ventures.
· *Soul Guard Service* relates the experiences of a black Watts detective who started a security guard service hoping to build his business on the high incidence of crime in the community.

The question of case selection was a difficult one since our major objective was to use representative cases. After looking at almost two hundred black-owned businesses assisted by CBDOs, we finally settled on the nine found in this volume. In each instance we chose situations in which the business had evolved to a point that clearly showed *learning experiences,* as well as typical relationships existing between entrepreneurs and CBDOs.

Because many of these businesses are still operational, we have changed the names of the businessmen and the CBDOs, and in several instances we have changed the locale and dates of the studies. In order to preserve both the form and the substance of the records of the CBDOs and the entrepreneurs, however, we made no changes in any of the original case data. Thus we made no alterations or corrections in the data contained in the financial statements, reports, proposals, or other materials of the businesses or the CBDOs. As one reads these cases, it is also necessary to keep in mind that they are not intended merely to present stories of successful or unsuccessful black businessmen. More properly, they reflect the invaluable learning experiences gained by the three groups concerned with the ventures: black community leaders and CBDO community-based boards of directors, the entrepreneurs assisted by the CBDO, and the CBDOs' executives and staffs. Furthermore, these case studies show that the greatest value to the three groups were the types and magnitudes of experiences they encountered rather than quantitative results based upon the number of businesses assisted, the total financial commitment made, or the profits of a business. Thus, in the final analysis it is these case examples which begin to demonstrate the extent to which the community groups must direct their efforts if they are to foster black business development in this country.

Part V summarizes the problems encountered by the nine black businesses and the CBDOs which assisted them. Following this summary of the problems of the entrepreneurs and CBDOs is an outline of several ways in which the black community might be helped to progress toward the goal of resident business ownership. While these suggestions represent only a start, they are intended to supplement greatly the current attempts already under way.

As the reader moves through this volume, it will become increasingly clear that we are concerned primarily with—in this initial effort—the results of CBDO efforts to start black-owned businesses. This is not to say that other areas of black economic development or CBDO development are unimportant or *even that black business development is a correct strategy for black economic development*. As indicated above, there is ample room for debate on these subjects. Each of these and other relevant subjects are beyond the scope of this initial work however. In this country there are many areas to cover on the development of the black community and organizations in the black community. We have limited ourselves to a very narrow examination—the task of illustrating through case studies how community-based organizations have assisted in the development of locally owned business enterprises. In later volumes we will evaluate fully these efforts, as well as present more details on how America's black communities might move into the mainstream of the country's economic life.

# 2

# A PRELUDE TO THE
# COMMUNITY BUSINESS
# DEVELOPMENT ORGANIZATION
# (CBDO)

## INTRODUCTION

Initially, one might understandably question why a chapter on black business development will begin with a section on white business. As one reads further he might also wonder why the authors treated such involved subjects as American capitalism and black business development with such brevity. Our response to both inquiries is that this chapter is intended simply to place the remainder of the book in perspective. For to understand CBDOs' involvement with the nine cases of black entrepreneurs, one should be able to recall— if only briefly—the growth of the American capitalist system, and to understand the parallel slower evolution of black business development in the same country. This historical excursion will set the stage for our presentation of Chapter 3 on the CBDOs' background as well as the nine case studies which describe the roles of CBDOs in the furtherance of black business development.

It is only fair to warn the reader again that this chapter—and this book—is not intended to debate the merits of the capitalist system or to evaluate the conditions which have been instrumental in retarding black business development. While this issue will undoubtedly raise serious questions on both capitalism and the future of the black American, our intention is only to give the reader sufficient background to enable him to have some appreciation for the tasks that CBDOs, as catalytic mechanisms, must accomplish.

BLACK ENTERPRISE, INC.

# AMERICAN CAPITALISM: A BRIEF HISTORY

*The Capitalist Foundation: 1776–1929*

The eighteenth-century American businessman was fortunate in that the country's natural resources and political and social value systems encouraged him to make a livelihood as an independent entrepreneur. Early Americans always seemed attuned to new opportunity for profits. Many ventures carried on originally as a matter of necessity—the production of woolens in the home, for example—were found to be attractive ways of making money. All that seemed to matter was that there was some "opportunity"—a byword of American free enterprise.

The emergence of a new industrial class and the American endorsement of a business way of life in the first half of the ninteenth century promoted business development in this country. In the years before the Civil War, American industry increasingly consolidated itself around the twin concepts of risk and profits as Americans continually seized upon new opportunities to provide goods and services to a new country and a demanding world. All that seemed necessary was desire, coupled with hard work, thrift, and industriousness. While American industry was evolving during the first half of the nineteenth century, it was during the post-Civil War period that capitalism finally came of age.

By the second half of the nineteenth century, the threat of an internal war became a reality as the country plunged into civil strife. Instead of slowing down growth, however, the war acted as a stimulus to the northern industrialists as the government purchased enormous quantities of goods and paid high prices. Its demand for uniforms and blankets afforded a market for cloth as had never been seen before. When cotton goods could not be furnished in sufficient quantities, northern woolen mills more than doubled their output. Similarly, the demand for munitions imparted a strong stimulus to the iron and steel industry. And so it went in other industries—copper, shoes, etc.—many of which had been barely saved from destruction by foreign competition in the early decades of the nineteenth century.

As America came of age during its bloodiest war, it ushered in a new type of leader whose style was to set the pattern in business for the next one hundred years and beyond. Most were drawn from the aggressive Yankees who had thrived in New England. In general, they were highly self-disciplined, with their strongest lust being the pecuniary appetite. These men—Jay Gould, James Fisk, J. P. Morgan, Philip Armour, Andrew Carnegie, John Rockefeller, Collis Huntington, Jay Cooke, and Leland Stanford—became known as the "robber barons" and probably did more to anchor firmly the idea and myth of business as a basic part of the American tradition than any other group of individuals.

They exhibited a zeal and shrewdness for business that made them crafty foes willing to do almost anything in order to best their competition. It is not surprising that by 1880 all were substantially wealthy and well on their way to becoming the captains of industry. What is significant about these robber barons is not simply that they amassed great wealth, but that they seemed totally occupied with business as a way of life. It is this total preoccupation that is characteristic of a capitalist system which seems to say that a man's profit potential is limitless, given his ability and willingness to pursue business opportunities.

As American industry developed and grew under the influence of the nineteenth-century industrialists, it became more sophisticated in its organizations and its operations. As smaller firms were consolidated into larger systems through trusts, mergers, and acquisitions, authority was decentralized in regional divisions and subsidiary offices. And things did not stop there, as in one industry after another the strongest competitors combined their forces and either absorbed or crushed the weaker concerns. Those few allowed to exist as independent companies were clearly no threat to the combination. In this process, for example, the American Tobacco Company gained control of three fourths of the country's tobacco trade.

The economic growth which continued into the twentieth century underwent a momentary strain as the United States felt the effects of World War I and the level of foreign trade was seriously threatened. However, instead of deflating American business, a chief result of the war was to stimulate American commerce and industry. For as during the Civil War, to meet growing war demands required extraordinary activity on the part of manufacturers and to make up for the loss of the men who left for the war required all the efficiency in production that could possibly be attained.

Once the war was over, trade and industry continued to flourish as the war left the industries of Europe in a paralyzed condition. The warring nations were compelled to turn to the American market for the supplies they needed. This new prosperity engendered, was to continue into the 1920s as America at last seemed to achieve a world-dominant position in business.

## Depression Survival and the Space Age: 1930–1980

The period of seemingly continuous prosperity that Americans had seen was brought to a screeching halt as a result of the 1929 stock market crash with its snowballing negative effect on the economy. Any other country's economy might never have withstood such an onslaught. In a way, perhaps, the Great Depression was a "final examination" of all of the business lessons learned during the country's first 150 years. If this is the case, then capitalism managed to pass the test. For while many banks did fail, the majority were able to sustain themselves through government intervention and a build-up of substantial reserves and adequate capital cushions. Of equal importance, many industrial concerns were also able to survive, through such techniques as austerity budgets, the reorientation of production from durable to replacement goods, the liquidation of high-cost inventories by price cutting, and the utilization of internal sources of capital. All in all, since most large manufacturers had a diversified market, they were able to continue in operation until the recovery of the economy at the outbreak of World War II. Thus while the Depression spelled a serious threat to American industry, by utilizing proven skills and improving management techniques, it was able to hold on and, in retrospect, not lose much of the ground gained in its evolution.

Probably the best indication of how sophisticated American business had become was not the Depression but its reaction to World War II. This war, like World War I and the Civil War, acted as a stimulus for American business. As before, the efforts of industry were channeled into meeting the demands of a war economy. In this instance, however, the giant corporations took over even more of the management of mass production and also coordinated the activities of many small firms working under sub-contracts for the government.

After the war, American industry recognized that pent-up demands for consumer goods had to be satisfied not only at home, but all over the world. The same ability to see and seize opportunity that had made earlier Americans successful dictated that American business cover the globe with its products. And as the free world continued to pull itself out of the throes of devastation into the 1950s and 1960s, American business was there to provide goods and services.

True to the American business tradition, as the profitability of new markets began to wane under revived foreign competition in the 1960s, business looked inward and began to consolidate on a scale that would have staggered even the imagination of a J. D. Rockefeller or an Andrew Carnegie. Combinations of several dissimilar businesses united: a steel company, an electronics manufacturer, and a meat producer—on and on, until the emergence of a giant conglomerate. These conglomerates appeared to have a nose for money as they rooted out opportunity wherever they found it: in casinos, in franchising, in hospitals and nursing homes, and even in cemeteries.

But one might ask what lies ahead for American business in the decades of the 1970s and 1980s and through to the end of this century. Will the American business sustain itself or have the last one hundred years been the exception instead of the rule? As we enter the 1970s, the following forces seem to be operative and will probably affect the character of the free enterprise system in this country:

1. The swinging pendulum in favor of the consumer as critics are becoming increasingly concerned about the quality of goods and services and less susceptible to the created demand that flourishes around advertising.

2. The theme of corporate social responsibility that includes a variety of subjects ranging from the rights of women and racial minorities to the legitimacy of a company to make a profit.

3. The attacks on American business because of its contribution of such environmental problems as noise and industrial pollution.

4. The government as a force with such issues as control of in-

　　　　　　　　BLACK ENTERPRISE, INC.

flation through wage and price controls and the maintenance of competition through a close review of mergers and acquisitions.

5. The demands of labor—both organized and unorganized—which limit some of the prerogatives of management.

6. The threat of foreign competition both at home and abroad.

It should be obvious to the reader that these and other influences are likely to have an effect on the development and future of American business as we know it today. *But for purposes of black Americans, the immediate future of American capitalism seems to be of less relative importance since black buiness development is almost totally outside of the framework of the business development we have just outlined. Perhaps this accounts for the reason that the work of Community Business Development Organizations and indeed the concept of black business development is often misunderstood; they are usually erroneously viewed within the context of American capitalism as it has evolved today.* While the gulf between American and black business development should be clear to anyone with a cursory knowledge of American history, we will devote the remainder of this chapter to a description of the development of the *black* free enterprise system. This should give a better indication of the environment giving rise to the CBDO and in which it must function presently.

## HUMBLE BEGINNINGS: 1619–1941

*Slaves and Quasi-Slaves: A Non-Enterprising Beginning*

Slavery was unjustified legally in this country until the 1660s when Virginia and Maryland passed laws making blacks "servants for life." While the great mass of these slaves were field hands, others engaged in such non-farming occupations as carpentry, shoemaking, tailoring, bricklaying, painting, plastering, and goldsmithing. Their abilities as skilled artisans on the plantation and in towns is attested to by the fact that white owners often hired them out by the year or for shorter periods of time. Moreover, even though the law frowned upon the practice, some masters encouraged their slaves to find their own jobs and keep a portion of the earnings. Given the opportunity and under more civilized conditions, American slaves would certainly have stood a chance of becoming successful entrepreneurs as did other early Americans.

In the period from 1790 to 1860, the number of free blacks in America rose from 60,000 to 500,000, equally divided between the North and the South. In the South as well as in the North, the status of all these free blacks deteriorated during the nineteenth century as they became "quasi-slaves." In the South as legislation grew increasingly more restrictive, the status of free blacks, who had never enjoyed many rights, became increasingly similar to that of slaves. In the North the plight of the free blacks was increased by urban white workingmen, who felt that they could improve their own lot by deprecating blacks. Thus, as a result of widespread discriminatory actions, even free blacks were prevented from gaining a foothold in the American economic system from the beginning.

## The Black Church as an Economic Institution

One significant reaction to white discrimination was the development of black economic institutions centered around the church—an early mechanism of black economic development. The church had always been a focal point for blacks—both slaves and free men. In addition to caring for their spiritual needs, it also created programs to deal with their economic needs and was instrumental in the development of black newspapers, schools, and mutual aid societies. These mutual aid societies evolved into economic institutions in the pre-emancipation black community.

The Free African Society, the first mutual aid society, was established in Philadelphia in 1787 to help blacks adjust to their hostile environment. Following its creation, societies multiplied all over the North, numbering approximately one hundred by the 1830s. Free blacks in the South also formed mutual aid societies fashioned after those in the North and by 1835 about thirty existed throughout the South. Since mutual aid societies paid sickness and death benefits, for the first time in American history a few blacks were able to inherit "wealth" from their parents. These benefits would usually pay funeral and other immediate obligations with the remaining possessions being distributed to the children. Moreover, the savings deposits of the mutual aid societies and benevolent associations served to inculcate a rudimentary knowledge of finance.

Beginning in the 1830s the black church started to sponsor black conventions designed to ameliorate the poor conditions of blacks. Led by ministers, lawyers, physicians, businessmen, and other black leaders, national conventions were held annually from 1830 to 1835 and sporadically thereafter. The delegates to these conventions condemned racial prejudices and urged blacks to stress schooling, good moral character, and economic accumulation. An important part of this program was a concern with training more blacks for the skilled trades, since this training led eventually to a means of becoming self-supporting artisans.

Discouragement with the political atmosphere, as well as the success of white immigrants in taking over many of the jobs traditionally held by blacks, led the Rochester Convention of 1850 to place an even stronger emphasis on racial solidarity and economic advancement. The convention held that black survival depended upon blacks using each other's economic services when possible and advocated the establishment of a national register of black businesses, mechanics, and laborers.

In the years preceding the Civil War, free blacks in northern cities discussed the establishment of credit and banking associations. In New York in 1851 a church-backed convention discussed plans for forming a bank, suggesting that its organization would assist black homesteaders and black men who wished to go into business. The convention recommended that a bank be established on the mutual principle, with power to deal in real estate, merchandise, bonds, mortgages, and commercial paper. In 1855 another church-backed New York convention encouraged cooperation among black businessmen and recommended that a fund be created to encourage those who wished to start businesses.

*Pre-Emancipation Black Business*

As one might expect in a slave economy, the beneficial effects of these early efforts to establish a black economic base were probably more psychological than quantitative. Before the Civil War, a few free blacks made a comfortable living through the ownership of small service businesses which catered principally to whites. And since these black entrepreneurs found it virtually impossible to obtain expansion capital and credit, they were destined to remain small. The limited state of black business development is summarized in the following excerpt:

During the early 1800s, the seat of black affluence was Philadelphia. As early as 1789, free blacks ran small shops throughout the city, and by 1820 the black population of 12,000 persons owned about $250,000 worth of property . . .

Perhaps the most successful Philadelphia entrepreneur was James Forten, a Revolutionary War veteran who made a fortune as a sail manufacturer. Starting as an errand boy around the docks, he learned the trade through apprenticeship to a white man . . . Upon the death of his mentor, Forten took over the business and expanded it until there were more than forty employees . . . The company continued to prosper until steam navigation came into general use . . .

By the time of Forten's death in 1842, *black business in Philadelphia had succumbed to a series of setbacks.* The influx of competitive European immigrants resulted in racial clashes that often erupted into riots. Black citizens in the City of Brotherly Love had been deprived of the right to vote in 1836, and subsequently the number of black businessmen and women there dropped sharply . . .

. . . a few black men had a natural business acumen that enabled them to achieve success in the Southern States. Lunsford Lane, a servant for a wealthy citizen in Raleigh, also ran errands for merchants and he learned much by observing their business operations. Since the state legislature met in Raleigh and its members were heavy smokers, he started a business to supply them with pipes and tobacco. Later he expanded to cover a large part of the state.

With his profits Lane bought freedom. Since that was still illegal in North Carolina, he went to New York with his master's agent to complete the transaction. Returning to Raleigh, he continued his tobacco business and opened a general merchandise store and lumberyard. Although he grew quite wealthy and counted the well-to-do people of Raleigh among his patrons, he was unpopular among poor whites, who demanded that he be expelled from the state under a law forbidding free blacks from other states to reside in North Carolina. Finally, all of his property was taken from him by force and he was tarred and feathered and driven out of town . . .

Black entrepreneurship emerged even in Washington, which was perhaps the most notorious slave market in the country until 1850. William Wormley was a wealthy man who owned and operated the largest livery stable in Washington. Unfortunately, Wormley's health and business declined after repeated acts of vandalism and persecution following the riots of 1835.[1]

Thus at a time when white America was ready to embark on the second half of the nineteenth-century growth which was to make it the business capital of the world, its black population was collectively struggling to keep itself and a few small businesses alive.

## The Bitter Fruits of Emancipation

With the freeing of the slaves and the end of the Civil War, whites tried to inculcate habits of thrift and enterprise in the black masses. It is the story of the first banking experience of the "freed blacks" that best illustrates the frustrations that were to characterize business development for the majority of blacks in the remainder of the nineteenth century.

Congress established the Freedmen's Bank as a depository for the savings of black soldiers and laborers. Incorporated as the Freedmen's Savings and Trust Company, the first branch was opened in May 1865, with a total of thirty-four branches being established between 1865 and 1871. Organized and controlled by whites, initially, few blacks were employed in any capacity. However, blacks were led to believe that the bank was a government institution or that at least the government was responsible for their funds.

From 1865 to 1869 the banks's central office was in New York where it was operated by men who managed it conservatively. But in 1870 the central office was moved to Washington where the bank fell into the hands of a group under whose management it carried the questionable commercial paper of the First National Bank of Washington. When the First National Bank failed, it precipitated a run on the Freedmen's Bank, which was looked upon as a branch of the First National Bank. When the bank closed its doors in June 1874, it owed almost $3 million to its 61,000 depositors.

Despite such fiascos as the Freedmen's Bank, the absence of an

[1] Burrell, Berkeley G., and John Seder, *Getting It Together*. New York: Harcourt Brace Jovanovich, Inc., 1971, pp. 12–15.

economic base, and the rising tide of white oppression and discrimination following Reconstruction, blacks continued to desire to become a part of the country's business community. A frequent complaint was their inability to secure money when it was needed. Growing out of this need was the beginning of the first black banks, which then, as today, controlled an infinitesimally small share of the country's assets.

The first banks organized and administered by blacks were the Capital Savings Bank of the Grand Fountain United Order of True Reformers in Richmond, Virginia (March 1888), and the Capital Savings Bank at Washington, D.C. (October 1888). In 1889 the Mutual Trust Company was organized at Chattanooga, Tennessee, and in 1890 the Alabama Penny Savings and Loan Company, in Birmingham, Alabama. The combined influence of the black fraternal order and the church stands out strikingly in the organization of these early banks. For example, the True Reformers Bank was a subsidiary organization and depositary of the Grand Fountain United Order of True Reformers founded by Reverend W. W. Brown. The Alabama Penny Savings Bank was founded by a church minister and the Nickel Savings Bank, organized in 1896 in Richmond, Virginia, was the depositary of the People's Insurance Company, of which the Reverend Evans Payne was the founder.

The roots of the black insurance company were initially a part of the death benefits of mutual aid societies and benevolent associations prevalent in the 1880s. By the end of the nineteenth century, however, these societies had been eclipsed by such fraternal orders as the Odd Fellows, which grew from 89 to 1,000 lodges between 1868 and 1886, the Masons, and the Negro Knights of Pythias, which also experienced significant expansion. Among the nonsecret, quasi-religious fraternal orders the most well-known was the Grand Fountain United Order of True Reformers founded in Virginia in 1881. By 1911 it had become a mutual benefit stock company with a membership of 100,000 persons operating a bank, five department stores, and a weekly newspaper in addition to its insurance department. The black insurance movement was further spurred in the last decade of the nineteenth century by the wholesale cancellation of black insurance policies by white insurance companies. The founding of the North Carolina Mutual Insurance Company, America's largest black insurance company, is one of

BLACK ENTERPRISE, INC.

the prime examples of the evolution of black insurance companies. In 1883 John Merick—a Durham barber who catered to upper-class whites—and some friends obtained control of a quasi-religious fraternal order, the Royal Knights of King David. In 1898 the business was twice reorganized, first as the North Carolina Mutual and Provident Association, and then as an insurance company.

As blacks continued fruitlessly to seek economic freedom during the last decade of the nineteenth century, their efforts carried them not only to the formation of banks and insurance companies, but to other small businesses as well. The state of the black business community was documented in a study by Dr. W. E. B. Du Bois in 1900 which examined almost two thousand enterprises with capital exceeding $500. It showed that most had evolved from occupations dictated by slavery: barbers, cooks, caterers, grocers, florists, builders, painters, and blacksmiths. Testimony to the seriousness of the turn-of-the-century status of blacks in business was that at this same time America was beginning to react to the giant trusts in oil, tobacco, steel, and other industries which had become too large and powerful.

## A Continuing Struggle and the Depression

Despite the poor racial and business conditions of the late nineteenth century, many blacks continued to feel that the route for black development lay in the economic realm. In this regard, the World War I period seemed to usher in a new era for blacks. Because of the depressed conditions of the South and northern industry's demands for a war in Europe, millions of blacks left the South for northern urban complexes where they thought that they would find better wages and living conditions. However, in this new "promised land" the black migrant encountered the initial problem of competition with whites for limited housing. When the war ended and the need for supplies and services was cut back sharply, contracts were canceled and many plants drastically reduced operations. This brought a worsening labor market and a return to the familiar pattern of racial discrimination in employment.

The downturn in blacks' employment and general economic statuses was reflected in the characteristically slow development of the black community's business enterprises. By 1920 black businesses numbered only 26,000, with the most successful ventures being in the field of small personal services—restaurants, beauty parlors, barbershops, and funeral parlors. Blacks were unable to organize large commercial and industrial enterprises, the backbone of American industry. The basic industries—steel, petroleum, transportation, communications, etc.—were owned and controlled by whites.

The existence of post-World War I black business as "small business" is summarized in a 1928 National Negro Business League study. The NNBL surveyed a total of 1,534 black businesses in thirty-three cities and found that the overwhelming bulk of the enterprises did an annual gross business of less than $5,000; less than 10 per cent of these enterprises even approached $10,000 in their annual gross. The survey also revealed that, on the average, only 3.9 persons were employed in each business establishment. Except for a few banks and insurance companies, blacks had no control over any significant enterprises functioning either in or outside of the black communities. Thus, in the years preceding the Great Depression, blacks were able to gain only a minor foothold in the starting of relatively small businesses. Furthermore, the earlier white capitalists had already dictated the terms of involvement in large-scale operations and with the exception of a few areas, there was little room for the entry of inexperienced blacks. And certainly the market place had little time for blacks to learn the new game of large business development. In a sense, all of this becomes a meaningless discussion, as the Depression wiped away even the small advances of the first three decades of the twentieth century.

The Great Depression which adversely affected the business structure of America hit black businesses with even more severity. The black banks and insurance companies that had grown during the last decade of the nineteenth century were decimated in the early 1930s. Where once there had been 56 black banks, there were now only 11; where there had been 110 insurance companies, only 30 were left. The adage that "blacks were the last hired and the first fired" came true, and as black employees lost their jobs, they were less able to purchase goods and services. Black service businesses were hit even harder, since they were totally dependent on these same blacks for their business. Thus the Depression wiped out the few gains that blacks had made economically as a group after emancipation. And again they were faced with the task of rebuilding.

BLACK ENTERPRISE, INC.

# A TASTE OF HONEY?: 1941–1967

World War II acted as a catalyst in getting a limited number of blacks into areas which had previously been closed. Although there continued to be racial segregation, they were at least able to gain slightly in the educational and employment areas.

Blacks saw education as a panacea which would give them strength. The number of college graduates multiplied as more and more departments of business administration were strengthened to cope with the problem of an aspiring population interested in business careers. While the relative number of black students graduating in business administration was small, and the majority of these went into business education, insurance, and banking, some few did begin seriously to attempt to become businessmen. Atlanta University, perceiving the trend in business and visualizing the need for additional training for blacks in business administration, instituted a Master's degree program in 1945. For several years the number of black business graduates produced by Atlanta University was more than those produced by all other business schools in the nation combined, as white business schools remained effectively closed to all but a few blacks.

Also, after World War II, blacks trained in the military services transferred their newly acquired skills to the production of peacetime goods. Industry was booming and skilled workers were needed in many industries to provide goods for a war-torn Europe, as well as satisfy the demands of returning servicemen. These post-war demands as well as a relative lessening in discrimination fostered new employment opportunities.

Just as some blacks got better education and jobs after the war, so did a few do well in business. As might be expected, service establishments blossomed and to an extent the banks and insurance businesses continued their revival. In the North and South businessmen such as L. D. Milton of Atlanta's Citizen's Trust Company, C. C. Spaulding of North Carolina Mutual Insurance Company, and Truman K. Gibson of Chicago's Supreme Life Insurance Company took the lead. They hired and trained clerks, accountants, and executives, and provided the black community with business leadership. Segregation in the South continued to serve as a catalyst for the development of black businesses. Hotels and motels, restaurants, nightclubs, and other service enterprises developed out of the need to provide for a segregated population. The cosmetics business that began around the turn of the century also grew steadily.

Perhaps one of the most significant areas of growth occurred in the mass media. In 1943 there were 164 black newspapers with a total circulation in excess of 2 million. In the years following the war, at least four of those emerged as important organs of opinion among blacks: the Pittsburgh *Courier,* the Baltimore *Afro-American,* the Chicago *Defender,* and the *Journal and Guide* of Norfolk, Virginia. At the same time that the black newspaper grew in importance, a number of black magazines with pictures and stories on the activities of blacks began to circulate widely. The most significant of these magazines were published by the Johnson Publishing Company of Chicago. Started by John H. Johnson in 1942, it initially published the *Negro Digest* and because of its success, in 1945 began *Ebony,* which now has a circulation in excess of 1.2 million.

Despite the relative spectacular success of some black-owned businesses during the 1940s, it was clear that mainstream black Americans were still not reaping the economic benefits of a profit-oriented system. For every publisher like Johnson, there were hundreds of thousands of blacks who had no opportunity to own even a candy store.

Ironically, the events that were to begin to promote the CBDO concept were not related to business per se, but to the apparent failure of the civil rights movement to help black people achieve equal opportunity. While the World War II struggle had lifted blacks' hopes that they could gain first-class citizenship, they quickly learned this was not so. Hope, however, continued into the 1950s, especially when the Supreme Court issued its landmark 1954 decision on *Brown et al.* v. *Board of Education of Topeka,* which held that in public education the doctrine of separate but equal was unconstitutional. Now blacks thought that things were going to get better, for education was the first step and other action would surely follow to provide them with equal opportunity. Yet little of significance really happened.

Another turning point in the civil rights movement seemed to come in 1957 when Martin Luther King, Jr., led an assault against a southern segregated bus system. King bested the Montgomery Transit Company by using an economic boycott that won the right for blacks to participate as equals on public facilities and to demand equal employment rights. Encouraged by this victory and the subsequent leadership of King's movement, the Congress of Racial Equality, the Student Non-Violent Coordinating Committee, and other emerging civil rights organizations, blacks continued to assault head-on the other inequities of the system.

Continuing the trend of the late 1940s and 1950s, a *limited* number of blacks continued to benefit into the 1960s, especially in education and employment. The number of college graduates continued to rise, with more going into business administration, not only to teach, but planning to become managers and businessmen. At the same time, white colleges began to accept more blacks into their professional programs, especially their business schools.

President John Kennedy, apparently sensing the mood of blacks in the country, called for the voluntary commitment of business to equal opportunity employment. A substantial number of companies endorsed the concept and, in theory, the employment barrier to blacks was broken. While unions continued to exclude blacks in the 1960s, even they seemed to realize by the end of the decade that blacks were here to stay. Accordingly, they began to institute token programs for black apprentices. At the same time, large industrial companies began training and hiring unemployed and unemployable blacks. Banks, insurance companies, and brokerage houses also instituted crash programs to train tellers and clerks, as well as managerial personnel.

Thus, during the 1945–1967 period, blacks made measurable gains in employment, education, and civil rights. *Still unanswered, however, was the question of whether and how such affirmative action was to give blacks the opportunity to own businesses.*

A PIECE OF THE ACTION: 1968–1980

A major government effort in the early 1960s to improve the conditions of blacks was the Office of Economic Opportunity's "War on Poverty." This effort which began in 1964 sponsored community agencies to dispense funds to blacks for job training, community organizing, and other non-business-related ways. As the black community continued to define its role and look closer at these programs, it began to question the relationship of these poverty programs to the real economic needs of the community. As black communities became more aware, they began to demand not simply handouts in the form of poverty funds, but control of businesses which would return a profit to the residents of the community.

Climaxing this and other discontent were the events that led to the riots in Newark, Watts, New York, Detroit, and other cities in the late 1960s. It was clear that things were not getting better for the masses of blacks, especially in business. This is not to say that efforts were not being made. Such diverse organizations as the Black Economic Union, the National Business League, the Interracial Council for Business Opportunity, the Urban Coalition, the Nation of Islam, the Small Business Administration, the Presbyterian Church, and the Department of Commerce sponsored or initiated programs designed to increase the number of black-owned businesses. Despite these efforts, however, there are still less than fifty thousand black businesses (out of 5.5 million) in America. Even in insurance—the largest black industry—the fifty companies' total insurance in force is *less than 1 per cent of the national total*.

Despite such dismal statistics and the obvious absence of a significantly large black entrepreneurial class, many might argue that blacks are progressing in business. For example, there are several black-owned advertising agencies and public relations firms. Approximately twenty-five blacks own new car dealerships. About fourteen blacks own radio stations. Life insurance companies are still prominent, with North Carolina Mutual, Atlanta Life, Supreme Life, Universal Life, and Golden Gate Mutual leading the pack. There are threescore black banks and savings and loan associations, though their combined financial leverage is still infinitesimally small. Cosmetics are a big business in the black community with Supreme Beauty Products and Johnson Products being among the leaders. In food processing, H. G. Parks, Inc., leads the way, while the publishing field is still dominated by Johnson Publications and the black newspapers mentioned earlier.

While the above list could probably be extended, the *majority* of the persons in the black community have still not been given the opportunity to begin to cash in on the American dream to start even

28                                        BLACK ENTERPRISE, INC.

a small business. In relating the stories of several successful black businessmen, Burrell and Seder point out that

. . . Every man whose story we have told is an exception. Most of them have exceptional intelligence. All of them have extraordinary patience, endurance, imagination, energy, drive—and luck. All of them had to sweat and strain and struggle many times as hard as their white counterparts for every sale, every achievement, every dollar . . .

In America, lots of ordinary white people make it. Why shouldn't an ordinary black man of average ability be able to make it, too? Why should he have to rise to heroic achievements in order to share in American life? . . . That's what black people are complaining about.[2]

What was still needed then was an instrument to give the masses of blacks the opportunity to move into the economic mainstream of the country. Such an instrument would accelerate the process through which blacks could become the owners of profit-making business enterprises. This new type of organization, which emerged in the late 1960s, took many forms, though they were always concerned with business development in the black community. It is with the operations of these organizations—CBDOs—and case studies of nine of the black businesses they assisted that the remainder of this book is concerned.

[2] Burrell and Seder, op. cit., p. 233.

# 3

# THE BLACK COMMUNITY
# ORGANIZES TO DEVELOP
# BUSINESSES

## INTRODUCTION

Chapter 2 traced briefly black business development in this country
from slavery through the 1960s, showing that it was not until the
latter part of the 1960s that the country began to deal with the
economic gulf existing between whites and most blacks. To the millions of black Americans living in depressed communities across the
country, it became increasingly clear that one major source of power in
America emanated from business profits. Since black residents controlled relatively little of these profits, there resulted a powerlessness
which manifested itself in dilapidated housing, substandard schools,
high unemployment rates, inadequate social services, and similar
social ills. Relatively few businesses were owned by black ghetto
residents, and as a result the residents' money left the community
at night with the white store owners. As one black leader in
Harlem remarked: "A dollar only spends one third of its time in
the black community; the other two thirds of the time it is in the
white community. And even when it is in our community, it is in
'Charlie's' pocket."

But as the black community became more cohesive, it began to
show its concern for the relevance of various institutions—including
business—in its midst, as well as the various government/commu-
nity programs which were designed with little or no input from the
community. From this concern came blacks' realization that they
would have to begin exerting themselves to be more instrumental
in determining their own destinies. In addition, they accepted the
fact that their community would have to develop a business base to

BLACK ENTERPRISE, INC.

allow it to prosper by keeping money within its environs, and thus contribute toward the solutions of its own problems. One necessary ingredient then was organizations which could provide a multiplicity of needed services to the community—services dealing with total economic development in general and business development in particular. These organizations would have to provide capital to spur the creation of profit-making institutions. Furthermore, since capital itself would not create entrepreneurs, and since many blacks lack management skills, the instrument would also have to make management assistance available to the residents. More importantly, these organizations would have to be influenced by the community. For if they were to have substantial impact, the community would have to decide its priorities. And while guidelines might come from the government, these guidelines would have to be broadly based and only establish reasonable parameters for the community.

All of these conditions have not been met fully, though the recognition of a need for an economic unifying force has generated the development of community-based economic development organizations. These organizations take many forms and emphasize several different programs, though a primary interest is always local business development. In this volume we have grouped all community-based organizations together and given them the generic designation of *Community Business Development Organization (CBDO)*.

We use the term CBDO to identify organizations controlled by black persons living in impoverished areas for the purpose of planning, stimulating, and financing businesses for the residents. Although there is no one CBDO prototype, but many different individual community organizations, certain characteristics seem common to them all. *They are usually engaged in all stages of economic development, acting as planners, providing technical assistance to local entrepreneurs, and making investments. They are controlled by residents or by representatives selected by the residents of the communities they serve. And their ultimate purpose is to increase the economic well-being of the community's residents.* In this chapter we will explore briefly the objectives, characteristics, and operations of such agencies of business development and then in succeeding chapters examine—through case studies—the results of their efforts to promote black-owned businesses.

# THE CBDO: ITS ORGANIZATION,
# ITS FUNDING, AND ITS OBJECTIVES

## The Organization of the CBDO

By the end of 1971, CBDOs were engaged in several phases of business development in black communities. The one similar characteristic in all of these efforts was that all CBDOs were relatively new and still evolving into a final program phase. Thus, while it is impossible to describe a "typical" CBDO, it is possible and necessary to examine briefly some of their distinguishing general characteristics. (See Appendix A for a history of the Bedford-Stuyvesant Restoration Corporation, America's largest CBDO.)

Though most CBDOs are controlled by blacks, a few, particularly those funded with federal money, make some attempt to include more than one ethnic group. By and large, though, the blacks who organize and support the organization consider it their own. At this early stage in the evolution of community development this orientation is probably inevitable and some think it psychologically beneficial.

Most CBDOs are concentrated in impoverished black urban communities where businesses they assist are likely to generate maximum benefits for the community. Concentrating in poor neighborhoods also helps to legitimize the CBDO in the view of the community and its sponsors, whether business, foundations, or government. Thus in the nine cases which follow the action takes place in the black sections of such cities as New York, Detroit, San Francisco, Chicago, Boston, Baltimore, and Atlanta.

The organization of CBDOs varies depending upon their size, scope of activities, and funds available. Generally, most CBDOs are incorporated with a board of directors to oversee operations. The size of the board is virtually unlimited, though it is usually composed of community residents who are prominent businessmen, social and civic figures, as well as black nationalists. In some few cases interested whites are involved, either as advisers or active board members.

Because they are to be representative of the community's interest in economic development, most CBDOs have deliberately tried to weigh representation on their boards in favor of community residents with interests useful to CBDO operations. The ways in which CBDOs have attempted to solve the problem of representation generally fall into three patterns: self-selected boards; boards elected through an assembly of the neighborhood; and boards selected by stockholders.

The *self-selected board* typically begins with a group of leaders in a community who form a non-profit corporation to promote business development. Since there is no direct, formal means of participation by community residents in such CBDOs, decision making is not a community affair per se. The *assembly-selected board* is chosen by election, with the typical pattern having the residents elect the members of the board of a neighborhood corporation, which in turn selects the board of the CBDO. This process tends to insulate the CBDO staff from the politics and patronage demands of the poor neighborhood and often results in a board with a relatively high degree of business expertise. In a *stockholder-elected board* the traditional corporate practice is followed. The selection of the board of directors and ultimate control of the corporation are in the hands of stockholders. Because few CBDOs have attempted to sell stock to date there are few stockholder-controlled CBDOs.

Regardless of the board selection mechanism, many CBDOs have separate non-profit and profit-making corporations built into their structures, the precise pattern depending upon the community and state laws. Often the non-profit corporation will be the "parent" organization holding all of the stock of the profit-making arm, the chief purpose being to provide a means by which the CBDO can receive tax-free grants and gifts and, at the same time, engage in financing and otherwise operate as a business.

The board usually sets the CBDO's policies—policies which should, in theory, derive from conversations and meetings with community residents and which should represent the crystallization of the community's needs. Where whites are involved—either as members of the CBDO board or as members of a separate board— a clear delineation of roles is developed. Usually the white partners come from big business and are charged with the responsibilities for taking the CBDO's message to the business community; encouraging outside business to invest in the area; seeking private funds; and assisting the CBDO by bringing their expertise to bear in solving the community's problems.

## The Funding of the CBDO

As with any board of directors, a real concern for a CBDO is securing the money it needs to operate. CBDOs need funds to recruit, train, and maintain staff; to plan; to negotiate financial arrangements; and to undertake other development work. Moreover, if CBDOs are to carry out investment programs, they also need investment money. While CBDOs receive funds from foundations, private businesses, and the community, the overwhelming majority of most CBDO funds come from the federal government.

A typical first step in all CBDO fund-raising—federal and non-federal—is the preparation of a proposal outlining program needs and their approximate costs. The CBDO sends this proposal to federal agencies, foundations, and private firms where it undergoes a rigorous review by the funding source. If initially impressed, the funding source then invites the CBDO to defend its proposal, with most questions centering on the projected impact of the CBDO program. Usually there are a substantial number of community groups vying for the same limited funds. For example, in 1969 a major government funding agency had about $30 million for CBDO-type agencies and over one hundred proposal requests. Obviously all of the proposals could not be funded, though there was probably a genuine need for funds by each applicant.

Among federal programs, the Office of Economic Opportunity (OEO), through its authority under the Title I-D Special Impact Program, has been a chief sponsor of CBDOs. Grants under Title I-D amounted to only about $7 million in fiscal 1967, with grants of $37 million budgeted for fiscal 1971 reflecting the growth in the program but still representing a small fraction of the total OEO budget of over $2 billion. The typical Special Impact grant provides administrative and planning funds for a two-year period and some funds for investment. By 1971 about forty CBDOs had been funded through this program.

Another example of CBDO support has been through the Model Cities Program. During the first two or three years of the Model Cities operation, economic development was not considered an integral part of its inner-city program, but pressures from neighborhood groups resulted in a growing number of Model Cities economic

34

development plans. Like the Special Impact Program, Model Cities supplies money for administration as well as investment. The precedent set by the Special Impact Program in making equity grants has been adopted by Model Cities, which also restricts such grants to broad-based CBDOs.

A third major government agency is the Small Business Administration (SBA). At present the typical CBDO, like the typical ghetto business, obtains much of its debt financing from the SBA, with most of this financing in the form of SBA guarantees of up to 90 per cent of commercial bank loans. The SBA's programs include *regular business loans* of up to $350,000 for up to ten years; *economic opportunity loans,* providing loans and loan guarantees of $25,000 for up to fifteen years for low-income or otherwise impoverished entrepreneurs; *local development corporation loans,* providing loans of up to $350,000 for twenty-five years to CBDOs for plant and equipment for small businesses; and Minority Enterprise Small Business Investment Company (MESBIC) assistance.

In addition to the government, CBDOs also get limited funds from foundations and private industrial concerns, though these funds are often restricted in their uses to the operations of specific programs. As foundations come to recognize the positive social impact of CBDOs, more of them will undoubtedly give these funds on a less restricted basis. Few CBDOs have been funded from within the black community because of the scarcity of capital and the reluctance of most CBDOs to seek funds from local residents until they have reasonably good investment records.

## The Objectives of the CBDO          1742191

Regardless of the event giving rise to the CBDO, once it is organized and funded, it begins to concern itself with setting clear objectives designed to lead to a solution of the community's economic problems. Usually the relationships between CBDOs and the businesses they assist vary from CBDO to CBDO. In some cases CBDOs act as bankers, lending or guaranteeing loans to individual entrepreneurs; in others they are landlords, securing land by virtue of its community support and its non-profit status and leasing it to an individual or a small black-owned business; or they may have a share of the equity in partnership with an entrepreneur; or they may own and operate an enterprise, with the degree of ownership depending on the nature of the business arrangement.

*In addition to sponsoring locally owned businesses,* most CBDOs also "sponsor" total economic development. While we are primarily concerned with business development, it is important that the reader get a brief perspective of the other related and important CBDO economic objectives. These objectives usually evolve around: becoming an economic focal point, setting economic priorities, providing capital and training, and becoming self-sufficient.

Most CBDOs, rather than seeing themselves as the sole developers of their communities, *view themselves as catalysts which mobilize activity to halt economic deterioration.* At the same time they become coordinating forces which bring together all of the available resources of the community. For example, they might sponsor manpower training programs which supply skilled workers for newly formed enterprises, they might create local contracting firms to provide inner-city building programs, or they might attempt to link national supermarket chains with wholesale food distribution or food-processing units.

Most CBDOs view *control over the setting of priorities* as particularly important in their economic development programs. Their demand for control over economic development is related to the community's demand for control over education, housing, welfare services, health, and other local activities. CBDO leaders recognize that no economic development program can succeed without community support, and in order to obtain it they attempt to share responsibility and decision-making power. Some CBDOs demand more control, some less, but there is general agreement on the principle that the community, not outsiders, should set priorities.

One of the most difficult obstacles for the black businessman to overcome is the need for capital. Community incomes and savings are so low that the capital is simply not available. Accordingly, most black businesses are usually financed with a high proportion of debt and are thus burdened with the necessity of loan repayments in the early, most critical stages of the business' life. In *generating equity or highly favorable debt* CBDOs see themselves providing one of the most crucial services required by the black businessman, though only unsophisticated CBDO officials see money as their *only* service. The ability to raise funds gives the CBDO one of its relative strengths and becomes a prime operating objective. Incorporated CBDOs, like other corporations, can sell stock. Through community stock sales they can tap equity money from local residents who have small savings and the desire to participate in self-help efforts. They also have the ability to draw capital from outside sources and convert it into capital under community control. Because they are broad-based, have social objectives, and are not usually organizations of a small number of businessmen who stand to make private profits, CBDOs become politically "legitimate" vehicles through which foundations, government agencies, and private donors can make contributions of capital.

Just as one prime objective of CBDOs is to secure capital, another is to *provide a means for assisting the community's labor force to gain experience and skills* that will enable it to compete in the larger economy. Because black-owned businesses are usually located in the black community and because their owners are usually familiar with ghetto conditions, they have the potential to attract and train the hard-core unemployed. Moreover, the existence of a black-owned business also increases the opportunity for local residents to become managers without all of the formal education credentials. While care is taken not to diminish the business' potential by the additional burden of training, the need to provide some training is emphasized by CBDOs.

In the final analysis, all of the objectives of CBDOs are related to their own survival through a *gradual and conscious program of self-sufficiency*. The concept of rising business profits—both for the CBDO and the independent black businessman—to furnish a flow of funds for the financial support of the community is an important principle. Some CBDO leaders even envision community business development programs as generating sufficient profits to pay for community services in the social and political arenas. Although self-sufficiency has obvious attractions, there has been a decline in the number of CBDOs regarding it as a realistic objective for the foreseeable future. Most think of self-sufficiency in terms of the more realistic goal of generating a flow of income to maintain the CBDO and enabling it to be independent of grants from federal agencies, foundations, churches, and other sources of funds.

Despite the fact that most of these objectives are tied to the economic development of the black community, some writers see a potential for serious conflicts between objectives. Geoffrey Faux, for example, in speaking of Community Development Corporations (CDCs), says:

> Some of the objectives of CDCs are in conflict. A concentration on self-sufficiency, for instance, demands maximization of profits, which in turn requires projects to be chosen on the basis of their profitability rather than their overall impact upon the ghetto economy. Yet if CDCs are to act as catalysts, they will have to make investments of time and money in activities whose returns are to the general economic health of the communities they serve and not the balance sheets of the CDCs.[1]

## THE STAFFING AND OPERATIONS
## OF THE CBDO

### The Staffing of the CBDO

Regardless of how sound the objectives and the organizing plan of a CBDO might be, in the final analysis the effectiveness of the CBDO depends upon its executive and operating staff. In the following discussion the reader is warned not to rely on titles but to seek to understand the staffing concept involved.

THE OPERATING EXECUTIVES. Perhaps the most crucial decision of the CBDO board of directors involves its selection of the CBDO's executive officer. Usually referred to as the *Executive Director, General Manager,* or *President,* this position might be filled by a social worker, a community organizer from the poverty programs, an executive in industry or government, a teacher, or a lawyer. The holder of the title might be male or female, young or old, or conservative or militant. He may or may not understand the business world. Above all, however, he must possess the charisma necessary to stimulate the community and have sufficient leadership qualities to supervise. He must also be able to deal effectively with business leaders and government officials.

Since most CBDO programs revolve around business develop-

[1] Faux, Geoffrey, *CDCs: New Hope for the Inner City.* New York: Twentieth Century Fund, 1971, p. 54.

ment, probably the singular most important senior management position in the CBDO is the *director of business development*. In smaller CBDOs the director of business development and the chief executive officer may be the same person. Regardless of the size of the CBDO, the person responsible for the operation of the business development activity is the one who takes the ideas, wishes, dreams, and policies of the board of directors (and the executive director) and translates them into realizable goals. To accomplish these tasks, he should be thoroughly grounded in business theory and operations and have good business experience.

Many CBDOs found that it took many months to locate a person to become a director of business development. One board member who headed the search committee of a Washington, D.C., CBDO said:

"Most of us on the board have little understanding of the intricacies of business. We know what we are interested in doing for our communities, but we don't know the proper way to go about doing it. The man we're looking for must know how to put together business proposals, what is required to get them funded, and how to go about setting these businesses up once the funds have been provided. We don't have time to be dillydallying around with some cat who has a bunch of degrees but no experience. We need to know like yesterday how to do it."

A Brooklyn board member who had been in a similar position said:

"We had this white fellow from Manhattan with all of his fancy degrees who talked about what he was going to do. When it came time to put up or shut up he didn't know nothing about setting up a black business. All he knew was what he had read in some book: talking about debt/equity ratios and floating $2 million worth of stock in Brooklyn for a brassiere factory."

Obviously one of the director of business development's primary responsibilities is the development of locally owned businesses within the community. In addition, he is also responsible for establishing a rapport with community businessmen, for explaining the role of business to the community residents, and for recruiting a staff.

THE OPERATING STAFF. Without a doubt a most difficult task is the recruiting of a staff to do business development. The director of business development must develop a cadre of business specialists who can evaluate and prepare financial proposals. In addition, his staff will have to be able to assist entrepreneurs who will be plagued with production, accounting, marketing, and similar problems relating to starting and operating a business.

Faced with the need to find blacks with business skills, directors of business development have sought them in industry, government, education, and other community organizations. While their preference has been for the holders of Master's degrees in business administration (MBA), the scarcity of black MBAs has caused many program directors to hire former Peace Corps volunteers, social workers, history teachers, insurance salesmen, or community organizers.

Most program directors point out that they have been quite fortunate in that many blacks are willing to leave positions in industry and government to join CBDOs. For example, in one year a large East Coast food manufacturer lost six of its eight black MBAs to CBDOs across the country. In talking with black MBAs about their reasons for joining CBDOs, it became apparent that they see the CBDO not only as a vehicle for allowing them to help the black community, but also as a means of gaining new experiences. One young MBA who joined a Baltimore CBDO said: "I know that I can only go as high as a manager earning about $17,000 a year. I didn't get my MBA because I only wanted to earn $17,000 a year, but because I believe that it would help me to really accomplish my goal—to own my own business. This agency [CBDO] provided me with an opportunity to use all of my training and to help my people—and not just a small portion of them. Once I get ready to go into business, I will have learned a lot about business; more than I could have ever learned before."

Another black MBA who has just joined a West Coast CBDO said: "Where else can you get the kind of experience and exposure that I'm getting here? I've developed a shoe store, a large bakery, a construction company and I'm working on a merger between two companies. A lot of this stuff even the books in grad school didn't deal with."

Because of the shortage of black MBAs, many CBDOs have attempted to recruit whites to work in their economic development programs, but with little success. One business development director put it bluntly when he said: "We've talked with a lot of whites with good academic backgrounds and business experience about coming to work for us. Most indicate that they would like the experience, but one thing that turns them off is the fear of being in the area after dark. Of course I have to explain to every prospective employee that this isn't a straight nine-to-five job and that they'll find themselves working late at night, Saturdays and Sundays even. Once they hear this, I can see their whole facial expression change. Although we do get a lot back as part-time volunteers—in the daytime."

A new CBDO employee usually undergoes a brief training program that introduces him to the CBDO's business development functions. He then joins other staff members who are divided into specialty areas depending upon their backgrounds and experiences. While job titles within the CBDO may vary, there seems to have developed a consensus about the functions to be carried out by the staff in helping a resident to start a business. Within most CBDOs the various functions are divided as follows:

· The *solicitation function* involves inducing businessmen and prospective entrepreneurs to use the CBDO's services.
· The *screening function* involves the scrutinizing of business propositions to ensure selection of those that seem viable and relevant to the objectives of the CDBO.
· The *loan packaging* function involves finding possible sources of funds and assisting the applicant in preparing a funding proposal.
· The *management assistance* function involves providing management and technical assistance to the businessman.

## The Operations of the CBDO

Because of the scarcity of resources and opportunities in the black community, CBDOs usually proceed on an opportunity strategy. An "opportunity" may be defined as an available building, a white businessman leaving the area, a white corporation's offer to help, or a potential entrepreneur who happens to walk in the door with an idea to start a business. In the exploitation of these opportunities, most CBDOs' activities can be divided into two distinct operations: *funding* and *management assistance*.

FUNDING. Funding applications come to the CBDO either solicited or unsolicited. Solicited applications result from the CBDO staff contacting businessmen, church groups, lodges, block associations, or residents who are interested in going into business. In these instances the staff man explains the CBDO's program and requests that interested persons complete and submit an application.

Most CBDO applications are unsolicited and come from a variety of sources. They may result from someone hearing about the CBDO's program and putting together the business facts on the proposed venture and delivering them to the CBDO. They may also come from a white businessman in the community who is interested in selling his business. Banks and other financial institutions also provide a source of unsolicited applications since they steer businessmen seeking financial assistance to the CBDO, which may be better able to handle the increased risk of ventures in the black community.

Regardless of how the applications come into the CBDO, most go through the following steps: application review, proposal writing, proposal review, and funds disbursement.

The *application review* process usually begins with an examination of the application which allows the CBDO to rule out obviously poor investments. In a case of an overly technical application, the CBDO will send it to a consultant who has the skills to do sufficient research to determine the reasonableness of the idea. Most CBDO officials agree that each application must be reviewed sufficiently to judge the viability of the venture, and if rejected, the decision must be an objective one.

Most CBDOs require that the funding application include a projection of the funds needed and how they are to be used, as well as the business' expected profit. Preparing such an application usually requires a great deal of work by the prospective entrepreneur. From the point of view of the CBDO, it forces him to think seriously about the venture, a requirement which discourages many would-be entrepreneurs who begin to appreciate the "price" of being in business.

Once the staff member has completed his preliminary analysis of the proposed venture, he submits his recommendation to a supervisor who may be a senior staff member or even the director of business development. The final decision of whether to commit the CBDO to investigate the venture further and assist in preparing a funding proposal usually rests with the director of business development. Finally, all applications deemed viable are then developed into proposal.

*Proposal writing* is a full examination of the areas necessary for the profitable operation of a business: management, markets, technical expertise, production, and finance. The proposal must give the CBDO's proposal review mechanism sufficient information to determine if the venture has a reasonable chance to be successful. The typical CBDO proposal, in effect, becomes the major effort to determine whether the venture is sound, based upon the nature of the market, the entrepreneur and his experience, and the amount of funds required. In the nine cases which follow, we have usually included a summary funding proposal for each venture.

The *proposal review* procedure varies from CBDO to CBDO, though in most cases the board of directors plays a significant role in making the final determination as to whether the CBDO will give financial assistance. While in a few CBDOs the final decision is left to the executive director, or even the director of business development, the prevailing pattern is a board committee upon which members of the operating staff may be included. Regardless of its composition, the committee's primary function is to review all proposals and to decide which get funded.

Although most review committees examine carefully such variables as management, marketing, and production, most CBDO officials generally agree that the most crucial consideration is finance. In addition to the level of funding, some other financial issues are debt vs. equity, outside participation, and personal loan guarantees.

While almost all CBDOs make loan funds available, some prefer to take equity positions in the businesses they assist. Though the overwhelming majority of our case studies initially involved loan situations, CBDOs have resorted increasingly to taking an equity position in order to guarantee some broad community ownership in the venture eventually. In essence, a portion of the equity gained by the CBDO would be resold to community residents with the CBDO retaining a portion for itself. Proponents argue that this portion would allow the CBDO to become self-sufficient at a later date. In addition, the equity position helps the CBDO to maintain greater control of the actual management of the company.

Often a CBDO proposal review committee is interested in bringing in other investors. In fact, many review committees *require* bank or SBA participation in their ventures. In addition to leveraging the CBDO's funds, outside participation provides the venture with a source of future short-term capital if the need arises.

Another area where many CBDOs differ is in the amount of risk they pass on to the entrepreneur. Some CBDOs make loans to a corporation formed by the applicant. As such, if the principal uses the funds injudiciously, the CBDO has no redress to the entrepreneur. Accordingly, many CBDOs have continued to make corporate loans only with the personal guarantee of the owner. In doing so, they theorize that the entrepreneur will realize that he is personally liable and take more precautions with the money.

According to several CBDO officials most proposals are not approved at their first presentation to the proposal review committee but have to be revised as a result of questions raised by the committee. However, even when a proposal has been approved, a final issue becomes that of method of *funds disbursement*. Some CBDOs do not disburse all of their funds to the businessman at once, but require a disbursement schedule prepared in conjunction with a member of the CBDO staff. Funds are then disbursed based on the disbursement schedule, with evidence of expenditures being required by the CBDO. Many CBDOs have embraced this idea of a disbursement schedule because of bad experiences they have had with ventures receiving lump sum disbursements. In several such cases the entrepreneur—not being used to controlling such a substantial sum at one time—used the funds imprudently. Once the funds are disbursed, the CBDO's real problems usually start. It must then provide some form of management assistance, an activity which often spells the difference between life and death for black-owned businesses.

MANAGEMENT ASSISTANCE. A CBDO's management assistance program is designed to ensure that a new business venture gets the non-financial support necessary to make it a success. Some CBDOs have specialists who provide this management assistance, while others utilize the staff persons who handled the original funding proposal. The management assistance programs of most CBDOs attempt to supplement the businessman's abilities with those of specialists trained in various business disciplines. These specialists are proficient in a range of fields and may be either on the staff of the CBDO or paid or volunteer consultants.

In the larger CBDOs a management assistance specialist—and in the smaller CBDOs, a staff member—is usually assigned to several businesses and given the over-all responsibility to help each entrepreneur in operating his business. From the day of the approval of the proposal, he helps the businessman to assess his needs, identify potential problems, and, in general, determine how the business will succeed. Once the funds are disbursed, he ideally plans a total program with the operator of the new venture. This program would include such aspects as the accounting systems, inventory control, production, display, bank relations, personnel policies and practices, marketing, and even the grand opening ceremony.

As an operation continues, a management assistance specialist becomes increasingly familiar with the business. His mere presence lends depth to the management and encourages discussion of ideas and problems and their solutions. In a few cases, the management assistance specialists have even been called upon to run a company. This could result because of a personal crisis in the life of the entrepreneur or because the entrepreneur has lost interest in running the operation. Even with a going concern, the specialist may be called upon to serve in such positions as a salesman, fiscal officer, or government liaison man.

Since most CBDOs have many businesses and small staffs, they lean heavily on the use of outside assistance. In addition, a new venture often needs services that cannot be provided by the CBDO's staff and it has to resort to the use of consultants. In these instances, CBDOs are often torn between using *paid* or *volunteer consultants*. The volunteer consultants usually fall into two groups: active or retired businessmen and graduate business students.

Looking first at the volunteer businessmen, CBDO officials have indicated that they often lack the proper attitudes to deal with a black businessman. Many of them assume that because they have knowledge and experience, the black businessman should automatically look to them for assistance. Thus, many consultants seem to find it difficult to deal effectively with an aggressive and confident black who has made the best of his circumstances. As a result, the black businessman often does not accept the volunteer consultant's advice, and consequently, problems are not only unsolved, but in many cases made worse.

Some CBDO directors confide that even worse is the volunteer consultant who is always agreeing with the black businessman. One recent example of this happened in Chicago, where a CBDO asked a volunteer to determine if a black cosmetics wholesaler's inventory turnover and sales projections were reasonable. The consultant walked into the cosmetics warehouse and came face to face with $30,000 worth of cosmetics inventory. At that instant, he exclaimed that the businessman "could capture the market with such an ethnic product" and launched into a long monologue about how more blacks needed to go into the wholesale business. Later he confided to the CBDO official that the owner's sales projections could not be met, being highly optimistic for even an established company. He defended his dubious actions with the view that because blacks had been victimized so long, the owner should have a chance even though it might mean failure. By the time that the CBDO analyst convinced the owner that the projections were too optimistic and his operations should be scaled down, the business had failed.

While student volunteers often have the commitment to help, the majority have never had any business experience nor been involved in the start-up of an operation, and many CBDO officers claim that they are often more fascinated than helpful. As a result, most of their advice is based on the theory that the business has unlimited capital and a triple-A credit rating. As one black businessman said: "Business school teaches you how to deal once you have gotten that nice capitalization, have a good P & L, and a nice D & B rating. But it does *not* teach you how to go about getting a business started. As a result, most graduate students don't have the faintest notion about starting a business from scratch and all that is involved in getting it to the point where people are willing to invest in it. How can they help someone else?"

With poor experiences behind them, many CBDOs have used volunteer consultants—businessmen and students—only under very strict restrictions. These include:

· providing him with sensitivity training
· having him work directly under a staff man who understands the situation and the entrepreneur
· providing him with background material on similar firms started by the CBDO
· arranging pre-interviews between him and the entrepreneur
· making it clear that the CBDO is looking for objective opinions based on his knowledge and/or experience.

CBDOs feel somewhat more secure with paid professional consultants. Though they might fall into bad habits, the CBDO is able to exercise far more control because they are being paid. Also, most paid consultants recognize that the CBDOs have continuing needs for consultants and if they do a good job, they may well expect more business. Accordingly, the paid consultant has fewer problems about working with the CBDO staff and in being restricted by procedures that the CBDO feels are necessary.


## CONCLUSION

In many respects, the frustrations of the management assistance specialists and consultants are reflective of the CBDOs, which are struggling to help blacks get started and to stay in business. Their task is a difficult one and they have not been crowned with great success. But given the bleakness of the situation, they have made tremendous strides.

One could successfully argue that the bulk of this chapter has dealt with theoretical concepts and presents a broad picture of how CBDOs *should* operate. The question still remains as to how effective they have been in *their* business—helping blacks to be successful entrepreneurs. In the cases which follow, we will look at several black businessmen and their and the CBDOs' problems and we will see that CBDOs do have problems with funding, recruitment of good staff, financing and follow-up procedures, and a host of other difficulties.

In recent years, CBDOs have assisted in the development of a variety of business ventures. We have grouped these businesses into franchises, manufacturing, and non-manufacturing operations. In Chapters 4 through 12 the reader will get a firsthand view of nine cases which illustrate the kinds of problems that CBDOs faced as they and the businessman tried to create profitable businesses in the black community.

# I

# Franchises: Guaranteed Black Capitalism?

This section looks at the attempts of two CBDOs to promote black business development through franchising. At the outset many CBDOs viewed franchises as attractive business opportunities because of their time-tested operating systems and the assistance that the franchisor would provide. Since most CBDOs had inexperienced staffs, the franchise seemed to be a reasonable way to ensure success in a new business. The two cases in Part II mirror the learning experiences that took place in the CBDOs as they attempted to come to grips with the problem of the two black franchises. The cases also reflect the CBDOs' recognition that the problems of a franchisee are not dissimilar from those of the operators of other businesses.

# 4

# BAILEY'S ARC TRANSMISSIONS

Bailey's ARC Transmissions, our first case, focuses on the problems of a black junior accountant who started a transmission repair franchise business in July 1970 in a location that had already been abandoned by at least one other franchisee. About one half of the financing for Bailey's was provided by a Detroit CBDO which found out later that the franchisor had a questionable reputation.

The Detroit CBDO in this case was a not-for-profit corporation which began operations in May 1969 with its primary purpose being to develop businesses with black ownership. The Detroit CBDO had a thirty-man board of directors, all of whom lived in the black community and all of whom were elected by community organizations. Primary responsibility for the CBDO's total operations lay with the CBDO's president, who delegated much of the development of locally owned business to an economic development director. The funds to support the CBDO's business development program came mostly from private Detroit firms and foundations, though the CBDO had a state planning grant.

At the time that the CBDO began offering assistance to Robert Bailey, it had "looked into the merits of franchise operations for underskilled black residents." During Bailey's initial visit to the CBDO in October 1969, it had already given financial assistance to a greeting card manufacturer, a men's retail store, and a service station.

# THE CASE

*Introduction*

On May 5, 1971, William Joyner, president of the Detroit CBDO, received the following letter from ARC Transmissions advising him that ARC was considering revoking Robert Bailey's franchise:

May 3, 1971
Mr. William Joyner
President, Detroit CBDO

Dear Mr. Joyner:

During the summer of 1970, Robert Bailey opened his ARC Transmission Center. ARC and all others involved in this very important undertaking were hopeful that this would turn out to be a very successful and gratifying experience. We regret that this was not the case. Instead, we find it necessary to reluctantly list the following undesirable situations:

1. We have had ARC representatives at Bailey's Center on several occasions totalling approximately nine weeks in an attempt to help him acquire the ability and the motivation to properly run his Center. It is customary for ARC to send such a representative to a new center for a period of one week. The men that we have sent have reported that he was very difficult to get along with, was uncooperative and did not spend the required time in his Center.
2. He did not cooperate with the other ARC centers in his marketing area in advertising programs where the interest from such advertising would accrue to him as well as the other centers involved . . .
3. Since the first of the year, Mr. Bailey has not been sending in the weekly business reports required under his Franchise Agreement.
4. Since the first of the year, Mr. Bailey has not been paying his franchise fees . . .
5. Since the first of the year, he has not paid the $480 monthly rental for the property, which at the end of April totalled $1,920.
6. He owes ARC over $1,000 for parts and over $700 for advertising.
7. He owes other ARC centers varying amounts for work they performed on the guarantees issued by him.
8. He has created a very unsatisfactory atmosphere among his fellow ARC operators . . .

52                                          BLACK ENTERPRISE, INC.

9. Contrary to and in violation of his Franchise Agreement, he has purchased a car wash across the street from his ARC Center. This must detract from the time and effort that he should be applying to his ARC Center . . .

In view of the violations of his Franchise Agreement and the wrongdoings as recited, we hereby tender notice that we desire to have the license granted to Robert Bailey revoked, Bailey's ARC Center discontinue business as ARC and the vacating of the property for which rent is due and payable to ARC.

Very truly yours,
Stanley Flowers
Vice-President

*Background*

ROBERT BAILEY. Robert Bailey was born on Chicago's South Side in 1928 and before finishing high school moved to Detroit in 1946. After moving to Detroit he took a high school equivalency examination to obtain his Michigan Equivalency Diploma to enable him to pursue an advanced educational degree. In 1948 he joined the United States Army and was trained in an administrative trade where he "learned most of the basics of administration."

After leaving the military in 1950, he studied at a local junior college and at Wayne State University, concentrating in accounting and corporate finance. At the junior college he received a diploma in accounting and general business.

After a series of odd jobs in the 1950s "because nobody would hire a black professional," he took a job at the University Medical Center in September 1964 as the accounting clerk to the project assistant at a salary of $5,200 a year. In September 1967 he left the Medical Center to work for Metropolitan Life Insurance Company as a special agent through April 1968. From April 1968 to May 1970 he was back at the Medical Center, first as a statistical clerk at a salary of $5,720 per year, rising finally to the position of cost accountant at a salary of $6,500 per year.

While at the Medical Center, Bailey became interested in "going into business." He had "done some reading on transmissions repair and believed that this was one place where blacks could really make it." Automatic transmission franchises were booming and he "thought that a franchise would be a real winner." After more research, Bailey finally decided that he wanted an ARC Transmission franchise.

ARC TRANSMISSIONS. ARC Transmissions, Inc., had started operations in Michigan in 1958 with eight company-owned shops. Two years later, John Igel, its founder and president, introduced a system of franchising that produced a chain of over 375 centers by 1970, making it one of the Midwest's largest chains of automatic transmission centers. In its literature, the company said that it had grown from sales of "less than $1 million in 1958 to over $100 million in 1970." It went on to say:

ARC has a complete line of parts warehoused in Pontiac which are shipped air freight to ARC distributors throughout the country . . .

ARC distributors come from all walks of life: accountants, retired military officers, engineers, insurance men. No mechanical experience or aptitudes required. ARC franchisees enjoy outstanding success rate.

ARC will spend over $10 million in 1970 in television, radio, newspaper and magazine advertising.

BAILEY AND THE CBDO. After completing his review of ARC, Bailey approached the Slip Company, a subsidiary of ARC, for financing. After the Slip credit analyst looked over Bailey's application in August 1969, he recommended against financing him. The slip analyst stated that "Mr. Bailey does not qualify for Slip participation because he does not have the background or experience necessary in the transmission field."

Not content with this negative response, Bailey went to the local CBDO in October 1969 for financial assistance. At the CBDO he met Dick Newsome, a young black lawyer, who had studied at Wayne State and the University of Michigan. In his capacity as the CBDO's director of economic development, Newsome listened to Bailey's description of ARC and requested that he (Bailey) complete an application form for financial assistance. With the information that Bailey supplied, Newsome then had a staff analyst prepare a proposal for financial assistance. (See Exhibit I on pages 74–76 for a summary of the Bailey proposal.[1])

[1] Exhibit I and all other Exhibits for Bailey's ARC Transmissions are found at the end of Chapter 4. Also, in the eight subsequent cases in Chapters 5 through 12, the relevant Exhibits are all found at the ends of the respective chapters.

In support of his contention that he "understood the ARC operations *and* that it made 'economic sense' to assist Bailey," Newsome sent the CBDO Loan Committee the proposal and the following information on ARC:

TO: Loan Committee
FROM: Richard Newsome
DATE: November 19, 1969

Re: Franchisee Program — ARC Transmissions, Inc.

| | |
|---|---|
| *Franchise Fee:* | $7,000 |
| *Royalty Fee:* | 7½% of weekly gross sales |
| *Operation Fee:* | 4% of weekly gross sales, refundable quarterly provided franchisee has complied with ARC rules and regulations. |
| *Capital Investment:* | $32,000 for a six-bay facility (including $7,000 franchise fee). |

In response to several questions on the prospects of a successful operation, Newsome sent the following projections on a "typical" ARC Center to the Loan Committee:

TO: Loan Committee
FROM: Richard Newsome
DATE: December 1, 1969

Projected Sales and Operation Expense
for Typical ARC Transmission Center

| | Calendar Year Ended | |
| --- | --- | --- |
| | 12/31/68 ($3,000 per week) | 12/31/69 ($4,000 per week) |
| Sales | $156,000.00 | $208,000.00 |
| Expenses: | | |
| Parts | $ 23,400.00 | $ 31,200.00 |
| Labor | 23,400.00 | 31,200.00 |
| Commissions | 8,400.00 | 11,400.00 |
| Payroll Taxes and Insurance | 2,340.00 | 3,120.00 |
| Advertising | 23,400.00 | 20,800.00 |
| Franchise Fee | 10,920.00 | 14,560.00 |
| Rent | 7,200.00 | 7,200.00 |
| Maintenance and Repairs | 1,200.00 | 1,200.00 |
| Telephone, Gas, Electricity | 2,400.00 | 2,400.00 |
| Insurance — Other Than Payroll | 1,200.00 | 1,200.00 |
| Legal and Accounting | 1,200.00 | 1,200.00 |
| Towing | 2,400.00 | 2,400.00 |
| Miscellaneous | 1,200.00 | 1,200.00 |
| Laundry, Towels, Etc. | 1,200.00 | 1,200.00 |
| Office Supplies | 750.00 | 750.00 |
| Total Operating Expenses | $110,610.00 | $131,030.00 |
| Net Profit on Operations | $ 45,390.00 | $ 76.970.00 |
| Owner's Salary | $ 15,000.00 | $ 15,000.00 |
| Net | $ 30,390.00 | $ 61,970.00 |

BLACK ENTERPRISE, INC.

During the period in which the CBDO loan committee was debating the merits of the Bailey proposal, a state investigator made several serious allegations about transmission franchises in general, and ARC in particular. In December 1969 Newsome read the following story which appeared in a Detroit newspaper:

. . . In a 400-page affidavit the Attorney General charged that irregularities in transmission shops and other repair shops are widespread in the City, and include overcharges, "repair" of non-existent problems and unnecessary replacement of parts . . .

During the investigation it was discovered that ARC had never filed proper papers for doing business in Detroit. The Court order told ARC to cease its business until they complied with city laws . . .

ARC was assessed and paid $36,000 for its share of the investigation.

Ralph Lee, an assistant attorney general, started his investigation by taking a training school course then spent ten months in the field checking repair shops, many of them ARC franchises.

In his affidavit, he said ARC trains sales people for its franchises in how to tell customers that their transmissions are shot, burned out, have deposits of scum on them or have other difficulties.

In one shop, Lee said, when he refused to pay for repairs, a worker handed the transmission parts back to him in a box.

At another ARC shop Lee said he found that the transmission which was replaced with one represented to be new was only repainted.

In Lakewood, Lee charged that ARC men were obtaining their replacement transmissions from junk shops.

Though "the article and other information raised several doubts" in Newsome's mind, he nevertheless "pushed for CBDO and bank acceptance of the proposal" and by March 1970 the financial package was set. The CBDO would lend Bailey $17,500 and the bank would lend him $16,398, repayable in sixty installments, forty-five days after disbursement at a rate of $237 per month.

ARC then went to work to locate a site for Bailey. In April 1970 it "identified a location that appeared suitable." The building had housed an ARC dealer from October 1969 to January 1970 and was at "a busy intersection near several other automotive stores and shops." The location still belonged to ARC but they agreed to sublet it to Bailey. Newsome also insisted that ARC provide Bailey with projected revenue for the location. In response to this request, Stanley Flowers, ARC vice-president, sent the following letter to Bailey:

April 13, 1970
Mr. Robert Bailey
39 Less Street
Detroit, Michigan

Dear Bob:
Here are the facts that Dick Newsome requested on the ARC Center. The center was opened the week of October 20, 1969.

| Week Ending | Gross Sales | No. of Cars |
|---|---|---|
| 10/24 | $ 3,132 | 17 |
| 10/31 | 3,564 | 17 |
| 11/7 | 3,047 | 18 |
| 11/14 | 3,220 | 16 |
| 11/21 | 3,046 | 13 |
| 11/28 | 2,898 | 16 |
| 12/5 | 4,247 | 20 |
| 12/12 | 1,975 | 15 |
| 12/19 | 1,309 | 8 |
| 12/26 | 3,460 | 17 |
| 1/2 | 888 | 4 |
| 1/9 | 1,289 | 6 |
| 1/16 | 1,265 | 8 |
| 1/23 | 601 | 8 |
| 1/30 | 2,450 | 13 |
| | $36,391 | 196 |

The figures for February and March are not available as they were not reported to ARC. This is the reason this center is available for sale.

Cordially,
Stanley Flowers, Vice-President



With the receipt of this letter Bailey was "anxious and impatient to get started." He signed a lease and "wanted to get going in the training program." By the middle of May 1970 Bailey was in Pontiac to begin his training program and on June 12, 1970, he sent the following letter to Newsome voicing his approval of the program:

June 12, 1970
Mr. Richard Newsome
Detroit CBDO
Detroit, Michigan

Dear Mr. Newsome:

This may be a little late but on the other hand, it's timely. Today we are exactly halfway through the course.

Up to now it has been intensive and interesting; at a fairly terrific pace. The student body of twelve comes from all over the U.S. and from equally varied professions or vocations. We have all learned by now that this is a course designed for more than to impart knowledge. There's a lot of built-in psychological pressure. In addition to testing men's ability to absorb and reproduce—a good deal verbatim—one's breaking point is also constantly tested. These people seem to be pretty well organized. Quite frankly, it's not exactly easy.

On the very first day we were warned that it was not unlikely that the group would suffer one or two fatalities. Since the beginning of the program the average fatality has been one and one half per group. Well, our group had its first victim today—its highest ranking member too, a Major General of the U. S. Air Force. He was quite broken and slipped away quietly this morning. He is a fine man and we were all very touched. However, we're not without rank. We still have an Air Force Colonel left.

Well, unless we are in contact before, I hope to see you as soon as possible after my arrival.

Trusting sincerely that you and your family are in good health,

Cordially yours,
Bob Bailey

Bailey graduated from the training center at the end of June and on July 1, 1970, signed a loan agreement with the CBDO. The CBDO had already issued approximately $5,000 to Bailey while he was still in school so that he could secure his equipment and inventory.

*Operations*

START-UP. On July 8, 1970, Bailey's ARC Transmissions opened for business with a large press party attended by CBDO and ARC officials. At this gathering, ARC president John Igel set the tone with the following speech:

"I would like to congratulate the members of the Detroit Business Development Corporation on the wonderful progress they are making in the areas of inner-city development.

"I feel that this achievement should act as a board of reckoning for the industries of the nation to come forth with a show of hands with active participation in community development. There is a need for providing lines of credit for entrepreneurs in ghetto areas and to provide management skills and technical skills to neighborhood groups to carry out specific projects. We at ARC look upon the concept of franchising as one of the tools available for the development of our nation's future.

"Franchising today represents about $75 billion or 12 per cent of the gross national product. There are 350,000 franchisees in operation now, accounting for 25 per cent of all the retail sales within this country.

"Now, what exactly can franchising do for community development? Franchising enables men with drive, and ability, to elevate themselves above their normal earning potentials within the inner city. Through franchising these men can realize an income above the limitations which society may have seemed to set for them. These entrepreneurs can now choose their own goals and they are given every tool necessary to achieve these goals.

"Through the franchise, one doesn't just invest in a business, and then open a business. He is trained, deliberately and comprehensively. His employees are trained. A system of procedures is established for his guidance. He is given constant direction throughout his entire career by the franchisor's home office.

"In short, the franchisee is like an adopted son. He has the stature of owning his own business. But he also commits himself to accepting constant direction from the parent company that will virtually assure his success, as it has done for many others.

"The world of franchising has a great deal to offer in the form of business opportunities, in the form of skilled training, and in the form of personal enrichments. Franchising is clearly a way for community development. We feel that this major success of this Business Development Corporation is a strong indication that progress can be made.

"No longer can lack of understanding be the reason for industries to tolerate the creeping paralysis of initiative within the ghetto communities. And no longer should industry sweep the inner-city problems, along with their consciences, under the rug.

60                                                                BLACK ENTERPRISE, INC.

"It is a mandate for the industries of the United States to grapple with the inner-city problems, rather than grope with them. When that time comes, when programs are efficiently executed, and not just set up —when there is greater achievement by the individuals in the ghettos as a direct result of our united efforts—then and only then will our great American dream of free enterprise be more than just that . . . a dream."

In September 1970, while reviewing the Bailey file, Newsome realized that there were several missing documents, including copies of Bailey's certificate of incorporation, corporate bylaws, and statement of assets and liabilities. In order to ascertain what had happened to these documents, Newsome asked Bailey to come to the CBDO's office on October 14 for a conference. Although Bailey indicated that he could make the appointment, he did not appear, nor did he call to cancel his appointment.

Bailey and Newsome next agreed on another appointment for October 23 at 2:30 P.M. At that meeting, in addition to Newsome and Bailey, was Joe Buggs, a white CBDO staff member who was a graduate of a Midwestern business school. During the conversation, Bailey said that he was thinking of expanding his operation to include a new auto preparation franchise, and he thought that it would be a profitable adjunct to the present business. Newsome counseled Bailey against expansion, advising him to "move slowly, since the ARC center is less than four months old." Newsome also suggested that there might be some legal obstacles against such an expansion, whereupon Bailey agreed to delay any move into a new business. Finally Buggs briefed Bailey on the terms of his CBDO contract with respect to use of funds, loan repayments, financial statements, employment, and insurance.

On October 29 Buggs sent a follow-up letter to Bailey reminding him he was to furnish the CBDO with quarterly financial statements for each of the first three fiscal quarters and a certified annual statement for each fiscal year.

FINANCIAL AND OPERATING PROBLEMS. At a meeting on November 9, Buggs asked Bailey about the status of his fire, theft, and liability insurance. Bailey said that he was "aware that [I] need to renew [my] insurance," and he was "in the process of acquiring a bank loan to pay for it." Bailey added that he had contacted his insurance broker, and had received an extension on his expired insurance policy. Bailey promised to contact Buggs as soon as the matter was completed.

On November 16 Buggs met Bailey at the ARC shop and several personnel and production problems came to light. Bailey stated that it was difficult to find qualified transmission specialists, that some of his employees lacked discipline, and that absenteeism and tardiness were common. Buggs advised Bailey to be firm with his employees and let them go after one or two warnings. He also suggested that Bailey "strive to develop a workshop spirit with pride of being part of the ARC team."

Bailey next pointed out that his service manager—Sidney—was not effective in controlling production. Buggs recommended that Sidney be reduced to a senior worker, and that production control be left to Ralph Cost, the general manager. Bailey agreed that this made sense and then pointed out that production was also adversely affected by limited work space. According to Bailey, the number of cars that the men could work on at any time was limited and he classified it as an "unsurmountable problem." Buggs advised him that with proper production control, output might be speeded up.

Next Bailey said that he had "some bills." He owed his lawyer $800 and the insurance company approximately $1,700. Furthermore, he said that if he did not pay the insurance premium by November 20 he would lose his coverage. Buggs advised Bailey to seek a bank loan, since it would "take too long for the CBDO to process a request for funds." As he left the office, Buggs reminded Bailey that he had to take the initiative and do better planning as far as paying his bills was concerned. He added that "you [Bailey] should have taken care of these matters months ago unless you were undercapitalized in the beginning."

After this episode it was clear to Buggs that the CBDO's reporting procedures were not effective in terms of management control. Bailey's financial statements were required on a quarterly basis, with a sixty-day grace period. Consequently, Bailey's or any business could operate for five months before submitting financial statements. Therefore, it was clear to Buggs that there was need for a change. Consequently, he sent a letter to Bailey explaining that effective January 1971 *monthly* financial statements would be needed to keep the CBDO abreast of developments.

On Thursday, January 7, 1971, Bailey walked into Buggs' office at 11 A.M. and said that he had insufficient funds to meet his payroll of $730 due the next day. He said that he had a bank balance at the end of 1970, but had not taken into consideration a number of checks which had not cleared. Buggs stated that there was not much he could do other than call in Newsome, the Director of Economic Development.

About noon on that same day, Newsome joined the meeting and said that unless Bailey had "financial statements or some concrete indication of immediate financial needs" there was very little the CBDO could do. Bailey in turn contended that his present situation was a consequence of having *"insufficient working capital from the very start."* He also argued that though he was not familiar with the current status of his accounts receivables, he felt "off the top of my head, they are $1,400 at most."

Before Newsome or Buggs could respond, Bailey became further incensed and began a tirade, categorizing all of his problems. First, he complained that Sidney, his senior rebuilder, was doing inferior work. He said that "everything Sidney touches comes back and costs me additional time and money." Next, Bailey complained about his new service manager, Ralph Cost. He said that "Ralph is a weak manager although he is technically proficient." And finally, Bailey complained bitterly about ARC Transmissions, Inc. According to Bailey, ARC "left me high and dry except when it wished to sell me parts."

Bothered by Bailey's attacks, Buggs responded that he had "gotten wind" that Bailey owned the car wash across the street from the transmission center "in direct contract violation of [your] contract." Buggs said, "Since you are discussing your problems, it might be appropriate to discuss the ownership of this car wash."

Bailey admitted readily that he and Ralph Cost (the service manager) had bought the car wash with "$1,000 each." According to Bailey, "the car wash is economically self-sufficient and is justified on the basis that it provides extra space for vehicles awaiting transmission service." Bailey further added that the ARC center was "doing okay" and then produced a four-month profit and loss statement and a balance sheet for October 31, 1970, which showed that the business had over $1,300 in cash *at that time.* Bailey explained that he had just received the statement and in the "heat of argument" had neglected to mention it. (See Exhibit II on pages 77–79 for the October 1970 financial statement.)

FRANCHISOR ASSISTANCE FOR BAILEY. After further discussions the CBDO officials and Bailey agreed that Bailey had violated his franchise and the CBDO agreements and that some corrective steps should be taken. Accordingly, on January 29 Buggs contacted ARC's director of franchising, Mr. Sam Morris, and apprised him of Bailey's situation. Buggs suggested that ARC "take action to provide Bailey with intensive management assistance since he seems to be falling by the wayside." Mr. Morris stated that ARC had "volunteered assistance to Bailey in late 1970" and that Bailey had "rebuffed these overtures to help" and said that he (Bailey) would "take the matter to the [ARC's] president." Morris then stated that he would "refer the case to Mr. Stanley Flowers, Vice-President of Operations, since Mr. Igel [ARC president] has been intimately involved from the beginning."

On February 12 Buggs received a telephone call from Flowers, who said that ARC was "not pleased with Bailey's operation at all." Buggs agreed that Bailey had some problems but again asked: "What can ARC do?" Flowers finally agreed that ARC would send a "top-notch individual to work with Bailey for a period of two weeks starting on February 22." Buggs cautioned Flowers that "a troubleshooter should offer his help in the spirit of cooperation and not in the spirit of condescension, the attitude that alienates blacks." Flowers agreed and said that the troubleshooter was "an indoctrinated man."

Flowers said he would ask the troubleshooter to make a recommendation on whether Bailey was capable of managing an ARC center and also whether the center still had potential. Flowers said if ARC found that the center had potential but Bailey was incapable, he "might recommend the transfer of ownership to another community resident."

Later that day, Buggs contacted Bailey to confirm an appointment they had scheduled for 3:30 P.M. Though he had indicated that he was coming, Bailey failed to appear. When Buggs finally contacted him at about 4:10 P.M. at his shop, Bailey said that he had been "too busy running around." During this conversation Buggs advised Bailey that ARC was going to provide the center with management assistance for a period of approximately two weeks starting Monday, February 22. Bailey replied that he was "willing to cooperate since I need help" and also informed Buggs that he had fired Sidney and hired a new rebuilder. Buggs and Bailey then rescheduled their meeting for February 16.

BLACK ENTERPRISE, INC.

On February 16 Bailey called to inform Buggs that he could not make the meeting, but that he had sent over financial statements for the period July through December 1970. (See Exhibit III on pages 80–82 for Bailey's year-end financial statement.) He added that he would see Buggs on February 22 when the "ARC expert comes to town."

On February 22 a meeting was held at the CBDO. Present were Bailey, Buggs, and Ron Kaneel of ARC. Buggs introduced Kaneel to Bailey, and explained that Kaneel was there to help Bailey in any way he could. At the meeting Bailey was very cooperative and highlighted briefly his major problems as personnel, space, competition, and working capital. He added, however, that business was generating enough income to make ends meet.

One week later on March 1, Buggs called Bailey to find out if Kaneel was helping to improve operations. According to Bailey, Kaneel was "not making much of a contribution." He felt that all Kaneel did was "stand around all day and observe."

To get a different point of view, Buggs next contacted Kaneel, who summarized his feelings in the following March 5 report:

Bob Bailey feels that his main problem in this center is the lack of operating capital. Although he is in trouble financially, I feel that this could have been avoided, for the most part, if he spent more time in the center where his customers are, and also if he used the Merchandising Procedure as he was taught. No matter how much more money he receives for operating this center, unless he himself handles more of these procedures and implements them as he was taught in the training course at ARC, he will never be able to get this center on a profit-making basis.

Bob, these past two weeks, never arrived at the center before 9:30 A.M. leaving his lead man, Cost, in charge. Cost knows the ARC Merchandising Procedures; however, I feel that he doesn't have the ability to use these procedures effectively. Even when Bob is in the center, and from what I have heard, that isn't too often, Cost is the one who usually handles the customer, at least up until the car delivery procedure. The few times I saw Bob handle the Service Recommendation Procedure with the customer, I found that he was able to convince the customer of the value of the Six-Month Exchange Rebuilt or the Car Ownership Exchange Rebuilt Services over the Ninety-Day Repair Service. I pointed this out to Bob, explaining that the extra money he got for these services meant that much more profit for him and that if he continued to do this, he would be able to make more profit and ease the financial position that he was in.

Another problem in this center is Bob's apparent lack of interest in its operation. When I point out a way to retain a car using the ARC Merchandising Procedure, he advises me that he already knows this. As far as I can detect, he isn't using all the tools at his command and doesn't retain as many leads as he should.

Bob feels that if he has to offer the customer a Customer Service Refund for the $23 inspection service, the chances are that he will have to put the transmission back together and in the car. I purposely handled a situation such as this myself, in order to show him how it can work effectively. Even with this example, I don't believe that he is convinced of the effectiveness of this method. He also doesn't believe that he should sell a Car Ownership Exchange Rebuilt because the extra $60 or $100 isn't worth it to him. I tried to point out to him that this extra profit is necessary right now so that he will be able to fulfill his present financial obligations and the chances of his having problems with these units in the future are not that great. His comebacks were running high until recently when he fired his rebuilder and hired one that can rebuild units with less trouble.

As I mentioned before, Cost, the lead man, knows the ARC Merchandising Procedures but doesn't have the sales ability to sell the better services. He is primarily a rebuilder but he doesn't have the knowledge of transmissions that he should. For example, he is in charge of parts but doesn't know all the parts he has on hand and often sends out for a part that he already has in stock. I spent an entire day in the parts department trying to straighten it out so that the parts on hand were more recognizable. When he disassembles a unit he doesn't take it all the way down first; instead he writes up the repair service as he goes, then he disassembles the unit the rest of the way. He usually finds much more damage in the unit; had this damage been recorded, the repair service price would have been closer to or more than the Six-Month Exchange Rebuilt price that he quoted to the customer. I pointed this out to him, and I believe that the services that were offered this past week were more in line with what was wrong with these units.

From what I can gather, Bob and his lead man, Cost, have a financial interest in the car wash across the street and spend considerable time attending to these interests and neglecting their interest in the ARC center.

In summation, I feel the center has four major problems:
1. It is out of advertising.
2. It will not be in the Yellow Pages until April.
3. It has a poor reputation for the large amount of comebacks. This has been corrected by hiring a new man recently.
4. Bob's apparent lack of cooperation and implementation of ARC's Merchandising Procedures.

All these problems, I feel, can easily be corrected, except for Bob's attitude.

THE DECLINE OF BAILEY'S ARC CENTER. John Sheffield was assigned by Newsome to the Bailey case in March. Sheffield, who had a Master's degree in sociology from Michigan State University, had known Newsome before entering the Peace Corps in 1968. He had joined the CBDO staff in late January 1971 and was assigned to the case because Newsome thought that a "black staff member might improve the CBDO's relations with Bailey." On March 15 Sheffield met with Bailey, who explained that his main problem was "lack of working capital." Having spoken to Buggs earlier, Sheffield was aware of the problem and suggested to Bailey that perhaps his ability to manage his finances was a major part of the problem.

Sheffield spent the next few days reviewing Bailey's over-all operation, trying to determine what went wrong. On March 26 Sheffield scheduled an important meeting. Present were Bailey, Simon Stuart (legal counsel for the CBDO), Van Johnson (a local C.P.A.), Joe Buggs (the former CBDO contact man), John McQueen (representative of the local bank), and Sheffield. The meeting was held to review Bailey ARC Transmissions' financial situation as of December 31, 1970. At this meeting Johnson, the accountant retained by the CBDO to audit Bailey's books, explained the financial transactions that were questionable. He covered the following points at the meeting:

*Records*—Mr. Bailey's records showed that he withdrew $1,000 in September and $3,000 in October for himself. The $4,000 cash transaction was not journalized until December of 1970 and at that time it was charged to the office loan account with no explanatory note. I surmise that Mr. Bailey used the money for the car wash.

*Present Bank & Loan Situation*—Bailey received about $30,000 in financial assistance, $27,000 of which went to ARC. Mr. Bailey argued that his problems arose because of initial insufficient working capital compounded by high initial cost in trying to recruit proper personnel. Mr. Bailey was several payments behind to the bank.

*Adjustments*—It was necessary to make several adjustments to Mr. Bailey's Balance Sheet since the insurance account, the equipment account, and the liabilities account were understated.

Johnson also highlighted Bailey's poor collection and credit controls; cars being left for repairs without an initial deposit on repair work; and an ineffective bookkeeping system. After Johnson finished, Bailey argued that he had to "supervise work as well as talk to customers, consequently, there is very little time for administrative matters."

On March 29 Sheffield visited Bailey at 9:15 A.M. Bailey was not in, but Sheffield spoke to Roy White, a new employee who seemed to be in charge. White informed Sheffield that he did not know what time Bailey would arrive. When Sheffield asked White about Cost, the service manager, he learned that he was working across the street. Sheffield visited Cost at the car wash, but was unable to speak to him because he was busy with a customer's car.

Sheffield left the car wash to visit another CBDO client and returned at 11:30 A.M. to find that Bailey had not yet arrived. White informed Sheffield that Bailey was "getting his hair cut and would call later." Sheffield returned to the office and received a call from Bailey at 12:30 P.M. Bailey explained that he still needed working capital and the CBDO had neglected him.

On March 31 Sheffield visited Bailey's shop at 3:30 P.M. As he approached the shop, he noticed that "it appeared closed for business." However, upon further inspection he saw that the garage door was merely shut. Upon entering the shop, Sheffield saw "White and another employee eating a late lunch of chicken." He inquired about Bailey's whereabouts and learned that White "did not know where he was or when he might be expected back."

On April 2 Sheffield again visited the shop. When he approached Bailey, the latter "became quite belligerent," stating that he thought Sheffield's visit to be "purposeless" if he did not come with the promise of more working capital. Sheffield reminded Bailey that in accordance with his contract with the CBDO, he still had "certain responsibilities such as the submission of financial statements and filing of employee reports." Bailey said that "these are not necessary."

On April 16 Sheffield again visited Bailey. Though it was approaching 12:30 P.M., Bailey had not yet arrived. When asked when he was expected, Bailey's employees would give no answer. Sheffield waited an hour and finally left.

### The Future of Bailey's ARC Transmissions

Upon securing ARC Transmissions, Inc.'s, May 3, 1971, letter advising him of the franchisor's plan regarding Bailey, William Joyner, the CBDO president, asked Dick Newsome to evaluate the situation. Though Newsome saw the alternatives as (1) closing the business, (2) providing additional assistance, or (3) getting a new franchisee, he did ask Joe Futrel, a black senior financial analyst with the CBDO, to "prepare an independent in-depth report on Bailey."

In the following memorandum to Newsome, Futrel summarized the Bailey case:

TO: Richard Newsome
FROM: Joe Futrel
DATE: June 17, 1971
RE: The Bailey Case

We have received two certified letters from ARC giving notice of the intent to revoke Mr. Bailey's license. I visited Mr. Bailey on June 11th for discussion of the current situation.

The following are Mr. Bailey's reactions in reference to various aspects of his business and to his relationships with ARC and us.

. . . He believes that he was doomed for failure from the beginning because he was not provided with sufficient working capital. His initial impression was that capital would be provided by us at quarterly intervals during the business' beginning. When funds were not forthcoming, he had to cut corners. This has resulted in the present situation.

. . . He said that he had received no written communications as to ARC's intentions. He did not receive letters similar to those sent to us. During the course of our conversation, however, notification of non-payment of rent was presented to Mr. Bailey. ARC gave him three days to pay $2,880 in overdue rent or to vacate the premises.

. . . He feels the other ARC shops—particularly the 663 Boggs Avenue location—are conspiring to put him out of business because he is black.

. . . He acknowledges ownership of the car wash located almost directly opposite his shop but contends that he is entitled to make such an investment, since none of his time or energy is involved in the operation of that business.

. . . He said ARC sent him improper inventory which he has not been able to exchange because he must purchase two items for every one he returns.

. . . Mr. Bailey stated that he has not paid fees due to ARC since the beginning of the year. He said he concentrated on paying those bills which would keep him open (labor, electricity, parts) and did not have funds with which to pay ARC.

. . . He stated that he did not know how much he owed or how much money he had in the bank.

The above reactions are presented so that a partial picture of Mr. Bailey's outlook can be obtained.

Subsequent to my conversations with Mr. Bailey, I spoke to Mr.

Flowers and Mr. Morris of ARC. They feel they have been extremely patient with Mr. Bailey and have provided him with a great deal of assistance. They have recently been pressured by the other franchisees to correct the present situation as it affects them. These franchisees share in advertising expenses. They feel Mr. Bailey is getting a free ride at their expense. This has created dissension in the organization and Messrs. Flowers and Morris are taking steps to stop it.

They stated that Mr. Bailey could keep the franchise only if all back payments were made and only if he agreed in writing to live up to the contract. During the course of the conversation, I expressed my belief that Mr. Bailey should be contacted directly concerning all of the problems that have developed.

On June 12th, I had another lengthy conversation with Mr. Bailey. I informed him that we would not consider giving him monetary assistance until his financial statements are available. Shortly thereafter he would be notified as to our decison.

Up to this point there has been no direct contact between Mr. Bailey and ARC. I urged him to telephone ARC so as to talk to someone directly about his situation. I was informed the following day by Mr. Bailey that he will attend a meeting with ARC the latter part of next week. He was told that further actions by ARC would await the outcome of this meeting.

I feel that mistakes made by each of the parties concerned—Mr. Bailey, ARC, and us—have led to the present situation.

Mr. Bailey will not accept full responsibility for the management of the business and will not accept suggestions for change. For example, when it was suggested that he should be present when the shop is opened, his reaction was that this is "an effort to cut down my independence as an owner and to make me punch a time clock like a laborer."

Mr. Bailey seeks to delegate his authority but does not follow up once this delegation is made. As a result he is not on top of things, but moves from one crisis to another.

Inquiries from independent sources have raised serious questions as to ARC's effectiveness. The SBA has found that ARC extracts excessive fees, they perform inadequate location analysis and their sales and profit projections have been overly optimistic.

When it is considered that it usually takes three to six months before income from the business will cover regular monthly expenses, it appears that we did not provide sufficient working capital to the firm. Add to this the fact that new businessmen (even those with good background experience) are likely to make one serious mistake during the first year of operation and it becomes clear that an adequate provision was not made.

In addition we should have made a more serious review of the ARC franchise operation. A hint of possible problems with the franchise was indicated last year, but there appears to have been no follow-up.

Because of the lack of financial data, it is impossible to reach a firm decision at this time. Mr. Johnson told me statements would have been available by June 16th.

The major questions are whether this shop can be made into a viable business and who would be most able to accomplish this goal. Mr. Bailey has had the advantage of day-to-day experience over the last 11 months but he has not been able to "take hold" of the problems and to work toward their resolutions. I have no confidence that he will be able to do this alone in the immediate future. If financial aid is to be given, it would have to be tied to closer managerial assistance from us.

An alternative is to seek an individual with the capacity to take over ownership and management of the business. Our past experience would have to be relied upon to determine whether a trained individual would be available for this purpose within a reasonably short period of time. The shop itself is located in a very competitive area. There is a nationally advertised transmission franchise located across the street and there are other transmission businesses in the area. Therefore, it is easy for the customer to shop around when he is not satisfied. This shop must be tightly managed if it is to survive.

On June 18—the day after the report—Sheffield received May 31 financial reports from Bailey. (See Exhibit IV on pages 83–85 for Bailey's May 31 financial statement.) He noticed that "they did not seem bad."

## EPILOGUE

After reviewing Futrel's report and Bailey's May 31, 1971, financial statements, Newsome passed them on to William Joyner, president of the CBDO. Joyner scheduled a meeting for June 29 which he began by asking Newsome if it would not be better to try and salvage some of the CBDO's investment since "it is always better to save an investment providing it can be saved." When Newsome answered in the negative, Joyner then raised the possibility of putting in another franchisee. Newsome replied that "the problem is more than the franchisee; another part of the problem is the franchisor." He then produced the December 1969 newspaper story on ARC Transmissions, Inc. Joyner also learned from Newsome that Bailey's facility only had enough space for serving three cars and no storage space, thus meaning that the facility could not service enough cars fast enough to make a profit. Newsome indicated that the only way that Bailey could make a profit was to keep the business open for a longer period of time and be able to run the cars in and out without a letup.

Finally convinced, Joyner instructed Newsome to notify Bailey that the CBDO could provide no further assistance. On July 1 Bailey received the following letter from Newsome:

Dear Mr. Bailey:

After a long and painstaking analysis of Bailey's ARC Transmissions' operations and management, we have reluctantly come to the conclusion that no useful purpose would be served by our investing additional monies in your business.

With kindest regards, I remain

Respectfully yours,
Richard Newsome
Director of Economic Development

After reading the letter Bailey spent the next two weeks fruitlessly seeking additional financial assistance. Finally, on July 20, 1971, he was evicted from Bailey's ARC Transmissions and took a job with a major oil company as a junior accountant. Within two months all traces of Bailey's ARC Transmissions were gone and the building was occupied by a used-tire dealer.

In a follow-up discussion with Dick Newsome he expressed his observations about ARC Transmissions and the CBDO. He said:

"I think in the beginning we made the mistake of believing that since this was a franchise it would not have to be monitored as closely as any other business venture, but we were really wrong. We should have watched this baby even more closely. Those franchisors always give you that song and dance about how great their programs are and what you can do with one of their franchises. Well, I'm here to tell you that most of that stuff is just pure bunk. Based on the franchisor's informations, we provided Bailey with some $30,000. Yet by November

Bailey needed more money. We thought Bailey could do $3,000 a week, but he was barely able to do $2,000. I was the guy that pushed so hard for Bailey to get in business even though I had seen the newspaper article and so I had to be the guy to take the position that no additional dollars be pumped into the business. My staff and I put together all the facts that we should have done in the beginning, and I came to the conclusion that Bailey did not have a snowball's chance in hell of making it in that transmission business. We found that there are five or six transmission repair shops in the same area. In fact, there is one next door to him and one right across the street.

"If Bailey came through the door today and I saw the same newspaper article, there is no way that I would make the loan to him. In the future, you can bet that any franchise deals that we get involved with will be thoroughly researched by our staff and every projection that the franchisor provides will be documented. We will never again take anything at face value."

Attempts to reach Bailey were unsuccessful, since there were a number of lawsuits outstanding against him personally.

## Exhibit I

## PROPOSAL OF ARC TRANSMISSION

## ROBERT BAILEY

*Introduction*

This is a proposal to lend $16,500 of our Economic Development funds. The funds would be advanced under a contract with a corporation to be organized for the sole purpose of owning and operating an ARC Automatic Transmissions franchise. The sole stockholder of the corporation will be Mr. Robert Bailey.

*Purpose of the Proposal*

Mr. Bailey plans to establish an ARC Transmissions franchise in our community. The purpose of this proposal is to assist Mr. Bailey in establishing this business.

*Employment*

The facility would employ six persons, including the owner, two automatic transmission builders, two automatic transmission removers and installers, and one salesman.

*Training*

Mr. Bailey will undergo a five-week training course sponsored by ARC in Pontiac, wherein he will receive extensive instruction in all phases of ARC's operation.

*Capital Requirement*

In order to become an ARC franchisee, Mr. Bailey will need $30,000. The bank has agreed to lend him $12,500. Mr. Bailey's capital contribution will be $1,000, leaving a balance to be financed of $16,500. Of the $30,000, approximately $26,000 will be used to purchase equipment, inventory, supplies and to pay fees. The balance will be used for operating capital. Annexed hereto is a copy of the equipment, inventory, supplies and fee schedule prepared by ARC. The said attachment is dated 8/1/69 and indicates a total schedule figure of $26,221.98, however, the schedule has been revised downward to $26,191.72.

## Implementing the Proposal

The actual financing of this enterprise will be prepared in conjunction with the bank. The reason for the submission of this proposal without the financial plan is to obtain the approval of the basic idea so as to enable Mr. Bailey to begin his training course on April 20, 1970.

Equipment, Inventory, Supplies and Fee Schedule

1. 6-ARC Twin Post Universal Transmission
   Lifts (installation not included)     $ 6,799.98
2. 2-T-2 Blackhawk Transmission Jacks     767.90
3. 2-ARC Rebuilding Facilities (Work Benches
   w/tanks)     600.00
4. 1-ARC Foot Press     189.50
5. 4-ARC Service Stands     174.60
6. 1-Ingersoll-Band Air Wrench ½" DR No. 405     159.50
7. 12 Sets—Tuflate Couplers 15-C     70.00
8. 3-Hoses ID-25' ⅜"—No. 406-25     27.45
9. 1 Wilton Bench Vise No. 645     26.50
10. 2 Brookins Drain Cans No. 405     44.00
11. 2 Brookins Oil Cans No. 805 AT     22.94
12. 2 Brookins Water Drain Cans No. 676     8.92
13. 1 Brookins Water Bucket No. 501     3.83
14. 1 American Gauge Come-Along-Jack No. 108     24.00

     Total Equipment     $ 8,919.12

15. ARC Service & License Fee     $ 7,000.00
16. Inventory (Parts)     9,373.76
17. Inventory Boxes     48.50
18. Steel Shelving 12×36×75     203.00
19. 4-Peg Boards—4 White Framed 4'×4' w/hooks     55.00
20. 1 Hexagon Sign—18'×25"     20.00
21. 1 Belveliner—No. 1437 Clock—14"×37"     25.00
22. 1 Shop Desk No. 2250     52.95
23. 1 Stool No. 1902     8.15
24. 1 Outside Salesman Kit     16.00
25. 2 Repair Order Racks     30.00
26. ARC Repair Orders—1,000 Printed     67.00
27. ARC Emblem Stationery—1,000 Sheets     17.50
28. ARC Emblem Business Envelopes—1,000     17.50
29. ARC Emblem Business Cards—Printed 1,000     14.00
30. 40 ARC Insignia Service Emblems     45.00
31. Outside Sales Package     128.50
32. Promotion Package     101.00
33. Bushing Driver Set     80.00

     Total Schedule     $26,221.98

## Exhibit II

## BAILEY'S ARC TRANSMISSIONS

Income Statement for the four months ended October 31, 1970

| | | |
|---|---:|---:|
| Net Sales | | $ 38,066.38 |
| Cost of Goods Sold: | | |
| Purchases | $ 24,228.53 | |
| Direct Labor | 11,290.56 | |
| Sub-Contract Labor | 900.00 | |
| Freight | 87.39 | |
| Factory Expense | 308.56 | |
| | 36,815.04 | |
| Less: Inventory 10/31/70 | 15,400.00 | |
| Cost of Goods Sold | | 21,415.04 |
| Gross Margin | | 16,651.34 |

Operating Expenses:

| | |
|---|---:|
| Officer's Salary | 2,000.00 |
| ARC Franchise Fees | 2,462.33 |
| Advertising | 3,764.72 |
| Laundry | 325.35 |
| Subscriptions | 103.85 |
| Office Expenses and Stationery | 260.73 |
| Dues | 27.00 |
| Insurance | 500.00 |
| Repairs | 104.16 |
| Rent | 1,920.00 |
| Travel | 371.56 |
| Interest and Bank Charges | 287.38 |
| Towing | 345.80 |
| Accounting | 120.00 |
| Rubbish Removal | 36.50 |
| Telephone | 410.34 |
| Parking and Storage | 140.80 |
| Auto Expense | 256.27 |
| Commission | 17.50 |
| Water | 59.50 |
| Intercompany Labor | 97.14 |
| Payroll Taxes | 1,094.07 |
| Sales Tax | 710.35 |
| Utilities | 313.61 |
| Depreciation | 120.00 |
| Miscellaneous | 33.60 |

| | |
|---|---:|
| Total Operating Expenses | $15,882.56 |
| Net Profit | $    768.78 |

# BAILEY'S ARC TRANSMISSIONS

## Balance Sheet as at October 31, 1970

### Assets

| | | |
|---|---:|---:|
| Cash | $ 1,331.56 | |
| Accounts Receivable | 837.94 | |
| Inventory | 15,400.00 | |
| ARC Transmissions Escrow Account | 981.00 | |
| Advance to Employees | 515.12 | |
| Deposits Receivable | 520.00 | |
| Advertising Escrow Account | 250.00 | |
| Prepaid Interest | 3,636.96 | |
| ARC License Fee | 7,000.00 | |
| Furniture and Fixtures | 434.54 | |
| Equipment | 4,403.68 | |
| | 35,310.80 | |
| Less: Accumulated Depreciation | 120.00 | |
| Total Assets | | $35,190.80 |

### Liabilities and Capital

| | | |
|---|---:|---:|
| Liabilities: | | |
| Accrued Expenses | $ 3,942.29 | |
| Bank Loan | 15,301.36 | |
| Loans Payable — CBDO | 13,372.24 | |
| Payroll Taxes Payable | 806.13 | |
| Total Liabilities | | $33,422.02 |
| Capital: | | |
| Capital Stock | 1,000.00 | |
| Profit for Period 7/1-10/31/70 | 768.78 | |
| Total Capital | | 1,768.78 |
| Total Liabilities and Capital | | $35,190.80 |

Exhibit III

## BAILEY'S ARC TRANSMISSIONS

Income Statement for the six months ended December 31, 1970

| | | |
|---|---|---|
| Net Sales | | $54,462.07 |
| Cost of Goods Sold: | | |
| Purchases | $26,421.59 | |
| Direct Labor | 20,913.89 | |
| Sub-Contract Labor | 1,150.00 | |
| Freight | 87.39 | |
| Factory Expense | 1,656.58 | |
| | 50,229.45 | |
| Less: Inventory 12/31/70 | 12,024.06 | |
| Cost of Goods Sold | | 38,205.39 |
| Gross Margin | | 16,256.68 |

Operating Expenses:

| | |
|---|---:|
| ARC Franchise Fees | 3,533.21 |
| Advertising | 5,966.87 |
| Laundry | 561.45 |
| Subscriptions | 103.85 |
| Office Supplies | 125.72 |
| Insurance | 300.00 |
| Utilities | 313.61 |
| Repairs | 151.41 |
| Rent | 2,880.00 |
| Travel | 452.83 |
| Legal | 108.60 |
| Towing | 666.00 |
| Interest and Bank Charges | 376.60 |
| Accounting | 200.00 |
| Rubbish Removal | 68.00 |
| Stationery | 135.01 |
| Telephone | 514.41 |
| Parking and Storage | 260.80 |
| Auto Expenses | 748.23 |
| Water | 59.50 |
| Taxes | 2,958.53 |
| Inter-Company Work | 456.45 |
| Depreciation | 240.00 |
| Miscellaneous | 82.50 |
| Total Operating Expenses | 21,263.58 |
| Net Profit (Loss) | ($5,006.90) |

# BAILEY'S ARC TRANSMISSIONS

## Balance Sheet as at December 31, 1970

### Assets

| | | |
|---|---:|---:|
| Accounts Receivable | $ 1,069.11 | |
| Inventory | 12,024.06 | |
| ARC Transmissions Escrow Account | 845.02 | |
| Deposits Receivable | 520.00 | |
| Advertising Escrow Account | 250.00 | |
| Prepaid Interest | 3,555.14 | |
| ARC License Fee | 7,000.00 | |
| Organization Expense | 600.00 | |
| Furniture and Fixtures | 434.54 | |
| Equipment | 4,462.20 | |
| | 30,760.07 | |
| Less: Accumulated Depreciation | 240.00 | |
| Total Assets | | $30,520.07 |

### Liabilities and Capital

| | | |
|---|---:|---:|
| Liabilities: | | |
| Cash — Overdrawn | $ 210.40 | |
| Accrued Expenses | 4,879.76 | |
| Payroll Taxes Payable | 825.40 | |
| Bank Loan | 14,727.42 | |
| Loans Payable — CBDO | 13,372.24 | |
| Officer's Loans | 511.75 | |
| Total Liabilities | | $34,526.97 |
| Capital: | | |
| Capital Stock | 1,000.00 | |
| Loss for Period 7/1-12/31/70 | (5,006.90) | |
| Total Capital | | (4,006.90) |
| Total Liabilities and Capital | | $30,520.07 |

Exhibit IV

## BAILEY'S ARC TRANSMISSIONS

Statement of Operations   January 1, 1971 – May 31, 1971

| | | |
|---|---:|---:|
| Net Sales | | $30,462.98 |
| Cost of Goods Sold: | | |
| Inventory – January 1, 1971 | $12,024.06 | |
| Purchases | 4,546.05 | |
| Direct Labor | 7,843.88 | |
| Sub-Contract Labor | 3,175.00 | |
| | 27,588.99 | |
| Less: Inventory – May 31, 1971 | 8,742.73 | |
| Cost of Goods Sold | | 18,846.26 |
| Gross Margin | | 11,616.72 |
| Operating Expenses: | | |
| Officer's Salary | 2,800.00 | |
| Office Help | 680.95 | |
| Utilities and Fuel | 1,499.03 | |
| ARC Franchise Fees | 4,253.91 | |
| Advertising | 876.88 | |
| Laundry | 226.20 | |
| Subscriptions | 32.00 | |
| Office Supplies | 140.00 | |
| Insurance | 849.57 | |
| Repairs | 225.97 | |
| Rent | 2,400.00 | |
| Legal | 25.00 | |
| Towing | 472.83 | |
| Accounting | 340.00 | |
| Rubbish Removal | 116.05 | |
| Telephone | 310.85 | |
| Parking and Storage | 262.50 | |
| Depreciation | 422.32 | |
| Payroll and Business Taxes | 824.36 | |
| Bank Charges and Interest Expense | 1,369.60 | |
| Total Operating Expenses | | 18,128.02 |
| Net Profit (Loss) | | $ 6,511.30 |

# BAILEY'S ARC TRANSMISSIONS

## Statement of Financial Position as at May 31, 1971

### Assets

| | | |
|---|---|---|
| **Current Assets:** | | |
| Cash on Hand and In Bank | $ 2,546.85 | |
| Accounts Receivable | 3,692.44 | |
| Inventory — Part and Supplies | 8,742.73 | |
| Prepaid Stationary and Supplies | 220.50 | |
| Prepaid Interest | 601.59 | |
| Prepaid Insurance | 299.00 | |
| Total Current Assets | | $16,103.11 |
| **Fixed Assets:** | | |
| Furniture and Fixtures — At Cost | 1,023.14 | |
| Equipment — At Cost | 9,176.10 | |
| Tools | 50.45 | |
| | 10,249.69 | |
| Less: Accumulated Depreciation | 929.12 | |
| Total Fixed Assets | | 9,320.57 |
| **Other Assets:** | | |
| ARC Franchise Cost | 7,000.00 | |
| Organization Costs | 600.00 | |
| Utilities Security Deposits | 520.00 | |
| Cost of Auctioned Autos | 350.00 | |
| Deferred Interest Costs | 1,709.59 | |
| Total Other Assets | | 10,179.59 |
| **Total Assets** | | $35,603.27 |

BLACK ENTERPRISE, INC.

Liabilities and Capital

Current Liabilities:
| | | |
|---|---|---|
| Notes Payable — Bank | $ 5,343.60 | |
| Payroll Tax Deduction | 1,614.05 | |
| Accrued Taxes | 1,823.80 | |
| Accrued Expenses and Accounts Payable | 11,046.34 | |
|     Total Current Liabilities | | $19,827.79 |

Long-Term Liabilities:
| | | |
|---|---|---|
| Notes Payable — Bank | 9,697.82 | |
| Notes Payable — CBDO | 17,500.00 | |
| Officers Loans | 136.75 | |
|     Total Long-Term Liabilities | | 27,334.57 |
|     Total Liabilities | | 47,162.36 |

Capital:
| | | |
|---|---|---|
| Capital Stock Issued and Outstanding | 1,000.00 | |
| Retained Earnings (Deficit) — 1/1/71 | (6,047.79) | |
| Loss from Operations 1/1-5/31/71 | (6,511.30) | |
|     Total Capital | | (11,559.09) |
| Total Liabilities and Capital | | $35,603.27 |

# 5

# JEFF'S ALL-STAR RIBS

## PROLOGUE

Jeff's All-Star Ribs is a case study of a black college counselor, Jefferson Davis, who started a rib restaurant in Baltimore in November 1970. The restaurant was part of a franchise system operated by a black Philadelphia franchisor who later tried to infringe on Jeff's territorial rights. A substantial portion of the venture— $20,000—was allocated by a Baltimore CBDO, which alerted Jefferson Davis to the infringement and was determined to see that his rights and money were protected.

The CBDO in this case was created by black professionals, clergy, and businessmen active in inner-city affairs in the aftermath of a 1967 riot in a Baltimore black ghetto. Incorporated as a nonprofit corporation in October 1967, it had since built a reputation as a leading economic development vehicle of the black community. Governed by a twenty-three-member board elected from the various community organizations, it represented a broad spectrum of the city's black residents. The funds to finance its business development program came from the city government, the Office of Economic Opportunity, and the Model Cities Program.

The operations of the CBDO were under an executive director, assisted by a loan director and a director of business consulting. Each director had a staff of four paid professionals and several volunteers to provide assistance to the various applicants. Loan requests were handled by a financial analyst who prepared a proposal to be sent to a loan review committee for its approval.

While Jeff's All-Star Ribs was the first franchise assisted by

    BLACK ENTERPRISE, INC.

the CBDO, it had previously made loans to four manufacturers, as well as several retail and service businesses.

# THE CASE

## Introduction

In September 1971 Jefferson Davis, owner of an All-Star Ribs franchise unit, was faced with a critical decision. Jeff's franchise agreement with the franchisor, All-Star Ribs, Inc., gave him exclusive territorial rights within a one-square-mile radius from his operation at 780 Auburn Avenue. Specifically, Section II of the franchise agreement read as follows:

> FRANCHISOR hereby grants FRANCHISEE a FRANCHISE to operate in *the City of Baltimore, State of Maryland, with an area which shall be a radius of one square mile from* a location which shall be mutually acceptable to the parties hereto.

However, the franchisor after reviewing Jeff's profitable operations realized the lucrative possibilities of selling ribs in the Baltimore area and contracted to put a company-owned restaurant about three quarters of a mile from Jeff's, in direct violation of their contractual agreement.

## Background

JEFFERSON DAVIS. Jeff's background, education, interests, and experiences before starting his franchise unit are best summarized by the following excerpts from an interview with Jeff:

I was born in Montgomery, Alabama, on May 6, 1941. My father has been a recreation director since 1949 while my mother returned to school in 1957 to complete her degree in home economics. I have one brother who is the director of a settlement house in Nashville, Tennessee, and a sister who is a teacher in the public school system in Montgomery.

I attended school in Montgomery and graduated from junior high school at the top of the class, and moved on to Alabama Preparatory High School, which is the college preparatory high school for Alabama

State. I think that a most significant thing occurred for me in high school, where I got much of what has been necessary for me to make it in this society. Primarily, I think the academic preparation that I received in high school was of such a nature as to allow me to perform some of the responsibilities that I have had to perform in recent years.

One aspect of my high school preparation was my participation in athletics, which led to my being able to receive a college scholarship in football. In high school I was an All-City Halfback. At that particular time I gained quite a bit of interest in athletics and felt that athletics was one real way of allowing me to do some of the extra-curricular-type things that I very much wanted to do.

From high school I went to Ohio State in 1959. I was particularly interested in attending Ohio State because of its football team and I was under the illusion that any person who was at least able to perform on a football field would be given all of the opportunities to make the team. I think this was one of my first real disillusions after having come out of the South—thinking that any young black person would be given the same opportunities given a white youth in the North.

At this point in life I think it is to the best advantage of any young person who is interested in athletics to completely look into the situation if they think athletics are going to allow them to make it in this society. I think that athletics—like anything else—relates a lot to who you know, and what kind of support you have. At Ohio State there were approximately 140 athletes on the freshman football team, forty of whom were black. We found that the black athletes were stuck into the same positions, and were competing with each other for what amounted to one or two positions on the varsity team.

The varsity team only chose about twenty-six individuals each year from the freshman team, which made the competition very great. My own feeling was that it was very possible for me to have made the team at Ohio State if I had been given a real opportunity to do so. But because of the lack of fair competition, the lack of any real support from anyone who really knew of my abilities, and coming from Alabama, it was not possible for me to play at Ohio State.

Having become unhappy about my experience at Ohio State—primarily in football, but also in terms of the kind of social situation in which I found myself—I spoke with the coaches at Nebraska State, where I had been offered a scholarship out of high school. They were ready to accept me on full scholarship, but since there was a ruling about the eligibility of transfers they suggested that I attend Oleans Junior College to be able to play in my sophomore year. I accepted their suggestion, and went directly to Oleans Junior College to play football in September 1960.

BLACK ENTERPRISE, INC.

Having arrived in a small town of fourteen thousand people with no black families, I recognized that it would be a very lonely place to reside for a year. After having been there one day, I suggested to the coaches that they give a scholarship to my roommate, who had remained at Ohio State, and had decided that he would not play football any more. The coaches agreed and I managed to get my former roommate out to Oleans.

At Oleans, I was a Junior-College All-American in football. At the end of the year I was able to choose from among several senior colleges in terms of which place I would care to spend the final two years of my college life. I finally decided to go to Nebraska State [in September 1961]. This choice was made on the basis that it was a good school academically and that they promised to protect me in case of any injury in football. Having had the experience previously at Ohio State, I began to understand that my real future should not be tied up in athletics alone, but should be related to what I could do academically, since if I was not going to play professionally, I would be in the market for a job. I felt that I should begin preparing for such a reality.

At Nebraska State I majored in physical education, and minored in the social and biological sciences. I also had a series of football injuries that resulted in my having surgery, but despite it all continued to play football with an eye to moving on in professional sports. I became known as the "Cinderella Kid," in the sense that when I was healthy I would manage to perform very well but managed to get more crippling injuries than most young people got on the athletic field.

The injuries resulted in my having operations on my ankle and my knee. So I went into my senior year having to sit out a football season. Despite the fact that I had gone to Nebraska with the understanding that I would not be taken off the scholarship in the event that I was to receive injuries, this was not the case. The athletic director and the coach took me off the athletic scholarship when I injured my ankle. They stated that it was just too expensive for the school to carry me on scholarship when in fact I wasn't playing as much football as they had expected. When I threatened to inform the commissioner about their taking me off athletic scholarship, despite the fact that my grades were being kept up, they simply let it slide and continued me on the scholarship.

I think that overall the college experience taught me a lot of things about promises that people make to young people. It taught me a lot about what's necessary to make it, and taught me a helluva lot about the dignity of work, and the need for work in order to guarantee one's survival.

I graduated from Nebraska State in June 1963, and went to Howard College School of Social Work. My interest in social work came about as a result of the experiences I had had working with young people in the housing projects on the playgrounds in Montgomery. I was also influenced by my brother, who had attended Howard College the previous year. I went directly to Howard without a scholarship and began working hard on an academic level to get the monies, in order to make it easier on myself and on my father, who was always willing to put out any monies that were available to help me with my education. I was fortunate enough at the end of my first year to receive a Foreign Study Scholarship to study social work and sociology abroad.

In July 1964 I went to the London School of Economics for one year. This was one of the more enjoyable experiences that I have ever had, in that it gave me the opportunity to meet many people from different countries, to get another perspective on social work in general, and to get some understanding about the different cultures and the way people live around the world.

I returned to Howard in September 1965 and graduated in June of 1966. After graduation, I went to work in a children's camp in New York which was funded by the people in the community and the federal government. I had a very good experience in a sense that I was able to perform in the way I liked in terms of being able to relate to young people and being able to guarantee some of the types of programs that we had set up for them.

I was also offered and accepted a position as a full-time employee in the community center that sponsored this particular camp. I worked there for two years, continuing some of the things we had started in camp.

I left there in July 1968 to go to work with the Welfare Action Group in Baltimore in order to get some experience on an administrative level. My brief experience at the Welfare Action Group proved further to me that the people with whom I was working were only poor economically. Their problems were the result of a system that had not made available to them the economic opportunities that they should have been able to enjoy.

In December 1968 I took advantage of the opportunity to come to Morgan University as a counselor. Just this September [1971] I was promoted to the position of Director of Counseling.

ALL-STAR RIBS. Sonny Locke is a young black executive who was raised in Los Angeles. Locke also attended Nebraska State and was a classmate, friend, and fraternity brother of Jeff. After graduation in 1963 he played for seven years with the

Philadelphia and Los Angeles teams of the National Basketball League. Initially during the off-seasons he had worked in his own real estate firm and as a personnel executive for Hughes Aircraft.

In 1966 he decided that barbecued ribs was a "hot" product. He researched the field, worked at a friend's rib restaurant, and in 1967 Sonny Locke's All-Star Ribs was born in a racially mixed neighborhood in Los Angeles. That Locke should select food as a business was natural to his experience. According to Locke, "It all started when I was a small boy playing basketball in the playgrounds. My mom would call me in at a certain hour each day and say, 'Now, Sonny, it's about time to be learning something worthwhile,' so she would teach me how to cook, sew, and keep house. The first thing I learned to cook was doughnuts. My mom wanted to make sure I'd keep my interest in it, and she knew I liked to eat doughnuts."

So when Locke wanted to look for a way to make some money, and decided that franchising would be profitable, the first thing that came to mind was the fact that he knew how to cook. He got together with his immediate family and they made up a formula for a rib sauce. After a 1967 All-Star game, he threw a party and served ribs made with this sauce. According to Locke, "all the guests loved it." This was the beginning of what was to be All-Star Ribs.

According to Locke, "In my first store there was no publicity, no advertising, no nothing. I wanted to see how the product would move under the most adverse conditions. Most businesses make their projections under the most favorable conditions, and that is why most businesses fail. Well, I started with two little cookers and in two weeks I had to put in two more, and in three months I had to tear up the place and put in new equipment."

Because of his success with the rib restaurant Locke decided to devote his energies to developing a franchise barbecue rib operation. According to company literature:

All-Star Ribs, Inc., a Pennsylvania Corporation, was incorporated in February 1969. The company prepares and sells barbecue ribs, hamburgers and related products in company-operated, take-home retail outlets. The company also grants franchises to operators of All-Star outlets, licensing them to prepare and sell All-Star's distinctive brand of barbecue ribs.

All-Star is an integrated, totally bi-racial company, which has, as one of its major objectives, the development of substantial minority group enterprises in "inner-city areas." The company feels strongly that a franchising program which provides a turn-key operation, buttressed by continuing technical, financial and management assistance, provides the best vehicle for minority groups to obtain a meaningful stake in our economic system.

The principal offices of the company are in Philadelphia. The company, in its initial developmental stage, established five units in Philadelphia, four in Buffalo, New York, and two in Los Angeles, California. The marketing and site selection data, and other technical information produced by these initial units, enabled the company to formulate a sophisticated franchise program, which has activated a new stage of highly accelerated national development. The company has successfully placed Area Directorships in the following areas: New York City, Kansas City, St. Louis, Pittsburgh, Newark, Trenton, and the states of Massachusetts and Connecticut. These Area Directorships were sold for a total of $390,000.00, but, more importantly, they contractually require the owners to collectively establish a minimum of eighty-three franchise units in their respective territories by 1973 . . .

The company is currently negotiating contracts for Area Directorships representing more than $1,000,000.00 in proceeds, including the cities of Oakland, Sacramento, Washington, D.C., Chicago, Gary and Richmond.

The company has successfully negotiated a two-step financing, involving an immediate $775,000.00 private placement, with one of the oldest and most prestigious Wall Street investment houses, to be followed by a three to four million dollar public offering, to take place in the Spring of 1972.

The funds that will be generated by a public offering in the Spring of 1972 will enable the company to take advantage of the many opportunities to assimilate profitable, black-owned companies, which, however, lack the technical ability, financial resources, and national image All-Star can provide, and thereby maximize profits. These funds will also permit the company to generally accelerate its operations, including the expansion of company-operated units, and to participate in related and unrelated ventures in both domestic and foreign markets.

Franchises are granted to both Area Directors for the development of geographic areas, and to unit franchisees for the operation of individual installations. Area Directorship groups are selected on the basis of their collective administrative and business ability, and the strength of their financial resources; unit franchisees are selected on the basis of their past business experience, honesty, and willingness to devote full time to the operation of their unit.

The cost of an Area Directorship is determined by an evaluation of population statistics, purchasing power, family formations, and other pertinent data indicative of the attractiveness of the area for franchise development. Unit franchises are sold for $33,000.00 per unit, which provides the franchisee with a "turn-key" operation. Neither land and construction costs for a free-standing building, nor renovations for existing structures are included in that fee, but in many cases, the building will be constructed and leased to the franchisee, either by the parent company or an approved real estate company. If the franchisee desires to construct an All-Star free-standing structure, his costs will be approximately $50,000.00, but will vary regionally, according to where the facility will be established.

In addition to the franchise costs, the company recommends that the franchisee start out with at least $7,000 working capital requirements. Thus, a franchised retail outlet, exclusive of land and building, requires a commitment of approximately $40,000 on the part of the franchisee.

Owing to All-Star's relationships with financial and governmental institutions, it is often possible for a franchisee in a minority group area to receive almost 100% leverage from agencies serving minority group areas. Presently, the Urban Coalition, Small Business Administration, and Equitable Insurance Company are among participants committed to franchisee loans in St. Louis, Philadelphia, New York City, Newark and Detroit. (See Exhibit I on pages 104–105 for more information on All-Star Ribs, Inc.)

JEFF DAVIS AND ALL-STAR RIBS. Jeff became acquainted initially with All-Star Ribs through his friendship with Locke, who had been a college classmate and friend. According to Jeff:

Sonny and I have been very good friends since 1961, and I've been in constant communication with him over the years. When he started his first rib business in Los Angeles, I was aware of this. He finally managed to get some capital to begin a franchise operation and was informing me of the progress being made. Whenever he came to Baltimore or Washington, D.C., he stayed at my apartment with my wife and me.

We generally spoke about All-Star and its possibilities, but he did not make any attempt to interest me directly in the business. He felt that I was not interested in business, having been a social worker and counselor. He felt that my interests lay outside the business area. However, in discussing this business thing with Sonny, and realizing myself that I would not be able to make a real buck by working in the college, even though I was doing what I really wanted to do, I felt that having an outside business interest would be in my best interest. It would make it possible for me to do some of the things right in the community that I would like to do.

I thought that I saw the need for employment for black people. And I've seen the need for ownership of black businesses by black people. And I've seen the need to have monies returned to the community rather than moved outside the community. So I felt that getting into All-Star Ribs was a real opportunity for me to be directly related to the black community on a basis other than social work or counseling.

JEFF AND THE CBDO. After mulling over the situation for a while, Jeff decided in July 1970 to open an All-Star Ribs restaurant in Baltimore. Because he and Locke wanted to open up the area they agreed to open a larger than ordinary facility which with more renovation required a total of about $80,000. In an attempt to raise the funds, Jeff contacted Citizens Trust Bank and the Baltimore Coalition. They responded with preliminary commitments of only $40,000—$30,000 from Citizens and $10,000 from the Coalition. Jeff's accountant, Jack Gibson, suggested that an additional $20,000 might be gotten from the local CBDO and in September 1970 Jeff applied to it for $20,000 to cover contingencies which might arise with respect to the opening or the operation of the business.

Norman Anderson, the CBDO loan director, was very impressed by Jeff's academic credentials and by the fact that All-Star Ribs was a minority franchisor. Therefore he prepared a funding proposal which called for the CBDO to provide Jeff with an additional $20,000 to be available when he opened his restaurant. (See Exhibit II on pages 105–106 for a summary of Jeff's funding proposal.)

Anderson was able to gain the loan review committee's approval of the proposal because of the expected return on investment and the training services provided by the franchisor. He showed the committee the following schedule in which All-Star Ribs projected that the average franchisee could expect to earn $30,000 on sales of only $150,000 and thus have a rate of return of 75 per cent on an investment of $40,000:

## Projected Franchise Unit Profit and Loss

| | | |
|---|---:|---:|
| Gross Sales | $150,000.00 | 100.00% |
| Cost of Sales: | | |
| Food Purchases | 60,000.00 | 40.00 |
| Paper and Supplies | 7,500.00 | 5.00 |
| Wages | 19,500.00 | 13.00 |
| Utilities | 3,750.00 | 2.50 |
| Rent | 6,000.00 | 4.00 |
| Franchise Fee | 7,500.00 | 5.00 |
| Delivery | 750.00 | .50 |
| Adv. Expense | 7,500.00 | 5.00 |
| Depreciation | 3,000.00 | 2.00 |
| Interest | 1,500.00 | 1.00 |
| Ins. and Misc. | 3,000.00 | 2.00 |
| | $120,000.00 | 80.00% |
| Profit | $ 30,000.00 | 20.00% |
| | | |
| Investment: | | |
| Franchise Fee | $ 2,000.00 | |
| Unit Fixtures, Decor and Equipment | 25,000.00 | |
| Grand Opening and Promotional material, Misc. Forms, Advertisement Kit, Opening Inventory & Training | 6,000.00 | |
| Total Franchise Package | $ 33,000.00 | |
| Operating Capital Estimate: | $ 7,000.00 | |
| (Property Improvements, Start-up Expense, and Working Capital) | $ 40,000.00 | |
| Percent Return on Investment | | 75.00% |

Anderson's second selling point was that All-Star was able to present a training and supervision program. Summarized below is the training schedule for a new franchisee.

*All-Star's Training Program* prepares the franchisee and his first manager to manage a unit. The Training Program consists of three weeks of on-the-job training in an All-Star unit and two weeks of intensive management training in Philadelphia, Pennsylvania, under the direction of City Talent Development Corporation, an organization specializing in management development. This organization specializes in preparing an individual for the management of a small business enterprise.

On-the-job training involves an overview of food preparation and service the All-Star way. Lectures and discussions complement on-the-job training. The trainee will also visit our local commissary and can observe how foods are being prepared before being sent to the unit. In addition, representatives of companies that service All-Star will hold special classes for the edification of those attending our training program.

Each student is furnished with an All-Star Operations and Accounting Manual, which is used as a textbook during training and as a reference book by the unit operator, once he has graduated. The All-Star Operations and Accounting Manual is the result of a process of evolution based on technical advances and refinements of methods of operating from year to year. The manual is periodically revised, as improvements in equipment and operating procedures are developed . . . Satisfactory completion is mandatory for the owner-operator of a franchised unit.

The five weeks of training are just the beginning. Prior to the opening of the new unit, the franchisee is assisted by an experienced Field Supervisor in organizing the new unit, training the personnel, and, in general, guiding and advising the franchisee until he feels confident that he is able to operate the unit on his own.

Depending upon the number of units in a given area, a full-time Field Supervisor will be furnished, at the expense of All-Star. The Field Supervisor keeps a close watch on the day-to-day activities of the unit under supervision, for the purpose of advising the franchisee of methods of reducing costs, improving service, increasing sales, and improving over-all unit performance.

The new unit is also guided through the grand opening period by a Field Supervisor, who advises and assists the operator in ordering foods, scheduling help, preparing production schedules, and promoting the grand opening.

*The equipment purchased by the franchisee* is delivered to the unit location, but is not installed by the manufacturer. *All-Star provides the franchisee with the complete service required* including receiving the equipment and checking for accuracy and condition, hook-up and installation, performance check, and replacement ordering, when required. This service also includes contacting local sources of maintenance and repair for future use by the franchisee.

Though the CBDO loan review committee was impressed with the potential of the operation, several members raised questions about such a large investment. One, for example, felt "that $60,000 is a lot of money for a 'rib joint.'" Furthermore, another felt that Jeff would not have an expected return on investment of 75 per cent on profits of $30,000 because his total investment was to be $60,000 and not $40,000 as was the average investment. Despite these objections, however, the loan was approved because "the bank and the Coalition are already involved and ours is just a contingency amount that he will draw down as he needs it."

## Operations

Jeff opened his All-Star Ribs restaurant on November 24, 1970, with a large press party since it was the first All-Star unit in Baltimore. In attendance at the grand opening were the director of the SBA; the chairman of the State Human Rights Commission; vice-presidents from the participating bank; and local community leaders, politicians, and several star athletes.

According to Jeff, despite the management assistance program, the restaurant had several problems initially. He said: "We opened with many of the kinds of problems I'm sure most young businesses have—learning how to do inventory, how to keep on top of monies, dealing with the labor market, and any number of different kinds of situations that young businessmen find themselves in. Fortunately, we were able to take off right away in terms of this business. We averaged $3,000 per week from the time we have been in business."

Jeff's problems were further complicated by the fact that All-Star Ribs was less than two years old and most of its work was done by people who were novices in the franchise area. Because the franchisor lacked sufficient capital, it was unable to provide a great deal of help to Jeff.

An additional contributing cause of Jeff's early problems was that because he still had a full-time job as counselor at Morgan University, he found it necessary to hire a manager to run the operation. Jeff best summarizes the management problem in the following statement:

We always hear the concern raised about management of any particular unit in the food franchises. In my own case I'm not what one might call a full-time person at All-Star, because I am involved in this counseling program at Morgan University. I spend approximately thirty to forty hours a week in my unit, attempting to guarantee the successful operation there.

However, we have found that it is difficult to guarantee the type of management that is necessary in order to run a successful unit. It is very difficult to depend on managers who do not necessarily have their own monies invested in the business. The types of problems that I've had with management are related to their handling of personnel and their unwillingness to take on the dirty jobs that may be done by other personnel, particularly in the absence of a staff member in the schedule to work that day. I found that the managers were not as willing to assume the responsibilities of selling the ribs and cooking ribs and packing ribs, in the same way that other employees are who are hired to do that job. As a result there are times when our operation doesn't move as smoothly as it should.

Despite Jeff's many personnel problems—including a $400 robbery by three former employees in January 1971—the restaurant prospered and averaged about $3,000 per week in sales through February 1971, actually showing a net profit after four months. (See financial statements for Jeff in Exhibit III on pages 107–110.)

Jeff's pattern for the next few months followed a similar course of sustained sales and sustained operating problems. With respect to operations, he showed a net profit of over $4,000 at the end of June 1971 on sales of $117,000. (See Exhibit IV on pages 111–114.) At the same time, he continued to experience labor problems with which the manager could not or would not deal. These problems centered around wages and poor employee attitudes and in May 1971 they forced Jeff to fire the manager and take over the operations of the store until he found another manager in June.

Though sales continued to climb in the second half of 1971, Jeff continued to experience problems in his operations. In August there was another robbery that resulted in the store losing $5,000 worth of equipment that was never replaced by the insurance company.

In September there was a fire in the apartment directly above the store. It caused severe smoke and water damage, forcing Jeff to spend $11,000 for remodeling. Jeff was forced to restrict the eating area, which accounted for approximately 25 per cent of the business, and to operate on a day-to-day basis in an unattractive store that had been damaged by smoke and water.

On September 27, 1971—ten months after his opening—Norman Anderson of the CBDO called Jeff to inquire if he knew that the franchisor was putting up another unit a few blocks away from his place. Jeff indicated that he did not know, but after checking the newspaper and calling the franchisor's headquarters he was able to substantiate the story. Later that day he called his attorney to seek his advice and to schedule a meeting between himself, his attorney, Anderson, and the CBDO attorney to decide on a course of action. Before the day of the scheduled meeting on October 7, however, Jeff received the following letter from Locke, stating that he did not want to hurt Jeff and that the new unit would actually help Jeff's business.

Mr. Jefferson Davis                              September 30, 1971
Jeff's All-Star Ribs
Baltimore, Maryland

Dear Jeff:

I am disturbed that you feel we are jeopardizing your unit by placing another All-Star unit near you. I am sure you realize that if your volume is jeopardized we are hurt just as much as anyone else. I am personally hurt because you are my friend and I went to bat for you in securing the loans and getting the franchise. On the other hand, I do appreciate your concern.

The purpose of this letter is to assure you that we have your interest in mind as well as our own. We estimate that it takes 50,000 population in a one-mile radius to support one of our units. Our competitor computes their unit projections on the basis of 30,000 population per unit. I think you will find that the population in the area around your unit comes close to exceeding 100,000. Also if you have looked over the site, you will find that a Carvel Ice Cream store is next door to the new site and one is across the street from your unit. You will also note that both Carvel units are doing very well for the simple reason that the marketing areas are very different and the people who live, shop and eat at one do not necessarily live, shop and eat in the marketing area around the other. Before I entered into the lease, I visited the second site and felt assured that the location would not hinder your unit.

I think the second unit can do nothing but help you in that we can spread the advertising dollar over two units and therefore increase the exposure of All-Star Ribs in the market area.

Enclosed you will find real estate demographics as I promised, which will indicate the density of the population in the immediate area. Also you will find a copy of in-store questionnaire tabulation for your unit.

I hope that this information proves further our ability to function as a franchisor, which includes by the way, selection of sites as well as advertising, marketing, training and the ever increasing necessity to be a successful franchisor.

Since we would like to bring other applicants into Baltimore, we are by no means going to jeopardize our position by placing a unit too close to your unit, therefore jeopardizing his existing volume.

I hope this meets with your approval.

My most sincere regards,<br>Sonny

Upon receiving this letter and talking to Sonny Locke later by telephone, Jeff felt that "things would be done right by me." However, he knew that he should protect his interest. As Jeff reflected on this latest turn of events, he said: "In terms of management, the thing is the desire to succeed, to be willing to invest your time, and to somehow make the effort to somehow overcome the adversity that one may experience."

## EPILOGUE

On October 7 Jeff and his attorney met at the CBDO headquarters. Anderson gave Jeff a list of alternatives which included: (1) to seek an injunction against the franchisor to prevent the new unit from opening; (2) to let the new unit open and sue for breach of contract and seek damages; (3) to sell Jeff's unit to the franchisor at a substantial profit; or (4) to allow the other store to open if the franchisor agreed to guarantee him a minimum volume and revenue level.

The parties agreed that they could not weigh the alternatives until their economic impact had been ascertained. Anderson stated that he would put the staff to work to determine the dollar impact of the options and lawyers would research franchise law to see what precedents existed. Anderson also stated that it would take about three weeks to get all the necessary information together and that the group should plan to meet again in early November.

On October 8 Anderson contacted All-Star Ribs by telephone to request information on the new store. He asked for a copy of the site survey of Jeff's All-Star Ribs, projections of the new unit, and All-Star's advertising plans for the new unit. Members of Anderson's staff contacted the city department of planning for a demographic survey of Baltimore as well as racial concentrations in the city. At the same time, other members of Anderson's staff were busily compiling statistics on the eating and spending habits of the blacks in the area.

As the days wore on and as it received information, the CBDO staff began to piece together the market universe and its potential value. Rumors also began to circulate that the new unit would be owned by a Baltimore Orioles baseball player. This new information changed many of the CBDO's assumptions since a sports figure's reputation might draw more business to an All-Star Ribs restaurant than one owned by Jefferson Davis. On November 3 everyone involved gathered at Anderson's office to discuss the various alternatives and their impact. After the evidence was presented and after much discussion, they agreed that it would be in the best interest of Jeff and the CBDO if a combination of the alternatives were used. The consensus was that Jeff's lawyer should secure an injunction preventing the opening of the new franchise unit and that Jeff should agree to allow it to open only if the franchisor guaranteed him a sales volume equal to a negotiated rate of growth for the business over a period of seven years. Jeff's and the CBDO's attorneys agreed to meet and draw up such an agreement based on the figures provided by the staff.

On November 11 the agreement was submitted to Sonny Locke of All-Star Ribs, Inc. Initially Locke was opposed to the idea, but when his lawyers advised him that Jeff could keep the new unit closed indefinitely, he relented and agreed to settle. The terms of the agreement guaranteed Jeff a level of sales that provided for an increase of at least 10 per cent per year for seven years.

After the signing of the agreement, the new store was opened on January 4, 1972, with much fanfare. In the interim, however, the ballplayer had decided against becoming involved in the venture and the sales of the new restaurant fell below projections. In April 1972 it was rumored that All-Star Ribs wanted to sell the store. When these rumors reached Jeff he stated that he "briefly considered buying the other unit since I felt that I had learned how to properly manage the business. After much discussion with my wife and realizing that it would mean a full-time commitment, I decided against purchasing the other unit."

In a subsequent discussion, Norman Anderson, CBDO loan director, said:

The problems of franchising are not dissimilar from those of any other business. Initially, the franchise is a good way to start profitable businesses, and it was only after we had become involved that we realized that the problems of franchising were like those of all other businesses. These problems revolve around the issues of money and management and motivation.

Jefferson Davis represented the kind of man that we like to see go into business. He had the drive and a record of accomplishment that were ideally suited for a franchising operation. Unfortunately, Jeff was unable to commit himself full-time to the venture and it is very difficult to make a go of a franchise if one is an absentee owner. I think based on our experiences, we would more than likely not go with another absentee owner because there is a built-in failure mechanism in the beginning since he would have to hire someone who might not be as concerned about the operation as the guy who has put his money in the venture.

Also, we would not allow a franchisee to take part in an experimental franchise—experimental in the sense that the size of the franchise is substantially larger than the ones that the franchisor is used to putting up and the franchisor is not familiar with those problems. The franchisor should be the one to eat the costs of developing experimental units. Also, if given the opportunity to do it all over again, we would demand a tighter contract from the franchisor.

With respect to his experiences Jeff said:

I feel that my own experiences with regard to adversity prior to All-Star have been meaningful to me. In our earlier discussion I spoke about being in institutions where there was virtually no social life, or being in places where I was completely isolated and had to address my attention to overcoming adversities. I think that these experiences helped me one helluva lot, in terms of dealing with the problems that I have had at All-Star. I think also my experience in working with people has had a lot to do with my ability to be successful. I think I know something about people and what people are capable of putting out.

On the other hand, I have been very fortunate in having a wife who has invested considerable time in the business and an accountant who has been able and willing to do whatever is necessary in order to assist the business from the financial end. The other thing is to have a very good lawyer, and I would suggest that anyone going into a franchise business get himself a very good lawyer. There are enough legal problems that require legal expertise in dealing with parent companies if you are in a franchise.

I think that despite the real problems that we may have in the black community in terms of getting employment, there are a lot of people in the community who really want to work, and who are willing to do what is necessary to guarantee themselves economic security.

At this time, I am not really sure that my future lies in business to the extent that I would want to open a number of All-Star units. I've been involved in a counseling program and in social work for a number of years and I am really interested in the field and have found that it helps me to enjoy some of the kinds of things that I want to do.

However, I think that the experience I've had in All-Star dictates that I somehow maintain a relationship to the business aspects of life, and that perhaps I ought to be looking forward to others kinds of possibilities for myself, where I may be able to pull all of these things together—a desire to work with people and a desire to be financially secure.

Exhibit I

# ALL-STAR RIBS, INC.

## Additional Information

### Franchise Revenues to Parent Company and Area Director

Of the initial franchise fee ($5,000.00 per unit) received by All-Star from franchisees, the Area Director receives $2,000.00.

Royalty income is based on 5% of the gross volume of each unit which reports directly to the parent company. Twenty-five per cent (1.25% gross volume) of this royalty income in an area owned by the Area Directorship will be remitted to the Area Director, in return for his continuing supervision, in conjunction with the parent company and other obligations to the franchisee under his contract with the parent company.

### Control

The company exercises control over its franchise operation through contracts undertaken with the area and unit franchisees and a continuing surveillance on the part of trained food service and operations experts from the parent company. Each Area Director and unit franchisee must attend in person, or send a representative, to All-Star's training facilities in Philadelphia for a course of instruction which will be of not less than one week in duration and can last up to three weeks, depending on the needs of the attendees. In addition, a company supervisor will conduct operations for at least two weeks when a franchise unit first opens. The company feels strongly that the proper training and supervision of the franchisees is essential for the ultimate success of its program.

### National Advertising, Marketing, and Public Relations

All-Star supports its franchised and company-owned units with a national advertising and public relations campaign. All-Star assumes the cost for the production of advertisements and will arrange for dissemination of these advertisements on an "as-needed" basis for unit franchisees. Franchisees will bear only the cost of local advertising which directly affects their units.

The company produces advertisements for radio, billboards, magazines, and television. The company also participates in all the major national franchising shows throughout the country and plans grand openings for each installation, featuring the appearance of leading professional athletes. Because of the company's sports orientation, it has attracted the participation, in the form of time, money, and effort, of many prominent sports celebrities.

Furthermore, the company is in the process of finalizing an agreement for a permanent affiliation with the National Basketball League, which will involve the participation of the Learning Corporation of America in merchandising, marketing, and public relations programs on behalf of the National Basketball League and All-Star Ribs. This is undoubtedly one of the most important developments, at the consumer level, since the company's inception.

*Institutional Resources*

The company has been the recipient of both financial support and active participation from institutions prominent throughout the country, such as the National Bank of New York, the Mercury Foundation, Equitable Insurance Company, the Small Business Administration, the Urban Coalition, and Eastern Pennsylvania National Bank. Negotiations are currently in progress involving the support of countless other national and regional agencies, for the purpose of providing funds for franchisees who would not otherwise be able to participate in the program.

Exhibit II

JEFF'S ALL-STAR RIBS, INC.

Final Proposal October 26, 1970

*Introduction*

This is a proposal to provide assistance to Mr. Jefferson Davis, who is purchasing an All-Star Ribs franchise. In order to complete the purchase and began operations, Mr. Davis will need a total of $60,000, $20,000 from the CBDO.

## Market

All-Star Ribs, Inc., a Pennsylvania Corporation, has nine restaurants in operation and eight under construction. This Corporation expects to have ninety units in operation by the middle of 1971.

Mr. Davis' operation will be the first to be established in the immediate Baltimore area, and with the heavily pedestrian traffic in this area of operation this will have a direct influence on his success. Mr. Davis is very optimistic that his unit will do well.

With All-Star personnel constantly supervising Mr. Davis in the preparation and control of the quality of the food served, this establishment should encounter no problems with its competitors, as well as having no difficulty in enhancing the reputation of All-Star Ribs.

## Funding

CITIZENS TRUST BANK. The bank has agreed (with a 90% SBA guaranty) to loan the company $30,000 at eight (8%) per cent, repayable in five (5) years, to be used for the purchasing of the franchise and renovation.

BALTIMORE COALITION. The Coalition has agreed to loan the company $10,000 at eight (8%) per cent, repayable in three (3) years, subordinate to bank loan, to be used for purchasing of the franchise and renovation.

CBDO FUNDS. As the company demonstrates a need for the remainder of $20,000, it will be paid out under an as-needed monthly plan.

Repayment of this loan will commence after repayment of the bank loan to run concurrent with Coalition payments.

| | | | |
|---|---|---|---|
| 61 through 84 months | @ $500 per month | = | $12,000 |
| 85 through 95 months | @ $675 per month | = | 7,425 |
| 96th month | @ $575 per month | = | 575 |
| | Total | | $20,000 |

Exhibit III
# JEFF'S ALL-STAR RIBS, INC.

### Income Statement   November 1970 — February 28, 1971

| | | |
|---|---:|---:|
| Sales | | $58,696.00 |
| Cost of Sales | | |
|     Inventory — Beginning | — 0 — | |
|     Purchases | $32,014.00 | |
|     Freight — In | 618.00 | |
|         Total | 32,632.00 | |
|         Less: Ending Inventory | 2,281.00 | |
|         Total Cost of Sales | | 30,351.00 |
|         Gross Profit on Sales | | $28,345.00 |
| Selling Expenses | | |
|     Salaries | $14,380.00 | |
|     Payroll Taxes | 448.00 | |
|     Royalty Fees | 2,935.00 | |
|     Repairs | 606.00 | |
|     Advertising | 294.00 | |
|     Light and Gas | 146.00 | |
|     Travel | 28.00 | |
|     Uniform Service | 269.00 | |
|     Depreciation | 2,933.00 | |
|     Licenses and Permits | 2.00 | |
|     Miscellaneous | 92.00 | |
|         Total Selling Expenses | $22,133.00 | |

General Expenses

| | | |
|---|---|---|
| Rent | $ 1,575.00 | |
| Interest | 632.00 | |
| Professional Fees | 858.00 | |
| Insurance | 336.00 | |
| Stationery, Mailing and Postage | 167.00 | |
| Office Supplies | 199.00 | |
| Telephone and Telegraph | 405.00 | |
| Maintenance and Cleaning | 141.00 | |
| Depreciation | 848.00 | |
| Cartage | 117.00 | |
| Exterminator | 54.00 | |
| Bank Charges | 29.00 | |
| Miscellaneous | 274.00 | |
| Casualty | 300.00 | |
| Total Selling and General Expenses | | 28,068.00 |
| Net Profit (Loss) | | $ 277.00 |

# JEFF'S ALL-STAR RIBS, INC.

## Balance Sheet as at February 28, 1971

### Assets

Current Assets:

| | | |
|---|---:|---:|
| Cash in Bank and on Hand | $ 9,559.00 | |
| Accounts Receivable | 898.00 | |
| Loans and Exchanges | 101.00 | |
| Inventory — Submitted | 2,281.00 | |
| Prepaid Expenses | 535.00 | |
| Prepaid Insurance | 136.00 | |
| Total Current Assets | | $13,510.00 |

Fixed Assets:

| | | |
|---|---:|---:|
| Auto | 3,794.00 | |
| Equipment, Decorations and Fixtures | 31,383.00 | |
| Furniture | 157.00 | |
| Leasehold Improvements | 17,354.00 | |
| | 52,688.00 | |
| Less: Accumulated Depreciation | 4,729.00 | |
| Net Fixed Assets | | 47,959.00 |

Other Assets:

| | | |
|---|---:|---:|
| Deposit and Security | 2,725.00 | |
| Franchise Fee | 5,000.00 | |
| Total Other Assets | | 7,725.00 |
| Total Assets | | $69,194.00 |

## Liabilities and Capital

Current Liabilities:

| | | |
|---|---|---|
| Notes Payable — Citizens Trust | $ 4,500.00 | |
| Notes Payable — GMAC | 1,147.00 | |
| Accounts Payable | 19,444.00 | |
| Accrued Expenses Payable | 1,584.00 | |
| Payroll Taxes Payable | 1,392.00 | |
| Sales Taxes Payable | 3,793.00 | |
|     Total Current Liabilities | | $31,860.00 |

Long-Term Liabilities:

| | | |
|---|---|---|
| Notes Payable — Citizens Trust | 24,000.00 | |
| Notes Payable — Coalition Corporation | 10,000.00 | |
| Notes Payable — GMAC | 2,109.00 | |
| Total Long-Term Liabilities | | 36,109.00 |

Other Liabilities:

| | | |
|---|---|---|
| Loans Payable — Officer | | 1,300.00 |
|     Total Liabilities | | 69,269.00 |

Capital:

| | | |
|---|---|---|
| Capital Stock — Common, $50 Par Value | 2,500.00 | |
| Retained Earnings (Deficit) | (2,575.00) | |
|     Total Capital — (Deficit) | | ( 75.00) |
| Total Liabilities and Capital | | $69,194.00 |

## Exhibit IV
## JEFF'S ALL-STAR RIBS, INC.

### Income Statement November 1, 1970 — June 30, 1971

| | | |
|---|---|---|
| Sales | | $117,367.00 |
| Cost of Sales: | | |
| Inventory — Beginning Food and Paper | — 0 — | |
| Purchases — Food and Paper | $61,060.00 | |
| Total Available for Sale | 61,060.00 | |
| Less — Inventory Ending | 2,349.00 | |
| Cost of Goods Sold | | 58,711.00 |
| Gross Profit on Sales | | $58,656.00 |

Selling and General Expenses:

| | |
|---|---:|
| Salaries | 26,564.00 |
| Royalty Fees | 5,868.00 |
| Rent | 3,675.00 |
| Repairs | 1,351.00 |
| Advertising | 1,239.00 |
| Freight | 1,090.00 |
| Store and Office Supplies | 1,113.00 |
| Light and Gas | 856.00 |
| Interest | 1,387.00 |
| Telephone and Telegraph | 564.00 |
| Uniform Service | 659.00 |
| Insurance | 671.00 |
| Cartage | 297.00 |
| Stationery, Mailing and Postage | 225.00 |
| Dues, Subscription, Licenses and Permits | 219.00 |
| Training | 305.00 |
| Outside Services | 210.00 |
| Professional Fees | 1,441.00 |
| Travel and Entertainment | 81.00 |
| Exterminator | 119.00 |
| Payroll Taxes | 1,659.00 |
| Maintenance and Cleaning | 337.00 |
| Bank Charges | 113.00 |
| Casualty Loss | 300.00 |
| Depreciation | 3,735.00 |
| Miscellaneous | 383.00 |

| | |
|---|---:|
| Total Selling and General Expenses | 54,461.00 |
| Net Profit (Loss) | 4,195.00 |
| Other Income—Interest | 27.00 |
| Total Profit (Loss) | $ 4,222.00 |

# JEFF'S ALL-STAR RIBS, INC.

## Balance Sheet as at June 30, 1971

### Assets

Current Assets:

| | | |
|---|---|---|
| Cash in Bank and on Hand | $ 8,210.00 | |
| Accounts Receivable | 724.00 | |
| Inventory – Submitted | 2,349.00 | |
| Prepaid Expenses | 1,107.00 | |
| Prepaid Insurance | 55.00 | |
| Loans and Exchanges | 204.00 | |
| Total Current Assets | | $12,649.00 |

Fixed Assets:

| | | |
|---|---|---|
| Auto | 3,794.00 | |
| Equipment, Decorations and Fixtures | 32,853.00 | |
| Furniture | 212.00 | |
| Leasehold Improvements | 17,354.00 | |
| | 54,213.00 | |
| Less: Accumulated Depreciation | 3,971.00 | |
| Net Fixed Assets | | 50,242.00 |

Intangible Assets:

| | | |
|---|---|---|
| Franchise | 5,000.00 | |
| Organization Cost | 100.00 | |
| Total Intangible Assets | | 5,100.00 |

Other Assets:

| | | |
|---|---|---|
| Deposit and Security | 2,725.00 | |
| Advances | 500.00 | |
| Total Other Assets | | 3,225.00 |
| Total Assets | | $71,216.00 |

## Liabilities and Capital

Current Liabilities:

| | | |
|---|---:|---:|
| Notes Payable — Citizens Trust | $ 7,500.00 | |
| Notes Payable — GMAC | 1,200.00 | |
| Accounts Payable | 16,730.00 | |
| Accrued Expenses Payable | 7,200.00 | |
| Payroll Taxes Payable | 1,359.00 | |
| Sales Taxes Payable | 1,195.00 | |
| Total Current Liabilities | | $35,184.00 |

Long-Term Liabilities:

| | | |
|---|---:|---:|
| Notes Payable — Citizens Trust | 18,500.00 | |
| Notes Payable — Coalition Corporation | 10,000.00 | |
| Notes Payable — GMAC | 1,651.00 | |
| Total Long-Term Liabilities | | 30,151.00 |

Other Liabilities:

| | | |
|---|---:|---:|
| Loans Payable — Officer | 1,300.00 | |
| Total Other Liabilities | | 1,300.00 |
| Total Liabilities | | 66,635.00 |

Capital:

| | | |
|---|---:|---:|
| Capital Stock — Common, $50 par Value | 2,500.00 | |
| Retained Earnings | 2,081.00 | |
| Total Capital | | 4,581.00 |
| Total Liabilities and Capital | | $71,216.00 |

# III

## Machinists Turned Manufacturers: More IBMS?

Part III focuses on the efforts of three CBDOs to develop larger black business enterprises and the problems they encountered. Clearly demonstrated is the need for management assistance to help entrepreneurs meet the complex problems of inventory control, production scheduling, cost accounting, market development, and resource management.

# 6

# MERRITT PLASTICS
# MANUFACTURING CORPORATION

## PROLOGUE

Merritt Plastics Manufacturing Corporation is a case study of a black real estate salesman who took over the development and management of a plastics operation after the death of his cousin. During his start-up period, the entrepreneur was faced with a number of problems that he was ill-prepared to handle. A Chicago CBDO provided about $210,000 in financing for the venture as well as management assistance in an attempt to make it viable.

The Chicago CBDO was a non-profit corporation formed in January 1968 by concerned citizens on Chicago's South Side in an attempt to foster business opportunities for blacks. Initially, interested black businessmen limited their efforts in assisting blacks to preparing the documents necessary for SBA applications. In October 1968 the Office of Economic Opportunity provided the CBDO with a planning grant of $150,000 to develop an experimental business development program. In January 1969 the OEO grant was increased to allow the program to provide start-up money to "worthwhile business opportunities." In addition, because of the widespread interest in the effort, the corporation also received $500,000 from several foundations.

The non-profit corporation was governed by a seventeen-member board of directors composed of lawyers, accountants, and community leaders. The board members, who were selected in a community election, named a president who was responsible for operations. In 1969 the president had a staff of seven people, including four professionals who assisted him in the development of businesses. All loan decisions were handled by the executive committee composed of the president, chairman of the board, treasurer, and six board members.

At the time of its loan to Merritt, the CBDO had previously made two $10,000 loans to retail stores. Merritt represented its first large-scale venture as well as its first attempt to help develop a manufacturing operation.

# THE CASE

*Background*

Clifton Merritt dreamed that one day there would be a Merritt Plastics Manufacturing Corporation. When he initially went to the CBDO in February 1969, he was working for the Harris Manufacturing Company, a manufacturer of plastic products. Though he had initially begun working for Harris in 1946 as a cutter, he subsequently resigned in 1951 when he started to believe that "there was no future for a black man with them." While he worked for several other employers over the next thirteen years, he kept in touch with Harris, later rejoining them as a production foreman in 1964.

After visiting the CBDO, Clifton prepared a $166,000 summary proposal which was submitted to the CBDO's executive committee in March 1969. (See Exhibit I on pages 142–143 for a summary of the Merritt proposal.) At the same time he was awaiting approval of the proposal, he sought contracts for his new business. He wrote to several suppliers explaining that he was in the process of setting up a plastics manufacturing facility, asking that they send him sample swatches of their complete line of plastics ranging from the lightest to the heaviest, as well as current prices per pound. Merritt also sent letters to several banks and insurance companies, requesting that they consider his firm as a supplier of plastic covers. He told them that he would be in a position to furnish them with price quotations and delivery schedules for the items in which they might be interested.

Throughout April and May, he visited with the purchasing director of vendors for the City of Chicago, the deputy director of the Office of Economic Advancement, and other officials who might help him. He believed that Chicago had 22,000 office machines which would require dust covers. He also visited the Department of Sanitation because it used large plastic bags. Furthermore, he believed that the city's Purchasing Department might possibly give a black manufacturer 10 per cent of their requirements to start his company off. By June 1969 Merritt was confident that there was a market for this particular product and he was "determined to get it."

In July 1969 the CBDO executive committee evaluated his proposal and agreed to lend him $136,000. The CBDO also sought participation from a local bank which independently evaluated Merritt's proposal and agreed to lend the company $29,500. Unfortunately, two weeks before he was scheduled to open his business, Merritt was killed in an accident.

## The New Organization

Ken Alston, Merritt's cousin, was born September 11, 1925, and educated in a Chicago high school. From high school he went to the South Side Community College, where he concentrated in real estate appraisal. At the time of his cousin's death, Alston was married, had five children, and was an employee of the City of Chicago. In addition, he was a licensed real estate broker.

According to Alston, he was "very much qualified to take over the reins of the Merritt Corporation" since he had been "very much involved in the Merritt proposal." In letters to Ted Vann, president of the CBDO, Alston argued that he had a significant interest in the business. In an August 22, 1969, letter he said:

The undersigned, Ken Alston, is the cousin of Clifton Merritt, deceased, who executed a contract with your agency. This contract culminated a series of conferences and negotiations in connection with a certain proposal by Merritt Plastics Manufacturing Corporation to manufacture plastic items and to provide a job training program for qualified community residents.

Clifton Merritt was President and principal stockholder of the corporation and he had some 25 years' experience in the plastics manufacturing field, which experience and knowledge was an essential ingredient to insure success of the proposed venture. Nevertheless, the Merritt Plastic Manufacturing Corporation continues and is anxious to fulfill the terms and conditions of this contract, and commence the business.

Needless to say, the death of my cousin has required corporate organizational changes and has also made mandatory some proposed personnel changes to insure a successful enterprise. It is hoped that the information we will supply will satisfy any requirements which you have in this connection.

One week later, on August 29, 1969, Alston sent a second letter to Vann which emphasized *his* right to operate the firm. In part, this letter said:

Due to the fact that I am employed by the City of Chicago certain steps were taken to protect the Merritt Plastics Manufacturing Corporation and myself so that a charge of conflict-of-interest could never be directed. We wanted to be able to go after business from the *city*, state and federal governments together with private sector, but there would create a conflict-of-interest if I appeared anywhere as having any interest in the Corporation, while doing business with the city government. This accounts for the absence of my name on all of the material that has been assembled and forwarded to you up to the time of the death of Clifton Merritt. This also accounts for the fact that Mrs. Jacqueline Fable is a stockholder with Clifton Merritt. Mrs. Fable, in fact, is my sister.

Every piece of material, every bit of research, including the literally hundreds of letters that have been dispatched for the Merritt Plastics Manufacturing Corporation, was done by my office. Enclosed find copies of day-to-day work sheets and letters which will show you the extent of my involvement in the building and creation of this corporation to date. This is not to say that Clifton Merritt did not take part in this massive undertaking. Thousands of dollars which have been invested in this corporation to date were equally done so by Clifton Merritt and myself. It is ironic that I have to go to such lengths to establish my true position in the Merritt Plastics Manufacturing Corporation, after taking such pains to show no legal attachment other than in the area of sales.

It is understood that the information and material I am furnishing will be held in confidence. Consider the fact that Clifton Merritt was duly employed by Harris Manufacturing Company prior to his death so naturally it would have been a physical impossibility for him to handle this volume of work, having neither staff nor time.

At the time of conception of this corporation it always was and still is my intention to phase out my city job during a period of three to six months, once we became productive. I have also arranged to sell several properties that I own and control due to the fact that I intend to devote my full time to the growth and development of this business.

120

However, I do not intend to draw a salary for the first three to six months from the corporation.

Vann reviewed Alston's claim that he was a "silent partner" in the Merritt Corporation and decided that he should formally present his claim to the CBDO executive committee.

KENNETH ALSTON'S PRESENTATION. "My background certainly doesn't fully qualify me to head a manufacturing company," Alston said, "but Clifton had put so much time and effort into the firm, and his ideas were so sound, that I thought the company shouldn't be liquidated without a fight." Thus on September 15, 1969, Alston met with the CBDO executive committee to present his plans for his cousin's factory. At that meeting, he explained that he intended to take over as president and chief operating officer and presented a list of the men who were to serve on the board of directors of the newly organized corporation. They were: (1) an attorney who was a local civil rights leader; (2) a successful insurance agency executive; (3) a leading attorney and active member of the Chicago Urban League; and (4) a marshal for the City of Chicago. In addition to this new board, Alston also presented a list of consultants who had agreed to serve the corporation when it got started. Among these consultants were Irving Salt, a plastics manufacturer, under whom Merritt had worked for fifteen years, and Dan Sampson, a plastics wholesaler. As Alston was to be only a part-time salesman, he planned to hire two salesmen to take up some of the sales duties.

Alston explained that as the president of the firm, he would be responsible for the over-all operation of the business. On the factory level there was to be a shop foreman—Robert Clandon—who had fourteen years' experience in plastics manufacturing. Clandon would be responsible for over-all plant supervision, including quality and production control, machinery and equipment utilization and maintenance, trucking, shipping and delivery schedules, purchasing product inspection, and standardization of new materials and finished products. A second supervisory job was to be filled by Pedro Lopez, as production manager. His primary responsibility would be with operations and the servicing of the heat-sealing department. A third important position was that of chief machine operator, who would be responsible for all machine operators. For this job Alston chose Mrs. Edie Dalton, who had twenty-two years experience in the plastics field. Not only was she to supervise the machine operators, but she was also responsible for pattern making, piece goods purchases, and quality control of products.

Alston indicated that he had learned much from his cousin and had gained valuable working knowledge of the various technical phases of manufacturing. He claimed familiarity with time and motion studies, purchasing, cost and production control, piece goods buying, and pattern making. He said that he had set up certain performance standards, and that they would "be achieved by one of several innovative methods."

Alston also made it clear that he "would make projections in each department for related maximum production capabilities." These projections were to be short- and long-term forecasts as well as analyses of cost on a breakdown basis, at appropriate stages of production. He said, "continual appraisal must be applied to maintain economical costs and maximum profits."

According to Alston:

. . . There is no doubt in my mind as to my capabilities in managing the day-to-day affairs of the factory, and in obtaining experienced technical supervisors to handle the two key departments: sewing and heat sealing. I have already been successful in engaging Mr. Clandon, Mrs. Dalton, and Mr. Lopez to take over as supervisors. I have set up a special Advisory Board with experienced men serving as consultants. Because my cousin had executed an August 1 [1969] lease for factory space and we have orders in hand, I hope that you [the CBDO] and the bank will respond favorably to this *new* proposal. For with the groundwork laid by Clifton, a good working organization, and the advice of our friends, the Merritt Plastics Manufacturing Corporation will become a viable organization and a credit to the man and his race.

## Operations

On October 2, 1969, the CBDO executive committee, after having reviewed the Alston proposal, decided to approve it by a vote of five to four. Consequently, during the month of October the necessary forms were completed by Alston. By December, five months after his cousin's death, Alston had submitted all the necessary documents and began receiving funds for his company.

BLACK ENTERPRISE, INC.

In accordance with CBDO guidelines, checks were issued to the company through a two-party check system. That is, the CBDO check was made payable to both the firm *and* its payee. According to Vann, this method guaranteed that "the funds are being used properly." Alston's first request for funds came in early December when he requested $79,100. Exhibit II on pages 143–144 is a statement forwarded to the CBDO by Alston which was prepared by his accountant. Vann did not honor this $79,100 request, but did give him $23,000 on December 18 to offset the initial start-up cost outside of machinery.

In January 1970 Alston brought up the matter of space allocation. He felt that it would be in the firm's best interests to lease an additional 11,000 square feet of space located on the second floor of his building. Although the original proposal called for $1,200 per month rent, he said that he was only paying $875.00 and declared that it "seemed logical" to take this additional floor space immediately. Though Vann stated that he did not think Alston should take more space than he needed, Alston could not be persuaded and he took over a second floor of the building.

During the same month he submitted a request for $38,500 to the CBDO. He indicated that he was now ready to begin production and received CBDO checks for the following equipment:

| | |
|---|---|
| $22,000 | Heat Sealing Machine |
| 2,000 | Sewing Machine |
| 8,000 | Die Cutting Machines & Equipment |
| 6,500 | Hot Stamping Machine and Office Equipment and Supplies |
| $38,500 | Total |

In February he returned to the CBDO for another $22,000 to cover the following items:

| | |
|---|---|
| $ 8,000 | Payroll |
| 11,000 | Rent, Supplies, Brochures, Raw Materials |
| 2,000 | Bender Slicer Machine |
| 1,000 | Snap Machine and Banding Attachment |
| $22,000 | Total |

By March 3 the company had received a total of $84,000 and was still not in operation. (See Exhibit III on pages 145–147 for financial position as of February 28, 1970.) The plant occupied the second floor where only a cutting machine and a cutting table were located. On the first floor were the administrative offices and the main sewing and heat-sealing plant. The factory had twenty machines (sewing machines, set-up, and six heat-sealing machines, and a heat-sealing cage) and "only needed customers to begin operations."

According to Alston's plant manager, they were "still waiting for replies from IBM concerning a final price on a February bid" and Alston had "identified skilled employees standing by to start once the orders begin to come in."

On March 21, 1970, because of the increasing number of businesses being assisted by the CBDO staff, Vann assigned Vince Edwards to be the permanent contact man for Alston. On March 23 Edwards visited the plant and was initially impressed by Alston's operations despite the fact that there were no sales. According to Edwards:

. . . On March 23, 1970, I visited the Merritt Plastics Manufacturing Corporation. The purpose of the visit was to get acquainted with Mr. Alston and to inform him that I was his contact man. He was very receptive and I was very impressed with the tour that was given.

Although business has not started, there are optimistic signs of tremendous possibilities for this organization. The present plant layout and general business outlook would indicate this trend. Mr. Alston anticipated that within the next few days he should have a contract from IBM. He has quoted on items for Sears Roebuck which seem very promising; General Electric, there are possibilities here; Smith-Corona and Underwood can go either way.

He mentioned that at the outset he had problems quoting on items, consequently he was not competitive. However, IBM has been very helpful in assisting him to arrive at meaningful quotations. As a result, he is now assured that he should have a contract from them.

He has all machines ready to go on a day's notice. He was also cautioned on the limited amount of funds in his reserve and that he should be somewhat cautious.

As I stated earlier, I was very impressed with what I saw and I left Mr. Alston and his workers with the thought that his business should succeed.

About a week later, on March 28, Edwards visited Alston to determine if there were any new developments. Alston said that

IBM had put in an order for 15,000 typewriter covers and stated that if that order was satisfactory, a larger order would follow. Though this was the plant's only firm order, he indicated that he was discussing a contract of 100,000 covers with Underwood, negotiating with Smith-Corona, and had prepared quotes on air conditioning covers for General Electric. He said that Sears Roebuck had mentioned that they were interested in Polybags, but his plant did not have the special heating machine needed to manufacture them. He hoped that the necessary machinery could be ordered and delivered by April. Alston indicated that he had given a quote to a local bank on 200,000 checkbook covers, but was notified that his price was too high. Because of the frustrations dealing with these large commercial companies, Alston indicated that he was "trying to become involved in government procurement." However, this was a field entirely new to him. Edwards assured him that the CBDO would inform him of the procedures to follow for the procurement of government contracts.

At the beginning of April, Alston sent Edwards a request for additional funds for April, May, and June totaling over $83,000, $31,000 of which would be needed in April. (See Exhibit IV on page 148 for the funds requested.) While Edwards and Vann were pondering how to deal with the cash situation, Alston—without their knowledge—drew down his $29,500 bank loan on April 2, "to buy machinery and supplies." In the meantime Vann decided that Alston "could get along for April and May on $39,500" and began processing the necessary papers on April 9.

On April 11 Edwards visited the plant "to see how things were coming along." He found that Alston was home with a back injury, but spoke to Lopez about the status of the business. According to Lopez, the material for the IBM job had not been delivered. Therefore, the operators would not report to work on April 15, but April 25 instead. In addition, he indicated that Alston had quoted on a number of contracts, but still had no firm decisions.

On April 14, when Alston went to the CBDO office to pick up the $39,500 check, he informed Edwards that he would be leaving the same day "for a trip to the South to garner some business." At this time Alston also informed Edwards that he had secured a contract from Underwood.

On April 23 Edwards visited the plant in order to give two new CBDO employees a tour of "one of its promising businesses."

Edwards' optimistic observations on that visit are summarized in the following memorandum:

On April 23rd, along with Messrs. Smith and North, I visited Merritt Plastics Manufacturing Corp. The purpose was to give Smith and North a tour of one of our promising businesses, and secondly to discuss general business conditions with Mr. Alston. Upon arrival, I noted that the factory was very busy. Operators were making IBM covers; the production man was scheduling samples to be made for presentation and in general business seems to be shaping up. The points discussed with Mr. Alston were:

1. Number of pending contracts he has—he stated that he has two firms; there is the likelihood that General Electric will be inclined to give a contract. Sears Roebuck and Chase Manhattan purchasing agents will be visiting the plant next week to see operations before commitments are made.
2. All machinery has been delivered and is set up for operation.
3. The production manager is preparing samples for the medical market, insurance industry disposal bags, and "suit containers."
4. Mr. Alston will be quoting on binders for an insurance company and because of my connections, I think I may be able to get him the contract.
5. As I stated earlier, business has started and I do think there are tremendous possibilities here.

The next meeting between Edwards and Alston was on May 8. Alston stated that he was busily developing a full line of disposal bags since the City of Chicago had proposed to discard the use of metal cans for collecting garbage and use plastic disposal bags instead. He also indicated that the Salvation Army was desirous of giving him a job for 500,000 vinyl bags and he was busily working on that proposal.

During Edwards' next visit on May 13, Alston informed him that the company had secured a contract with Acme Markets for 250,000 bags and had received confirmation from Underwood for typewriter covers. Alston also informed Edwards that his plastic bags would probably be used by the city and a meeting was to be scheduled with the mayor's office to discuss Merritt's bidding on them. From all indications it seemed to Edwards that the company was doing quite well since "it had a full line of products, a complete insurance package and a market that it could handle."

With respect to finances, Alston's accountant was preparing an in-depth study of cost needs. When Edwards asked him when it would be finished, the accountant replied: "It will be in your hands very soon." By the end of May, however, Edwards still had not received a cash projection for the company, though he did get a financial statement for April 30 which showed no sales (see Exhibit V on pages 149–151) because it *did not* reflect the "increased activity" in May.

During a visit on May 29, Alston told Edwards that sample copies of a three-ring "Black Is Beautiful" binder had been mailed to several department stores across the country, and he was waiting for some feedback. On another visit in late June, Edwards found that Alston was visiting a General Electric plant in Connecticut. Because Alston felt that this was a very competitive job, he wanted to make a personal appearance at the plant. Also according to his production manager, IBM had given Alston another small order because they were satisfied and from all indications would be giving them small jobs on a regular basis. The "Black Is Beautiful" binders had apparently met with tremendous response from several department stores in the area, and the company had received several tentative orders.

*The Financial Crisis*

In June Alston's accountant indicated that the firm would need about $17,000 for working capital that month. However, because there was only $11,000 left in the CBDO appropriation for Merritt, Alston decided to contact a bank to secure the additional funds. In the meantime, Edwards went about preparing a check requisition for the remaining $11,000. Before giving Alston the amount requested, Edwards decided to audit Merritt's operations. Upon reviewing the books and financial statements, he noted that Alston had been "spending a tremendous amount for machinery." When asked for an explanation, Alston replied, "I have plans for a very large plant, therefore I have to tool up for it."

Alston also submitted a formal proposal to Edwards for an additional $50,000 for machinery, equipment, and working capital. (See Exhibit VI on pages 152–154.) Because of the urgency of the firm's needs, Alston said that he was going to a bank for a short-term loan to meet the immediate obligations and he indicated that the CBDO should either give a portion of the funds requested or guarantee a bank loan. However, Edwards informed him that while he had no objections to Alston going to the bank, he could not say that funds or a guarantee would be forthcoming.

Edwards had decide to prepare a new funding proposal but it was not to be presented to the CBDO executive committee until June 18. In the meanwhile, Alston had informed Edwards that he had received a number of contracts from several department stores for his "Black Is Beautiful" binders and if he was to be able to fill the orders he would need some working capital to buy supplies. Another factor which made the money matters seem even more urgent was that the suppliers of the binder material would be closing down soon for summer vacation. Since the binders had to be in the store before the fall to meet the onrush of students going back to school, Alston needed the additional cash immediately.

On June 15, in an oral status report to Vann, Edwards defined the company's needs succinctly. He said: "Apart from additional cash, which is the most pressing need, Merritt Plastics has no immediate need." He went on to mention that a proposal was being prepared and would be presented to the executive committee on June 18, at which time he would defend the request.

By June 16 Alston informed Edwards that he had received letters from several food chains and department stores indicating their interest in purchasing items from the company. With the seemingly strong sales and additional funds, Edwards was "pretty confident that things would go well for the company."

On June 18 Edwards presented a proposal for additional funding in the amount of $87,000. In a verbal summary, he argued that: (1) Merritt Plastics was initially underfinanced; (2) the death of the original proprietor (Clifton Merritt) brought setbacks as a result of change in the organization; (3) due to the time lag between the submission of a proposal and its implementation, equipment needs and costs changed; (4) the firm was substantially under-financed in its initial equipment needs and this caused a severe drain on working capital to the point where the corporation could not move ahead on its firm orders because it had run out of money. (See Exhibit VII on pages 154–156 for a summary of Edwards' June 18 refunding proposal.)

A member of the CBDO executive committee found it difficult to believe that a "business could run through over $160,000 in such a short time." Vann asked Fred Frazier, senior economic analyst, to review Merritt's needs again and come back with a *final* proposal on June 25.

In his June 25 proposal, Frazier said that even the $87,000 was not enough. He felt that the projected collection period in the June 18 proposal was too optimistic. Thus, he felt that "a truer measure of funding support was $141,000." (See Exhibit VIII on pages 156–157 for a summary of Frazier's revised refunding proposal of June 25, 1970.) With this turn of events, the executive committee decided to table the proposal until a board decision could be made.

After getting negative reactions to the proposals, Edwards told Alston that he "should curtail his activities for a while and await the decision concerning the additional funds." He indicated that "it seems somewhat inopportune to seek additional accounts when it's clear that there is no working capital to fulfill any orders that would be received anyway."

By July 11 the financial situation was acknowledged as being critical as evidenced by a visit by Vann and Edwards to the Merritt Plastics plant. Vann visited the site so that he could make a decision as to whether or not the proposed funding was necessary and decided to take direct control until he could make a decision. Subsequent to his visit, Vann decided that only a limited amount of funds would be given to Alston during July and August. During that two-month period, he would make a decision as to whether more should be allocated.

Vann finally decided to give Alston $15,000 for working capital to meet his payroll and "his most pressing obligations." In addition, Vann instituted the following set of stringent rules to protect the CBDO's interest:

At the time we disburse the $15,000 to Alston he should be told the following:

1. The funds are to be allocated in three areas:
   a. $1,000 to the bank as a working capital base;
   b. Approximately $7,000 to support payroll expenses for three weeks;
   c. The balance of $6,800 to meet his most pressing debt obligations other than the purchase of additional capital equipment.
2. We want him to agree that we can have one or two people on his premises full-time working with him in making his business operate. We expect that he would be completely cooperative with our people.

3. We want him to agree to the following:
   a. That we may hire a professional accounting firm to immediately undertake a complete audit of the company at the expense of the company, which audit would include an evaluation of the accounting and reporting systems and if necessary, recommendations for changes.
   b. We will be furnished by Tuesday of next week with an employee profile which would include for each employee, the name, job title and or description, weekly salary and date employed.
   c. We will receive by next Tuesday morning detailed recommendations on all present management personnel.
   d. No machinery not yet on order be purchased and that we receive by Tuesday a short summary of the justification for all machinery either in the plant or on order and the manner in which it relates to the sales forecast.
   e. Ken Alston must agree to furnish us a monthly Profit and Loss Statement until we decide we no longer need such statements.

Finally, Alston should be told in the most positive terms he should get into production immediately on the approximately $47,000 worth of firm orders he now has on hand and he should get busy getting orders that he can produce with the equipment he has installed. And that without the affirmative action on Alston's part on all these areas, we are not going to put any more money in the business.

In addition Vann asked Edwards and two other staff men to visit Alston for a week and prepare a full report on the company. He felt that such a report "would give us the real facts on what is needed." On July 25 Edwards submitted a report which discussed over-all management, office procedures, record keeping, personnel, disbursement of the $15,000, status of firm orders, accounts receivable, production, and machine capacity. Among other things, the report mentioned that Alston was so sales-oriented that it was necessary for the company to have someone with knowledge of the over-all scheme of the operations. The report also showed shortcomings in the record-keeping system, management control system, the personnel system, and the office procedures and business in general. (See Exhibit IX on pages 157–159 for excerpts of Edwards' July 25 report.)

The $15,000 allocated to Merritt Plastics Manufacturing Corporation during July managed to cover some of its working capital needs but by August, Alston was again feeling financial pressures. Fred Frazier urged the bank to extend an additional loan to the company, but the bank representative replied that the bank "would be willing to do that only if the CBDO would guarantee it." However, the CBDO was unwilling to provide a guarantee.

By the middle of August Vann had decided that the CBDO might put more money into the firm if Alston would relinquish some of his controls. Accordingly he dispatched the following letter to Alston:

Dear Mr. Alston:                                        August 14, 1970

This will confirm the understanding which we reached with respect to your application for an additional $100,000 loan.

We have already loaned you $15,000 on a short-term basis, pending our review of your loan application. We are ready to loan you an additional $10,000 on a short-term basis and submit a proposal to our Board for approval of a total commitment of $65,000.00, providing you agree to the terms of the $10,000 loan. If our Board approves this proposal, you will, of course, only be receiving $40,000 of additional money as you will be required to liquidate your two short-term notes to us in the total amount of $25,000 . . . If we make the loan, it will be made with the specific understanding that this is the limit of our foreseeable credit line to your company.

Thus, it should be clear to you, if we are able to lend you an additional $65,000.00, you must get your company on its feet and operating profitably with the money that will have been made available for your business.

We are willing to advance the additional $10,000.00 short-term loan and to submit the loan proposal to the Board, if, and only if, you agree to the following terms and conditions:
1. That we be permitted to assign Vince Edwards of our staff as part of your management team and that you agree
   a. to make no payroll additions without prior approval of Mr. Edwards;
   b. to make no purchases of supplies or services in excess of $300.00 without prior approval of Mr. Edwards;
   c. to issue no company check in excess of $300.00 without prior approval of Mr. Edwards;
   d. to work out with Mr. Edwards specific and detailed budget of expenditures for the next 12 weeks and to observe that budget to the letter in your company's operation.
2. That we be permitted to assign an outside consultant as part of your management team and that you will agree
   a. to work with him on estimating, production, and marketing matters;

b. to place no order for machinery or equipment except for a $3,000.00 riveting machine and a $200.00 up and down cutter, without prior approval of the consultant.

3. That we be permitted to assign a team of accountants to independently audit your books to date and to establish a simple, conservative internal bookkeeping system for your company.

4. That we be permitted to maintain your internal bookkeeping system until such time we are satisfied you have an employee capable of maintaining it independently.

If this letter sets forth our understanding, and if you agree to it, please indicate your agreement by signing a copy of this letter after noting that you have read and agreed to the terms of the $10,000 loan set forth in this letter, receipt of which $10,000 is hereby acknowledged.

Alston agreed to the terms of Vann's August 14 letter and the latter made the necessary arrangements to secure the $65,000 for Alston.

The CBDO staff spent most of September and October trying to understand and assist the Merritt operation. In a September 23 meeting, Vann set as the CBDO's objective the obtaining of $100,000 in sales for the company:

At a meeting this morning, we agreed that we would provide assistance in generating sales for Merritt Plastics Manufacturing Corporation. Specifically, the following will be done during the next two weeks.

1. I will write selected industrial leaders to ask for contacts in obtaining orders for Merritt.
2. Fred Frazier and Vince Edwards will work to develop sales to the City of Chicago.
3. Peter Greene will prepare a list of Boards of Directors and also identify key contacts at retailers in Chicago.

Our objective is to obtain $100,000 in orders for Merritt by the end of September. Sales will be generated from three groups of companies: industrial companies, financial companies and retail companies, each of which reflects a specific Merritt product area.

However, despite these efforts, the CBDO was not too successful in obtaining business for Alston, as is indicated by the following excerpts from a memorandum from Frazier:

TO: Ted Vann                                        October 14, 1970
FROM: Fred Frazier

Merritt Plastics Manufacturing through the end of August suffered a deficit from operations of $86,584 and continued to operate at a deficit during September. I estimate that the company needs $45,000 in monthly sales to break even.

Merritt Plastics Manufacturing should record sales of over $30,000 during October. Its order backlog beyond October is thin, perhaps $10,000 (this figure depends on how much is shipped during October). It has obtained tentative commitments from IBM and from General Electric for orders during 1971. We are attempting to obtain $100,000 in orders for Merritt setting as our target date October 20th (this $100,000 includes about $20,000 in October sales and current backlog).

Merritt Plastics Manufacturing may make it, but only if our sales efforts are successful in generating a break-even sales volume for the company.

In late October and November the CBDO became somewhat encouraged with the Merritt situation as Edwards began to have some success with government officials in the "8-A" program about contracts for Alston. In an October 23 memorandum to Vann he said:

As of today the picture looks favorable for Merritt getting a government "8-A" contract.

I have been in touch with a SBA representative many times in the past week. Our last conversation, which was held at 9:00 this morning, was to firm up those products that Merritt could produce. At the time of this conversation, the government procurement representative of the General Services Administration was present. He is going to take the products we have agreed upon and match them up to GSA requirements during the next four months.

As GSA is constantly in a "buy" position on litter bags, office equipment covers, binders, etc., I feel it is just a matter of time before Merritt gets a contract.

One week later, on October 30, Edwards reported that the "8-A" still looked positive though it would be a few months before a contract could be awarded:

I received a call from our contact man on the "8-A" program. He advised me that GSA had identified three procurements that Merritt could possibly bid on. They were:

1. Polybags;
2. Plastic mattresses and pillow case covers;
3. Binders.

Exact details as to quantities required, delivery dates, etc. would not be available until sometime next week, but the total procurement for the three products could run upwards to $200,000. Merritt could receive any or all of this amount. Based upon the information at hand, the contracts, if awarded, would probably be let around the 1st of February.

In November Vann asked the CBDO board of directors to solicit orders for Merritt. In a November 1 memorandum to his board, he said, in part:

. . . You will recall that in mid-September, we determined to put our weight behind a sales effort for Merritt Plastics with a short-term goal of $100,000 in orders to be shipped by the end of the year 1970 . . .

. . . We have not yet exhausted potential for short run pre-December 31 business. We believe we can reach our goal of $100,000 if we can penetrate the checkbook cover business; with the help of the banks, I am sure we will do it. For the long run, the picture is still far from encouraging . . .

In view of the importance of this loan and this business to our overall operation and in view of what has been done to date, I would like to suggest that the following directors undertake the following assignments:

1. That Mr. Mason contact several department chain stores to see if we can get an opening for business.
2. Mr. Otto consider whether he can get us any help with Sears.
3. Mr. Moses and his staff assist us in following up on the checkbook business.
4. That Mr. Wallace help us penetrate the dust cover business on the basis of Merritt's performance with IBM to date.

As a result of these efforts, American Foods, a major food manufacturer, came back with optimistic outlook in the following November 12 letter:

Mr. Ted Vann
President, CBDO
Chicago, Illinois

Dear Ted:

We have identified five business opportunities, all of which are moving forward and all of which involve possible opportunities for Merritt Plastics. These are:

1. Bin liners for Newark, Delaware.
2. Bin liners for Trenton, New Jersey.
3. Drum liners for Wellesley, Massachusetts.
4. Plastic bags for East St. Louis, Illinois.
5. Ring binders for this office.

My staff is following up on all five of these possibilities and I feel sure that some of them are going to result in profitable business for Merritt.

At this point in time I am very optimistic about the outlook.

Cordially yours,
Richard Cunningham
Vice-President, Operations

## The Future of Merritt

Despite these favorable signs, by the end of November things had reached a very critical stage. Merritt missed scheduled delivery dates; expected orders did not come through; and in-house orders were calculated to be only marginally profitable, at best. Alston was not approaching breakeven and his money had run out. (See Exhibit X on pages 160–163 for Merritt's November 1970 financial statements.)

Again, on December 4, 1970, Alston turned to the CBDO for assistance. In a telegram to Vann he said:

YOUR RELUCTANCE TO RELEASE FUNDS WILL SURELY CAUSE US TO FAIL. I KNOW THAT WITH THE FEW PRODUCTION CHANGES AND ADMINISTRATIVE ADDITION WE CAN SUCCEED. WE HAVE PASSED OUR TEST PERIOD REGARDING OUR PRINCIPAL CUSTOMERS AND THE ORDERS ARE NOW COMING IN. YOU CAN CONSIDER THIS NOW MY LAST APPEAL IN TERMS OF GETTING YOU TO CHANGE YOUR POSITION AND RELEASE THE FUNDS FOR THE PURPOSE OF A GUAR-TEE TO THE BANK SO THAT THEY CAN MAKE THE LOAN.

In a December 7, 1970, letter Vann replied in the negative to Alston, thus effectively eliminating the CBDO as a source of funds. In this letter to Alston, he said:

This is in reply to your telegram of December 4, 1970 . . .

. . . Your company was not able to utilize this money in a way that would enable it to earn the funds necessary to pay current obligations. This was due in part to the fact that your capital expenditures exceeded by about 100% the amount you budgeted in the initial loan application for such expenditures. Because of the company's critical financial condition, you made application for an additional term loan from us.

Following the series of conferences with you in July and early August of 1970, we wrote you a detailed letter with respect to your pending loan application. In that letter we said we would recommend approval of a firm commitment of $65,000 to you if you would agree to certain conditions specifically spelled out in this letter.

That letter made it clear that this was the limit of our foreseeable credit line to your company . . .

You agreed to this proposal.

We call your attention to our letter to you of August 19, 1970, which sets forth the terms and conditions of this loan. You accepted the loan and agreed to the conditions . . .

You have not yet been able to get your company moving in the right direction . . .

Since August we have worked closely with you, providing you with marketing, production and bookkeeping assistance.

We have found that your costing has been inaccurate; that your overhead is too high for the type of business you are in; that you have not shown the necessary respect for bookkeeping, accounting and business procedures; that you have failed, in spite of our insistence, to properly pay your federal withholding taxes.

You will recall that at the beginning of October, after we had assisted you in developing a substantial number of firm orders, you stated that you would ship $30,000.00 in goods during that month.

In the latter part of October your company ran out of cash to meet your current payroll. At that time, so as to give you every opportunity to make your October shipment goals, we made an emergency $10,000 thirty-day loan to you. It has not been repaid, nor is there any prospect that it can be repaid in the near future.

It is worth noting that you shipped about $13,000 in goods in October and have never come near approaching the $30,000 per month figure.

We have, therefore, concluded that no more funds can be committed to you. It follows that we are in no position to guarantee a loan from a bank.

During this same month the authorities sent the marshal to Alston's office to serve an eviction notice for non-payment of taxes and rent. Alston was given ten days in which to show cause why he should not be evicted. On December 20, 1970, Alston was scheduled to go to court to fight an eviction notice that he knew could signal the death knell for his company.

Meanwhile, the CBDO had decided that the firm was finished and was in the process of attempting to salvage something out of its investment. It saw its alternatives as represented in Vann's December 18 report to the board of directors:

. . . On a workout basis, we form a corporation and

1. At a private sale offer to buy out the bank's first mortgage. A deal could be made with the bank at about $15,000. (The face value of this first chattel mortgage is $25,000.) This is preferable to letting the bank sell the machinery at a foreclosure sale.
2. Make a deal with the landlord to rent the present premises on a month to month basis with a long-term option. This probably would require our cleaning up some back rent and might cost $4–$5,000.
3. We would then attempt to find someone to operate the business with a commitment from us that he could acquire stock and eventual control if he performed.

My basic reason for this recommendation is that whatever else Alston did not do, he did build a factory capable of employing 40–60 people if a manager could develop a need for that kind of employee and that kind of product.

Upon hearing of this decision, Alston knew that only a miracle could "save his cousin's dream."

# EPILOGUE

On January 4, 1971, Dick Cunningham, vice-president of American Foods, sent the following letter to Ted Vann:

Dear Ted:

My staff has completed the follow-up on the five business opportunities that I identified for you in my letter of November 12, 1970. As a result of their search, we can confirm that our firm will require bin liners for Newark, Delaware and Trenton; drum liners for Wellesley, Massachusetts; and plastic bags for East St. Louis, Illinois.

We expect the cost of these materials to range from $225,000 to $275,000. I should like to have our purchasing agent sit down with your Mr. Alston within the next two weeks to negotiate a price. Of course, because of the level of business that we are doing with our consumer products, we might need more.

Vann realized that the letter virtually guaranteed Merritt Plastics $250,000 in sales over twelve months. Moreover, he recognized that there were some grave implications if the CBDO were not able to participate after the CBDO's board had secured the business. He decided to call a meeting of the board of directors and discuss the most recent development. The meeting was scheduled for Friday, January 8.

The meeting began with Vann reading the letter he had received from Dick Cunningham. A board member immediately asked: "Does the letter change the substance of the report that you sent to us on December 18?" According to Vann he indicated that it did not change the report, but it did necessitate a speedy decision on the course that the CBDO wanted to follow regarding Merritt. He added: "I think that we do a great disservice to our efforts if we do not respond in the affirmative to this offer. We were the ones that sought the assistance, and for us to back out now might put a crimp in any other efforts that we might want the corporations to help us in. And you know as well as I that the word will get around if we can't come through." Vann reported that "the board members were at a loss for words," finally asking his advice. He suggested that Merritt specialize only in Polybags, its most profitable item. In response to a question about the role of Alston, he said: "I think we can work out a deal so that Mr. Alston could get out of all of this and he would probably accept it. If this happens, then we can bring in someone to run the enterprise."

138

When the board seemed to agree that this was the best alternative, Vann made the following recommendations:

A few days ago we received a proposal from David Bruce, who had previously operated a Polybag business for an absentee owner. He has an impressive résumé. He was trained as an accountant, but because of some problems in getting a job in the fifties, he was able to land a job in the plastics business, as a supervisor. From there he worked himself up through foreman and became manager of an operation employing some sixty people. The owner—who was in poor health—left the business about eight years ago and spends all of his time in Florida. Now he has a son about twenty-four or twenty-five who has just come out of graduate school, after getting a degree in Engineering, and he is going to take over the operation. Mr. Bruce is totally disillusioned with the firm and is interested in setting up his own shop. He also says that there are a lot of customers that he can take with him. I have checked out Bruce's credentials and everyone I talked to thought that he owned the company. One man said, "Bruce knows more about the business than all of the others put together." I think we should negotiate with him.

As far as the bank is concerned, if we agree to pay them for their investment, they would have no choice but to go along, since it would not stand to lose any money. The excess machinery could be sold and the funds from the sale of the machinery could be used to operate the business. Of course, we will not need all of the space that is in the building, but we can partition it off and rent the rest as storage space.

The board members agreed with Vann's view and instructed him to work out the details.

Immediately after the meeting, Vann placed a call to Alston and scheduled a meeting for the following Monday, January 11. On the day of the meeting Vann indicated to Alston that the CBDO did not think it prudent to invest any more funds in Merritt Plastics as it was presently constituted. He then showed Alston a copy of the letter from Cunningham. Upon being questioned by Alston on his role in bidding on this "lucrative contract," Vann indicated that the CBDO had already put "a quarter of a million dollars" in the firm with little likelihood of success, and felt that if "it could run the way it ought to be run," there was some likelihood for success. Vann also added that the CBDO was prepared to absolve Alston of any personal liability and indicated that he would have the CBDO attorney send such a statement to Alston's lawyer.

By January 21 Alston had agreed to "sell" his assets and

liabilities in the company to the CBDO. Vann then met with Bruce to offer him a management position with the reorganized and sharply limited company. Bruce accepted the position of general manager, with the provision that he would share in profits after the first year. Bruce and Vann later met with the purchasing agent of the food manufacturer and agreed upon an initial order of $233,000.

Subsequently, the CBDO hired an auctioneer to get rid of the excess equipment and advertised in the local papers that it had space to let. By February 10 the CBDO had received several firm offers for the machinery and several moving companies had indicated their interest in the excess space.

A few months after the CBDO had taken over the company and started production on the Polybag order, Vann said:

Merritt was quite an experience for us. It taught us a lot of lessons about what we ought to be doing and what we ought not be doing. One thing is for sure, we should never have funded the business once Merritt was killed. Everything about the business had substantially changed. Alston had no knowledge or experience about running a manufacturing business, especially a plastics business. And although he gave the business his all, he just did not have it. In addition, we continuously provided money, when there was no market, believing like he did that if someone said that they were impressed with his work a contract would be forthcoming. And if you look at some of the early reports under business, you will see some $400,000 in contracts pending.

But you know, even if Alston had the necessary skills to run the business, he would have caught hell trying to make it go, because of insufficient funds. Our projections were overly optimistic and we saw the business reaching break-even in five months. But the amount of money he had to do it with was $166,000. We know now that it is nearly impossible to start any kind of manufacturing operation with less than $250,000.

Also little attention was given to the whole area of marketing the products, which we have learned is the key area. I have made sure that all of the employees understand what happened here, and we have discussed various parts of Merritt in some detail at our staff meetings. We know that some good analysis was done, but because of a breakdown in communications, the recommendations were not implemented. This will never happen again. We made some mistakes in Merritt and these mistakes taught us some very important lessons. You can bet that we will know how to handle our next manufacturer.

Initially Alston was very hesitant to discuss the business that he had left, but after a rather lengthy exchange on business and the community he relaxed and agreed to talk about Merritt Plastics. He said:

I should not have attempted to take over and run the company. I know now that it just was not my cup of tea. I am a real estate man. I guess I was so emotionally concerned about all the work that Cliff had put into this thing that I did not want to see it go. You know I was very naïve about a lot of things. I had thought that by getting myself a good board of directors and advisers, that they would help me operate the company, but I never saw any of those people more than once or twice. Every time I looked around there was a problem: rent was due, salaries were due, material had to be paid for. And these things were high. I never realized that a business could eat up so much money. Then everybody wanted me to make decisions. Here I was paying people to handle various areas and any time something happened, they would save it for me. I could be gone two weeks and come back and the problem was still there. Just traveling and making sales pitches took most of my time and by the time I got back to the office, I had problems to work on, so I never got ahead of the game. I was always behind.

One thing I can truthfully say: if those people up at the agency [CBDO] give everybody as much assistance as they gave me, a guy with his head screwed on right has a good chance of making it. Most of the things I learned about the manufacturing business I learned from them and their questions. After a while, they had a question for everything and they sure were stingy with that money. One of those guys used to act like it was his money.

I thought that I was having problems with the corporations being unresponsive and believed that if I went after government business, things would be better. Well, brother, let me tell you, the government has ninety different ways of jerking you around. And they can have that government business; the time and effort just ain't worth it.

But of all the problems I had, the problems with trying to run four or five different operations almost ran me ragged. In sewing there were these women and women are something to deal with. This woman does not talk to this one and if you say more to this woman than the other one, then one gets peeved and shows her evil streak.

Well, I have learned my lesson, and the manufacturing business you can have. People talk about business as though there is something romantic about it, but business is a lot more than a notion—a hell of a lot more.

# Exhibit I

## MERRITT PLASTICS MANUFACTURING CORPORATION

### March 19, 1969

This is a proposal to request $166,000 of the Development Fund administered by your organization.

We plan to manufacture protective plastic dust covers for commercial and industrial items. The purpose of this proposal is to request assistance in establishing this business which will provide an on-the-job training program for indigenous residents.

The stock of the company is owned by Mrs. Fable and myself. In addition to manufacturing protective plastic dust covers, other related plastic and cloth items will be manufactured. The process used by the company is the ordinary sewing and heat-sealing process.

We anticipate gross sales of $25,000 to $50,000 per month when the business becomes established. Based on the initial investment the business will require gross sales of $22,623 per month to break even. A twenty-week period is projected in the Pro Forma Balance Sheet to reach breakeven:

### Operation at Breakeven

#### Assets

| | | |
|---|---:|---:|
| Current Assets: | | |
| Cash | $ 13,575.00 | |
| Accounts Receivable | 27,150.00 | |
| Inventory | 13,575.00 | |
| Total Current Assets | | $ 54,300.00 |
| Property, Plant and Equipment: | | |
| Machinery, Equipment and Furniture | 56,752.00 | |
| Fixtures, Renovation and Other Capitalized Items | 8,500.00 | |
| Total Property, Plant and Equipment | | 65,252.00 |
| Total Assets | | $119,552.00 |

BLACK ENTERPRISE, INC.

Liabilities

| | | |
|---|---|---|
| Accounts Payable, Accrued | | |
| Liabilities, Taxes Payable | 9,050.00 | |
| Notes Payable | 136,142.00 | |
| Stockholders' Capital Investment | 5,000.00 | |
| Operating Loss until Breakeven | (30,640.00) | |
| Total Liabilities | | $119,552.00 |

I have 25 years' experience in the plastics field.

The business will eventually employ eighty-four full-time employees. We plan to maintain an on-going training program where we will employ indigenous residents, regardless of their past backgrounds.

Exhibit II

Mr. Ken Alston            November 26, 1969
President
Merritt Plastics Manufacturing Corp.
Chicago, Illinois

Dear Mr. Alston:

At your request I have prepared a schedule summarizing the capital needed to get the plant started immediately. The costs and expenses outlined reflect the minimum deposit and/or amount needed to effect installation of equipment and provide services over the next several weeks as follows:

| | |
|---|---|
| Rent: October, November and December | $ 2,625.00 |
| Salary—Production Manager 6 weeks | 1,500.00 |
| Electric—Deposit | 300.00 |
| Workmen's Compensation Insurances | 1,200.00 |
| Stationery—Preliminary | 100.00 |
| Rubbish Removal | 50.00 |
| Legal Expenses | 1,250.00 |
| Dues—Plastics Manufacturers Assn. | 100.00 |
| Accounting-Systems Installation | 500.00 |
| Advertising and Signs | 200.00 |
| Improvements—Carpentry | 2,000.00 |
| Electrical | 3,500.00 |
| Flooring | 2,000.00 |

## Machinery and Equipment

| | |
|---|---:|
| Cutting Room Appliances | 1,000.00 |
| 5 Heat Sealing Machines | 23,175.00 |
| 10 Sewing Machines | 5,975.00 |
| 1 Hot Stamping Machine | 2,200.00 |
| 1 Die Cutting Machine | 2,000.00 |
| 1 Shell Dol Poly-Bag Machine | 21,000.00 |
| 1 Cutting Drum-Custom Made | 1,275.00 |
| Cutting Room Tables | 750.00 |
| Office Equipment (Desks, Chairs, Typewriter) | 1,500.00 |
| Sewing Machine Tables | 3,900.00 |
| Air Compressor | 1,000.00 |
| | $79,100.00 |

Please do not hesitate to contact this office in the event that you have any questions.

Respectfully submitted,
Ezell Clander, C.P.A.

Exhibit III

# MERRITT PLASTICS MANUFACTURING CORPORATION

## Income Statement for Period Ended February 28, 1970

| | | |
|---|---|---|
| Net Sales | | – 0 – |
| Cost of Sales | | – 0 – |
| Gross Profit | | – 0 – |
| Operating Expenses: | | |
| Selling | $ 455.12 | |
| Administrative | 6,445.62 | |
| Travel and Entertainment | 119.75 | |
| Officer's Salaries | 1,700.50 | |
| Total Operating Expenses | | $8,720.99 |
| Profit (Loss) | | ($8,720.99) |

# MERRITT PLASTICS MANUFACTURING CORPORATION

## Balance Sheet as at February 28, 1970

### Assets

| | | |
|---|---:|---:|
| **Current Assets:** | | |
| Cash | $11,973.63 | |
| Prepaid Expenses | 1,200.00 | |
| Other Current Assets | 250.00 | |
| Total Current Assets | | $13,423.63 |
| **Plant Property and Equipment:** | | |
| Machinery and Equipment | 61,420.57 | |
| Other Property | 1,013.77 | |
| Total Property, Plant and Equipment, Net | | 62,434.34 |
| **Other Assets:** | | |
| Security Deposits | | |
| Utilities | 300.00 | |
| Rent | 875.00 | |
| Telephone | 150.00 | |
| Deferred Assets | 14,424.21 | |
| Total Other Assets | | 15,749.21 |
| **Total Assets** | | $91,607.18 |

## Liabilities and Net Worth

| | | |
|---|---:|---:|
| Current Liabilities: | | |
|    Accounts Payable — Trade | $ 8,325.62 | |
|    Accrued Liabilities | 220.17 | |
|    Other Current Liabilities | 1,252.27 | |
|       Total Current Liabilities | | $ 9,798.06 |
| Long-Term Liabilities: | | |
|    Loan Payable — CBDO | 83,459.86 | |
|       Total Long-Term Liabilities | | 83,459.86 |
|       Total Liabilities | | 93,257.92 |
| Net Worth: | | |
|    Common Stock 21 Shs. Outstanding | 5,250.00 | |
|    Earned Surplus | (6,900.74) | |
|       Total Net Worth | | (1,650.74) |
| Total Liabilities and Net Worth | | $91,607.18 |

## Exhibit IV

Mr. Ken Alston                                  March 31, 1970
President
Merritt Plastics Manufacturing Corporation
Chicago, Illinois

Dear Mr. Alston:

    Please be advised that you will need funds during the months of April, May and June 1970 to cover the following expenses:

| | April | May | June |
|---|---|---|---|
| **Payroll:** | | | |
| Cutter | $ 400.00 | $ 400.00 | $ 400.00 |
| Production Manager | 1,000.00 | 1,000.00 | 1,000.00 |
| Bookkeeper-Gal Friday | 500.00 | 500.00 | 500.00 |
| Shipping Clerk | 340.00 | 340.00 | 340.00 |
| Floor Lady | 460.00 | 460.00 | 460.00 |
| Sewing Machine Operators | (10) 3,200.00 | (15) 4,800.00 | (20) 6,400.00 |
| Floor Boy | 272.00 | 272.00 | 272.00 |
| Foreman | 1,020.00 | 1,020.00 | 1,020.00 |
| Total Payroll | 7,192.00 | 8,792.00 | 10,392.00 |
| Payroll Taxes 10% | 720.00 | 880.00 | 1,040.00 |
| Fringe Benefits 17% | 1,222.00 | 1,495.00 | 1,770.00 |
| Rent | 1,750.00 | 1,750.00 | 1,750.00 |
| Stationery | 100.00 | 100.00 | 100.00 |
| Brochures | 1,050.00 | —0— | —0— |
| Rubbish Removal | 50.00 | 50.00 | 50.00 |
| Advertising | 200.00 | 200.00 | 200.00 |
| Utilities | 200.00 | 200.00 | 200.00 |
| Business Taxes | 87.00 | 87.00 | 87.00 |
| Accounting Fees | 150.00 | 150.00 | 150.00 |
| Raw Material | 6,000.00 | 9,000.00 | 12,000.00 |
| Postage & Express | 500.00 | 800.00 | 1,200.00 |
| Total for Working Capital | 19,221.00 | | |
| **Machinery & Equipment:** | | | |
| Turntable | 8,000.00 | | |
| Dies | 2,300.00 | | |
| Patents | 300.00 | | |
| Baggers & Sealers | 1,648.00 | | |
| Total Funds Needed | $31,469.00 | $23,504.00 | $28,939.00 |

Respectfully submitted,
Ezell Clander, C.P.A

Exhibit V

## MERRITT PLASTICS MANUFACTURING CORPORATION

Statement of Operations March 1, 1970 — April 30, 1970

| | | |
|---|---:|---:|
| Sales | | —0— |
| Selling Expenses: | | |
| Shipping Supplies | $393.20 | |
| Travel | 409.03 | |
| Auto and Carfares | 834.37 | |
| Sample Expense | 393.64 | |
| Total Selling Expenses | 2,030.24 | |
| Administrative Expenses: | | |
| Officer's Salary | 1,156.00 | |
| Office Payroll | 1,000.00 | |
| Payroll Taxes | 265.60 | |
| Telephone | 471.82 | |
| Legal and Accounting | 493.50 | |
| Office Supplies and Expenses | 682.04 | |
| Help Wanted Advertising | 337.89 | |
| Deprcciation — Office Equipment | 85.78 | |
| Dues and Subscriptions | 51.00 | |
| Total Selling and Administrative Expenses | | 6,573.87 |
| Net Income (Loss) | | ($6,573.87) |

# MERRITT PLASTICS MANUFACTURING CORPORATION

## Balance Sheet as at April 30, 1970

### Assets

| | | |
|---|---:|---:|
| **Current Assets:** | | |
| Cash on Hand | – 0 – | |
| Cash in Bank | $ 26,568.25 | |
| Inventories: | | |
|   Raw Material – Sewing | 700.00 | |
|   Work in Process – Sewing | 5,643.63 | |
|   Work in Process – Heat Sealing | 3,114.04 | |
|   Work in Process – Polybag | 1,817.66 | |
| | 37,843.58 | |
| Tools and Dies | 4,709.15 | |
| Prepaid Expenses | 3,200.00 | |
|   Total Current Assets | | $ 45,752.73 |
| **Fixed Assets:** | | |
| Office Equipment and Improvements | 5,396.33 | |
| Plant and Equipment | 99,422.06 | |
| | 104,818.39 | |
|   Less: Accumulated Depreciation | 1,742.84 | |
|   Total Fixed Assets | | 103,075.55 |
| **Other Assets:** | | |
| Security Deposits: | | |
|   Utilities | 300.00 | |
|   Rent | 875.00 | |
|   Telephone | 150.00 | |
| Deferred Costs | 17,043.10 | |
| Organization Expense | 232.00 | |
| Deferred Interest | 7,844.81 | |
|   Total Other Assets | | 26,444.91 |
| **Total Assets** | | $175,273.19 |

BLACK ENTERPRISE, INC.

## Liabilities and Stockholders' Equity

Current Liabilities:

| | | |
|---|---|---|
| Accounts Payable | $ 17,508.14 | |
| Payroll Taxes Payable | 1,158.17 | |
| Accrued Expenses | 28.15 | |
| Payroll Accrued | 359.92 | |
| Notes Payable | 12,543.24 | |
| Total Current Liabilities | | $ 31,597.62 |

Long-Term Liabilities:

| | | |
|---|---|---|
| Loan Payable — CBDO | 151,900.18 | |
| Total Long-Term Liabilities | | 151,900.18 |
| Total Liabilities | | 183,497.80 |

Stockholders' Equity:

| | | |
|---|---|---|
| Common Stock Issued and Outstanding | 5,250.00 | |
| Net Worth — Beginning | (6,900.74) | |
| Income (Loss) for Period | (6,573.87) | |
| Total Stockholders' Equity | | (8,224.61) |
| Total Liabilities and Stockholders' Equity | | $175,273.19 |

## Exhibit VI

## PROPOSAL

## June 1, 1970

Due to the additional cost of machinery and equipment, which is over and above our original budget, the Merritt Plastics Manufacturing Corporation is requesting additional working capital of $50,000.

Method: Separate short-term loan from a bank for a period of 90 days until necessary paper work can be processed to increase the amount of funds provided for in the contract between the CBDO and Merritt Plastics Manufacturing Corporation.

#### Additional Machinery & Equipment That Is Needed and Partially Ordered

| | |
|---|---:|
| Semi Automatic Silk Screen Machine and Rack | $ 2,400.00 |
| 11 inch gluing machine | 400.00 |
| Up and Down Cutting Machine | 200.00 |
| Automatic Eyelet Machine for Polybag including Installation Snaps | 1,700.00 |
| 10 additional 111W153 Sewing Machine @ $225.00 | 2,250.00 |
| Wicket Puncher for Poly Machine | 1,200.00 |
| Automatic Rivet Machine for Ringbinder | 2,400.00 |
| Factory Fans and Office Air Conditioners | 600.00 |
| | $11,150.00 |
| Machinery & Equipment Purchased | 84,465.65 |
| | $95,615.65 |
| Original amount for machinery | 56,000.00 |
| Amount of machinery over original budget | $39,615.65 |

# SPECIAL PROJECTS

*Polybag Department*

We have developed under our own label plastic trash bags, garbage bags and rubbish bags, which will be distributed in various department stores, chain stores and supermarkets. We will be ready for distribution in the latter part of June. We project a market of approximately $350,000 for the first year.

*Sewing Department*

We have developed our own air conditioner covers under our own label and will be ready for distribution the latter part of June for the department stores and chain stores. We have produced our own garment bags which will be available for distribution the latter part of June for department and chain stores.

*Heat-Sealing*

We have developed our own ring binders under the title of "Black Is Beautiful" and "The American Flag." First orders are expected from various department stores. We have designed our own catalog and have tooled up for some 20 separate items for the insurance industry. We are about to distribute our catalog to some 8,000 insurance companies and agents.

Special sorting and bagging of picture book covers under license of well-known record companies—$16,000.00 every 10 weeks. Extensive line of medical disposal items now being developed, coupled with our Certificate of Eligibility will place us in good position to do business with United States Government.

## SPECIAL REMARKS FROM THE
## PRESIDENT AND SUMMARY

We started receiving our initial funding in January of 1970. We are tooled and are in production. In all three departments, ninety per cent of our original projection in terms of potential customers has held up. We are about to or have started production for some of the largest companies in the country today such as IBM, General Electric, Royal, Prudential, Remington, Westinghouse, Sears, Veterans Administration, Woolworth, Western Electric, and many others.

Training schedules now being prepared by Illinois State Department of Labor will entitle our company to receive certain tax benefits.

Samples of most of our work are readily available for inspection. Funds under our original budget will last us until June 27, 1970. We respectfully request immediate consideration on our proposal.

Exhibit VII

## REFUNDING PROPOSAL
## MERRITT PLASTICS MANUFACTURING CORPORATION

June 18, 1970

*Purpose of the Proposal*

This is a proposal to provide additional capitalization to the Merritt Plastics Manufacturing Corporation for approximately $87,000.00.

*The Proposal*

Merritt Plastics Manufacturing Corporation is a manufacturing concern which produces plastic and vinyl covers, binders, booklets, bags, packages, etc. for commercial and industrial use. Its proposal was first presented to the CBDO in February of 1969, approved in July but did not receive its first funding until late December of that same year. We provided $136,000 and the bank $29,500.

Unfortunately in July 1969, Mr. Clifton Merritt died in an accident. His cousin, Mr. Kenneth Alston, was able to take up the reins and with the approval of the bank and the CBDO continue to build the operation which Merritt was in the process of getting off the ground.

However, when organizations change presidents under as unpleasant circumstances as were these, more often than not things do not initially run smoothly; e.g., where it should have taken five months for the company to reach a breakeven level of operation it appears as though it will be closer to a year before that happens. Still further when there is a significant time lag between the submittal of a proposal and its implementation, equipment needs, styles and cost change. In the case of the Merritt company it was close to a year before its proposal was to be implemented which resulted in their being underfinanced by approximately $56,000 for their initial equipment needs. The cost, needs, and styles of equipment had changed considerably which also caused the cost of the plant renovations to change significantly.

The underfinancing of equipment needs of the company caused a severe drain on the working capital appropriation to the point where, now, when the company has *firm orders of approximately $400,000* and bids of $1.4 million it can not move ahead on these orders because it has run out of funds.

*Financials*

The company has demonstrated its abilities to reach its market but, as very clearly demonstrated in its cash flow statement, being undercapitalized in its equipment needs not only meant drawing on the working capital appropriations to meet these needs but also that the working capital needs were understated. This is clearly demonstrated by the turn-table attachment to the heat-sealing operation which increased productivity by 300% and therefore material and labor needs as well.

*Capital Requirements*

To reach a monthly breakeven level of approximately $53,000 sometime between October and November the company will need $86,825.00 to finance its operational loss position until breakeven.

*Funding*

BANK PARTICIPATION. A local bank has tentatively agreed to lend Merritt $30,000 on a short-term loan basis if we will come in either on a subordinated loan basis or equity position for the remaining $57,000.00.

CBDO FUNDS. We will provide $57,000 toward the financing of this operation to be paid back if a loan position is taken after final payment of the original loan at a rate of $5,000 a month for ten months and a final monthly payment of $7,000 in the eleventh month.

Exhibit VIII

REFUNDING PROPOSAL (REVISED)

June 25, 1970

*Purpose of the Proposal*

This is a revised proposal to provide additional funding to the Merritt Plastics Manufacturing Corporation for approximately $141,000.00.

*Nature of the Proposal*

(See June 18th Proposal)

*Financials*

(See June 18th Proposal)

*Capital Requirements*

To reach a monthly breakeven level of approximately $53,000 sometime between October and November the company will need $141,000.00 to finance its operational loss position until breakeven.

*Funding*

BANK PARTICIPATION. The bank has agreed to lend the Merritt Corporation $40,000 on a three-year loan basis if we will come in either on a subordinated loan basis or equity position for the remaining $101,000.00.

FUNDS. We will provide $101,000 toward the financing of this operation to be paid back if a loan position is taken after final payment of the original loan at a rate of $5,000 a month for nineteen months and a final monthly payment of $6,000 in the twentieth month.

## Exhibit IX

TO: Mr. Ted Vann                                            July 25, 1970
FROM: Vince Edwards
RE: Merritt Plastics Manufacturing Corporation

. . . On July 21st, I took up residence at the place of business. Areas which needed observation were:

*Overall Management*

. . . In my judgment Mr. Alston is an excellent salesman and has tremendous capabilities of reaching his prospective clients, as is evidenced by the contact he has established with the larger companies . . .

. . . I do think that there is a void in the operation which should be filled by a general manager for the operation because in the absence of Mr. Alston everything seems to be at a standstill. Now, I do realize that because of the shortage of working capital it would be difficult to employ such an individual at this time but I have mentioned to Mr. Alston that this is a necessity and as soon as there are sufficient funds, this person should be hired . . .

*Office Procedure*

Presently, there is one girl in the office who is more or less a Girl Friday. She does the billing, typing, invoicing, bookkeeping and answers

the phones. I do think this is too much for one person to handle . . .
I am recommending that Mr. Alston get a general bookkeeper who
would be capable of supervising the office functions . . .

### Record Keeping

. . . In this situation definitely insufficient records are kept.

### Personnel

Within the establishment there are 17 people that are presently
employed . . . The operators are paid a salary between $1.75 and
$2.00 per hour according to their skills . . . In my curiosity to see
whether these girls were performing sufficiently, I did a spot check
every hour and can safely say that these girls are doing an excellent
job . . .

### Disbursement of $15,000

On Monday . . . I sat down with Mr. Alston and we covered the
accounts payable that were to be paid based on the $15,000 that was
funded to the company . . . Attached is a listing of the disbursements
made and to be made . . .

### Firm Orders

When I presented the proposal for $140,000 over a month ago,
I . . . stated that the orders presented were not presented as firm
orders but to demonstrate that Mr. Alston had the ability to market his
material and to show the potential of this company.

. . . Because Mr. Alston did not know if he would be funded, he
reneged on some of his quotations. As a result, some of the firm orders
presented previously were canceled.

. . . I can foresee where there will be a deluge of orders and Mr.
Alston will be unable to acquiesce.

### Production

. . . On my first day at the company I detected one major flaw
in the system. There wasn't a production chart or a specification sheet.

## Machine Capacity

Presently there is over $95,000 worth of machinery in the company. We may argue that the company has bought too much machinery but . . . I do think that in order to be competitive a concern must have the very best machinery.

Originally $56,000 was earmarked for this company, but in going out to purchase the machines, management found that it was better to buy these machines than cheaper machines which would likely hamper the growth of the company . . .

## Costing

. . . The system developed . . . in pricing each specific item is very adequate.

## General Comments

In summary, I'll add that this company, as it is, has loopholes but its virtues definitely outweigh its flaws. I believe in this company. I know that this company will succeed if given the working capital and if controls are instituted to govern the spending of the money that is funded . . .

## Exhibit X

## MERRITT PLASTICS MANUFACTURING CORPORATION

### Statement of Operations March 1, 1970 — November 30, 1970

| | | |
|---|---:|---:|
| Sales: | | |
| Sewing | $20,426.93 | |
| Heat-Sealing | 29,872.04 | |
| Polybag | 6,247.49 | |
| Cutting | 514.50 | |
| Total Sales | | $57,060.96 |
| Cost of Goods Sold: | | |
| Sewing | 39,413.17 | |
| Heat Sealing | 54,076.83 | |
| Polybag | 19,834.54 | |
| Cutting | 1,832.65 | |
| Total Cost of Goods Sold | | 115,157.19 |
| Gross Profit (Loss) on Sales | | ($58,096.23) |

BLACK ENTERPRISE, INC.

Selling Expenses:
| | |
|---|---|
| Shipping Salaries | 2,488.65 |
| Shipping Supplies | 3,244.92 |
| Freight Out | 2,089.85 |
| Credit and Collection | 937.68 |
| Travel | 1,096.55 |
| Advertising and Promotion | 2,311.21 |
| Auto and Carfares | 1,246.60 |
| Sample Expenses | 1,057.69 |
| Total Selling Expenses | 14,473.15 |

Administrative Expenses:
| | |
|---|---|
| Officer's Salary | 5,346.50 |
| Office Payroll | 7,572.25 |
| Payroll Taxes | 709.11 |
| Telephone | 2,275.68 |
| Legal and Accounting | 2,383.50 |
| Office Supplies and Expenses | 2,467.75 |
| Help Wanted Advertising | 337.89 |
| Depreciation — Office Equipment | 455.94 |
| Interest Expense | 1,423.12 |
| Dues and Subscriptions | 336.77 |
| Business Taxes | 24.00 |

| | |
|---|---|
| Total Selling and Administrative Expenses | 37,805.66 |
| Net Profit (Loss) | ($95,901.89) |

# MERRITT PLASTICS MANUFACTURING CORPORATION

## Statement of Financial Position as at November 30, 1970

### Assets

Current Assets:
| | | |
|---|---|---|
| Cash on Hand | — 0 — | |
| Accounts Receivable | $ 29,078.80 | |

Inventories:
| | | |
|---|---|---|
| Raw Material — Sewing | 2,080.30 | |
| Raw Material — Heat-Sealing | 7,130.07 | |
| Raw Material — Polybag | 1,125.15 | |
| Work in Process — Sewing | 3,082.00 | |
| Work in Process — Heat Sealing | 10,147.49 | |
| Work in Process — Polybag | — 0 — | |
| Finished Goods — Sewing | 1,400.00 | |
| Finished Goods — Heat Sealing | 1,266.59 | |
| Finished Goods — Polybag | 3,860.23 | |
| | 59,170.63 | |
| Tools and Dies | 15,237.20 | |
| Prepaid Expenses | 3,200.00 | |
| **Total Current Assets** | | $ 77,607.83 |

Fixed Assets:
| | | |
|---|---|---|
| Office Equipment and Improvements | 6,346.33 | |
| Plant and Equipment | 91,449.30 | |
| Less: Accumulated Depreciation | 8,106.21 | |
| **Net Fixed Assets** | | 89,689.42 |

Other Assets:
| | | |
|---|---|---|
| Total Security Deposits | 2,175.00 | |
| Deferred Costs | 17,043.10 | |
| Organization Expenses | 232.00 | |
| Deferred Interest | 6,806.27 | |
| Exchanges | 1,389.36 | |
| **Total Other Assets** | | 27,645.73 |
| **Total Assets** | | $194,942.98 |

BLACK ENTERPRISE, INC.

## Liabilities and Stockholders' Equity

| | | |
|---|---:|---:|
| Current Liabilities: | | |
| Accounts Payable | $21,641.31 | |
| Payroll Taxes Payable | 10,241.92 | |
| Bank Overdraft | 10,542.27 | |
| Accrued Expenses | 4,166.37 | |
| Notes Payable | 20,563.24 | |
| Total Current Liabilities | | $ 67,154.31 |
| Long-Term Liabilities: | 225,360.50 | |
| Total Long-Term Liabilities | | 225,360.50 |
| Total Liabilities | | 292,515.61 |
| Stockholders' Equity: | | |
| Common Stock Issued and Outstanding | 5,250.00 | |
| Retained Earnings—Beginning | (6,900.74) | |
| Less — for Period | (95,921.89) | |
| Total Stockholders' Equity | | ( 97,572.63) |
| Total Liabilities and Stockholders' Equity: | | $194,942.98 |

# 7

# ALBERT'S ORIGINALS

## PROLOGUE

The Albert's Originals case relates the experiences of a black hand-bag maker who had unsuccessfully attempted to start his own opera-tion on several occasions. Finally, he was assisted by a New York City CBDO in 1970 with a loan of $120,000, though the CBDO later learned that along with money, Albert Douglas needed manage-ment assistance.

The West Side CBDO was organized in May 1970 to serve a predominantly black community in New York. The CBDO wanted to stress manufacturing operations in accord with its belief that "black communities need to move from their role as consumers to producers in the nation's economy and in recognition of the marketable value of technical skills." A fifteen-man board of direc-tors directed the operations of the corporation and governed the allocation of surplus funds generated by the corporation's business ventures. Eight of the directors were residents of the black com-munity, while the other seven were selected for their positions in New York City's business community. The board appointed a presi-dent to carry out policy decisions. The major portion of the CBDO's funds came from foundations, churches, and private corporations.

The CBDO actively sought new ventures that had good profit potential. In addition, residents needing financial support were encouraged to submit requests for financial assistance. All requests for financial assistance went to a manager of business development, whose staff was responsible for determining the feasibility of the loan request and developing a proposal for a finance committee. Once approved, a business was then the responsibility of a management follow-up specialist, who provided management assistance to the new venture.

## THE CASE

*Introduction*

On April 14, 1972, Albert Douglas, president of Albert's Originals, Inc., met with Rick Haver of Haver & Haver Sales, Inc., to discuss Albert's line of ladies' handbags. Haver had called Albert the previous day and requested the meeting in order to "find out how [Albert] would be leaning and what [his] biggest lines would be."

During the meeting, Albert stated that his plant "can produce a maximum of fifteen hundred gross per year and I expect to use the same styles with slight modifications." Haver replied: "Albert, I agree that you should continue to make the same line, especially since your bags are a standard item that doesn't change from year to year. The fabric may change, but not the bag."

Haver went on to say that the main reason for the meeting was to discuss an offer that Haver had received from National Stores to buy fourteen hundred gross of handbags per year from Albert. In addition National was willing to pay Albert's invoices ten days after receipt of shipment, providing Albert agreed to manufacture handbags for National only. Also because Haver knew that Albert was having cash problems he indicated that he would be "willing to finance the order for a small piece of the business." Albert's first reaction was: "Sounds just like a dream; too good to be true. Where were these kind of offers a year ago? I'll get back to you in a few days with my answer." After Haver left, however, Albert was more cautious in his original appraisal because he was concerned about producing for only one buyer and about whether he had the ability and funds to produce continually at his maximum capacity. Before he made his decision, he called to arrange a meeting with the CBDO which had given him financial assistance.

*Background*

ALBERT DOUGLAS. Albert was born in Camden, South Carolina, in 1922 in a family of four sisters and five brothers. After completing high school in Camden, and working on a farm for two years, he joined the U. S. Army in 1942.

After his discharge in 1944, Albert went to New York, where he began an apprenticeship training program with Apex Plastics in the assembly of plastic and leather handbags. After he completed his training, he went to work as a sewing machine operator for the American Leather and Zipper Bag Company. Over the next twelve years he rose from a handbag framer to a cutter and finally made foreman in 1955.

In 1956 Albert took a foreman's job with the Goodrich Bag Company, where he was in charge of a much larger manufacturing operation. In 1957 he became superintendent of operations, a job in which he remained for three years. During those years, he began thinking about starting his own operation and finally left Goodrich in 1960 to try his luck in business.

For three years Albert ran a small but unsuccessful contract (the stores supplied the material) handbag business in the Bronx. Finally, he closed down the Bronx operation and moved to Brooklyn, where he opened another handbag operation in 1963. Mounting problems in the industry and lack of funds finally forced him also to close down this operation and he took a job with Drake Handbags as production manager in 1966.

At Drake, Albert designed handbags, purchased machinery and inventory, and supervised twenty to thirty-five employees for an absentee owner. During this time he began to believe that if he could run a profitable operation for an absentee owner, he could do it for himself. He was determined to go back into business as soon as he had enough money. Since he believed that it would be "a long time before I could muster enough funds to go into business full-time, I decided to begin small and increase the size of the business that I would do on the side." For the next three years, while Albert continued as production manager for Drake Handbags during the day, he ran his own operation at night.

By 1969, when he had seven part-time employees in his night operation and a backlog of orders, he decided to devote himself full-time to the venture. This decision to go into business a third time was also influenced by a potential partner, Edward Faison, who was willing to invest $2,000. Albert decided that "the timing was finally right" and left Drake to devote himself full-time to Albert's Originals.

Albert's handbag operation consisted of two machine operators and three sewing machine operators and Albert, who filled in at various positions. In addition, he was also responsible for the generation of new business, the collection of accounts, and payment of all bills. Faison was a limited partner and did not participate in the operation of the business. Because he did not agree with Albert's "business methods," Faison decided he "wanted to withdraw" and Albert agreed to repay him his initial $2,000 investment in installments of $100 a month, beginning in April 1970.

ALBERT AND THE CBDO. In July of 1970 sales for Albert's Originals "were around $900 a month" when Albert's accountant told him about a new program to assist black businessmen and suggested that he pay a visit to the CBDO. On July 13, 1970, Albert visited the West Side CBDO, where he met Bill Boone, the manager of business development. Boone explained the CBDO's program to help minority entrepreneurs and gave Albert a chance to discuss his business. Boone was "quite impressed with Albert's willingness to stick to it" and asked him to submit the following information:

General description of the business and the product, including:
  · Square feet needed
  · Special requirements such as high ceiling, loading dock, etc.
  · Insurance needs: city, state or local requirements; licenses, permits or certificates needed
History and description of company (if existing), including:
  · Where incorporated
  · Planned facilities (owned or leased)
  · Patents
  · Union affiliations
  · Job descriptions
  · Wages
Ownership and Management:
  · Résumé of owners, officers or key personnel in the company including:

1. Length of service
2. Experience
3. Qualifications
4. Share in business
5. Names of stockholders, state office held and working position if any

Sales:
- List of places where product will be sold
- Amount of sales anticipated weekly
- Furnish sales literature
- List of 10 largest customers (existing companies only)
- Future plans and projections

Description of on-the-job training (if this is planned in your proposal)
Amount you will invest
Raw material as % of sales
Principal competitors and position in industry
Financial information (existing companies only):
- Furnish Balance Sheet
- Furnish Income Statement

Pricing policy:
- List of items to be sold (if large selection, group by categories)
- List selling price per item (if a large selection give an average price per category)
- Compare your selling price with the average competitive selling price.

Complete the following forms:
- Weekly Payroll Expense (Based on Proposal)
- Monthly Operating Expenses
- Machinery, Equipment & Furniture Inventory
- Merchandise and/or Raw Material Inventory
- Fixtures, Renovation and Other Expenses
- Personal Financial Statement
- Family Cost-Of-Living Budget
- Personal References

Boone implored Albert to "get them done as soon as possible because time is of the essence."

Albert returned to his shop and telephoned his accountant to put together the financial statements of his company, as well as projections for the future. The accountant agreed, though Albert later stated that he did not know how he "would be able to come up with all the financial information because the records of the firm consisted of a bag of paid and unpaid bills." After the accountant completed his work, Albert presented the May 1970 financial statements to Boone. (See Exhibit I on pages 185–187 for Albert's May 1970 financial statements.) After some delay, Albert also gave Boone most of the other information requested and on August 27, 1970, Boone's staff prepared a $149,000 proposal for Albert. (See Exhibit II on pages 188–196 for a summary of the Albert's Originals proposal.)

Boone presented the proposal to the CBDO finance committee on September 7, 1970. Because the proposal called for "so much money and 'nothing' coming from Douglas," the finance committee requested additional information on the handbag industry and how this information would affect Albert's Originals. Accordingly, Boone submitted the following report to the committee on September 21:

TO: CBDO Finance Committee                    September 21, 1970
FROM: Wm. Boone

There are at least 1,000 handbag manufacturers in the New York Metropolitan area. A tremendous demand for handbags exists on a continuing basis. Considering the fact that each female above the age of 14 years old has at least two handbags, in itself provides a very lucrative market. The average woman will purchase from two to four handbags per year in the popular price range. Our handbag company manufactures the popular-price bag.

Ruby Leather Goods, one of the top handbag manufacturers in the Metropolitan area, specializes in the popular-price bags. They employ between 225 to 250 people. Their gross sales are in the area of $2½ million per year. This business is operated by the owner and his two sons, however, each of them performs working tasks in addition to supervision, which is characteristic of the industry. Other floor supervisors working in the company are individuals who have had experience in the handbag industry, however, the wages they receive are less than $100 per week. They perform as working supervisors. The ratio of supervisors to workers is one to twenty-five. Albert has more than adequate supervision in his proposal. The office personnel is adequate to provide the clerical assistance needed. The bookkeeper handles payroll, accounts payable and receivable, and inventory control. The secretary-receptionist will assist the bookkeeper and salesmen in addition to handling communications and the telephone. At regular intervals a Certified Public Accountant will visit the business to do the more complicated accounting work. The sales outlets for handbags are numerous throughout the country. Most large retail stores carry handbags, in addition to the numerous specialty shops. Stores will vary in the price range that they carry, but your popular-price bag which is the bag being manufactured by Albert's is the largest-selling bag. Each company salesman will concentrate on retail outlets and jobbers. The Manufacturers Exchange in Manhattan will give the line an additional push by making buyers aware that they are in business and are capable of manufacturing in large volumes. Normal trade terms are 2% discount on cash deliveries or net in 10 days from the end of the month. The ability to carry accounts is what primarily cuts out your jobbers and allows for direct sales to retailers at a much higher profit.

Albert's Originals specializes in frame handbags. Normal anticipated production is a minimum of 15 bags per floor employee, all employees are considered floor employees except office workers, salesmen and drivers. Price Breakdowns: (Sold in gross lots: 12 dozen per gross or 144 bags)

Prices at Retail $1.98, $2.98, and $3.98

Sales to Jobber:
$1.98 bag for $9.00 per dozen or $.75 each
$2.98 bag for $17.00 per dozen or $1.41 each
$3.98 bag for $24.00 per dozen or $1.91 each

Sales to Retailer:
$1.98 bag for $14.50 per dozen or $1.20 each
$2.98 bag for $21.00 per dozen or $1.75 each
$3.98 bag for $27.00 per dozen or $2.25 each

Even with this additional information several committee members were not satisfied with the proposal and instructed Boone to get bank participation. Four weeks after submitting the proposal to a local bank, Boone received the following letter from an officer who specialized in minority loans:

Dear Bill:                                                    October 23, 1970

This will confirm that we have approved a Monthly Payment Business Loan for Albert Douglas for $29,000, proceeds to be repaid in forty-eight monthly installments. In the event Mr. Douglas incorporates his business the loan will be made to the new corporation with his endorsement. Loan proceeds will be used to purchase equipment costing approximately $28,500 and we will draw checks to the sellers in payment of specific invoices. We shall also secure the loan with liens on presently owned equipment.

Prior to, or at the time of disbursement, we will require evidence that your Corporation has loaned to our borrower no less than $70,000 which loan must be subordinated to ours and require no principal repayment until our loan is paid. Evidence must be supplied that the $70,000 has been credited to the business account which hopefully will be opened with us. We will also require evidence that an additional $50,000 has been approved by you and will be held available for the subject.

If you are in agreement with the foregoing proposal, I would appreciate you so informing me so that Mr. Douglas may be advised of the disposition of the loan request.

Sincerely yours,
Dave Young
Minority Representative

With this bank commitment, Boone went back to the finance committee with the addition to his proposal:

TO: Finance Committee                        November 2, 1970
FROM: Wm. Boone

The bank has agreed to advance the company a loan of $29,000 at a 6% add-on rate, repayable in forty-eight months. We will make available a total of $120,000 to the company to be paid out over two periods. The initial appropriation of $70,000 will be paid out under a monthly payment plan; this provides for an operation that will produce 20 gross per week. When the business demonstrates the ability to produce over 20 gross per week the additional $50,000 will be made available, again paid out under a monthly plan.

Repayment of the total loan will commence after repayment (48 months) of the bank loan. The repayment will be as follows:

$$49th\text{--}105th \text{ month } @ \ \$1,200 \text{ per month}=\$ \ 68,400$$
$$106th \text{ month}= \ \ \ \ 1,600$$
$$\overline{\$ \ 70,000}$$

$$107th\text{--}119th \text{ month } @ \ \$1,200 \text{ per month}=\$ \ 15,600$$
$$120th \text{ month}= \ \ 34,400$$
$$\overline{\$ \ 50,000}$$

$$Total=\$120,000$$

Though some members of the finance committee thought that the analysis was "too general" and the bank's loan "too small," the majority voted to approve the loan on January 19, 1971. On January 22, 1971, Albert received a $17,650 disbursement from the

CBDO. He said, "It took a lot of work and a lot of waiting, but it was worth it."

## Operations

Immediately upon releasing the CBDO funds, Boone assigned Sam Stiff to the Albert's Originals account. Stiff was a black economist who had recently joined the CBDO from CBS Laboratories. On February 26 the bank released $29,000 to Albert's Originals and Stiff prepared the following report:

TO: Bill Boone
FROM: Sam Stiff
DATE: February 26, 1971

Today I visited Albert's Originals which is in a six story affair which appears to be an abandoned building. The general interior and stairways do very little to dispel this original impression.

Albert's is located on the second floor and its physical plant is a well-organized, maintained and brightly colored arrangement. Its facilities are well arranged in a comprehensive work-flow pattern. Mr. Douglas, on Monday, hired his ninth employee and is presently building for inventory while training and breaking in his new employees.

All of his space is well utilized with the lighting facilities being well placed so as to prevent any portion of his operation from being darkened or hidden from view.

Albert's has two basic problems: (1) sales and, (2) space. The first will be a problem for a little while yet because the primary sales sources—a commission salesman and a handbag jobber—have not picked up samples as yet to canvass some sales sources. Albert's presently makes two styles of handbags with a third to be introduced next week. He expects to get up to a fairly sizable sales level within a few months.

The second problem has more immediate possibilities in that there is additional space available in the building for storage or shipping. I told Mr. Douglas I would talk to the landlord both about additional space and the general condition of the building. Mr. Douglas presently has no signs on the building, but will have some made up in a short time. The mailing facilities leave much to be desired and I suggest that he purchase a large mail box with a lock and place it where it is accessible to the mailman.

The next problem is generating sales without falling back on the sales-image of a new black venture requiring patronization. This business will have to be able to make it on its own.

Despite these problems, Albert ordered new cutting machines, sewing machines, and heat sealers and learned that it would take two months for delivery. In the meantime, he began to increase the number of employees in order to build up inventory. Because he found few skilled employees, he hired persons with no skills but who seemed to be willing to work and learn. However, because he "was strapped in dealing with the problems of hiring and training, I was unable to go out and do any selling during the first two months of operation."

Stiff found that record keeping in the firm was poor and suggested that Albert set up an adequate bookkeeping and filing system. In addition he saw that the areas of costing, inventory control, purchasing, and accounts receivable collection needed systematizing. Consequently during March and April Stiff and his secretary spent a great deal of time setting up a filing and record-keeping system for Albert's operation.

Though Albert drew down another $21,350 from the CBDO in March, he was continually experiencing cash problems. Though his sales terms called for payment within thirty days, many of his receivables were over forty-five days old. Therefore Albert tended to collect money from his clients—all of whom he knew—on an as-needed basis. For example, if $3,000 was needed to meet payroll expenses, he would go through his list of customers who owed him money and go out to see them and collect as much as possible from each until he got the $3,000. This and other problems were documented by Stiff:

TO: Bill Boone                                        April 16, 1971
FROM: Sam Stiff

On April 14, I visited Mr. Douglas at his factory. We discussed the following things:
1. The upcoming visit in May by a number of businessmen, domestic and foreign, on a tour sponsored by the Time and Life organization.
2. The current financial position including sales, receivables and expenses.
3. The present need for a secretary-bookkeeper type of person.

His financial position is as follows: He has sold approximately $10,000 worth of handbags in the past 2½ months. He has received approximately $2,000 in cash and has a remaining $8,000 in receivables. His whole system of record keeping and control needs to be better systematized.

Because Stiff was assigned to several other accounts and Boone felt that Albert's would be "a time consumer," he decided to put another CBDO management assistance specialist on the case. Thus, on April 26 Albert's got Charles Alexander, who was "fresh from the corporate world." First, Alexander attempted to complete the systems job that Stiff had started. He developed production and billing procedures and questioned Albert's accountant about the absence of such basic financial records as sales, cash receipts journals, and accounts receivable and accounts payable ledgers. The accountant said: "The company is not of sufficient size to go into a more detailed set of books." Alexander countered that "size is not a qualification since the company is a manufacturer and of necessity has to price its goods so that they can make a profit; the only way I know this can be done is with a cost system." The accountant contended that "a bookkeeper would be necessary to keep the books but her cost would be prohibitive." Alexander reasoned that Douglas could hire a girl as a secretary and an accounting system could be designed simply enough for her to handle. Finally, the accountant relented and agreed "to develop the type of accounting system that was needed."

On May 5, 1971, Alexander received financial statements from Albert's accounts which showed that the company lost over $7,000 on sales of only $12,000 in the first four months of 1971. (See Exhibit III on pages 197–199 for Albert's April 1971 financial statements.)

Because of the urgency of the situation and evidence of several large orders, Alexander released $11,331 to Albert and began developing a marketing plan. In this regard, Alexander sent the following memorandum to Boone:

TO: William Boone                                          May 12, 1971
FROM: C. Alexander

The past week has found me spending most of my time at Albert's Originals, devising primarily and developing a marketing plan. This plan consists of the following:
1. Direct mail to the presidents of the 25 largest department stores in the city.
2. Direct mail to an additional 500 department and specialty stores in the New York area.
3. Salesmen to zero in on the stores.
4. A direct mail campaign to the major metropolitan cities.
5. Utilization of the jobbers as an additional method of distribution.

Hopefully, one of these or all of these is expected to increase sales.

Finally, the cost system that was devised for Albert has not been installed since I felt that it was not as crucial as the other problem. It is felt, however, that it will be installed within the next week.

In an effort to stimulate Albert's sales, Alexander asked the CBDO president—Wyman Johnson—to write directly to the heads of department stores which had given donations to the CBDO. When Johnson agreed, Alexander prepared the following letter for his signature:

Dear Mr.

Your company has contributed greatly to our effort to develop the minority community. Not only has it provided a market for the products of our businesses, but it has also lent the talents of its employees to them as an aid in developing a saleable product. For this we salute you.

Recently we made a loan to Mr. Albert Douglas of Albert's Originals, Inc., to enable him to enlarge his scope of handbag manufacturing. He has developed a fine work force capable of producing exquisite ladies' handbags.

We would appreciate an opportunity to have Mr. Douglas display samples of his handbags to your chief buyer of handbags. I will take the first available opportunity of calling you to arrange an acceptable conference date.

Thank you for your cooperation.

Yours truly,
Wyman Johnson

At the same time, Alexander accompanied Albert on his various sales visits to the department stores. During one of these visits a related problem was brought out in an Alexander report:

TO: William Boone                                      May 17, 1971
FROM: C. Alexander

On Tuesday, May 14, I went with Mr. Douglas to visit United Girl Headwear Corporation. The purpose of this visit was to view the new fall line of goods and get 3 or 4 samples to produce for United Girl.

The samples to be produced were all children's styles and really big items. The only problem as I see it is that Mr. Douglas must be able to produce the bags for less than the bags are currently being purchased, $14.00 a dozen.

I see this as a problem simply because he is not able to calculate his actual cost of production. Consequently, he might not include all of his costs in the finished product. To this end, it is imperative that I am there and put together the total cost of production.

In talking with the representatives at United Girl Headwear and Dean's Department Stores, two things are apparent:

1. That Mr. Douglas' basis of styling bags is poor, i.e., he goes into a store and decides which styles are going to be sellers and copies them.

2. He began to produce summer bags *when most stores had purchased most of their bags, and has just gone to producing fall samples.*

I am going to contact a few additional stores to get data on styling from their handbag buyers, and possibly bring in a consultant.

From subsequent conversations with other buyers, Alexander "became convinced that Albert's was operating behind the season and as such could not do any business with the large stores, since they bought all of their merchandise three to four months before the season began."

At the same time that Albert was experiencing sales problems, he also began to have increased problems with his personnel. According to Alexander:

The Company experienced a voluminous turnover rate, with people beginning work on Monday and quitting two days later. The next week they would come back to work and do the same thing again. Finally, Mr. Douglas put his foot down and declared that anyone who was absent without reporting it was automatically fired. This did not alleviate the high turnover rate, but it did lower it. I suggested that rather than Mr. Douglas and his foreman doing the screening, it could be done by a local manpower development agency. This suggestion was adopted by Mr. Douglas, who later found that all the people the agency sent him were either excellent or satisfactory.

Subsequent reports by Alexander during the summer of 1971 continued to verify that Albert was having serious production, sales, and personnel problems. Alexander's summer reports to Boone were as follows:

June 28, 1971

Probably, the most pressing need Albert's has is for salesmen. This outweighs all the others, since we know the product is marketable, the

176                                          BLACK ENTERPRISE, INC.

only problem is having someone to present it to the stores. "A good mousetrap is fine, but if no one knows about it what good is it?"

Of secondary importance is the need for an experienced cutter. Presently, various other employees are doing the cutting, but it will be a matter of weeks before proficiency is achieved.

Thirdly, there is the need for a cost system of some sort, but at the present time, putting one in is impossible because of the operating levels.

We are making every effort to find a cutter and salesmen, but it appears that we will have to resort to training them, as people who have these skills are leary of taking a job with a budding business.

July 16, 1971

At present, Albert's is producing strictly for orders, but he still has a surplus of handbags. Our greatest concern is with getting rid of the summer bags, some 10–15 gross. We are attempting to have a closeout before August 1 or he will certainly be stuck with them.

In the meantime I have suggested that he cut his workforce, contrary to what I said about six weeks ago. This move is prompted by the fact that I do not want him to produce any bags for inventory, but with his labor force a surplus is inevitable. Moreover, this could reduce his payroll to about $800 a week.

A salesman is still an elusive commodity but I am considering training a young man who has done some selling. However, there are some details that must be worked out if this is to be done.

July 23, 1971

A much awaited order for 13,000 pieces has been secured by Albert's, but the terms remain to be worked out. Of course, Mr. Douglas has said if they desire more than 50% of his productive capacity he will certainly refuse it, as it will not allow him to develop the type of business he wants in the long run. I concur with him wholeheartedly.

He has also lost his shipping clerk/deliveryman, a blow that could have serious repercussions. However, we have contacted various employment agencies and it appears that we should have a replacement soon. In addition, we had a check bounce this week but it has forced Mr. Douglas to have a more stringent collection policy.

It appears that after much consternation I will be able to put in a hybrid cost system sufficient for Albert's needs.

July 29, 1971

Now that the terms for the 13,000 piece order have been satisfactorily worked out, it seems that Albert will be operating at nearly 75% capacity. Thus, the problems that he is expected to have will center around:

1. Collection of accounts receivables
2. Personnel
3. Production

Mr. Douglas is hopeful that he can collect enough funds per week thereby being able to pay his weekly payroll. Of course, with money being so hard to come by this remains to be seen. In the event he is able to collect enough funds weekly to meet his payroll expenses, it will only be a short time until I can cut my visits to once a week.

In another view we have secured a shipping clerk who seems to be quite capable. Hopefully, we can tie him to the business by the use of various benefits.

August 12, 1971

As orders continue to roll in, there are two problem areas that I shall address this letter to:

1. Finance
2. Personnel

The brunt of the financial problem revolves around the collection period of accounts receivables, currently some 60 days. Concomitant with this is a slowness in meeting payments for materials that could have disastrous results in the future. The absence of adequate planning in terms of purchasing has caused the situation to deteriorate even more. Then, too, the collection policy of Albert's is much too flexible, thereby allowing his customers too much latitude for payment.

The newly found shipping clerk did not report to work on Monday, and it appears that he will not return. For one reason or another, the "brother" is not interested in steady work, just a few days. I have noticed, and I think the employment statistics will show, that Puerto Ricans on a whole have tried to deal fairly with the company. I do not think it necessary to go any further.

More and more each day I am firmly convinced that it is not possible to exist without a staff accountant or bookkeeper to get cost, production, and inventory information.

All of my findings here have been communicated, or will be, to Mr. Douglas.

By September Alexander had completed the installation of Albert's cost and production system. He then began to teach Albert's daughter how to keep the system and what it could do for the company. He told Miss Douglas that while the system did not go into great detail, it would give Albert's all the information that was needed about the products, production costs, accounts payable, accounts receivable, and inventory.

In October W.E.J. Associates, a large jobber, expressed an interest in handling the Albert's line. The jobber representative stated that he had distribution all over the United States and Puerto Rico and indicated that he would handle the line for a 10 per cent commission. Albert gave the jobber the line with some hesitation, because he still wanted to hire black salesmen. He felt that if he had his own salesmen he "could make demands, but had little control over the jobber." Eventually, however, Albert dismissed the idea of a black salesman because "I knew from experience that whites controlled the buying offices and they would never buy from a black salesman." According to Alexander a more relevant reason for using W.E.J. was the financial statements he received from Albert's accountant. They showed a $43,000 loss for the first nine months on sales of only $57,000. (See Exhibit IV on pages 200–202 for Albert's September 1971 financial statement.)

By late November W.E.J. had sold enough of Albert's bags to cause the company to have production trouble—a two-week order backlog. This was especially true since most of Albert's employees "stayed out of work on cold days because of a lack of proper clothing and because they were very often sick with colds because they said they had little or no heat in their apartments." Alexander's reactions to Albert's problems are summarized as follows:

TO: Bill Boone                                    November 12, 1971
FROM: Chuck Alexander

Currently there are two problems facing this manufacturer—production and the availability of cash.

Handbags are being produced at the rate of 6½ gross per day, but this is not enough to satisfy the demand for them. It is estimated that deliveries are running at least a week behind schedule. This is primarily the result of huge orders that were placed by two large chains (about 600 dozen apiece) and a 13,000 piece order by American Leather Goods. Similarly, it appears that one of the hottest bags this season—crinkle patent—is being produced by Albert's.

The increased demand for handbags has wrought havoc on the resources of the company. Money has to be tied up in huge inventories of fabrics, locks, and frames as well as the increased cost of labor, even though the collection period has lengthened into 60 days. And of course, very little can be purchased on credit.

From December 1971 through March 1972, Albert continued to have production and cash problems, but managed to survive. Indicative of his attitude was an incident related by Alexander:

In December, a salesman from W.E.J. brought Mr. Douglas copies of bags that he wanted him to make samples of on a Friday and they had to have the samples by Saturday to show the buyer. Mr. Douglas worked all night to make the samples and spent the better part of Saturday making other samples that were needed for a Monday morning showing. He said, "All I have ever asked for is a chance to show what I can do and I am willing to do whatever is necessary to deliver the goods once I get the chance."

By April 1972 Albert no longer had a problem with sales or production. His greatest concern was cash. From October 1971 through March 1972 he had drawn a total of $24,000 from the CBDO, so that by April only $15,000 of the $120,000 remained. Of greater significance, his financial statements (Exhibit V on pages 203–205) showed that his bank account was overdrawn by almost $4,000, though his sales from October 1 through March 31 had totaled almost $131,000 and resulted in a six-month profit of almost $6,000. The key to his problem was that he had accounts receivable of $41,000.

Alexander reported Albert's critical cash situation to Boone:

TO: Bill Boone                                    April 12, 1972
FROM: Chuck Alexander

It is gratifying indeed to note that Albert's has reached profitability in the last six months. Yet, there are some problems that have cropped up that appear to be omnipresent, at least for the duration of the depressed economic situation.

The single largest problem facing Albert's is that of liquidity. An inspection of the balance sheet for March shows some $41,000 in accounts receivables, but over 80% of this money will take an average of 70 days to collect, according to the industry. Certainly then, this problem has had a detrimental effect on the firm's ability to meet its obligations, i.e., taxes, accounts payables and at times payroll.

My examination further shows that as a result of labor turnover, labor costs are $12 higher than they should be, but in discussing this with Mr. Douglas he is aware of it and we expect to see marked improvement in the next quarter.

While the next two months are supposed to be slow ones, business continues to be good and with the expected change in employee productivity coupled with changing designs, it looks like the second year's operation will far surpass the first. Of course, what will be invaluable at this point is a mechanism that would ease the liquidity problem. In the absence of such a mechanism, I will have to request additional funds.

## The Future of Albert's Originals

In April, when Albert and Alexander were attempting to find a solution to Albert's cash problem, Albert began to deal with Rick Haver, who had seen Albert's line in the Goldsmith Department Store and was interested in representing him. Haver indicated that he sold to Woolworth's, Kinney Shoes, Topp Stores, J. M. Fields, National, and other shops and that together they could do a lot of business. Albert agreed though he did mention his cash problems to Haver. Meanwhile, Alexander had figured that the company needed accounts receivable financing to allow the company to continue to grow and to meet its current obligations.

While Alexander was negotiating to get the money for accounts receivable financing, Albert received a call from Haver requesting that they get together on April 14 to discuss "a new deal."

## EPILOGUE

On April 14 immediately after Haver left him, Albert called Charles Alexander to tell him of Haver's offer. Alexander advised Albert not to accept Haver's offer since the CBDO was "formulating a new short-term financing system." He stated that the CBDO would be able to provide Albert with "accounts receivable financing if he merited it." He reported that he had told Bill Boone that "the need for accounts receivable financing was not going to diminish, but rather increase." Therefore, Alexander had suggested that the CBDO set aside a portion of its funds to provide accounts receivable financing. This service would not only be to the companies that the CBDO had assisted, but to other companies as well. Alexander indicated that Albert would be receiving financial assistance as soon as the CBDO approved the working capital fund.

During their conversation, Albert also told Alexander that his son, Albert, Jr., would be returning from Vietnam before May and that he had expressed an interest in joining the business. Since his son had had two years of business training before being drafted, Albert felt he would make a contribution to the administration of the firm.

On April 18 Alexander attempted to find out the status of the working capital fund proposal that he submitted to Boone. Boone indicated that it was with the CBDO president—Wyman Johnson —for approval and that a meeting was scheduled that afternoon to discuss it. In that meeting Johnson and Boone agreed that "funds should be set aside for accounts receivable financing" and that Alexander should administer the fund. When informed of the decision, Alexander indicated that "it would be bad timing to hand over to Albert another man who would have to start all over." Johnson and Boone agreed with Alexander's assessment and gave him three weeks "to get things in shape with Albert before taking on the working capital fund."

On April 20 Albert informed Alexander that Albert, Jr., was en route home and would arrive on April 27. Alexander then discussed his new assignment and said that he had three weeks to get Albert's Originals in good working order. With respect to Haver's offer, Albert indicated he would "never allow anybody to get more than 50 per cent of production, because on too many occasions the manufacturer becomes a captive shop of some large chain." He added that the CBDO's arrangement to finance his receivables made him even more determined not to accept Haver's offer of money and market.

During early May Alexander worked closely with Albert, Jr., to get him acquainted with his new administrative duties. He found Albert, Jr.,'s training had given him good experience and Alexander was able to get him to the point where he was reasonably sure that he could handle the administrative duties, thus freeing his father for designing, taking trips to the buyers' offices, and providing supervision. By the middle of May, Alexander was satisfied that

Albert, Jr., was ready to handle the administrative matters of the firm and he had been able to get the company continual short-term financing through the CBDO.

Subsequent discussions with Alexander elicited the following responses:

As I look back on my dealings with Albert's Originals I think I've grown a lot in terms of my own development. I made some mistakes but thank goodness they were not major ones. I realize now that in some areas I gave too much assistance, especially in talking to banks for Albert, or in talking to his landlord. These things Albert should have done, since he needed to develop the confidence that comes with dealing in problematic situations. You can bet I'll not do those things in this job. I will try to let the entrepreneur handle the situation with me along for assistance if needed, but I will not be the main spokesman.

I also know that I was too soft in several instances in dealing with Albert. Mr. Douglas is an easy-going man and I just couldn't bring myself to get tough with him. But this was wrong, for he needs to toughen up some, too. Even more importantly, he wasted a lot of resources by my not being firm with him. There were times when records and cost data were needed but since I knew what was going on I didn't hold my ground. In contradiction to everything I learned in school about management I allowed myself to participate in crisis management. Whenever a crisis developed there we reacted and this is not the way it should happen. They tell you all of those things in school, but they don't tell you how to go about doing them. I guess it is something you have just got to learn for yourself. But all in all I think it was a good decision to lend Albert the money, because he knew manufacturing backwards and forwards and this was the thing that saved his chestnuts many a time. He had been in the business so long that he just had rules of thumb yardsticks that he could use that were pretty accurate. He was also intuitive enough to know when something was amiss, without the aid of a cost system.

Albert Douglas' comments on his relations with the CBDO and his first two years in business were also revealing. He said:

Without the help of the agency, and especially Mr. Alexander, I could not have made it this far. The only problem that they have is that sometimes it takes too long to make a decision. But any way you cut it, they do a good job. I can remember one time they sent out about a hundred letters for me and then Charles [Alexander] went around with a suitcase full of handbags trying to sell some of my bags. We had just started then and sales weren't too much.

I have been in this business a long time but there are still some new things that I have learned. You've got to have a policy for most major things; otherwise, you do things on an as-needed basis. Take for instance my relationship with the small jobbers. The only time I collected from them was when I needed money and they knew this, so sometimes they would owe me money for sixty days. But not any more, all of my bills say "2/10 net 30"; and if I don't get my money in thirty days I go and get it or they don't get any more bags. I also know now that you can't get too close to your workers. At first I tried to be almost like a father to my workers, but they just took advantage of it. Now they don't even come into contact with me. The foreman does all of that. This way they don't know me and I don't know them and they don't feel that they can do things here that they would not anywhere else.

One other thing. If you have salesmen on commission like I have, then one way to get around having to collect all of your own money yourself is to tell them they get their commissions when you collect some money. This way they will put some pressure on the firms to pay so they can get their money.

You can be sure of one thing, if I had it to do, I'd do it all over again. There is nothing like having your whole family involved in a business and one day this will belong to my kids and maybe even my grandkids.

Exhibit I

# ALBERT'S ORIGINALS

Statement of Operations for the period January 1, 1970 — May 31, 1970

| | | |
|---|---:|---:|
| Sales Income | | $ 4,712.50 |
| Cost of Goods Sold: | | |
| Purchases — Material | $ 2,213.51 | |
| Payroll | 2,347.93 | |
| Factory Expense | 105.70 | |
| Machinery Repair | 31.46 | |
| Utilities | 340.59 | |
| Rentals | 900.00 | |
| Depreciation of Machinery | 106.25 | |
| Payroll Taxes | 178.44 | |
| Total Manufacturing Costs | 6,223.88 | |
| Less: Ending Inventory | 1,350.00 | |
| Cost of Goods Manufactured | 4,873.88 | |
| Less: Inventory Finished Goods | 960.00 | |
| Net Cost of Goods Sold | | 3,913.88 |
| Gross Profit from Operations | | $ 798.62 |
| Selling and Administrative Expenses: | | |
| Telephone and Telegrams | 87.54 | |
| Carfare and Travel | 20.00 | |
| Sanitation Service | 41.00 | |
| Rentals | 100.00 | |
| Professional Fees | 250.00 | |
| Business Taxes | 27.00 | |
| Bank Charges and Office Expenses | 36.00 | |
| Total Selling and Administrative Expenses | | 561.54 |
| Net Income | | $ 237.08 |

# ALBERT'S ORIGINALS

## Statement of Financial Position as at May 31, 1970

### Assets

Current Assets:
| | | |
|---|---:|---:|
| Cash on Hand and in Bank | $ 226.51 | |
| Accounts Receivable | 176.00 | |
| Inventories: | | |
|   Raw Materials | 740.00 | |
|   Work in Process | 610.00 | |
|   Finished Goods | 960.00 | |
|     Total Current Assets | | $ 2,712.51 |
| Plant and Equipment: | | |
|   Cost of Machinery | 2,550.00 | |
|   Less: Accumulated Depreciation | 106.25 | |
|     Total Plant and Equipment | | 2,443.75 |
| Other Assets: | | |
|   Security Deposits | 100.00 | |
|     Total Other Assets | | 100.00 |
| Total Assets | | $ 5,256.26 |

BLACK ENTERPRISE, INC.

## Liabilities and Stockholders' Equity

Current Liabilities:

| | | |
|---|---:|---:|
| Accounts Payable — Trade | $ 393.13 | |
| Payroll Tax Deductions Payable | 280.61 | |
| Taxes Accrued | 205.44 | |
| Expenses Accrued | 1,130.00 | |
| Notes Payable — Edward Faison | 1,200.00 | |
| Notes Payable — Equipment | 540.00 | |
| Total Current Liabilities | | $ 3,749.18 |

Long-Term Liabilities:

| | | |
|---|---:|---:|
| Notes Payable — Edward Faison | 800.00 | |
| Total Long-Term Liabilities | | 800.00 |
| Total Liabilities | | 4,549.18 |

Stockholders' Equity:

| | | |
|---|---:|---:|
| Net Worth (Albert Douglas) January 1, 1970 | 470.00 | |
| Income for period | 237.08 | |
| Total Stockholders' Equity | | 707.08 |
| Total Liabilities and Stockholders' Equity | | $ 5,256.26 |

Exhibit II

## ALBERT'S ORIGINALS

### August 27, 1970

*Introduction*

This is a proposal to provide assistance to Albert's Originals. The company plans an expansion of its operations which will require approximately $150,000. The company is a manufacturer of small handbags. It is interested in expanding its operation to include adding 50 new employees who will be residents. It intends to lease approximately 12,000 square feet. In order to make this expansion, the company will need $149,241, which is not otherwise available to it. The purpose of this proposal, therefore, is to assist in the development of a minority-owned business and thereby create new employment opportunities.

*Nature of the Proposal*

Albert's Originals was formed as a partnership in December, 1969 between Albert Douglas and Edward Faison. Douglas was to manage the plant and Faison to finance operations with a cash contribution of $2,000. Since the cash contribution was grossly inadequate, production was modest. The company designs, manufactures and sells a complete and diverse line of ladies' handbags in the $1.98 to $3.98 retail price range. Sales are made to jobbers and retailers. An important factor in this business is being able to produce in large volume and carry your customer for at least thirty (30) days.

Floor space currently is 6,000 square feet on a second-story loft. A total of 12,000 square feet would be needed. Space is available at the current location (an additional floor). Building has freight elevator service and should be adequate. The lack of operating capital resulted in low capacity production with five people on the payroll in addition to Mr. Douglas. The payroll consisted of two machine operators and three sewing machine operators. There is no union affiliation.

The company anticipates gross sales of $50,000 to $60,000 per month when the business is tooled up to manufacture in large volume. Based on the initial projected investment the business will require gross sales of $37,791 per month to break even. The business will require approximately one year to tool up, staff, and reach the projected breakeven sales point. A gradual payout system will be devised to be implemented in conjunction with increased sales volume.

Mr. Douglas has sold to jobbers and retailers in the course of his business. While self-employed he has been able to sell all he could produce. He has designed and manufactured all types of ladies' handbags and several types of light luggage. Aside from the extensive management and marketing assistance that will be provided by our staff, Mr. Douglas has two handbag manufacturers that have been in business for years who will provide him with whatever guidance he needs. These two manufacturers are not benevolent do-gooders, but sincere businessmen who have a personal friendship and knowledge of Mr. Douglas' capabilities.

It is indicative of the handbag industry, even when union contracts are involved, to pay marginal wages. The industry depends upon a migrant labor market whose needs and personal stability need not be taken into consideration. It is with this in mind that Mr. Douglas has agreed to establish a business that gives marginal employees more security and personal dignity. The beginning pay scale (Attachment 1) is above the normal starting salaries in the industry. In addition, each employee receives a ten cent per hour increase every three months for a period of 15 months, a total of fifty cents.

The business will institute a health insurance plan and share half the cost. The company plans to institute a program of on-the-job training on the designing of handbags, power sewing machines, light welding, light riveting, and sales, as well as training in various specialty machinery such as framing machines, stapling machines, paint spraying, eyelet machines, cutters, etc. Some trainees will find some of the floor jobs more amenable to their abilities, whereas others will find the more demanding jobs suitable to their abilities and desires.

Trainees will be required to take initial instruction about the proper maintenance and operation of the machinery they will work with, proper factory discipline, and safety rules and regulations. Initial machine indoctrination will start with simple operations and graduate to full use and application of the equipment in question.

A plan to rotate will be devised to allow trainees to master as many pieces of equipment as possible.

*Capital Requirements*

To support a breakeven sales volume estimated to be $453,492 per year, the company will need $149,241 to be used as follows:

| | |
|---|---:|
| Increase in Cash Balance | $ 22,453.00 |
| Increase in Accounts Receivable | 45,184.00 |
| Increase in Inventory | 43,050.00 |
| Increase in Machinery, Equipment and Furniture | 35,900.00 |
| Fixtures, Renovation and Organizational Cost | 14,025.00 |
| | $160,612.00 |

The expansion of trade accounts will provide approximately $11,371, leaving a balance of $149,241 to be financed.

The following are attached:
1. Employment Profile
2. Weekly Payroll Expense
3. Monthly Operating Expense
4. Machinery, Equipment, & Furniture
5. Fixtures, Renovation, & Organizational Cost
6. Pro Forma Balance Sheet at Breakeven

## Attachment 1 — Employment Profile

| Job Title | Starting Wage Hourly | Starting Wage Weekly | After 15 Months Hourly | After 15 Months Weekly |
|---|---|---|---|---|
| Production Manager | $5.00 | $200.00 | $5.00 | $200.00 |
| Foreman | 2.50 | 100.00 | 3.00 | 120.00 |
| Assistant Foreman | 2.00 | 80.00 | 2.50 | 100.00 |
| Cutter | 2.50 | 100.00 | 3.00 | 120.00 |
| Shipping Clerk | 2.50 | 100.00 | 3.00 | 120.00 |
| Assistant Shipping Clerk | 1.75 | 70.00 | 2.25 | 90.00 |
| Bookkeeper | 2.50 | 100.00 | 3.00 | 120.00 |
| Secretary Receptionist | 1.75 | 70.00 | 2.25 | 90.00 |
| Truck Driver | 2.00 | 80.00 | 2.50 | 100.00 |
| Floorman | 1.75 | 70.00 | 2.25 | 90.00 |
| Framer | 2.50 | 100.00 | 3.00 | 120.00 |
| Assistant Framer | 1.75 | 70.00 | 2.25 | 90.00 |
| Packer | 1.75 | 70.00 | 2.25 | 90.00 |
| Rivet Machine Operator | 1.75 | 70.00 | 2.25 | 90.00 |
| Turners | 1.75 | 70.00 | 2.25 | 90.00 |
| Trimmer | 1.75 | 70.00 | 2.25 | 90.00 |
| Boxers and Labeling | 1.75 | 70.00 | 2.25 | 90.00 |
| Stapler | 1.75 | 70.00 | 2.25 | 90.00 |
| Cementer | 1.75 | 70.00 | 2.25 | 90.00 |
| Heat Sealing Machine Operator | 1.75 | 70.00 | 2.25 | 90.00 |
| Sewing Machine Operator | 1.90 | 76.00 | 2.40 | 96.00 |
| Salesman (Draw & Comm.) | 2.50 | 100.00 | 2.50 | 100.00 |
| Salesman Trainee | 2.00 | 80.00 | | |
| Trainees | 1.60 | 64.00 | | |

Each employee receives a ten cent per hour increase every three months for a period of 15 months. This includes trainees, however, a trainee may move into a particular job after a period of a few months, thereby receiving an increase to the new job scale.

# Attachment 2 — Weekly Payroll Expense

| | | | |
|---|---|---|---|
| 1 | Production Manager | $ | 200 |
| 1 | Foreman | | 100 |
| 1 | Assistant Foreman | | 80 |
| 1 | Cutter | | 100 |
| 1 | Shipping Clerk | | 100 |
| 1 | Assistant Shipping Clerk | | 280 |
| 1 | Bookkeeper | | 100 |
| 1 | Secretary/Receptionist | | 70 |
| 1 | Truck Driver | | 80 |
| 2 | Floormen @ $70 | | 140 |
| 3 | Packers @ $70 | | 210 |
| 3 | Rivet Machine Operators @ $70 | | 210 |
| 2 | Turners @ $70 | | 140 |
| 2 | Trimmers @ $70 | | 140 |
| 2 | Boxers & Labeling @ $70 | | 140 |
| 2 | Staplers @ $70 | | 140 |
| 2 | Cementers @ $70 | | 140 |
| 1 | Heat Sealing Machine Operator | | 70 |
| 2 | Framers @ $100 | | 200 |
| 2 | Assistant Framers @ $70 | | 140 |
| 10 | Sewing Machine Operators @ $76 | | 760 |
| 1 | Salesman | | 100 |
| 1 | Salesman Trainee | | 80 |
| 10 | Trainees @ $64 | | 640 |
| 54 | Total Employees and Payroll | $ | 4,360 |
| | Fringe Benefits — 15% | | 654 |
| | Total Weekly Payroll | $ | 5,014 |
| | Monthly Payroll: $5,014 x 4.3 = | | $21,560 |

BLACK ENTERPRISE, INC.

## Attachment 3 — Monthly Operating Expenses

| | |
|---|---:|
| Rent | $ 700 |
| Telephone and Telegraph | 100 |
| Heat, Light, Power, and Water | 250 |
| Insurance | 360 |
| Stationery and Supplies | 60 |
| Advertising | 100 |
| Repairs | 100 |
| Accounting Fee | 200 |
| Sanitation and Carting | 20 |
| Cartons and Packaging | 200 |
| Legal | 50 |
| Postage and Express | 275 |
| Business Taxes — General | 25 |
| Truck Expenses and Maintenance | 120 |
| Total Monthly Operating Expenses | $2,560 |
| Weekly Operating Expenses: $2,560 ÷ 4.3 = | $ 595 |

## Attachment 4 — Machinery, Equipment and Furniture

| | | |
|---|---|---:|
| 4 | Framing Machines @ $350 | $ 1,400 |
| 3 | Staple Machines @ $350 | 1,050 |
| 2 | Latex Pasting Machines @ $600 | 1,200 |
| 1 | Paint Spray Booth | 300 |
| 2 | Rosley Machines @ $150 | 300 |
| 2 | Rivet Machines @ $500 | 1,000 |
| 2 | Gum Paper Machines @ $120 | 240 |
| 2 | Eyelet Machines @ $250 | 500 |
| 1 | Handle Making Machine | 700 |
| 2 | Welding Machines and Equipment @ $300 | 600 |
| 1 | Rapid Clicker | 3,500 |
| 1 | Heat Sealer (Seal-O-Matic) | 6,000 |
| 1 | Dinker Cutting Machine | 7,500 |
| 1 | Conveyor Belt | 1,000 |
| 1 | Air Compressor | 1,000 |
| 7 | Power Sewing Machines @ $300 | 2,100 |
| 6 | Bins @ $50 | 300 |
| 10 | Wooden Chairs @ $7 | 70 |
| 1 | Ford Econ-O-Van | 2,600 |
| 3 | Tables @ $200 | 600 |
| 1 | IBM Typewriter | 500 |
| 2 | File Cabinets @ $60 | 120 |
| 2 | Desks @ $320 | 640 |
| 2 | Swivel Chairs @ $60 | 120 |
| 1 | Calculator | 700 |
| 1 | Safe | 150 |
| | | $34,190 |
| | Estimated Sales Tax — 5% | 1,710 |
| | Total Machinery, Equipment and Furniture | $35,900 |

## Attachment 5 — Fixtures, Renovation and Organizational Cost

| | |
|---|---:|
| Light Fixtures and Electrical Wiring | $ 5,500 |
| Sign | 75 |
| Showcase | 250 |
| Work Benches and Tables | 400 |
| Plumbing | 400 |
| Telephone Deposit | 200 |
| Painting | 500 |
| Security Deposit | 1,400 |
| Legal Fee | 500 |
| Accounting Fee | 300 |
| Promotion Merchandise | 1,000 |
| Moving Cost | 1,000 |
| Installation Cost | 1,200 |
| Heat Sealing Certification | 300 |
| Heat Sealing Cage | 1,000 |
| Total Fixtures, Renovation and Organizational Cost | $14,025 |

## Attachment 6 — Pro Forma Balance Sheet at Breakeven

| Assets | Present Operation | Proposed Expansion at Breakeven | Additional Capital Requirements |
|---|---|---|---|
| Cash | $ 227 | $ 22,680 | $ 22,453 |
| Accounts Receivable | 176 | 45,360 | 45,184 |
| Inventory | 2,310 | 45,360 | 43.050 |
| Total Current Assets | $2,713 | $113,400 | $110,687 |
| Machinery, Equipment, and Furniture | $2,444 | $ 38,344 | $ 35,900 |
| Fixtures, Renovation, Organizational Cost | —0— | 14,025 | 14,025 |
| Deposit on Security | 100 | 100 | —0— |
| Total Fixed Assets | $2,544 | $ 52,469 | $ 49,925 |
| Total Assets | $5,257 | $165,869 | $160,612 |
| Liabilities and Equity | | | |
| Current Liabilities | $3,749 | $ 15,120 | $ 11,371 |
| Notes Payable | 800 | 150,041 | 149,241 |
| Equity | 708 | 708 | —0— |
| Total Liabilities and Equity | $5,257 | $165,869 | $160,612 |

BLACK ENTERPRISE, INC.

## Exhibit III
## ALBERT'S ORIGINALS

Statement of Operations for the period January 1, 1971 – April 30, 1971

| | | |
|---|---:|---:|
| Sales Income | | $12,393.60 |
| Cost of Goods Sold: | | |
| Raw Material Inventory – Beginning | $ 780.00 | |
| Purchases | 18,621.87 | |
| Freight In | –0– | |
| Total Material Available | 19,401.87 | |
| Less: Raw Material – Ending | 6,600.00 | |
| Raw Material Used | 12,801.87 | |
| Add: Inventory in Process – Beginning | 550.00 | |
| Manufacturing Overhead: | | |
| Direct Labor | 10,253.55 | |
| Payroll Taxes and Benefits | 820.28 | |
| Rent | 1,375.00 | |
| Light and Power | 184.99 | |
| Factory Supplies | 138.35 | |
| Tools and Dies | 782.57 | |
| Depreciation – Plant | 604.30 | |
| Insurance | 1,334.70 | |
| Factory Maintenance | 633.23 | |
| Total | 29,478.84 | |
| Less: Inventory in Process – Ending | 6,500.00 | |
| Total Goods Produced | 22,978.84 | |
| Add: Finished Goods – Beginning | 975.00 | |
| Total Goods Available | 23,953.84 | |
| Less: Finished Goods – Ending | 13,600.00 | |
| Cost of Goods Sold | | 10,353.84 |
| Gross Profit | | $ 2,039.76 |
| Less: Selling and Administrative Costs | | 9,450.01 |
| Net Income (Loss) | | ($ 7,410.25) |

# ALBERT'S ORIGINALS

## Statement of Financial Position as at April 30, 1971

### Assets

Current Assets:
| | | |
|---|---|---|
| Cash on Hand and in Bank | $ 3,496.18 | |
| Accounts Receivable | 9,214.40 | |
| Inventories: | | |
|   Raw Materials | 6,600.00 | |
|   Work in Process | 6,500.00 | |
|   Finished Goods | 13,600.00 | |
| Prepaid Expenses | 560.01 | |
|     Total Current Assets | | $39,970.59 |

Fixed Assets:
| | | |
|---|---|---|
| Plant and Equipment | 27,599.53 | |
| Vehicles | 2,856.95 | |
| Office Furniture and Fixtures | 647.32 | |
| | 31,103.80 | |
|   Less: Accumulated Depreciation | 799.04 | |
|     Total Fixed Assets | | 30,304.76 |

Other Assets:
| | | |
|---|---|---|
| Deferred Interest | 7,110.28 | |
| Security Deposits | 150.00 | |
| Organization Expenses | 500.00 | |
|     Total Other Assets | | 7,760.28 |
| Total Assets | | $78,035.63 |

BLACK ENTERPRISE, INC.

## Liabilities and Stockholders' Equity

Current Liabilities:

| | | |
|---|---:|---:|
| Accounts Payable | $ 5,742.43 | |
| Payroll Tax Deductions | 1,785.77 | |
| Accrued Payroll Taxes | 1,564.33 | |
| Notes Payable — Bank | 9,104.88 | |
| Notes Payable — Other | 2,367.49 | |
| Total Current Liabilities | | $20,564.90 |

Long-Term Liabilities:

| | | |
|---|---:|---:|
| Notes Payable — Bank | 25,797.16 | |
| Notes Payable — CBDO | 38,500.00 | |
| Total Long-Term Liabilities | | 64,297.16 |
| Total Liabilities | | 84,862.06 |

Stockholders' Equity:

| | | |
|---|---:|---:|
| Common Stock — No Par | 583.82 | |
| Retained Earnings — Beginning | —0— | |
| Income (Loss) for period | (7,410.25) | |
| Total Stockholders' Equity | | (6,826.43) |
| Total Liabilities and Stockholders' Equity | | $78,035.63 |

## Exhibit IV

## ALBERT'S ORIGINALS

Statement of Operations for the period January 1, 1971 — September 30, 1971

| | | |
|---|---:|---:|
| Sales Income | | $56,806.01 |
| Cost of Goods Sold: | | |
|     Raw Material Inventory — Beginning | $ 780.00 | |
|     Purchases | 57,811.71 | |
|         Total Material Available | 58,591.71 | |
|         Less: Raw Material — Ending | 22,911.00 | |
|         Raw Material Used | 35,680.71 | |
|         Add: Work in Process — Beginning | 550.00 | |
| Manufacturing Overhead: | 36,230.71 | |
|     Direct Labor | 38,997.14 | |
|     Payroll Taxes and Benefits | 3,359.19 | |
|     Rent | 3,370.00 | |
|     Light and Power | 467.60 | |
|     Factory Supplies | 940.61 | |
|     Tools and Dies | 300.00 | |
|     Depreciation — Plant | 1,611.45 | |
|     Insurance | 1,661.27 | |
|     Factory Maintenance | 1,461.23 | |
|     Carting | 243.80 | |
| | 88,643.00 | |
|         Less: Work in Process — Ending | 3,635.00 | |
|         Total Goods Produced | 85,008.00 | |
|         Add: Finished Goods — Beginning | 975.00 | |
|         Total Goods Available | 85,983.00 | |
|         Less: Finished Goods — Ending | 10,350.00 | |
| Cost of Goods Sold | | 75,633.00 |
| Gross Profit (Loss) | | ($18,826.99) |
| Less: Selling and Administrative Costs | | 24,005.41 |
| Net Income (Loss) | | ($42,832.40) |

BLACK ENTERPRISE, INC.

# ALBERT'S ORIGINALS

## Statement of Financial Position as at September 30, 1971

### Assets

| | | |
|---|---:|---:|
| **Current Assets:** | | |
| Cash on Hand and in Bank | $ 6,479.17 | |
| Accounts Receivable | 20,332.24 | |
| Inventories: | | |
| Raw Material | 22,911.00 | |
| Work in Process | 3,635.00 | |
| Finished Goods | 10,350.00 | |
| Prepaid Expenses and Dies | 2,636.31 | |
| Total Current Assets | | $66,343.72 |
| **Fixed Assets:** | | |
| Plant and Equipment | 28,192.41 | |
| Truck | 2,856.95 | |
| Office Furniture and Fixtures | 655.27 | |
| | 31,704.63 | |
| Less: Accumulated Depreciation | 1,979.74 | |
| Total Fixed Assets | | 29,724.89 |
| **Other Assets:** | | |
| Deferred Interest | 6,337.18 | |
| Security Deposits | 150.00 | |
| Organization Costs | 400.00 | |
| Total Other Assets | | 6,887.18 |
| Total Assets | | $102,955.79 |

## Liabilities and Stockholders' Equity

Current Liabilities:

| | | |
|---|---|---|
| Accounts Payable | $13,217.53 | |
| Payroll Tax Deductions Payable | 5,460.91 | |
| Accrued Taxes and Expenses | 4,557.85 | |
| Other Payables | 8,759.52 | |
| Notes Payable — Bank | 9,104.88 | |
|     Total Current Liabilities | | $ 41,100.69 |
| Long-Term Liabilities: | | |
| Notes Payable — Bank | 22,762.20 | |
| Notes Payable — CBDO | 81,396.48 | |
|     Total Long-Term Liabilities | | 104,158.68 |
|     Total Liabilities | | 145,259.37 |
| Stockholders' Equity: | | |
| Common Stock — No Par | 528.82 | |
| Retained Earnings | —0— | |
| Add: Income for Period | (42,832.40) | |
|     Total Stockholders' Equity | | (42,303.58) |
| Total Liabilities and Stockholders' Equity | | $102,955.79 |

BLACK ENTERPRISE, INC.

## Exhibit V

## ALBERT'S ORIGINALS

Statement of Operations for the period October 1, 1971 – March 31, 1972

| | | |
|---|---:|---:|
| Sales Income | | $130,907.26 |
| Cost of Goods Sold: | | |
|     Raw Material – Beginning | $22,911.00 | |
|     Purchases | 49,864.80 | |
|         Total Materials Available | 72,775.80 | |
|         Less: Raw Material – Ending | 29,436.25 | |
|         Raw Material Used | 43,339.55 | |
|         Add: Work in Process – Beginning | 3,635.00 | |
| | 46,974.55 | |
| Manufacturing Overhead: | | |
|     Direct Labor | 55,230.55 | |
|     Payroll Taxes and Benefits | 6,016.30 | |
|     Rent | 2,550.00 | |
|     Light and Power | 250.21 | |
|     Factory Supplies | 4,647.38 | |
|     Tools and Dies | 652.86 | |
|     Depreciation – Plant | 1,208.58 | |
|     Insurance | 1,527.68 | |
|     Factory Maintenance | 482.33 | |
|     Carting | 405.38 | |
| | 119,945.82 | |
|         Less: Work in Process – Ending | 12,308.00 | |
|         Total Goods Produced | 107,637.82 | |
|         Add: Finished Goods – Beginning | 10,350.00 | |
|         Total Goods Available | 117,987.82 | |
|         Less: Finished Goods – Ending | 19,004.50 | |
| Cost of Goods Sold | | 98,983.32 |
| Gross Profit | | $31,923.94 |
| Less: Selling and Administrative | | 26,059.12 |
| Net Income | | $ 5,864.82 |

# ALBERT'S ORIGINALS

## Statement of Financial Position as at March 31, 1972

### Assets

Current Assets:
| | | |
|---|---|---|
| Cash on Hand | $    150.00 | |
| Cash in Banks | (3,691.27) | |
| Accounts Receivable | 41,219.95 | |
| Inventories: | | |
| Raw Material | 29,436.25 | |
| Work in Process | 12,308.00 | |
| Finished Goods | 19,004.50 | |
| Prepaid Expenses and Dies | 2,636.31 | |
| Total Current Assets | | $101,063.74 |
| Fixed Assets: | | |
| Plant and Equipment | 28,192.41 | |
| Truck | 2,856.95 | |
| Office Furniture and Fixtures | 655.27 | |
| | 31,704.63 | |
| Less: Accumulated Depreciation | 3,396.58 | |
| Total Fixed Assets | | 28,308.05 |
| Other Assets: | | |
| Deferred Interest | 5,409.46 | |
| Security Deposits | 150.00 | |
| Organization Costs | 359.78 | |
| Total Other Assets | | 5,919.24 |
| Total Assets | | $135,291.03 |

Liabilities and Stockholders' Equity

| | | |
|---|---:|---:|
| **Current Liabilities:** | | |
| Accounts Payable | $ 21,409.46 | |
| Payroll Tax Deductions | 11,449.45 | |
| Accrued Payroll Taxes and Expenses | 4,565.58 | |
| Accrued Payroll | 835.47 | |
| Notes Payable — Bank | 9,104.88 | |
| Total Current Liabilities | | $ 47,364.84 |
| **Long-Term Liabilities:** | | |
| Notes Payable — Bank | 18,968.47 | |
| Notes Payable — CBDO | 105,396.48 | |
| Total Long-Term Liabilities | | 124,364.95 |
| Total Liabilities | | 171,729.79 |
| **Stockholders' Equity:** | | |
| Common Stock — No Par | 528.82 | |
| Retained Earnings — Beginning | (42,832.40) | |
| Add: Income for Period | 5,864.82 | |
| Total Stockholders' Equity | | (36,438.76) |
| Total Liabilities and Stockholders' Equity | | $135,291.03 |

# 8

# CLARK'S CREATIONS

## PROLOGUE

Clark's Creations is a study of a black silk screen designer who started a manufacturing operation in 1970 with a $45,000 loan from an Atlanta CBDO only to learn later that he did not have enough money. Later the CBDO provided additional funds coupled with technical assistance, but it learned that a major part of the problem was getting Clark to accept sound advice.

The CBDO in this case was a non-profit organization founded in 1967 to concentrate on mobilizing the black community around housing and education problems, an effort that resulted in the hiring of black administrators and the introduction of black studies in the area's public schools. After succeeding to a degree on both these issues, in 1969 the organization decided to tackle the serious economic problems of the black community in the greater Atlanta area.

The organization had a thirty-member biracial board that included community leaders and prominent businessmen and churchmen. The board was responsible for the development of policy and selection of a president to implement the policy decisions. Financial commitments up to $100,000 could be approved by the president, with those exceeding $100,000 being approved by the board of directors.

The initial funds for the CBDO's Economic Development Program came from the Department of Labor and amounted to $1 million to create jobs for minority residents. Later, substantial funds were provided by the Office of Economic Opportunity with additional

BLACK ENTERPRISE, INC.

grants coming from a Small Business Administration grant. In addition, significant funds were also provided by several foundations.

Prior to making the loan to Clark's Creations, the CBDO had not made any loans to manufacturers, though it had assisted a shoe store, a hardware store, and a janitorial service, among other service businesses.

## THE CASE

### Introduction

On August 2, 1971, Frank McNeill, the president of the Atlanta CBDO, held a meeting with his senior staff members to determine the future of Clark's Creations, a black-owned manufacturer of ladies' dresses. After two hours of discussion, Ray Patrick, the CBDO's director of economic development, contended that there were only three alternatives open to the CBDO: (1) not to provide additional funds and be prepared to write off the loan; (2) to seek a partner for Clark who could supplement Clark's managerial skills; or (3) to merge Clark's with another business the CBDO was in the process of developing.

Patrick went on to say that the most feasible course was to "write off the loan as a total loss and not provide any additional dollars." McNeill, however, indicated that "too many dollars had been committed to Clark's Creations not to attempt to salvage the business." To this end, he was still interested in having the total CBDO senior staff "come up with some way of getting the CBDO out of a bad situation. It's tough to give up $95,000 without a fight."

### Background

CALVIN CLARK. Clark was born in Macon, Georgia, in 1915 and spent most of his childhood there. He attended high school there and it was during this time that he began to display his artistic talents by doing all of the poster work for the school plays and bulletin board illustrations.

After graduating from high school in 1934 he attended Lincoln

University, majoring in fine arts. At Lincoln, one of his instructors suggested that he attend a "northern school" that specialized in art illustrating. Clark took this advice and went to New York in 1936.

Upon arriving in New York he found living quarters with the aunt of a friend from Macon who lived in Harlem. Clark indicated that: "It took me almost a year to land a job. Finally I got one as a shipping clerk in a shoe factory. At the same time I started making plans to get into an art school. I attended Cooper Union on and off for three years and in 1940 submitted an application to Pratt Institute. After several applications, I was admitted in 1942."

From 1942 through 1945 Clark took only evening classes as he continued to work at the shoe factory. At the same time he tried to develop his "artistic ability" by painting portraits. He says: "I did a painting of Billie Holiday for the YMCA that was auctioned off. Later I did a second painting that she liked so well she kissed me. I didn't wash my face for two weeks." In 1945 Clark switched to the day session "in order to get finished." It was at that time he was introduced to the silk screen process of printing fabrics.

It seems that in a conversation with a fellow student the subject of silk screen printing came up. Clark later asked his teachers some questions about silk screen printing and gradually became fascinated with the whole process. He began to examine garments and talked to the silk screen printers to learn more about the business. Unfortunately, the printers would not hire blacks at this time, though Clark began to make his own designs, and kept trying to penetrate the printing business.

Finally, in 1946, Clark said: "I decided to go full-steam into the silk screening business. I quit school and succeeded in getting into a small shop by letting the owners put me to work as an illustrator. I said, 'Okay, at least I'm inside now, and I can work as an illustrator; perhaps in time they will see that I am qualified to be a designer. Hopefully, from time to time I will be able to show them my designs, and perhaps someone will like them.'"

Clark found that "selling a design was a lot harder than designing a design." Finally in 1949 he managed to sell a design to Screen Creations, a company which had refused to hire him two years earlier. When Clark attempted to follow up on this success with another application, he found that "a black face was still a big disadvantage in cracking the garment district." Therefore, he continued working as a printer, making and selling a few designs, and trying to get employed in the designing department of a New York manufacturer.

In 1953, after years of frustration, Clark was able to land a job in the designing department of Jo-Mar Productions. "I was not satisfied with this setup, however, because they treated me like an apprentice and I went to work at Puiltex Creations in 1955, where I thought there was a great opportunity, not only to use my designs, but to be in the business. This did not work out and I left in 1958 to take a job with Zyula Designs. This too did not pan out and I began to look for another job. In 1961 I landed a job with Screen Creations." Previously Screen Creations, like the other design houses, had refused to give him a job, but once they saw his ability in the field they took a chance and hired him. Clark worked for Screen Creations for five years and was "relatively happy, but wanted to branch out and accomplish something." While he was working for Screen Creations he heard of the Atlanta Youth Corps program through a sister who was a supervisor in the program.

After talking with his sister, Clark decided to apply for a job with the Youth Corps. He said: "I thought if I could get in there I could give some of my 'northern' knowledge to Georgia kids and help them to earn a good living. At the Youth Corps the people were overwhelmed with my talent. I was hired in 1966 as an instructor in silk screening and after four months was promoted to supervisor and ran the whole department."

He stayed with the Youth Corps for four years. Then "one cold day in November [1969] while I was doing some free-lance work, I mentioned to my assistant that I wanted to produce garments using silk screening techniques. My assistant said that there should be some way that I could get started and suggested that I go to a bank. I called my bank and they suggested that the local CBDO would be better able to assist me, especially since I had indicated that I knew nothing about business. The bank representative gave me the name of Ashley Weston at the CBDO to contact."

CLARK AND THE CBDO. Clark called Weston, who seemed to be quite enthused about getting a garment manufacturer in Atlanta. Weston suggested that they meet December 11, 1969. Clark agreed to that date and indicated that he would also bring some of his designs.

When Clark and Weston met, the latter explained that the

CBDO was starting to make business loans "to enterprising black entrepreneurs." He outlined the structure of the economic development division, beginning with Ray Patrick, the director, and indicated that he (Weston) was a Columbia-trained MBA who had worked for IBM for four years before taking a leave-of-absence to be chief business developer with the CBDO. With respect to the loan processing, he explained that he would screen and prepare the proposal and that it would be reviewed by Patrick and then passed to Frank McNeill, the president of the CBDO, for a final decision if it required less than $100,000. Proposals calling for more than $100,000 had to be approved by the board of directors and the Office of Economic Opportunity.

After some additional talk "about the value of community development" Weston stated that he would do a feasibility study on Clark's proposed business. He would need specific information on the amount of money and space required, number of people needed, machinery, and supplies, as well as some idea of the kind of volume that Clark expected to do. Weston suggested that Clark gather the necessary materials and submit them to him within a couple of weeks. After Christmas, Clark sent the information to Weston and requested that Weston "do a proposal as soon as possible." By January 16, 1970, Weston had prepared a proposal calling for $45,000. (See Exhibit I on pages 237–238 for a summary of the Clark's Creations proposal.)

On January 19 Weston and Patrick met to discuss Clark's Creations. While Patrick found many merits with the proposal, he refused to consider the proposal unless there was indication of bank participation. He explained that the bank served two purposes: to leverage the CBDO's funds and to act as an "evaluator" of the loans. Weston agreed and "took the proposal and hastily contacted Clark's bank to discuss its participation in his proposal."

After negotiation sessions over a three-week period, the bank finally agreed to lend Clark some money, "though it had some reservations about the business making it." The bank manager indicated that the bank would be willing to participate only if it received a subordinated agreement from the CBDO and then only to the extent of assisting in the purchasing of equipment. Patrick indicated that this was agreeable to the CBDO and on February 12 Patrick sent the proposal to Frank McNeill for his approval. When

McNeill approved the package, Clark had $45,000 from the CBDO and $13,000 from the bank.

## *Operations*

SECOND QUARTER—1970. Clark acquired a loft for his new business late in March and drew down $10,500 from the CBDO and $2,650 from the bank to start operations in April. As he went about setting up his factory for production, he had little success in identifying the necessary employees to staff his operation and found that most of the machinery he had ordered would take at least six weeks for delivery; therefore, based upon the most optimistic projections it would be June before the plant could begin operating. In the meantime, Clark busied himself with taking care of other details: obtaining supplies, cleaning the factory building, and viewing the trade's offering for the season. By June he had set up for business and Weston, realizing that he had limited knowledge of the clothing business, had contacted several groups about providing technical assistance.

On June 16, 1970, Weston called a meeting to discuss means of assisting Clark to establish a successful business. Present at the meeting were representatives of the Kenance Fibres Corporation and SCORE (a SBA technical-assistance program), Clark, and Weston and Patrick of the CBDO. The outcome of the meeting is summarized in Weston's June 18 memorandum:

TO: File                                                        June 18, 1970
FROM: Ash Weston

On June 16, 1970, the following individuals met in our conference room: Ken Kerkoort, Vice President of Kenance Fibres Corporation; Cary Lineman from SCORE; Mr. Clark, Ray Patrick and myself.

The conference was held to discuss the means of assisting Mr. Clark in establishing a successful business. An open discussion was held, each individual contributing freely to the conversation to outline the goal we were attempting to achieve during this meeting. Mr. Patrick outlined some of the things we are attempting to do in terms of working with the consultants and how we would like to approach our relationship with the consultants. A general review was given by Mr. Clark to bring everyone up to date on exactly what position the company is in at the present time. Mr. Lineman interjected many things that he felt could not be done; for example, he feels that Clark is still trying to do too many things at one time and felt that he should concentrate on printing, which is not at all acceptable to Mr. Clark. Mr. Kerkoort contributed in terms of what he knows of the market and how he can establish customers.

The general agreement that was really developed from the conference was that Mr. Lineman would be helpful in assisting Mr. Clark in terms of administration and developing the intricate details which go into the production of the product.

Mr. Kerkoort would be useful in going into the market and obtaining business. This does not preclude that each would not be able to contribute something in both respective areas, it only indicates that one has a greater expertise in a particular area. *Throughout the conversation Mr. Clark was very emphatic that he did not intend to do just printing.*

We summarized the conference by coming to the following conclusions before visiting the factory:

1. Clark will continue to prepare his line to be displayed, however, he will not attempt to initially manufacture his garments. He will wait until a later date to begin the manufacturing aspect. This, in effect, means that Mr. Clark will design, put the original patterns together, do the printing where necessary, cut the garments and then send them out to be sewn by outside contractors.

2. Both Mr. Lineman and Mr. Kerkoort will assist in getting a top-rated contractor which will be a very important facet. The reason for this is that when initially going into the market as a new designer, it is best to go in with a quality product. It was felt through consensus of opinion that to attempt to do the manufacturing with new labor, not necessarily all skilled labor, will not necessarily make a quality product.

3. In order to begin realizing some income immediately, Mr. Clark will proceed to take in contracts to do printing. He should receive his oven which will enable him to do the complete processing in the printing operation within the next month. As soon as he has received the oven, Mr. Lineman will immediately attempt to bring in contracts for printing.

The group then visited the factory which gave us the opportunity to walk around and talk to some of the workers. Mr. Kerkoort was impressed with the determination and the desire to move on in the line that Mr. Clark is preparing. Mr. Lineman is still extremely reluctant in that Mr. Clark may be taking on too much considering the amount of money he actually has to invest into the operation. The feasibility and the profitability of a successful operation was reached assuming that the money that is available now will give Clark the opportunity to begin producing at such a level that he will be able to sustain himself and eventually go into a profitable operation.

The total conference and tour and discussions proved very fruitful and I do believe that this company is now ready to follow a constructive course of action.

At the conclusion of the meeting Patrick also released a check in the amount of $15,000 to Clark, who had drawn $3,000 from the bank earlier that day.

THIRD QUARTER—1970. Despite the fact that Clark had "agreed" not to attempt any direct manufacturing operations, Weston found that: "Mr. Clark continued to attempt to develop the business' manufacturing capabilities, in direct opposition to what had been agreed upon. He had designed several lines of dresses and was interested in producing all of them at the same time. I pointed out to Mr. Clark that it was financially unfeasible for him to attempt such a move, since there was a limited amount of capital, more importantly, several of his designs had dubious marketability. He was vehemently opposed to my idea. However, he finally relented but only until he was able to start producing his own garments."

In August Clark hired several employees and while they were able to assist Clark in producing the garments, their skills were only fair and Clark "had no one to help him in running the business in the areas of purchasing, marketing, production or management." Consequently, even when orders came in, he had great difficulty in producing the goods, as well as in hiring and screening personnel, and in costing and pricing his goods. By the end of August Weston attempted to solve Clark's problems by bringing in a consultant in garment manufacturing. The consultant was "to assist Mr. Clark in screening and hiring, help refine his cost price structure and develop a smooth production flow." The scope of the consultant's tasks is spelled out in Weston's September 7 memorandum to Patrick:

TO: Ray Patrick                                    September 7, 1970
FROM: Ash Weston

On August 25, 1970, I set out to find a production consultant for Clark's Creations. I contacted such a consultant and arranged a meeting with Mr. Clark for August 27, 1970. After a preliminary discussion with Mr. Aaron, the consultant, Mr. Clark concluded that he could indeed use his services, and expressed his appreciation for the promptness with which we had provided consultant services. Mr. Aaron and I have come to a tentative agreement as to fees and duration of his services, and a letter of agreement is being prepared as per this oral agreement.

Mr. Clark's chief problem at the present time is a shortage of trained personnel. He has had great success in obtaining orders (orders to be delivered by September 15 total $10,260), however, he has had some difficulty in meeting his delivery date. Mr. Aaron indicated that the first order of business, upon being retained, would be to assist in the screening and hiring of the needed personnel. He also intends to help refine cost-price structure and develop a smooth production operation. Mr. Aaron indicated that he would be able to put Mr. Clark in touch with several buyers who would be very receptive to his product. His evaluation of Mr. Clark's product was quite favorable, as he pointed out that Mr. Clark should have no trouble selling since he offers a unique product.

On the basis of this preliminary meeting, it was unanimously agreed that Mr. Aaron seemed to be the man for the job, and that he should prove quite helpful to Mr. Clark's operation.

Aaron indicated to Weston that it would take him "at least four weeks to complete a report and to bring about the necessary changes." In the meantime, financial problems became apparent to Weston, even though he had given Clark another $9,500 in August. The firm could not get credit since it was a new business, and since Clark had tied up his funds in inventories, accounts receivable, and raw materials, a cash shortage became imminent. Realizing this, Weston reminded Clark that he only had $10,000 left in his CBDO appropriation together with about $7,000 with the bank. He felt that since Clark had not begun "to even approach breakeven, it would be necessary to begin to secure more funds." Weston's concern is voiced in the following memo to Patrick:

TO: Ray Patrick                                    September 14, 1970
FROM: Ash Weston

On September 11, 1970, I attended a meeting with Mr. Clark who had asked me to meet with him in order to discuss the means available to him of getting additional financial assistance.

He indicated that he will be having no difficulty obtaining orders but that he needs operating capital to sustain him until he has collected on accounts receivable. At present, the company is able to ship 200–

250 pieces of merchandise a week, while he only needs 150 pieces per week to cover costs. He has been in touch with the bank for the purpose of borrowing against his accounts receivable if necessary.

The other major problem confronting Clark's Creations aside from lack of operating capital, is the difficulty he is having in obtaining credit. The company does not have a credit rating and he has had some difficulty obtaining one. As by his request, I contacted Dun & Bradstreet's group manager and he assured me that he would send someone out to see Mr. Clark immediately. Mr. Clark was contacted, as promised on September 11.

In an effort to assist Clark, Weston arranged to release the CBDO's remaining $10,000 and the bank's $6,413. Thus, in less than six months of operation Clark had now exhausted his initial funds. Also prohibiting Weston "from moving forward with a new financing package" was the absence of any financial statements from the company. The severity of the situation is clear in Weston's following memo:

TO: Ray Patrick                              September 23, 1970
FROM: Ash Weston

On September 17, 1970, I met with Messrs. Cross and Morgan [of the bank].

The purpose of this meeting was to determine what means are available for financing accounts receivable. As was indicated in my memorandum dated September 14, Mr. Clark is having financial difficulties. He is presently able to deliver on all of the orders he has received to date, however, he is afraid that he will not be able to handle the reorders expected after October 30. All of the present orders are for sample shipments, and are for relatively small quantities. However, the anticipated reorders may be for 200–300 pieces each, and Mr. Clark does not have the needed personnel or equipment to meet such large orders. I suggested that he consider not accepting such large orders, but he felt that this would only lose future orders. I also suggested that the sales income that he receives on orders to be delivered by October 30 should cover some of the costs of filling reorders; however, he pointed out that payment on orders usually takes from 45–60 days, and that he would not have any working capital to sustain him during this period.

Consequently, it was agreed that Mr. Clark's situation indicates two needs: (1) the need for additional current financial assistance to allow him to continue to operate for the next 60 days; and (2) the need for some continuous factoring arrangement whereby he would be able to continue production during future payment lags.

Ways of satisfying these needs were discussed. First, Mr. Morgan said that he felt that the bank might be able to assist in financing accounts receivable, but that he could not make any commitment at the time. He also indicated that there would be a need for immediate financing in order to meet expenses coming due in the next week or so. I indicated that we had released our funds.

It seemed to be the consensus of opinion that any additional funds might be "too little, too late," however, I informed Mr. Clark that we had responded to his request for additional funds as quickly as possible in view of the fact that we had not received the necessary financial statements. Specifically, on August 28 Mr. Clark indicated a need for additional funds. At this time, he was asked to furnish us with financial statements.

On September 14 (2 weeks later), we received the statements, however, they proved to be quite unsatisfactory in that they did not show anything; and on September 17, Mr. Clark was informed of this and instructed to get another accountant to prepare an acceptable set of statements.

As of today, September 23, 3½ weeks after the initial request by Mr. Clark, we are still awaiting the financial statements requested at that time.

Mr. Morgan contacted Mr. Clark on September 21 and told him that he was still looking into possible ways of obtaining the necessary financial assistance, and that he would contact me regarding any possibilities he came up with. To date, I have not heard from Mr. Morgan.

FOURTH QUARTER—1970. Weston decided in early October that he would have to go back to Patrick "and the CBDO board if necessary" to get Clark more money. His first move was to talk with the consultant the CBDO had retained to assist Clark. The results of that discussion are outlined in the following memorandum:

TO: Ray Patrick                                    October 2, 1970
FROM: Ash Weston

On October 1 I met with Mr. Aaron. We briefly discussed Mr. Clark's personnel problems, and discussed the preliminary measures that would have to be taken in order to alleviate these problems. Mr. Clark needs immediately, two additional workers: a floor lady and a head cutter. Mr. Aaron said that he would put two ads in the newspaper; and I agreed to put in a personnel requisition with the local employment office.

We also discussed the measures that would have to be taken in order to prevent an operating capital crisis next month. Along these lines, we worked up a draft of a cash flow that would show Mr. Clark's capital needs for the next few months. Based on a cash flow for the period from October to January, the company will need approximately $25,000 in order to generate enough sales income to render the company self-sustaining after January. We then discussed the means available to the company of obtaining the needed additional capital.

Following his discussion with Aaron, Weston "did some further analysis of the Clark situation" and concluded that $25,000 would not be sufficient funds. Before he could decide upon his course of action, however, he learned that Clark had already began attempting to raise money on his own. Weston's October 8 memorandum discusses this aspect of the case:

TO: Ray Patrick                                    October 8, 1970
FROM: Ash Weston

On October 7, Mr. Elridge Wolf of the Urban Coalition contacted me in reference to Clark's Creations. Mr. Clark had approached the Coalition for possible additional financing, and had asked Mr. Wolf to call me. When he did call, he indicated a desire to assist Mr. Clark and we set a date for today.

Today I visited Clark's and had a brief discussion with Messrs. Clark and Aaron. Based on a cash flow prepared by the consultant, the company will have to produce at least 800 garments a month in order to realize a profit. However, in order to support this expanded staff for a two-month period, the company will need approximately $18,000. It is felt that if the company can produce and ship 800 garments per month for October and November, sales income on these and prior shipments will render the operation self-supporting. For a six-month period, sales volume would total $96,000 with total expenses for that period at $76,000. This should produce a profit of $20,000 after six months of operating at this level.

It was for the purpose of obtaining the needed $18,000 that I met with Mr. Wolf today. Mr. Wolf indicated that he felt that the Urban Coalition would be willing to advance the needed funds, but that he would need documentation. I told him that I would contact him in the next few days.

When further discussions with the Urban Coalition indicated that money would not be forthcoming because of "questions on Clark's management ability," Weston decided to "attempt to get the money from the CBDO." Accordingly, on October 26 he presented a proposal to Patrick which said that "to show a profit by the middle of 1971, [the company] will need an additional $50,000." (See Exhibit II on pages 239–240 for a copy of the funding proposal.)

When Patrick saw Weston's new proposal he was concerned about "the continued absence of financial statements." Weston indicated that October 1970 statements were almost ready. He agreed with Patrick that McNeill would probably not approve additional loan funds until financial statements were available. Weston indicated that McNeill was beginning to take "a very conservative attitude on loan proposals because of negative board reaction on some poor loans."

Finally on November 12 Weston was able to get "preliminary financial statements" for Clark's Creations. These statements, which are in Exhibit III on pages 240–242, show a very low cash balance ($242) and a net loss of over $9,000 on sales of almost $15,000. When presented with the statements, Patrick said: "Give these to Mr. McNeill and keep me informed until he approves the loan."

After giving McNeill the financial information, Weston turned to other problems of Clark. In addition to finances, it appeared that a great deal of discussion had gone into the question of a market for Clark's goods. In a memorandum to McNeill and Patrick, Weston discussed this issue:

TO: Mr. McNeill and Mr. Patrick        November 13, 1970
FROM: Ash Weston

On November 11, I visited Clark's to discuss the company's marketing plans. Present at this meeting, in addition to Mr. Clark and myself, was Mr. George, a salesman.

Mr. George has been in the process of developing a marketing plan for some time, and I wanted to know what progress he had made. He pointed out that the key ingredients in any marketing plan for a ready-to-wear concern are: (1) location, (2) sales personnel, (3) an identifiable market, and (4) advertising and promotion. We discussed each item:

1. LOCATION. Location of the plant is not critical; however, what is critical is the establishment of a centrally-located showroom. This show-

room is essential because it is a meeting place for buyers and must be located in the industry center. Presently, Clark has access to a showroom at 1400 Broadway in New York, which is a prime location in the garment center, and is available at a minimum rate. Because of his lack of capital, Clark is not able at present to take advantage of this opportunity, but hopes to be able to do same in the near future.

2. SALES PERSONNEL. Mr. George feels that in order to adequately cover the market area, a sales force of two or three traveling salesmen should be developed. All members of the sales force would be paid strictly on a commission basis, with only the sales manager drawing a salary. This is the minimum requirement for a sales force since the market area for Clark's produce goes to New York and as far west as California. Development of this sales force will be done gradually and is a long-term goal.

3. MARKET. The market area for the company's product extends across the country, and includes the resort areas of the south and west. The resort areas are important because the company's product can serve as patio wear and cruise wear. However, there is great market potential in the north and east also, as the garments can be worn as indoor loungewear, etc. In addition, the company has found several outlets for damaged goods, which run about 2% of production.

4. ADVERTISING. Company expects that advertising expenses will be kept at a minimum since the Kenance Corporation has offered to underwrite most of these expenses. At most, the company will spend a maximum 1% of sales on independent advertising. In addition to the Kenance sponsorship, much advertising is expected to come from the larger department stores that buy Clark's goods.

On November 16 Weston followed up with a report to McNeill and Patrick which said that Clark had run out of funds:

TO: Messrs. McNeill and Patrick            November 16, 1970
FROM: Mr. Weston

On November 13, 1970, I received a call from Mr. Clark. He wanted to inform me that as of November 13, 1970, the company will be approximately $1,200 overdrawn on its account at the bank.

The bank had advanced the company $4,000 on November 2, 1970, for operating capital until it began to collect on its accounts receivable. The company had anticipated collections on its outstanding receivables ($11,000) for goods shipped during September and October; however, the company has not yet collected an amount sufficient to cover operating expenses for the month.

Hence, the current position of the company is one of a lack of operating capital due to slow collection of accounts receivable.

For the remainder of November and most of December, Weston devoted his efforts to convincing McNeill to approve the loan for Clark. In a November 20 memo he says:

TO: Ray Patrick                                          November 20, 1970
FROM: Ash Weston

On November 18, I accompanied Mr. McNeill on a visit to Clark's. The purpose of this visit was to enlighten him as to the company's present position, and also to seek answers to questions he raised subsequent to his review of the proposal to obtain $50,000 in additional financing for the company.

Mr. McNeill's chief concern seemed to center around the manner in which prior funds have been used. He was also interested in the company's anticipated sales volume, and the degree to which a market for the company's product has been identified.

He queried Mr. Clark as to his current financial position, as a means of determining how long the company could maintain its operation without additional funds. Based upon the approximate figures given by Mr. Clark, he concluded that the company could hold out for another week or so. This is completely contingent upon collection of some of the larger accounts rceivable.

Later Weston sent a similar memo to Patrick which reiterated the position that McNeill was taking before approving the Clark loan:

TO: Ray Patrick                                          November 30, 1970
FROM: Ash Weston

On November 27, I spoke to Mr. McNeill in reference to the above named company. He said that he had been in contact with Mr. Clark to find out how things were doing. He said that he was not yet in a position to act on the proposal for additional funds, as he wanted to be sure that Clark's operation was on firm footing; however, he also mentioned that he did not want the company to "go under" because of his delay. He therefore asked me to find out what the company's immediate needs are so that interim assistance could be given if needed.

I called Mr. Clark following my conversation with Mr. McNeill to get an idea of his immediate financial needs. Mr. Clark informed me that most of the checks that he has written are at the bank, however, there are insufficient funds to cover all of them. As of the payroll period ending November 27, 1970, the company was about $400 overdrawn in its account. The November rent which was due on the 15th has not been paid: $500. There is $4,970.35 payable and due on fabrics purchased. Operational expenses and supplies total $2,946.32. Hence, *immediate* financial needs total:

| | |
|---|---|
| Bank Overdraft | $ 400.00 |
| Rent | 500.00 |
| Fabrics | 4,970.30 |
| Operating Expenses/Supplies | 2,946.32 |
| Total | $8,816.62 |

I also received from Mr. Clark a projection of cash needs for the next eight weeks. This figure includes the $8,816.62 above: total capital requirements for the next eight weeks: $16,651.44.

The seriousness of the Clark situation and the resulting confusion in the CBDO on the matter is reflected in another Weston memorandum:

TO: Ray Patrick                                    December 8, 1970
FROM: Ash Weston

On December 3, 1970, I spoke to Mr. McNeill concerning the current financial condition of Clark's Creations. He again asked for a projection of the company's cash requirements through the end of next week. I reiterated the substance of a prior conversation in which I outlined the company's immediate cash requirements . . .

In addition to these expenses, the company has been billed for fabrics, and payment is due, however, Mr. McNeill did not feel that the fabrics bill had to be paid immediately. Consequently, based upon the above figures, he suggested that we consider advancing $2,000 to the company, to be deducted from funds forthcoming. This advance would be to cover the company's immediate expenses through the end of next week, by which time some decision should have been made on the pending proposal for additional funds.

I spoke to Mr. McNeill again on December 4, to find out what decision he had made on advancing the $2,000. He told me that he had spoken to you, and that you agreed with his suggestions, and would be taking steps to implement it. *However, after speaking to you on December 7, it is now my understanding that you did not agree* *with his suggestion. Instead, you told him that we wanted a total commitment for $50,000 now. The net result of this new position is that the company is still without funds, and consequently the business is suffering.*

Some $5,385.10 in merchandise has been returned this week because of late shipments. Due to his lack of operating capital, Mr. Clark has been forced to reduce his labor force in an effort to reduce payroll expenses. Consequently, payroll is approximately $1,200 per week. Because of this reduced labor force, the company was unable to meet delivery dates, and therefore, the merchandise was returned. Mr. Clark is in the process of trying to get the respective buyers to accept the merchandise. At the time of this writing, however, he has had no success.

In an effort to increase his sales, Mr. Clark has only one sales representative, Sam George. Conceivably, if Mr. George decided to "slow down," there would be a marked drop in sales. I have advised Mr. Clark to take steps to eliminate this dependence on one man for all sales. Following my suggestion, he has contacted a salesman in Miami, one in Pennsylvania, and another in New York. These three people, if retained, would cover the southern region, the mid-Atlantic region, and the northeastern region. Moreover, all three are willing to work on a straight commission basis of 7% of the sales they bring in, with no draws against their commissions; they would be paid when the goods were shipped, not when the order was received. Mr. Clark is seriously considering hiring these three people, and retaining Mr. George to work exclusively with the larger department stores. No commitment has been made by Mr. Clark, nor has he signed any contracts. He has been instructed not to commit himself, in any way, until it has been cleared by us. Further, Mr. Clark was waiting for final disposition of his proposal before implementing my suggestions, however, since it is taking an inordinate length of time for us to act, and sales are suffering, he may be forced to proceed with these new plans before getting additional funds. I am in favor of this move, as no payouts would have to be made to the salesmen until orders had been confirmed and shipped. Thus, hiring the new sales personnel would not immediately increase his payroll expenses.

The important thing here is that the company must increase its sales, and it must develop a viable sales organization, not dependent upon one man. I don't think that Mr. Clark should wait until he receives additional funds from us, as there may be no business to finance if we wait too much longer; or, less drastically, *if we wait too long, the business may need much more than $50,000 to put it in a favorable financial position.*

Shortly after this report, McNeill received the following rather threatening letter from Clark requesting financial assistance to ensure the survival of Clark's Creations:

Mr. Frank McNeill                                    December 12, 1970
President, CBDO
Atlanta, Georgia

Dear Mr. McNeill:

Clark's Creations, Incorporated was given birth by the kind reception afforded our proposal as submitted to you, and it has been my constant concern to establish a permanent as well as a profitable organization. There is no doubt in my mind that ours is such an organization as of this date. However, as you are well aware, the firm must have additional assistance in order to continue its operation. In light of the advice given to me, we did not turn to "outsiders" for help with the difficulties we are experiencing, but as we were counseled, we came to you for assistance.

We should also like to point out that in all ways we have spoken well of you in all the various media to which we have been exposed. Also, that said exposure has created great interest in the firm by the media itself as well as the general public. Our communications with the media as well as the sales we have accomplished attest to this. I must admit, however, that I am hard pressed by the media for the straightforward answers to such questions, "Does the CBDO properly back you? Are they there when you need them without the usual red tape? Will they let you fail?" As you well know I have been able to forestall any public evidence of any lack of support or rather any delays in support by the CBDO thus far. This will soon be impossible, and the true situation will become obvious to all concerned when assistance is not immediately forthcoming.

I was promised financial assistance by Mr. Weston many long weeks ago. To date none has materialized. I do not know the reason for the continued delay, however, I must point out that we are now in a state of emergency. Unless immediate assistance is forthcoming I will have no choice but to close the doors and discontinue operations.

I sincerely believe that the board of directors and you are deeply concerned with the future of Clark's Creations as a functioning business and not a defunct failure.

Sincerely yours,
Calvin Clark

Since Clark also sent copies of this letter to the board of directors, McNeill and Patrick agreed that "some action would have to be taken before it became an explosive community problem." Because of his concern about Clark's ability to run a dress-manufacturing concern, McNeill contacted the president of Kenance —James Bell—to get the "expert opinion" of someone who knew the production and merchandising of ladies' dresses. Weston welcomed the advice of Mr. Bell if it would result in a decision being made on the Clark loan. In the interim, he did release $2,000 to Clark on December 15 and "until a decision was made on the $50,000." Finally Weston sent the following progress report to Patrick on the involvement of Bell and McNeill's apparent next move:

TO: Ray Patrick                               December 18, 1970
FROM: Ash Weston

On December 16, 1970, I accompanied Mr. McNeill on a visit to Clark's Creations. He had suggested that we meet with Mr. Clark so that he could clarify his reasons for inviting Mr. Bell of Kenance to see Mr. Clark. I had made Mr. McNeill aware that Mr. Clark questioned Mr. Bell's interest in his company.

Mr. McNeill explained to Mr. Clark that Mr. Bell had no interest in the company, other than his desire to help make the business a success. He explained that his only reason for inviting Mr. Bell was because he felt that Kenance could assist in the area of market development. Mr. Clark seemed to accept what he said and by the end of our meeting, he seemed a little less concerned about meeting with Mr. Bell.

On December 17, I again visited the company. In addition to myself was Mr. Bell, Mr. Art Blount—merchandising manager of Kenance— and Mr. McNeill.

Mr. Bell got right down to cases by clearing the air about his interest in the company. He said that he had absolutely no interest in the company other than in doing everything he could to make the venture a success. He asked about the capital structure of the company, production capacity, sales and current financial position. He concluded, on the basis of the October financial statements, that the company had done quite well, as the statements showed that over a 7-month period the company had only lost about $10,000. He said that even if he had lost $15,000 over this same period of time, he would have been doing quite well.

Mr. Blount examined Clark's product carefully, and concluded that he had a good product, a timely design, and a saleable product. However, he said that the silk screen process always has "bugs" in it, and the one in Clark's garments was that the colors were not fast and would run with working. He suggested improvements in the curing process, by which the prints are baked into the fabric. The only other observation was that Mr. Clark is using a high-quality fabric which has increased his unit costs of production.

After Mr. Blount had completed his investigation, he was asked if Kenance could sell Clark's product. He replied that at the present price, and with the print defect, his company could not sell the garment. He added that this was not the final word, as he could not determine the exact unit cost of the garments. However, he suggested that Mr. Clark could produce a cheaper line to be sold to Kenance, and at the same time continue with his present line to be sold to the better department stores and specialty shops. If these suggestions are followed, Kenance could purchase as many as 800 garments of the 1,600 garments Clark could produce per month. Further, Mr. Bell said that he was willing to provide technical and distribution assistance to the company.

Finally, Mr. McNeill and I met alone to discuss his next move. He said that we should issue another check of about $1,000 to the company to meet expenses until such time as he could make a decision on the full amount. I told him that I was opposed to such a disbursement as I did not want to see the whole $50,000 doled out $1,000 at a time. I told him that I had made all of the input necessary for him to act, and that now that he has met Mr. Bell, the only thing left for him to do is to approve the loan.

FIRST QUARTER—1971. By the end of December, McNeill felt that he "had enough facts to make a decision on the entire Clark matter." Accordingly, (1) he had Patrick remove Weston from the case because "too much personal involvement had clouded the issue"; (2) effective January 1, 1971, "and until further notice, Patrick was to handle the Clark's Creations case"; and (3) he approved the Clark allocation of $50,000, subject to his (McNeill's) approval on the release of all funds. Patrick assumed responsibility for Clark's Creations and a few days later sent the following note to McNeill:

TO: Frank McNeill                                            January 4, 1971
FROM: Ray Patrick

This morning, January 4, I met with Mr. Clark and advised him that you had approved another contract whereby we were authorized to loan Clark's Creations up to an additional $50,000 for working capital.

I explained to him that the funds were to be disbursed monthly after the submission by him of specific working capital needs and up-to-date financial data and after we are satisfied with the data he has submitted and with his progress.

I said for the first disbursement I would take a list of his needs to review with yourself and thereafter issue the appropriate check.

I recommend that we advance Mr. Clark $15,000 to be used as follows:

| | |
|---|---:|
| Bank Note | $ 4,000.00 |
| Rent Due January 15 | 500.00 |
| Withholding Taxes Due Third Quarter '70 | 2,144.76 |
| Edmonds Company on Account | 3,000.00 |
| Dan River Mills | 793.48 |
| Seco Mills | 322.78 |
| Brookhaven Mills | 270.54 |
| Gen Instrument | 325.00 |
| Payroll 1/8 | 718.56 |
| Payroll 1/15 (estimate) | 900.00 |
| Oven Installation (estimate) | 700.00 |
| Reserve | 1,324.88 |
| Total | $15,000.00 |

In addition to releasing the $15,000 to Clark, Patrick also arranged to get an updated financial statement on the business. Exhibit IV on pages 243–245 is a financial statement for Clark's Creations as of December 31, 1970. For the operating period since April 1, 1970, the business had lost almost $39,000 on sales of just over $20,000.

On January 15, 1971, Patrick requested that McNeill release another $7,500 to Clark's Creations to pay wages and purchase supplies. McNeill approved the payment. Two weeks later he received the following memo requesting another $14,000 payout and stating Clark's difficulty at getting his price down:

TO: Frank McNeill                         January 29, 1971
FROM: Ray Patrick

I would like to report on Clark's Creations and recommend the advancement of additional funds from the loan that has heretofore been approved. To date, we have loaned Mr. Clark a total of $69,500 out of a total of $95,000 authorized.

At this time, I would like to recommend that an additional $14,000 be advanced to Mr. Clark for the following purposes:

| | | |
|---|---|---|
| 1. Bank Overdraft | | $ 2,900.00 |
| 2. Specific Accounts Payable | | |
|     Standard Machine | 335.00 | |
|     Telephone | 126.75 | |
|     Despatch Oven Corp. | 655.00 | |
|     State Empl. Ins. | 425.00 | |
|     State Withholding | 1,275.00 | |
|     Edmonds | 3,000.00 | |
| | | 5,816.75 |
| 3. Payroll Expenses for | | |
|     January 29 | | |
|     February 5 | | 3,500.00 |
|     February 12 | | |
| 4. Working Capital | | 1,783.25 |
| | | $14,000.00 |

Edmonds is the major supplier of material. At the present time, Clark owes them $9,180.00 and as they would be the material supplier for the Kenance job, I would think that a payment should be made to reduce this high balance.

Mr. Clark is meeting with Kenance tomorrow and is prepared to submit a proposal on a garment they are interested in. He has determined that he can make this garment at a price of $8.50. However, the Kenance people have told him that their top price is $6.25. We are going to have to get Kenance to adjust the price or figure out some way Mr. Clark can make this garment at a lower cost.

By the second week of February "Kenance and Clark reached a compromise position on price" and Clark contracted to provide Kenance with 800 garments. Kenance agreed to the $8.50 unit price with the stipulation that the CBDO would monitor the accounting and "pass back any savings to Kenance."

Despite the Kenance order Clark continued to draw upon the remainder of the CBDO allocation, a condition which continued to worry Patrick. In the following memorandum he requests another $7,500 for Clark and begins to anticipate the cash problem:

Yesterday I had a conference with Mr. Clark at his plant. Based upon that conference, I recommend that we approve the advancement to Clark, immediately, of $7,500.

At the present time, Clark has a bank balance of $300. He has ordered $6,000 of additional material to complete the Kenance order and in order to obtain release of this material, he has to send $5,000 to Edmonds immediately. Most of the remaining money will be needed to pay payroll for the period ending February 26.

Clark's weekly payroll has increased substantially to the point of being approximately $1,600 per week. Most of this payroll goes for operators in the factory. He also pays a commission salesman $125 per week and the balance goes into factory labor and has contributed to the amount of shipments he is now making per week. He estimates that by the end of February, or shortly thereafter, he will have shipped another $10,000 worth of goods; by the second week in March, he will have accounts receivable approaching $20,000. He believes he will face a cash emergency during March because of the lag in payments of the accounts receivable, and the heavy payroll during March.

If my figures are correct, the balance that we will now have for Clark is $4,000 and this may not be enough. He understands that this is all that he can expect from us and therefore, he should skimp as much as possible during March. Also, I have told him that he should get his financial records in shape so that he can seek a short-term loan of $5,000 or $10,000 from a bank.

I asked Mr. Clark to close the books promptly on February 28 and to give us a P & L statement and balance sheet, promptly. He agreed to do this.

The big problem now—besides the cash shortage—is the labor force's productivity; the operators are not on piece work. Clark believes that if they were on piece work, he could reduce his labor costs 25%. The problem is that Clark does not know how to set this up and neither do I. If you have any suggestions, I would appreciate hearing them.

By March 15, 1971, Patrick received February 28 financial statements from Clark (Exhibit V on pages 246–248) which showed that while total sales since April 1970 had risen to $34,000 (versus $20,000 on December 31), the firm's cash position was still very low. In a memorandum to McNeill, Patrick had the following observations, including a need for $15,000 in additional funds for Clark:

It is requested that a 90-day short-term working capital loan in the amount of $15,000 be made to Clark's Creations. The purpose of this loan would be to cover payroll and operating expenses for that period of time between shipment of merchandise on various orders and receipt of monies.

The following financial data is presented to support this request:

1. *Sales and Accounts Receivable*
   a. As of February 28, 1971, net accounts receivable were approximately $12,500. About 85% of this amount represents February billing with the remainder identifiable to prior months.
   b. As of February 28, finished goods (ready for shipment) amounted to approximately $10,500. About 50% is scheduled for shipment by March 15.
   c. Clark is currently starting work on a $18,600 order for Kenance. This order is scheduled for completion and delivery by April 15, 1971. It is the understanding of the parties concerned that payment of this order will be handled in a period less than the normal 30-day "lag" time.
   d. On March 16, a manufacturer's representative handling Clark's line is coming to Atlanta. The purpose of this visit is to meet with the senior buyers from Allied Stores who have expressed an interest in Mr. Clark's goods. At this time, the "holiday" line will be shown and the results, i.e., expected orders from Allied, should be known within the week.
   e. Clark has a back-order commitment total about $15,000.

2. *Accounts Payable*
   a. As of March 8, 1971, Mr. Clark owed $13,787.88. Of this amount $3,235.92 can be considered current or due within a thirty-day period.
   b. Mr. Clark's operating expenses for this five-week period of time are projected as follows:

|  |  |
|---|---|
| Week of 3/15 | $ 2,773 |
| Week of 3/22 | 2,852 |
| Week of 3/29 | 2,100 |
| Week of 4/5 | 3,100 |
| Week of 4/12 | 4,225 |
| Total | $15,050 |

McNeill reacted to this report by authorizing Patrick to "use the CBDO's bank contacts to arrange a line of credit for Clark." On March 30 Patrick informed McNeill that he was "successful in arranging a $15,000 line of credit for Clark, with $6,500 being drawn down for April needs." On that same day McNeill and Patrick agreed that Rollie Davenport, a CBDO staff member, should be given "day-to-day" responsibility for Clark.

SECOND QUARTER—1971. Davenport was a thirty-one-year-old white staff member whose family owned several department stores in the Atlanta area. McNeill felt that this connection might be of assistance to Clark in the creation of a market. Using his family contacts, Davenport "made the rounds" with Clark during the month of April, introducing him to buyers and giving some advice on seasonal lines, production, and pricing. Finally in a May 3 report, Davenport expressed a very great concern on the long-term future of Clark's Creations, particularly in the areas of marketing and production:

TO: Mr. McNeill and Mr. Patrick                    May 3, 1971
FROM: Rollie Davenport

My view is that given its present structure, Clark's Creations is bound to fail. Furthermore, radical surgery may, at best, result in the firm having a 50/50 chance of success. I am not addressing myself to the firm's ability to simply survive. It appears the firm can continue for from four to seven weeks, depending on the capacity of the company to deliver orders on hand and the degree to which variable expenses are incurred over the next two weeks (such as fabric purchases). My concern here is with the long-range future of the company.

There appear to be five critical interrelated elements necessary to be a success in the apparel manufacturing business:

1. *External Financial Support*
   This is the least of Mr. Clark's problems. If the business were being run properly, he could expand his present line of credit with the bank, particularly with the assistance of our good offices.

2. *Internal Financial Management*
   This constitutes a problem, but for the foreseeable future, Mr. Clark could rely on us to provide the basic necessities.

3. *Design Talent*
   In this area we have been simplistic in our assessment. It is true that Mr. Clark has talent as a silk-screen designer, but to date, he has

not shown that he is capable of modifying his creative ideas so that they can be directed toward a specific "hole" in the market place. For instance, Mr. Clark has been told that many of his hand silk-screen designs have already been "knocked off" by machine silk-screeners who achieve a remarkably similar effect for much less money. They make many of Clark's things non-competitive. Mr. Clark has also been told that regarding pant and top outfits, long, slim silhouettes are selling, stove type pant styles are selling, mix and match pant and top combinations are selling. This kind of information seems to have no effect on the direction of Clark's creativity. The problem then, is that he is creating in a vacuum. He is not creating for any specific customer. He is not creating for any specific area of the market, or kind of store, or kind of department. Some clear direction is needed urgently. This situation is not atypical of designers but in a normal apparel manufacturing business there are sales managers and general management people who channel and direct the energies of the design department. There is frequently friction between the two elements but the compromise that results from this is absolutely essential to a successful apparel manufacturing business dealing in fashion merchandise.

4. *Production Capacity*

To date, this company has been totally devoid of a stable capacity to produce merchandise at a dependable rate. Mr. Clark appears to know a lot about the quality of a given garment but little about the smooth production of many unit copies of the garment. There is a tremendous difference. Clark has not been able to hire a dependable production person, or one in whom he had confidence. It remains unclear as to whether he has had incompetents running the production department or whether he has interfered so capriciously with production efforts that competent people have quit, or both.

5. *Marketing Ability*

Of course, some of the marketing problems related directly to the product—its design, its quality, and its relevance to the market place. But assuming all these things were in order or could be put in order, there remains the more fundamental problem of no sales organization or strategy. As of this moment, there is no salesman. Other than our effort, there is no plan or notion as to how to go about getting sales. One could, for example, continue to canvass the stores in an orderly, cyclical fashion. One could hire an agent in New York City to show the sample line on a regular basis and take orders. One could hire a road representative to sell the line across the country.

Perhaps, the most disturbing conclusion I reach is that it is impossible to persuade Clark to establish priorities, to make decisions, to tackle problems in any organized fashion. Mr. Clark is a designer who enjoys creating and simply ignores the many other aspects of an apparel manufacturing business which he finds distasteful.

It appears to me that there are two clear alternatives:
1. Close the operation, cut our losses and make every effort to place the various individuals in jobs.
2. Commit to the venture more funds in the form of an equity investment which would constitute a take-over of the operation—51% of the stock and control. Given this control, I would do the following:
   a. Limit Mr. Clark to the designing of screen prints and garments with a clear understanding that his responsibilities would cease after the design concept was complete.
   b. Continue to supply the internal financial management.
   c. Identify and hire a production manager.
   d. Utilize the services of a New York sales agent and hire a sales manager.
   e. Seek out opportunities to do subcontract work simply to help meet overhead expenses.
   f. Continue to press for government work for the same reason under (e).

During the remainder of May and all of June, Davenport continued with his efforts to promote Clark's line of ladies' clothing. While no further financial crises erupted, it seemed clear to Davenport that "the company is not growing, just surviving."

THIRD QUARTER—1971. In July Patrick "began to focus on the Clark situation in an effort to salvage some of the $95,000 loan." After extensive interviews with Davenport, Weston, bank officials, and Clark, he tentatively decided that Clark's primary problem was production. In a July 22 memo he outlined his concern and suggested a merger:

TO: Frank McNeill                                          July 22, 1971
FROM: Ray Patrick

Mr. Clark has received favorable response on both his display in Martin's department store window and the news feature in the January 19 issue of the New York *Sunday News*. In addition to the possibility of Martin's reordering, the Gimbels and Sears and Roebuck chains have expressed interest in his line and have set up appointments with him.

While I have no doubt that Mr. Clark's fashions will meet with the wholehearted approval of these companies, *I am deeply worried as to his ability to produce a quality garment.* His past record bears out this apprehension. If there would ever be a time when a merger, etc., would be given serious consideration, it should be at this time. If we can find somebody who has the production talent and ability to complement Mr. Clark's forte, we would probably wind up with a much stronger company than we have right now.

Financially, Mr. Clark will probably be able to meet this week's payroll and in turn has about $4,000 in backlog orders. The bank will probably go along for another $1,000 but I believe the well will dry up at that point. Mr. Clark as made an application to the Small Business Administration for an Economic Opportunity loan. I believe he could probably get from $15,000 to $25,000 under this vehicle, but wonder if it will do any good. Even with Rollie opening up various sales avenues to Mr. Clark, his apparent inability to produce a quality garment on a production basis would probably close that avenue once the first orders were examined.

Patrick's pessimism increased a few days later when he received Second Quarter 1971 statements on the business. (See Exhibit VI on pages 249–252 for Clark's Creations' June 30, 1971, financial statements.) After reviewing the statements he sent the following report to McNeill:

TO: Frank McNeill                                              July 28, 1971
FROM: Ray Patrick

Attached is a Quarterly Income Statement and Balance Sheet for June 30, 1971, for Clark's Creations. The picture is discouraging.
1. Clark lost over $13,000 plus an additional bookkeeping loss of $4,000 because of fringe benefits not recorded during the previous periods and because of returned items sold during that period.
2. Clark sold only $28,000 worth of merchandise during the period and about $19,000 of this was from Kenance's order.
3. Clark had a lousy month in June. Clark is hanging on by the skin of his teeth; he has about a $1,000 credit line left at the bank and he is trying to get an SBA loan. Davenport has been working very hard on sales with Clark and there is some encouragement but he won't start moving goods until spring.

I doubt very much that he can survive without additional capital and I don't see that the marketing or production-cost-profitability picture is encouraging even if he could get additional capital.

After reading Patrick's memorandum, McNeill decided that a decision had to be made about the future of Clark's Creations. He called a meeting for August 2 and invited the CBDO's senior staff members as well as Davenport and Weston, two staff members who had worked with Clark. He was "determined that the meeting would go until the thing resolved itself."

## EPILOGUE

By 3 P.M. on August 2 it was clear to the participants discussing Clark's Creations that there was no easy solution to the problem. Frank McNeill suggested that Ray Patrick indicate why he felt that the option to seek a partner for Clark was unfeasible. Patrick replied: "In order to find a partner, Clark must be able to provide some advantage to a company, which he can't do. He is incapable of accepting criticism; he designs what he wants to design, not what he can sell; he is difficult to get along with; and our Economic Development staff has been searching for a partner for some time and it could literally take years before we can find someone." Patrick also suggested that "there is a cost of searching for someone to merge with since additional funds would have to be provided to Clark's to keep it in operation. We should not be willing to incur the additional costs of keeping Clark's afloat since it could cost as much as the total of the loan itself. Are we willing to incur these costs? And if we are unsuccessful, where are we then? We could be in twice as bad shape than if we face the reality of the situation and let him go."

After hearing Patrick's comments, Davenport and Weston, who had worked with Clark, both said that they agreed with Patrick. Weston added: "There are times when we must draw the line and not continue with a bad situation. This is one of them." With all of the staff members agreeing with Patrick's view, McNeill reluctantly agreed that the CBDO would not provide any additional assistance to Clark's Creations. Two days later he sent a certified letter to Clark informing him of the CBDO's decision.

When Clark received the letter on August 5, he called McNeill and indicated that he wanted to discuss the letter and they agreed to meet on August 11.

In the week before the scheduled meeting, Clark called his congressional representative, the mayor's office, the local bank, and several members of the CBDO's board of directors. By the day of the meeting, McNeill had received calls from several persons inquiring about the status of Clark's Creations. Despite the calls McNeill kept his appointment with Clark and stated the reasons why the CBDO could not afford to provide any additional assistance. Clark listened and according to McNeill said that: "All of the reports were wrong and none of the people [CBDO staff] knew the business." The meeting finally ended with Clark saying that he would go elsewhere to get assistance.

On October 1 Clark's Creations was still in business, having gotten a government contract to manufacture shirts. It was during this period that Clark agreed to discuss his experiences with the CBDO. During the interview, Clark said:

I have had my designs compared to those of Pucci, so what can those people tell me about my business. Of course I don't know much about running a business but that's what they [the CBDO] are supposed to be for. Costing and that kind of stuff I can do without. I'm in the process of finding a good contractor to manufacture my designs because manufacturing has too many problems: people don't come to work; the fabric is cut the wrong way; everybody screams about money. Just too many problems. Maybe I should have stayed in New York . . .

This last time was not the first time that they [the CBDO] had attempted to leave me out on a limb. They tried the same thing last winter and forced me to threaten to close the doors and tell the whole story to the press [see Clark's December 12, 1970, letter]. They came through with some money in a hurry.

I'm still not out of business. The bank has helped me land a contract for government shirts and also provided me with working capital. With the proceeds of the government contract I am able to meet my payments to the bank.

In an interview on the Clark's Creations affair, Ray Patrick of the CBDO said:

We had no business in the world making that loan to Cal Clark. He was a designer with no manufacturing experience. We've learned the hard way that unless you know something about manufacturing from the start, you are wasting your time and money. Besides, we should have known better than to think that we could start a manufacturing operation for $45,000. You can't even start a grocery for that kind of money. No wonder he came back to us for money so quickly. On a number of occasions we released money when there was no justification in the world for doing so.

I see now that our original strategy was correct where we attempted to have Clark only design. But we didn't provide the follow-up and when he decided he wanted to manufacture, we did nothing to stop him. I know now that there have to be some controls that we can exercise over the company so we can protect our investment speedily. There is no doubt in my mind about it. We should have stopped Clark cold when he started to manufacture.

Many of us here did not want to take a firm position, but I know that we'll not be 100 per cent successful in our efforts and there are going to be some projects that must be terminated. When that day comes, you just have to do it with no ands, ifs, or buts. Otherwise, the program is compromised and there is no real assistance being provided. I think all of us here on the staff will be far wiser as a result of the Clark's Creations involvement. It taught us valuable lessons—some of which we probably thought we knew but really didn't. We'll really be able to help the next man who comes along.

Exhibit I

# CLARK'S CREATIONS

## January 16, 1970

### *Purpose of the Proposal*

Mr. Calvin Clark plans to establish a silk screening and manufacturing facility. The items to be manufactured will be wearing apparel, i.e. baby bibs, blouses, aprons, T-shirts, sweat shirts, shifts, mini dresses and play suits, with designs impressed thereon utilizing the silk screening processing. In addition, towels, beach bags and children's novelties will also be manufactured. The purpose of this proposal is to assist him in establishing this business and provide an on-the-job training program for indigenous residents.

### *Nature and Background of the Proposed Subcontractor*

THE COMPANY. Mr. Clark will be the sole owner of the business.

FINANCIAL PROSPECT. Mr. Clark anticipates gross sales of $15,000 to $20,000 per month when the business becomes established in the community. Based on the initial investment the business will require gross sales of $14,318 per month to breakeven. A twenty (20) week period is projected to reach the breakeven point.

MANAGEMENT QUALIFICATIONS. Mr. Clark, the prospective proprietor, was a resident of New York for a long period of time and has had 15 years' experience in the silk screening field.

EMPLOYMENT. The plant will eventually employ twenty-four (24) full-time employees, including Mr. Clark. He plans to maintain an ongoing training program where he will employ indigenous residents interested in silk screening.

### *The Proposal*

TRAINING FUNCTIONS. Indigenous youth will be given the

opportunity to learn silk screening through on-the-job training. Where openings are available in the company, trainees will be given the first opportunity to fill the job. A training schedule showing the time and cost of training employees for silk screening printers will be prepared by Mr. Clark.

CAPITAL REQUIREMENTS. To support a breakeven sales volume estimated to be $171,816 per year, Mr. Clark will need $44,912 to be used as follows:

| | |
|---|---|
| Cash Balance | $ 7,155 |
| Accounts Receivable | 14,310 |
| Inventory | 14,310 |
| Machinery, Equipment & Furniture | 6,532 |
| Fixtures, Renovation | 2,750 |
| Operating Loss Until Breakeven | 8,010 |
| | $53,067 |

Approximately $7,155 will be generated from the expansion of trade accounts and $1,000 from Mr. Clark's capital investment, leaving a balance of approximately $44,912 to be financed.

## Exhibit II

## CLARK'S CREATIONS

### October 26, 1970

*Purpose of the Proposal*

This is a proposal to provide an additional $50,000 to Clark's Creations, Inc. The company was originally given $45,000. Allocation of an additional $50,000 will bring the total allocation to $95,000.

It is felt that in order for the company to show a profit by the middle of 1971, it will need an additional $50,000.

The company would have to produce at least 1,000 garments per month in order to cover expenses and realize a small profit. Presently, the company produces approximately 500 garments per month.

In order for the company to produce 1,000 garments, it must have at least six additional full-time sewing machine operators. Presently, there are two full-time operators and six part-time operators. The six part-time operators are high school seniors and will be hired as full-time operators beginning in January 1971. With the additional personnel, the company should be able to produce an average of 1,800 garments per month by the middle of 1971. This level of production represents the optimum level given the existing plant size and productive facilities. (Production at this level will result in a monthly net profit of approximately $12,000.) In order to reach this level of production by next June, the company will need an additional $50,000 to cover the increased production operating costs resulting from an increased output.

It is proposed that these additional funds be granted since the company will continue to operate at a loss if it does not significantly increase its output. Sufficient sales have been obtained to justify this increase in production. It is also felt that the company was under-capitalized ($45,000) as too little consideration was given to unexpected contingencies inherent in a new business; no room was provided for the expansion and acceleration of the operation; and no provision was made for the increase in job creation that would be required by the expanded operation. The proof of this under-capitalization is the frequency with which the company has had to seek additional funds in the past few weeks. An additional $50,000 would eliminate a recurrence of this situation, and would provide a strong base upon which a solid manufacturing firm could be built.

## Funding

The CBDO originally allocated and disbursed $45,000 to the company. The bank allocated, and has partially disbursed $13,338, for the purchase of equipment. An additional $50,000 would bring the total capital allocated to $108,338.

Repayment of the $50,000 from the CBDO will begin after the scheduled completion of the original bank and CBDO loans.

Exhibit III

CLARK'S CREATIONS

Income Statement April 1, 1970 — October 31, 1970

| | |
|---|---|
| Gross Sales | $14,711 |
| Cost of Goods Sold | 13,388 |
| Gross Profit | $ 1,323 |
| Operating Expenses | 10,374 |
| Operating Profit (Loss) | (9,051) |
| Non-Operating Expenses | 186 |
| Income (Loss) Before Taxes | (9,237) |
| Net Income (Loss) | ($ 9,237) |

## CLARK'S CREATIONS

### Balance Sheet as at October 30, 1970

#### Assets

| | | |
|---|---:|---:|
| **Current Assets:** | | |
| Cash | $ 242 | |
| Accounts Receivable | 11,698 | |
| Inventories: | | |
| Raw Material and Supplies | 9,000 | |
| Work in Process | 12,000 | |
| Finished Goods | 8,000 | |
| Prepaid Expenses | 1,170 | |
| Total Current Assets | | $42,110 |
| **Property, Plant and Equipment:** | | |
| Machinery and Equipment | 6,786 | |
| Other Property | 6,296 | |
| | 13,082 | |
| Less: Accumulated Depreciation | 516 | |
| Total Property, Plant and Equipment | | 12,566 |
| **Other Assets** | 1,765 | |
| Total Other Assets | | 1,765 |
| **Total Assets** | | $56,441 |

## Liabilities and Stockholders' Equity

Current Liabilities:

| | | |
|---|---:|---:|
| Notes Payable — Banks | $ 8,127 | |
| Accounts Payable — Trade | 10,023 | |
| Accrued Liabilities | 1,853 | |
| Total Current Liabilities | | $20,003 |

Long-Term Liabilities:

| | | |
|---|---:|---:|
| Notes Payable | 45,000 | |
| Total Long-Term Liabilities | | 45,000 |
| Total Liabilities | | 65,003 |

Stockholders' Equity:

| | | |
|---|---:|---:|
| Common Stock | 675 | |
| Accumulated Deficit | (9,237) | |
| Total Stockholders' Equity | | (8,562) |
| Total Liabilities and Stockholders' Equity | | $56,441 |

BLACK ENTERPRISE, INC.

Exhibit IV
## CLARK'S CREATIONS

### Income Statement April 1, 1970 – December 31, 1970

| | | |
|---|---:|---:|
| Gross Sales | | $20,307.40 |
| Discounts | $ 874.35 | |
| Returns and Allowances | 4,612.05 | 5,486.40 |
| Net Sales | | 14,821.00 |
| Cost of Goods Sold: | | |
| Finished Goods Inventory, 4/1/70 | –0– | |
| Cost of Goods Manufactured | 47,285.98 | |
| Goods Available for Sale | 47,285.98 | |
| Finished Goods Inventory, 12/31/70 | 11,066.00 | |
| Cost of Goods Sold | | 36,219.98 |
| Gross Loss | | ($21,398.98) |
| Operating Expenses: | | |
| Administrative Salaries | 3,621.47 | |
| Salesmen Commission | 5,676.58 | |
| Advertising and Selling | 2,058.69 | |
| Stationery and Supplies | 218.31 | |
| Telephone | 1,007.97 | |
| Postage and Shipping | 1,023.00 | |
| Legal and Accounting | 1,765.36 | |
| Interest | 222.95 | |
| Sundry | 970.99 | |
| Depreciation Office Equip., Furn. and Fix. | 221.18 | |
| Bad Debt Expense | 101.54 | |
| Depreciation of Leasehold Improvements | 696.83 | |
| Total Operating Expenses | | 17,584.87 |
| Net Loss | | ($38,983.85) |

# CLARK'S CREATIONS

## Balance Sheet December 31, 1970

### Assets

| Current Assets: | | |
|---|---:|---:|
| Cash in Bank | | ($ 177.99) |
| Accounts Receivable | $ 2,993.12 | |
| Less: Anticipated Discounts | 239.44 | |
| Less: Allowance for Bad Debt | 101.54 | |
| Net Accounts Receivable | | 2,652.14 |
| Inventories: | | |
| Finished Goods | 11,066.00 | |
| Work in Process | 7,200.00 | |
| Raw Material | 8,661.00 | 26,927.00 |
| Prepaid Expenses | | 4,538.00 |
| Total Current Assets | | 33,939.15 |
| Fixed Assets: | | |
| Machinery and Equipment | 12,000.83 | |
| Office Equipment, Furniture and Fixtures | 4,418.16 | |
| Leasehold Improvements | 6,968.28 | |
| | 23,387.27 | |
| Less: Accumulated Depreciation | 1,518.05 | |
| Total Fixed Assets | | 21,869.22 |
| Other Assets: | | |
| Security Deposits | 1,275.00 | |
| Total Other Assets | | 1,275.00 |
| Total Assets | | $57,083.37 |

## Liabilities and Stockholders' Equity

| | | |
|---|---:|---:|
| Current Liabilities: | | |
| Notes Payable — Bank | $ 2,667.60 | |
| Payroll Tax Deductions | 2,957.13 | |
| Accounts Payable | 17,319.39 | |
| Total Current Liabilities | | $22,944.12 |
| Long-Term Liabilities: | | |
| Notes Payable — Bank | 10,448.10 | |
| Notes Payable — CBDO | 62,000.00 | 72,448.10 |
| Total Long-Term Liabilities | | 95,392.22 |
| Stockholders' Equity: | | |
| Capital Stock Issued and Outstanding | 675.00 | |
| Accumulated Deficit | (38,983.85) | |
| Total Stockholders' Equity | | (38,308.85) |
| Total Liabilities and Stockholders' Equity | | $57,083.37 |

## Exhibit V

## CLARK'S CREATIONS

### Income Statement April 1, 1970 – February 28, 1971

| | | |
|---|---|---|
| Gross Sales | $34,321.80 | |
| Discounts | 1,126.94 | |
| Returns and Allowances | 3,842.99 | |
| Net Sales | | $29,351.87 |
| Cost of Goods Sold: | | |
| Finished Goods – Inventory 4/1/70 | –0– | |
| Cost of Goods Manufactured | 83,621.93 | |
| Goods Available for Sale | 83,621.93 | |
| Less: Finished Goods – Inventory 2/28/71 | 10,526.25 | |
| Cost of Goods Sold | | 73,095.68 |
| Gross Profit (Loss) | | ($43,743.81) |
| Operating Expenses: | | |
| Administrative Salaries | 4,491.47 | |
| Salesmen Commission | 6,626.58 | |
| Advertising and Selling | 2,113.05 | |
| Stationery and Supplies | 373.98 | |
| Telephone | 1,243.29 | |
| Postage and Shipping | 1,545.23 | |
| Legal and Accounting | 2,265.36 | |
| Interest | 400.33 | |
| Sundry | 1,259.09 | |
| Bad Debts | 384.30 | |
| Depreciation of Office Equipment, Furniture and Fixtures | 1,183.63 | |
| Depreciation of Leasehold Improvements | 885.82 | |
| Total Operating Expenses | | 22,772.13 |
| Net Profit (Loss) | | ($66,515.94) |

# CLARK'S CREATIONS

## Balance Sheet as at February 28, 1971

### Assets

**Current Assets:**

| | | |
|---|---|---|
| Cash in Bank | ($ 758.77) | |
| Accounts Receivable | 13,956.95 | |
| Inventories: | | |
| Raw Material | 6,917.95 | |
| Work in Process | 3,000.00 | |
| Finished Goods | 10,526.25 | |
| Prepaid Expenses | 1,264.00 | |
| Total Current Assets | | $34,906.38 |

**Fixed Assets:**

| | | |
|---|---|---|
| Factory Equipment | 9,000.83 | |
| Office Equipment | 4,418.16 | |
| Leasehold Improvements | 4,429.10 | |
| | 17,848.09 | |
| Less: Accumulated Depreciation | 4,369.62 | |
| Total Fixed Assets | | 13,478.47 |

**Other Assets:**

| | | |
|---|---|---|
| Security Deposits | 1,275.00 | |
| Total Other Assets | | 1,275.00 |
| Total Assets | | $49,659.85 |

## Liabilities and Stockholders' Equity

| | | |
|---|---:|---:|
| Current Liabilities: | | |
| Notes Payable — Bank | $ 2,667.60 | |
| Accounts Payable | 11,975.86 | |
| Total Current Liabilities | | $ 14,643.46 |
| Long-Term Liabilities: | | |
| Notes Payable — Bank | 10,225.80 | |
| Notes Payable — CBDO | 90,631.53 | |
| Total Long-Term Liabilities | | 100,857.33 |
| Total Liabilities | | 115,500.79 |
| Stockholders' Equity: | | |
| Capital Stock Issued and Outstanding | 675.00 | |
| Accumulated Deficit | (66,515.94) | |
| Total Stockholders' Equity | | (65,840.94) |
| Total Liabilities and Stockholders' Equity | | $ 49,659.85 |

Exhibit VI

## CLARK'S CREATIONS

Income Statement

| | Month of June 1971 | | April – June 1971 | |
|---|---|---|---|---|
| Sales | $3,771.25 | | $27,819.43 | |
| Less: Discounts | 179.90 | | 570.63 | |
| Less: Returns and | | | | |
| Allowances | 274.45 | | 5,721.67 | |
| Net Sales | | $3,316.90 | | $21,527.13 |
| Cost of Goods Sold: | | | | |
| Raw Material 4/1/71 | 7,596.29 | | 6,917.95 | |
| Purchases | –0– | | 10,658.61 | |
| Less: Raw Material | | | | |
| 6/30/71 | 7,200.00 | | 7,200.00 | |
| Cost of Material | | | | |
| Used | 396.29 | | 10,376.56 | |
| Factory Wages | 3,174.42 | | 13,032.72 | |
| Contract Labor | 191.00 | | 846.25 | |
| Manufacturing Overhead: | | | | |
| Accessory Supplies | 459.40 | | 161.62 | |
| Factory Supplies | 165.00 | | | |
| Rent | 500.00 | | 1,500.00 | |
| Rent Tax | –0– | | –0– | |
| Utility | 55.35 | | 150.43 | |
| Machine Rental and | | | | |
| Repair | 25.75 | | 264.33 | |
| Fringe Benefits | 176.36 | | 1,862.27 | |
| Insurance Expense | 59.50 | | 170.88 | |
| Cleaning and | | | | |
| Maintenance | 51.20 | | 102.40 | |
| Total Manufacturing | | | | |
| Cost | 5,254.27 | | 28,467.46 | |
| Goods in Process Used | 876.00 | | 1,500.00 | |
| Finished Goods Used | 3,320.00 | | 3,260.00 | |
| Cost of Goods Sold | | 9,450.27 | | 33,227.46 |
| Gross Profit (Loss) | | ($6,133.37) | | ($11,700.33) |

Selling and
  Administrative Costs:

| | | | |
|---|---|---|---|
| Officer's Salary | 500.00 | | 1,450.00 |
| Selling Expense and | | | |
|   Commission. | 59.66 | | 444.01 |
| Shipping and Postage | 72.65 | | 313.27 |
| Office Supplies and | | | |
|   Miscellaneous | 70.02 | | 512.85 |
| Telephone Expenses | 102.16 | | 301.45 |
| Interest Expenses | 128.40 | | 368.41 |
| Travel and Enter- | | | |
|   tainment | 153.98 | | 658.96 |
|   Total Selling and | | | |
|   Administrative | | | |
|   Expenses | | 1,086.87 | 4,048.95 |
| Profit (Loss) for Month | | ($7,220.24) | |
| Profit (Loss) for Quarter | | | ($15,749.28) |

# CLARK'S CREATIONS

## Balance Sheet as at June 30, 1971

### Assets

| | | |
|---|---:|---:|
| **Current Assets:** | | |
| Cash | $ 1,458.43 | |
| Accounts Receivable | 7,957.43 | |
| Inventories: | | |
| Raw Material | 7,200.00 | |
| Work in Process | 1,500.00 | |
| Finished Goods | 2,200.00 | |
| Total Current Assets | | $20,315.86 |
| **Fixed Assets:** | | |
| Factory Equipment | 9,000.83 | |
| Office Equipment | 4,418.16 | |
| Leasehold Improvements | 4,429.10 | |
| | 17,848.09 | |
| Less: Accumulated Depreciation | 4,369.62 | |
| Total Fixed Assets | | 13,478.47 |
| **Other Assets:** | | |
| Security Deposits | 1,275.00 | |
| Life Insurance — Officer | 156.24 | |
| Prepaid Expenses | 638.75 | |
| Total Other Assets | | 2,069.99 |
| **Total Assets** | | $35,864.32 |

## Liabilities and Stockholders' Equity

Current Liabilities:
| | | |
|---|---|---|
| Accounts Payable | $23,098.48 | |
| Taxes Payable | 2,180.59 | |
| Notes Payable — Bank | 5,000.04 | |
| Total Current Liabilities | | $30,279.11 |

Long-Term Liabilities:
| | | |
|---|---|---|
| Note Payable — Bank | 7,000.14 | |
| Note Payable — CBDO | 95,000.00 | |
| Total Long-Term Liabilities | | 102,000.14 |
| Total Liabilities | | 132,279.25 |

Stockholders' Equity:
| | | |
|---|---|---|
| Capital Stock | 675.00 | |
| Accumulated Deficit | (81,340.65) | |
| Loss for 3 months ending 6/30/71 | (15,749.28) | |
| Total Stockholders' Equity | | (96,414.93) |
| Total Liabilities and Stockholders' Equity | | $35,864.32 |

# IV

## Ghetto Services:
## Miracles or Myths?

Part IV presents case studies of four non-manufacturing businesses assisted by CBDOs. An examination of such businesses is especially relevant since the service sector is the fastest growing in the country and any serious attempt to foster black business development must delve into this area. These cases enable the reader to reflect on the widely held notion that services businesses cannot prosper in the ghetto because of outside competition and the inferior purchasing power of local residents. It also suggests that black firms can survive and profit if sound business principles are learned and adhered to and discusses the role of the CBDO in bringing resources to the non-manufacturing entrepreneur.

# 9

# FOUR BROTHERS TRUCKING
# COMPANY

## PROLOGUE

Four Brothers Trucking Company is a case study of four young blacks who started a moving company in 1967 with little capital and managerial skill but lots of determination. In the fall of 1968 the partners approached a Roxbury CBDO for assistance and eventually received almost $100,000. Despite this infusion of capital and the partners' hard work, the company was near failure two and a half years later.

The Roxbury CBDO was started in 1965 with its primary function being to find meaningful employment for the area's youth. As a result, most of the CBDO's funds usually supported business enterprises which were able to offer training and jobs to unemployed residents. Membership in the CBDO was open to all community residents, with open meetings being held every six to eight weeks. The CBDO's governing board was elected by the community and restricted to community residents. The CBDO had a seventy-five-man staff which included community organizers, loan officers, youth counselors, vocational trainers, and program administrators. Funds to operate the CBDO came from a variety of public and private sources, being given mainly on a project basis. The bulk of the CBDO's $2 million annual operating budget came from private foundations, the Departments of Labor and HUD, and the EDA.

In selecting its business undertakings, the CBDO placed the question of profitability and the consideration of the number of jobs to be created on an equal basis. The chief responsibility for reviewing requests and providing management assistance rested with several loan officers, all of whom held MBA degrees. The 1969 loan to Four Brothers Trucking Company represented one of CBDO's largest loans.

## THE CASE

### Introduction

In July 1971 the five partners of Four Brothers Trucking Company, a Roxbury (Boston) trucking company, were reviewing a proposal for additional funds which had been prepared by a local CBDO. They had previously borrowed a total of $78,000 from the CBDO and had to decide whether or not they would accept this latest offer of financial assistance. They felt that a significant difference with this proposal was that the CBDO would be assuming an equity position in the company, whereas the previous funding was in the form of loans.

### Background

THE PARTNERS OF FOUR BROTHERS TRUCKING COMPANY. Four Brothers Trucking Company is a Roxbury trucking company which is owned by five community residents, four of whom are driver-operators in the company. Like many minority-owned enterprises, this company is a reflection of its owners and their backgrounds. This is especially true in the cases of the owner-operators who were the principal movers in the formation of the company.

*James Bonds,* the president, was born in Roxbury in 1944 and had lived there all of his life. After graduating from high school in 1961, he attended Boston Community College during the evening from September 1963 to June 1965. While in college, he worked as a salesman and stock manager for a floor-covering firm.

After two years of college, he enlisted in the Air Force in June 1965, where he graduated from the Technical School as an air traffic control operator and achieved the rank of Airman Second Class. His military experience only lasted eleven months and in May 1966 he received an honorable discharge because of a service-incurred injury. Upon returning home, he got a job with King Moving and Storage Company, where he remained until he went into the trucking business with Richard Casey in 1967.

*Richard Casey,* the vice-president, who is four years younger than Bonds, was also born in Roxbury. After graduating from high school in 1966, he worked in the traffic department of American Merchants and Manufacturers, where he traced lost shipments for the firm. While working he also attended Boston Community College in 1966 and 1967 until he quit school to organize Four Brothers Trucking Company. Shortly after the company was organized, however, he was drafted into the Army. While Bonds continued to run the company, Casey was serving with the Army in Vietnam.

*Jim Evans,* secretary, who was twenty-four years old when the company started in 1967, was married and lived in Roxbury. Evans lived in Hampton, Virginia, until he graduated from high school in June 1961. After graduation he went to Boston, where he worked at a lamp shade company until September 1963, when he received a scholarship to attend Wesleyan University. Because of financial problems he only attended college for three years, returning to Boston in 1966 to accept a position as a children's counselor with the Department of Health. In an unsuccessful attempt to secure his college degree in sociology, he attended Northeastern University in 1966 and 1967. In 1967 he married a former schoolmate who also worked with the Department of Health. That same year Evans resigned his job to become a full partner.

*Larry Manley* became treasurer in November 1967 at the age of twenty-nine. A native of Cofield, North Carolina, he graduated from high school in 1956 and attended college in South Carolina for three years. After college he spent two more years in the Army serving as a company clerk in Korea. After obtaining an honorable discharge in 1961, he moved to Boston, where he worked for the Department of Health for six years, finally rising to a supervisor of children counselors before quitting to become the fourth operating partner.

*Andrew Scott* became a non-operating stockholder in 1967 when he was forty-four years old. A native of Roxbury, he graduated from high school in June 1944 and attended Harvard in 1943 and 1944. In August 1945 he was inducted into the U. S. Army, serving as a legal technician until he was discharged in January 1947.

Scott returned to Harvard for six more months from January 1947 to June 1947 and transferred to Northeastern University in September 1947, from which he graduated in October 1949. After graduation he worked with the Department of Health for one year before deciding to continue his education. In September 1950 he enrolled in law school and following graduation in June 1953 he set up a private practice in Roxbury. In 1967 he met James Bonds and decided that he would give financial support to "four struggling young businessmen."

EARLY HISTORY OF THE FOUR BROTHERS TRUCK-ING COMPANY. Both Bonds and Casey were men who "seriously wanted to go into business." At the suggestions of their respective employers, the two decided to form a trucking company. Bonds "brought to the partnership my experience as a trucker that I got while working for King Moving and Storage Company." Casey "lent some expertise because I was employed in the traffic department of American Merchants and Manufacturers." Although the two of them "did not have all of the necessary management skills, we did have the desire and the hopes that we would learn as we went along." Consequently, they resigned their jobs in 1967 and made a down payment on a new tractor trailer.

According to Casey, "We decided to go into business after offers were made to us by Paul Van Lines of Providence, Rhode Island, to transport furniture locally." Also Casey indicated that "Transport Service Company of Lynn promised to give us some business in transporting produce both on a short- and long-haul basis."

When the two partners started in the fall of 1967, they were both actively engaged in driving the diesel truck. When National Movers of Brockton approached them with an offer to provide a

BLACK ENTERPRISE, INC.

contract for full-time transportation of household goods, they knew they would need another driver because of the greater volume of work. Therefore, they asked Evans and Manley to join with them and just prior to Casey being drafted, they decided to incorporate their business. For the remainder of 1967 and much of 1968 the majority of their work originated in Brockton and was performed by the partners and occasional part-time help. With respect to maintenance, "most of the major work was done by International Harvester. Minor work was done by the National Movers mechanics who could tackle whatever problems we were confronted with."

FOUR BROTHERS AND THE CBDO. In November 1968 the partners of Four Brothers approached Emery Turner, executive director of the Roxbury CBDO, to secure expansion funding. They indicated that during "the five-and-a-half-month period prior to August of 1968, Four Brothers Trucking Company was doing about $4,000 per month worth of business. Consequently we felt that we should increase our operation."

At the time of the initial proposal to the CBDO (see Exhibit I on pages 282–285), the company's prime contract was with National Movers and it could not make major commitments to other contractors because of a lack of adequate rolling stock. In addition to the National Movers account, Four Brothers also had a contract with Hustings Products, Inc., to pick up and deliver plastics within the city. This activity required the part-time use of one 12-ton straight truck which also provided services for Hustings. In addition to these jobs, Four Brothers had obtained day-by-day transportation jobs from other companies in the Boston area. All of these activities involved the pickup and delivery of plastics. According to Bonds, "The ease with which Four Brothers was getting these accounts led to our desire to expand."

Upon receiving the November 15 proposal from Four Brothers Trucking Company, Turner assigned it to Lee Wright, a CBDO loan officer, who began to analyze the $135,000 request for funds. However, before completing his analysis, Wright received the following January 15, 1969, addendum to the November proposal which indicated that the company had purchased three used trucks through funds provided by Scott:

Dear Mr. Wright:

Since the last proposal was submitted, Four Brothers pursued its plan to expand by purchasing 3 used 12-ton trucks. The down payments for these vehicles were obtained through private sources. As of January 15, 1969, their activities are as follows: 2 trucks haul cellophane, grass, and wax paper at $75 daily each, and the other is to transport plastic at $300 weekly for 3–4 days' work. As of February 1, 1969, it is expected that Roe and Co. will use 2 full-time trucks at $100 daily. In addition, by February 1st, Hustings will lease the trailer for runs between Boston and Los Angeles, transporting finished plastic products and returning raw plastic. It is expected that 2 trips or 4 runs will be made monthly at about $1,200 per run. Roe has also requested a third truck at some time during the latter part of February.

By March 1st, the anticipated weekly income should be $3,200 for the 4 trucks and 1 trailer. The expected weekly expenses would be as follows:

| | |
|---|---:|
| 2 drivers for trailer @ $175 | $  350.00 |
| 4 drivers for 12 ton trucks @ $125 | 500.00 |
| Maintenance for 4 trucks | 80.00 |
| Maintenance & food allowance on roundtrip for trailer | 500.00 |
| Notes payable on 4 trucks | 260.00 |
| Notes payable on trailer | 165.25 |
| | $1,855.25 |

Though Four Brothers had included an income statement in their proposal to the CBDO, Wright wanted an up-to-date financial view of the company. When they received this request in April, the partners retained a local C.P.A. to prepare and submit the requested statements. (See Exhibit II on pages 286–288 for a March 31, 1969, balance sheet and an income statement for the period from October 1968 through March 1969.) Wright was "very impressed with the efforts of the young trucking company executives and the fact that the company had apparently made a profit over the six-month period."

Though there were several trucking companies in the community, Wright was anxious to give aid to this company because of the obvious ambition of the partners. By August 1969 he was able to prepare a proposal which requested a total of $147,000, slightly more than the firm had requested almost a year earlier. (See Exhibit III on pages 289–290 for a summary of the August 8 funding proposal.)

Before the CBDO executive committee acted on the proposal, it had Wright send copies to two consultants, who were considered knowledgeable about small business development. One consultant —James Smith—raised questions about (1) the level of any bank participation, (2) the role of Scott's ownership and financing, and (3) the validity of the potential business in the proposal. The second consultant—Amos Spellman—was mainly concerned about "whether or not there was a market for the proposed expansion of Four Brothers Trucking Company." He also raised questions "about the wages for the drivers, whether they were comparable to the union scale and whether the company was willing to commit itself to the schedule of salary increases."

These and other questions raised by the consultants, as well as the relatively large sum of money requested, caused the CBDO executive committee to hesitate in approving the proposal. Because no one on the CBDO staff had any experience with the trucking industry, Wright then sent the proposal to the First Boston Bank, asking it to participate in the project. Approximately two months later, on October 22, 1969, Pat Dand of the bank sent the following letter to Wright:

Dear Lee:

This letter is to confirm our commitment to advance 80% of invoice price not to exceed $25,000 to Four Brothers Trucking Company for the purpose of purchasing two 24-foot vans and one tractor. However, this commitment is subject to the receipt of a chattel mortgage covering the purchased trucks; your confirmation of the CBDO's willingness to advance up to $40,000–$50,000 to Four Brothers for Working Capital needs, with such advances being subordinated to us; and your satisfaction of the explanations of the credit experience and litigations outstanding against James Bonds and Jim Evans.

Our commitment will carry a 5% add-on rate and the borrowings will be amortized monthly over a five-year period. The exact amount of these payments cannot be determined until the invoice prices are known.

If you have any questions concerning the arrangement, feel free to call me at any time.

Sincerely,
Pat

Upon receiving bank confirmation that it would lend Four Brothers only $25,000, the CBDO executive committee requested that Four Brothers "cut back on its projects" in order to hold the total funding level "under $100,000." The partners agreed that by controlling their purchases of rolling stock they would be able to get by on less money. With this point cleared up, the CBDO executive committee on October 29, 1969, approved the following revised proposal "for $66,500 with the provision that ⅓ would be released immediately, ⅓ when a suitable location was found, and ⅓ when equipment and supplies were purchased":

Four Brothers Trucking Company, Inc., is a small trucking firm that intends to expand its operation in Roxbury. In order to make this move, the company will need $91,500. The First Boston Bank has agreed to loan the company up to $25,000 at a 5% add-on rate, repayable in four (4) years including a six-month grace period As the company demonstrates a need for the remainder ($66,500) it will be paid out on a "one-third" plan.

Repayment of this loan will commence after repayment (4 years) of the bank loan. The repayment will be as follows:

$$49\text{--}84 \text{ months @ } \$1,500 \text{ per month} = \$54,000$$
$$85\text{th month} \qquad\qquad\qquad = \ \underline{\ 12,500}$$
$$\$66,500$$

The partners of Four Brothers initially balked at this payment arrangement as well as the fact that they only had three years to repay the loan (vs. four years at the bank), but finally agreed and signed the loan agreement.

## Start-up

Thus by December 1969 the Four Brothers loan was approved and Turner assigned Barry Lewis, a business school graduate, to monitor its account with the company. In this capacity, he was instructed to assist Four Brothers in finding a location, employees, etc.

Lewis was new to the CBDO and knew very little about the history of the Four Brothers transactions. However, while in the process of assisting Bonds in securing a permanent facility, he decided that the CBDO should hire someone who understood the trucking business enough to help the CBDO evaluate Four Brothers and their prospects. Following the recommendations of the First Boston Bank in December 1969, he retained Joe Conyers, president of Transport Traffic and Sales, to give the CBDO a report on Four Brothers. In the meantime, on December 18, John King, for whom Bonds had worked, indicated that he was willing to sell his building and equipment to Four Brothers. Over the next few months, Lewis was to be kept busy dealing with the problems raised by Conyers' report, securing the building, and reviewing Four Brothers' financial situation.

CONSULTANT'S REPORT. Lewis had signed on the consultant in late December 1969 with a view toward receiving his report in January 1970. In the following memo to Turner, Lewis reported that things were looking very bright for Four Brothers because of the potential for new accounts, the availability of a building at favorable terms, and the assistance of King:

TO: Emery Turner                                    January 17, 1970
FROM: Barry Lewis

On January 16, 1970, I introduced Messrs. Bonds, Casey and Evans to Mr. Joe Conyers. We spent approximately two hours in my office getting acquainted and another three hours visiting with Mr. King who is interested in selling his building to Four Brothers. Below are the highlights of what transpired:

1. I advised Four Brothers that we had retained Mr. Conyers as an expert in the transportation industry (i.e., over forty years' experience in the industry) to work with them as a consultant. Initially, Mr. Conyers will review the situation and make recommendations on how they can strengthen their business operation. Most likely, he will be retained on a continuing basis for the next several months. Four Brothers was extremely pleased to have a person as knowledgeable as Mr. Conyers working with them.
2. James Bonds briefed Mr. Conyers on the present situation of Four Brothers . . .
3. A tour of the King Moving and Storage building reveals that it is in excellent condition. According to Mr. King, it is one of the few

buildings in the area which is approved for storage by the Department of Defense and as such he does a lot of business with the government.

Mr. King is asking for $25,000 down and $60,000 to be paid over a ten-year period at seven per cent. According to Mr. King, the building has been assessed at $114,000. Mr. Conyers asked him if that was as low as he would go. Mr. King responded that he would not come down from $85,000 but would take as little as $20,000 down. Mr. King after talking with his lawyer in our presence said that he would also agree (1) to a ninety-day deferred payment arrangement (i.e., Four Brothers would make their first payment ninety days after the closing) and (2) to a sixty-grace period (i.e., Four Brothers would be sixty days late in making their payment).

Mr. King explained that he looks on James Bonds as his "adopted son." James has worked for him off and on for several years. He feels so fond of James that he wants to give him whatever business he cannot take with him to Lynn, where he intends to operate a smaller moving and storage business. He offered the following:

· To secure a $10–12,000 a year account with Paul Van Lines, Inc. (Providence, R.I.). This $10–12,000 represents earned commissions for booking and packing loads. In order to demonstrate his good faith he said he would call the vice president of Paul Van Lines and ask him if he would transfer his arrangement to Four Brothers.
· To remain with Four Brothers for a month or so to help maintain the continuity of the business. During this time he would introduce Four Brothers to most of his customers (governmental and private) and counsel them over the rough spots in getting settled.
· To offer Four Brothers an opportunity to buy storage rights on what is presently being stored in the building.
· To offer Four Brothers an opportunity to buy some of his International Harvester trucks at discounted prices. These trucks are in excellent condition.

Thus, Mr. King is offering Four Brothers more than just a building. He is offering them an opportunity to cash in on some of the business which he has developed over a thirty-year period. Incidentally, Mr. King showed us his financial statements for the past several years. His business has shown a substantial profit and his warehousing, alone, generates income of $40–50,000 per year.

The question remains as to whether Four Brothers has sufficient capital to invest $20,000 in a building and pay an estimated $1,000 a month (insurance, mortgage, taxes and miscellaneous charges) on the building for ten years. The original proposal did not comprehend the purchase of a building and budgeted only $800 a month for rent. Nevertheless, the $20,000 may be an excellent investment in view of the opportunities which it can buy.

Mr. Conyers will submit a written report to us with his recommendations concerning this matter. He did say, however, that *"this is the best deal I've seen in ten years."*

Unfortunately, Mr. Conyers had been somewhat premature in his evaluation of the situation, for in his report which arrived one week later on January 23, 1970, he concluded with "We are very sorry to make this report such a . . . dismal affair but . . . we conscientiously tried to unravel the facts and make it understandable." In his report, he indicated that (1) given the present debt structure, the business "could not prove self-sustaining, let alone make a profit"; (2) the company required an I.C.C. and/or P.S.C. licenses which it would find difficult to obtain; and (3) even if it had the necessary approvals, it was probably overextended because of its limited resources. (See Exhibit IV on pages 291–293 for excerpts from the consultant's report.)

FINANCES. On the same day that he received the consultant's report, Lewis received a "second shock" in the following letter from a local accountant who indicated that Four Brothers urgently needed more than $100,000 to pay its current accounts payable and to set up its operations:

January 21, 1970

Dear Mr. Lewis:

Please see below a schedule of funds needed to revive Four Brothers' operations. Although my office has not audited the books and records in detail since September, 1969, it appears that substantial cash outlays have been made for truck rentals. Mr. Evans has stated to me that he is trying to service existing accounts, thereby protecting his good image, until such time as the company can afford good equipment. In my opinion, the cost of truck rentals on a regular basis is prohibitive. As the weeks pass the deficits from operations will continue to grow.

Sincerely yours,
Howard Felan

Accounts and Taxes Payable:

| | | |
|---|---|---:|
| Truck Rentals — Moon Rental Corp. | | $ 1,600.00 |
| | Granite Auto Leasing | 475.30 |
| | Hertz Rentals | 452.00 |
| | Avis | 232.00 |
| | One Plus Rental | 265.00 |
| Total Unpaid Truck Rentals | | 3,024.30 |
| International Harvester (Repair) | | 301.00 |
| Insurance | | 772.00 |
| Unpaid Wages | | 750.00 |
| Payroll Taxes (Estimated) | | 1,500.00 |
| Total Funds for Bills Rendered and Taxes | | $ 6,347.30 |

Funds Needed for New Operations:

| | |
|---|---:|
| Down Payment on Building and Equipment Including Closing Costs | 20,000.00 |
| 1 Tractor | 7,000.00 |
| 4 Trucks | 48,000.00 |
| 2 Low Lifts | 500.00 |
| Insurance — Workmens Comp., Fire, and Truck Liability | 6,500.00 |
| Signs | 200.00 |
| Telephone Deposit and Month Service | 300.00 |
| Legal | 1,000.00 |
| Accounting — One Year Service and Application and Reports | 1,000.00 |
| Tires and Fire Extinguishers | 2,800.00 |
| Utilities — Deposit | 200.00 |
| Fuel | 220.00 |
| Carting and Sanitation | 60.00 |
| Truck Fuel and Oil | 1,450.00 |
| Truck Repair and Maintenance | 300.00 |
| Registrations and Permits | 400.00 |
| Tolls | 50.00 |
| Highway Use and Mileage Tax | 500.00 |
| Payroll — Drivers — 5 @ 160.00 for 4 weeks | 2,400.00 |
| Payroll — Officers — Drivers 3 @ 200.00 for 4 weeks | 2,400.00 |
| Payroll Taxes | 575.00 |
| Office Stationery and Printing | 200.00 |

| | |
|---|---:|
| Total Cash Needed for New Operations | 96,055.00 |
| Total Cash Needed | $102,402.30 |

THE KING BUILDING. A few days after receiving these reports, Lewis met with Bonds to review the whole situation including the proposed purchase of the King building. Bonds acknowledged that they "were fully aware that we did not have the I.C.C. and P.S.C. licenses." However, he assured Lewis that their present operation would be in a "non-exempt" zone; consequently, Four Brothers would not be affected by the absence of these licenses. Moreover, he said that their lawyer was working on such permits. Further, Bonds pointed out that because King wanted to sell his building because of ill health, he had agreed to sell his P.S.C. license along with other assets of his company. According to Bonds, the most pressing concern was to close the deal for the purchase of the King building. He told Lewis that Four Brothers would be leasing the building until the CBDO approved the purchase and released the funds to make a down payment.

On February 9, 1970, the partners of Four Brothers and King met to negotiate the signing of a lease which enabled Four Brothers to rent the facilities at a monthly rental of $100. The lease also contained an option whereby Four Brothers could purchase the building on or before the termination of the lease. The lease was so favorable because King believed that Four Brothers intended to buy the building, at a later date, when funds could be allocated properly.

Since there was no provision for the purchase of a building in the Four Brothers funding proposal, Lewis found it necessary to show the CBDO executive committee why and how funds could be used for this purpose. So that a fair appraisal could be made of the building, he asked the attorney for Four Brothers to submit to him a formal statement as to the condition of the building. In his letter the attorney said:

March 11, 1970

Dear Mr. Lewis:

I inspected the premises on March 8, 1970, and based on said inspection and title search made by American Abstract Company, I make the following report:

The premises consist of a plot on Howard Avenue being 50 by 100 feet. The building erected on the premises occupies the entire lot and is three stories high. A heating room is located in the cellar, entrance from sidewalk, in which an oil burner, not more than two years old, is located together with a 275 gallon oil storage tank. Utilities meters are also located in this cellar area. The entire building has a recently installed sprinkler system and all floors are serviced by a freight elevator.

In addition to the truck storage area, the first floor contains an office which is wood paneled and is entirely suitable for business purposes. Additionally, on the first floor are located work benches, crating supplies, and a storage rack, erected on steel beams and pipes for equipment and supplies.

The upper two floors are used solely for storage facilities, and contain racks and bins for that function.

This brick building is well maintained, exceptionally clean throughout and based upon the inspection certificates and permits exhibited by the owner, apparently complies with all rules and regulations of governmental departments and agencies having jurisdiction of the same.

The building is owned by King Moving and Storage, Inc., with no more mortgages of record.

Real estate taxes are $2,001.84 per year.

There are two water meters on the premises.

This building is offered for sale on the following terms and conditions:

| | |
|---|---|
| Selling price | $85,000 |
| First Mortgage (to be taken back by owner) | 60,000 |
| Terms, 7% interest; 10-year self-liquidating, monthly payments approximately $700. | |

Personal property included in sale consists of office furniture, office air conditioner, PA system, large safe, file cabinets, two work benches, etc.

In my opinion, the price and terms of sale for these premises are fair and reasonable, and I have so advised my client, Four Brothers Trucking Company, Inc.

Yours truly,
Saul Lynch
Attorney-at-Law

At the same time that Four Brothers was negotiating for the purchase of the building, they had also put in an order with International Harvester for several trucks. In April 1970 the trucks were finally delivered and the Four Brothers partners signed a subordination agreement to the First Boston Bank and received the money to be used for the payment of the trucks.

Though they were able to start the trucks in the operation on April 2, 1970, the building situation still had not been settled. The CBDO executive committee was not satisfied that the company needed or had the funds necessary to make a down payment of

$20,000. Furthermore, they were not convinced that the building was worth the purchase price of $85,000. Therefore, the CBDO president, Emery Turner, requested an independent appraisal from the National Society of Appraisers (NSA). A representative of NSA sent the following report to Turner:

April 8, 1970

Dear Mr. Turner:

Pursuant to your authorization we have made a thorough inspection and investigation of the property hereinafter designated and commonly known at 244 Howard Avenue for the purpose of making an estimate of value.

It is our opinion that the building is in very good physical condition, and is not in need of any repair. The value of the subject property as of the 8th of April 1970 is as follows:

EIGHTY-SEVEN THOUSAND DOLLARS
($87,000.00)

Your attention is invited to the data, photographs, maps, and discussion following and from which in part, the conclusions were derived.

Cordially yours,
Richard Simon

This favorable appraisal, along with that of the attorney, was used by Lewis to recommend that the CBDO permit Four Brothers to use working capital as a down payment. He argued that: (1) Four Brothers would not decrease its cash flow if it used $25,000 of their working capital to buy the building because of the $2,400 income to be generated by the building's storage facilities; (2) the purchase was a good one, because it provided for furniture, air conditioning, and other equipment. He reasoned that Four Brothers would be "saving the $5,145 it had been allowed for furniture and renovation since it was being included in the purchase price of the building"; and (3) the mortgage payments of $700 per month would be $100 less in rent to be charged on the rented building.

At the same time that Lewis was making arguments for the purchase of the building, the CBDO received an abbreviated financial report from Four Brothers which covered operations from September 1969–February 1970 and showed an operating loss of almost $18,000. (See Exhibit V on pages 294–296 for the Four Brothers financial statements.) When questioned about these discouraging figures, Bonds indicated that the bad weather had reduced the movement of their vehicles. He also said that their accountant had not included one week's receipts in the gross receipts. Though these statements did not seem to argue favorably for the purchase of the building, the partners and King continued to negotiate until June 1970 when the CBDO executive committee finally agreed that Four Brothers could purchase the building.

## Operations

During the summer of 1970 it seemed that things were going well with the young trucking company. According to financial statements received by the CBDO, the firm showed a $10,000 profit in June and a relatively small loss for the last ten months of the fiscal year ending in June 1970. (See Exhibit VI on pages 297–299). The July income statement with its $7,000 monthly profit (see Exhibit VII on page 300) also reflected this upsurge in business. Even the August, September, and October income statements—on the surface—did not indicate any real difficulties, though the firm incurred small losses in each of the three months. (See Exhibits VIII, IX, and X on pages 301–305).

It was not until November 1970 that Turner began to sense a change in the conditions of Four Brothers. By that time Turner had assigned Ed Holmes, a new member of the CBDO staff, to the Four Brothers case. Holmes was to replace Lewis, who returned to school in October to seek a Ph.D. degree. Soon after taking the case, Holmes sent the following memorandum asking the CBDO executive committee to guarantee a $31,000 loan for Four Brothers to purchase two additional trucks:

TO: Executive Committee
FROM: Ed Holmes
DATE: November 13, 1970

On November 10, 1970, a meeting was held at the bank between members of Four Brothers and a representative of the loan department. I also attended this meeting as our representative. The purpose of the meeting was to secure a loan for $31,000 in order to purchase two additional trucks. These trucks are badly needed in order to service new IBM and ABC accounts.

The bank looked upon the proposal and supporting information very favorably but requests a 10% guarantee of the loan by us. This amounts to a guarantee of $3,100.

Based upon Four Brothers' past performance and their potential future outlook, I therefore propose that a letter guaranteeing 10% of the loan be sent immediately to the bank.

Urgency is required for this matter as the letter appears to be the final obstacle. An immediate demand exists for the trucks.

In looking at Four Brothers' over-all picture, Holmes felt that they had "passed through the first stages of development." Now he argued that "the company is facing the dual problems of expansion and lack of working capital because of slowness in collecting its accounts receivable from the government." In order to offset this problem, he thought that the company should acquire more commercial accounts, thus requiring additional equipment to service these new accounts. According to Four Brothers' projections, the additional net incomes from IBM and ABC would be $15,000 and $8,000 per month, respectively.

Because the CBDO had never previously guaranteed a bank loan, it was reluctant to initiate this new procedure in the Four Brothers case. Therefore, Turner asked Holmes "to substantiate his argument with some facts." In the following memorandum, Holmes gave additional operating details on the proposed new business:

TO: Executive Committee                            November 19, 1970
FROM: Ed Holmes

This is an accurate representation of what I feel is the profitability outlook of Four Brothers.

The company is definitely on the upswing. In the month of August it experienced a loss of $2,521.97, but the operation was able to pull itself up to a net loss of only $145.58 for the month of September, 1970. These two months were the beginning of the slack season for the trucking industry and followed months of $10,305.68 and $7,026.81 in profits for June and July respectively.

The future figures are based or substantial new business which has been acquired from IBM and ABC. The October figure of $456.51 net loss is based on the fact that the new accounts were just begun at the latter part of October. The November 1970 to March 1971 projections of $2,000.00 net profit is based on the fact that the profit from these accounts will take up the slack of the slow winter season.

The figures from April 1971 on show an increase due to the fact that this is the start of the trucking season and Four Brothers have cracked the market and have an established reputation. Sales during the winter months should average $13,000 per month versus approximately $11,000 per month in operating costs.

It must be stated that this projection is based on the assumption that Four Brothers will acquire three additional trucks and $25,000 of working capital before 1971. If this does not happen, Four Brothers will continue making or losing $100 to $150 a month because it will not be able to handle the new business and survive.

Despite Holmes' efforts, however, the CBDO executive committee took no affirmative action with respect to Four Brothers, deciding to wait until the company submitted new financial statements at the end of 1970. Because of what they interpreted as being a "negative attitude" on the part of the CBDO, the partners of Four Brothers began to "lose faith in the CBDO," and according to Holmes "developed a hostile attitude" toward him.

Despite the problems he was having in getting financial assistance for the company, Holmes prepared a *new* funding proposal for the company on January 25, 1971. In this new proposal he requested that the CBDO lend Four Brothers an additional $58,500 "to reduce its short-term debts and increase its working capital." He argued that the company was undercapitalized from the beginning, the original proposal of $147,168 being "shaved" to $91,500. He also indicated that additional management assistance "in the form of power to approve or disapprove capital budgeting decisions" was needed by Four Brothers since he felt that the company made "many serious capital budgeting decisions" by buying too much additional equipment. (See Exhibit XI on pages 306–308 for a copy of Holmes' refunding proposal.)

In subsequent discussions of his proposal with the executive commitee Holmes emphasized that Four Brothers needed the $58,000 because:

1. The consultant's January 1970 report on Four Brothers said that the company would need more than $91,000 and the Public Service Commission license was essential to the organization.
2. There was a large divergence between the estimated and actual sales figures for the company as projected in the original proposal.
3. There was a large divergence between the original stated collection period and the actual collection period of approximately 60% of Four Brothers' accounts receivable.

Looking at Four Brothers' over-all marketing position he explained that the company "had provided moving and storage services for households as well as for commercial and military clients." He estimated that sales volumes for the next twelve months would be approximately $145,000. He did not see this as being too unrealistic, as the company had generated sales of over $125,000 for the twelve months of 1970. He also argued that "the company had lost a great deal of money because of its inability to service some of the accounts that were offered it."

Finally, looking at the financial situation in 1970, he indicated that "during the slack season, 90% were government military accounts and unfortunately, the government did not pay its bills promptly." Holmes felt that upon reduction of short-term debts and acquisition of working capital, Four Brothers could acquire more commercial accounts by canvassing shipping firms, especially since the trucking season was approaching. He said: "Whereas with government accounts, the collection period is a rather long 60–90 days, household accounts are on a cash basis and commercial accounts are payable on a 30-day basis. By emphasizing the commercial market, they could do financially better than what they did."

As Holmes continued to insist that the company needed cash "to survive the winter," the CBDO executive committee finally granted the company a six-month secured loan for $12,000 on March 10, 1971. By accepting this loan, the company pledged its accounts receivable of approximately $14,000.

On March 11, 1971, Holmes presented an addendum to his January 25 proposal to the CBDO board—this new proposal would give the CBDO 80 per cent equity interest in Four Brothers for $63,500 and full control of the company's operations. In part, Holmes' addition said:

The following information is submitted as an addendum to the proposal in an attempt to allay certain well-founded fears expressed by members of the CBDO executive committee.

A. MANAGEMENT

We intend to take complete control of the firm and by doing so it is expected that the company can become self-sustaining and profitable. This will be accomplished by placing a duly authorized representative in charge of the operation. His duties will be coordination, planning, fiscal control, statement preparation and the direction of the marketing effort. It is contemplated that this will require 50% of the representative's time and this amount shall be added to the amount of equity funds, thereby increasing the amount of the equity in the firm from $58,500 to $63,500. Furthermore, it is contemplated that this will be necessary for twelve months. (Or until the company becomes self-sustaining.)

The current managers will then become working co-managers and their duties will consist of work supervision, sales, and backup for the manager.

B. CONTROLS

1. We will own 80% of the company's stock as a result of the investment of $63,500; with a buy back option that cannot be exercised for one year after the contract. This buy back option will allow the four working partners to purchase stock from us with the value of the Corporation being $65,000 and shares will be sold on this basis.

2. All income earned by Four Brothers while we have an equity interest will be shared on a 3:1 basis, with the remaining portion accruing to the Corporation. In the event that shares are purchased by the partners the value of the accrued earnings will be added to the purchasing price.

3. If our equity falls below 51%, the Corporation (Four Brothers) must take over total ownership and give a personal note for the balance of the funds.

4. All the company's disbursements will be controlled by our representative.

5. Separate tax and payroll accounts will be established and maintained.

6. An operation plan will be established and followed.

C. RECOMMENDATIONS TO BE APPLIED TO OUR REPRESENTATIVE

1. This representative will be totally responsible for the success or failure of Four Brothers.

2. The representative is required to spend not more than 50% of a working week at Four Brothers.

Before the CBDO executive committee could react to Holmes' proposal, the partners demanded to see the CBDO management. In a meeting on March 15, 1971, the partners of Four Brothers did not discuss their financial problems but proceeded to attack the efforts of Holmes, who four days later sent the following memo to the CBDO executive director, asking to be removed from the case:

TO: Emery Turner                                                    March 19, 1971
FROM: Ed Holmes

The purpose of this memo is to make a formal recommendation that another employee be assigned to Four Brothers *immediately, if not sooner.*

The basis for this recommendation is as follows: A considerable amount of distrust and ill-feeling exists on the part of the company toward me. The reasons for this seem to be the following:

1. The partners feel that our [CBDO's] present attitude towards their company is mostly due to me. Even though I was not hired until October 14, 1970, and did not take over my duties with the company until the last week of October, this feeling still persists. The present situation of the company is one which began and existed before I was hired.

2. The partners feel that I did not show an interest in the company due to infrequent visits. In addition, the partners were perturbed by my constantly emphasizing the gravity of the situation by reviewing financial statements, accounts receivable and accounts payable balances. The partners do not seem aware that I immediately began to press for additional funds, which included a new proposal less than a month after my employment.

3. The partners feel that I damaged their bank relations. A conversation between the bank representative and myself supposedly damaged the relationship and cancelled a potential loan. Yet in this alleged conversation I was besieged with an unneeded lesson in the financial analysis of a sick financially structured company of which Four Brothers was used as the model. I ended the conversation by assuring the banker that figures do not tell the whole story and that the potential of the company was outstanding.

4. The partners felt that I may have injured their chances for receiving their P.S.C. license. (The partners have since received the license.) They felt this may have occurred when I called to ascertain the status of the application. I had no way of knowing a hearing had already been held or secret measures had been implemented.

5. In the presence of the CBDO executive committee and others, the partners reiterated that I was the source of a communication breakdown. Yet, as you are aware, constant memos and discussions had been initiated by me in an effort to make the position of the company known. In the same meeting, the partners stated that I had stated that the acquisition of a P.S.C. license was "totally impossible." In actuality I had stated that the acquisition of the P.S.C. license was "close to impossible."

6. In the same meeting, the partners stated that I had told them to "close their doors." In actuality, in advising the company to reduce or eliminate temporarily work due to the cash flow crisis, I had stated that at a certain point it is even sometimes more economical for a company to stop operation than continue.

7. I was represented as being not interested in pushing the $12,000 request and also of not seeing them for a period of over one week. As you are aware, I did "ride herd" and personally hand carried the material from point-to-point while the contract was still being prepared. As for not visiting the company for over one week, I visited the company last on March 6. I was contacted by phone by the company on Tuesday, March 9. I stated that I was avoiding their call (in a half joking manner) because I had been constantly following up on the loan procedure and the agreement.

For the above mentioned reasons, the company-Holmes relationship has greatly deteriorated. Further relationship would only be a waste of resources. I consequently also retract my recommendation that I be the representative to the company under an equity arrangement.

I do still feel that with the influx of additional funds and management, Four Brothers can be a highly viable company.

At his request, Turner removed Holmes as the CBDO's representative to Four Brothers and turned to the question of how to help Four Brothers and/or save its investment in the company. After a series of meetings on the subject the CBDO executive committee decided that it could risk no more of its loan money without more control over the affairs of Four Brothers.

In late April 1971 Turner assigned a new staff member to the Four Brothers' case. This new man was John Dahms, who had recently joined the CBDO after working in a local bank. Upon receiving the assignment, Dahms spent several weeks reviewing the history of the company and talking with staff, consultants, bank officials, and the partners. On June 4 he submitted the following summary report on the company which outlined its background and discussed his efforts in securing a $50,000 bank loan from his former bank and his recommendation that the CBDO contribute another $20,000 as an equity investment with several restrictions being placed on the present management:

TO: Emery Turner                                    June 4, 1971
FROM: John Dahms

Sales for the Company's last nine months of operation were approximately $110,000 with a net profit of about $27,000 before depreciation. This was accomplished largely without a Public Service Commission license, which is considered crucial in the trucking industry. The Company received its P.S.C. license in March, 1971. Due to a tight cash structure, the Company has not been able to take full advantage of the large market available. With the advent of warmer weather, and the trucking season, the Company's monthly sales are on the upsurge as can be seen in May's sales of $15,977.38, and net profit before depreciation of $8,151.83. [See Exhibit XII on pages 309–311 for Four Brothers' May 1971 financial statements.]

The management of this Company can best be summarized as poor. Even though the four partners are probably good truck drivers, their financial planning for the Company has been so inadequate that the Company finds itself in serious condition, even though it generated $125,000 in annual sales, had a small loss, and now possesses a P.S.C. license. Trucks, trailers, and equipment were purchased without consideration of return on investment, cash flow effects, or alternative uses of funds.

I have assisted Four Brothers in applying for a $50,000 loan from the Penny Bank. The loan has been approved, but the funds will not be released until we put in $20,000. In line with Ed Holmes' earlier recommendation I think that we should guarantee the bank loan and receive 80% equity, with a buy-out option.

In addition to financial assistance, I propose tight managerial restrictions, which include the bank and our taking positions on the Four Brothers Board; a restricted bank account; and restricted purchasing ability.

On June 15, 1971, the CBDO executive committee approved Dahms' recommendation and transmitted these terms to Four Brothers. After one month of studying the CBDO's terms for releasing the $70,000, the partners of Four Brothers were still uncertain about whether they should surrender control of their company for the money.

278

# EPILOGUE

By July 20, 1971, John Dahms had become quite concerned about the failure of the CBDO to reach an agreement with Four Brothers, since he realized that without the $70,000, the company would have little chance of surviving. Therefore he contacted the partners of Four Brothers to find out why they were reluctant to come to terms with the CBDO.

In a meeting on July 21 he found that the partners had problems with the amount of the 80 per cent equity that the CBDO wanted. Specifically he learned that the partners felt that "because of the work and sacrifices put into the operation, under no circumstances would [they] give up 80% of the company." Dahms indicated to the partners that he understood their rationale and would attempt to develop a new proposal more acceptable to the firm.

Dahms returned to his office and discussed the matter with Emery Turner. Turner agreed that unless the company got additional funds, it would be hard pressed to succeed, but because of its record he "would be reluctant to provide the funds without some type of veto power over the management with regard to capital decisions." Dahms suggested controls could be effected without owning 80 per cent of the stock of the company by the use of various negative covenants. In effect, the CBDO would spell out contractually the rights of the company with respect to spending decisions. Turner agreed with Dahms and indicated that the CBDO should get at least 40 per cent in equity and two seats on the board of directors.

With these guidelines from Turner, Dahms scheduled another meeting with the partners on July 23. The partners agreed to the new provisions and an agreement was reached one week later. At that time Four Brothers received $50,000 from the CBDO and $20,000 from the bank. With the funds, the company was able to pay off most of its pressing outstanding obligations and operate the additional trucks it had acquired. Subsequently it was able to acquire on I.C.C. license.

In August, when the trucking season was slow, the owners of

Four Brothers provided information on their experiences with the CBDO and their business. James Bonds, the president, summed up the group feelings as follows:

Many of the problems that we faced were as a result of our not having sufficient management talent to do the planning and analysis that were needed. Oftentimes we were on the road at the same time and the secretary had to take care of any things that came up. This was the only way that we could make it. But at the same time we were not planning and looking over our operation the way we should in order to make sure of what was happening. Now we are in a better position. We have some money so we can afford to have one of us spend all of his time in the office looking after the business. Sometimes, we would buy a truck because we had the business only to find out later that we did not have enough money to operate it; or to meet all of the expenses that had to be met, which are considerable.

This business has grown tremendously and we are getting to the point where we have got to decide how fast we want to grow. Mr. Holmes, who was not the greatest guy in the world, if you know what I mean, once told us that we could go out of business by having so much business. At the time we thought he was some kind of nut, but he was right. And the time he suggested that we shut down the operation in order to have some capital we almost threw him out. But no matter how much money you have, that money will only allow you to do so much business. This is probably why we never had enough money.

But you can believe this, if we had it to do over again, we would still do it. In addition to the profits that we hope to make, we have given a lot of youngsters who live in this neighborhood part-time work, and made them want to go into business and be like us.

In a subsequent conversation, Turner gave the following observations about the partners:

When I first received the proposal from the boys I was gung ho over it. Here was a group of young black men who were interested in going into business at the age which most young men are still trying to prove their manhood. But these guys not only wanted to go into business, they were serious. I remember how they used to sleep in their trucks and how they would pay themselves small salaries to keep money in the company. Given the same situation, I would help them again, because they were a go-getting bunch of guys.

But as often happens, some mistakes were made that could have wiped them out; some were made by the owners and some were made by us. For the kind of operation that we had talked about initially, we did not give them enough money. I admit that as they continued to scale up the size of the operation, their problems were magnified, but still they did not have enough cash in the beginning. For example, we should not have agreed to let them purchase that building without some additional funds. Funds were already meager and investing $20,000 of that in a building did not help.

The only other thing that I really regret was our inability to decide at several points what we were willing to do. I think that was because of the amount of money that we were dealing with and our reluctance to put any more in and at the same time our concern with saving that which we had already put in. I think now we realize that these businesses are going to experience problems like any other business and when they do, we should be ready to deal with them in a speedy manner.

Exhibit I

# A PLAN FOR EXPANSION OF OPERATIONS
# BY FOUR BROTHERS TRUCKING COMPANY, INC.

## November 15, 1968

This proposal outlines a general expansion program contemplated by the trucking firm of Four Brothers Trucking Company. A short history of the origins of the organization will be presented as well as a review of its present operations. A detailed report of envisioned increases in range and volume of activities and estimates of capitalization funds will be submitted. It is to be understood that this undertaking is attempted in a field which has by no means reached its saturation point as far as the number and size of organizations involved is concerned and that it is believed to be entirely feasible within the scope of activities presented.

### Present Operations

Early in 1968, the need for expansion became evident when the following offers were made to the group:
1. To pick up and deliver freight throughout the Metropolitan area for Cooper-Counte.
2. To pick up, deliver and store cellophane, grass and wax paper for Carl Maker.
3. To pick up, deliver and store freight, especially textiles for American Merchants and Manufacturers. This operation would involve long distance as well as local trucking.
4. To pick up and deliver plastics as the sole agent performing same for Hustings Plastic Company.
5. In this connection the prospects of transporting freight for Eastern Airlines and Johnson Motor Lines were also considered.

At this point, the following decisions were made:
1. That to cope with such an anticipated increase in activity, a more expanded permanent and eventually self-owned base of operations would have to be acquired. This was most important when the aspect of freight storage was taken into consideration.
2. That since all members of the group were from the community

and the company incorporated in Boston such a base would best be located in this section and that needed additional personnel would be recruited from here.

## Expansion Plans

It was agreed that to conduct trucking activities on a scale anticipated in the foregoing outline, certain minimum requirements as far as equipment, a base of operations and additional personnel are necessary. These will be detailed in the following sections:

## Equipment

These trucks will provide for local and middle distance hauling.

| Quantity | Description | Sale Price |
|---|---|---|
| 1 | 4-wheel drive Panel Truck | $ 3,890.54 |
| 1 | 12-foot Metro Van | 5,007.43 |
| 4 | 22-foot body - 175" CA | 7,469.80 |
| 1 | F-1800 A 6-wheel truck | 12,400.79 |
| 1 | CF 50 Hilo | 6,850.00 |

The trucks are to be purchased from International Harvester, the hilo from Clark Equipment Co. The sale price of the trucks includes $2,141 sales tax. Complete sales analyses are enclosed.

## Building

An adequate base of operations would have to provide an area for—
1. Parking facilities for the diesel, panel truck, Metro Van, hilo and at least 4 of the other vehicles.
2. Space for anticipated short-term storage.
3. Space for a small emergency repair and maintenance area.
4. Small office space—Several prospects for a suitable building in the community have been investigated, but at this writing, no firm commitments have been made. It is felt that the equipment and activities described would probably require an area of at

least 6,000 to 6,500 feet. The going rental rate in the area appears to vary between $0.50 and $1.00 per square foot per month for fireproof facilities.

*Personnel*

| Number | Job Description | Capitalization Estimate |
|--------|-----------------|-------------------------|
| 1 | Mechanic—part time | $2,000 |
| 5 | Full time drivers—in addition to present members | @  3,500 |
| 1 | Office clerk-bookkeeper | 3,000 |

*Total Capitalization Estimates—One Year Basis:*

| | | |
|---|---|---|
| Equipment | Trucks | $ 42,816.00 |
| | Sales tax | 2,141.00 |
| | Hilo | 6,850.00 |
| Salaries | | 29,000.00 |
| Rent of building (6,000 sq. ft. @ $0.50/sq. ft.) | | 36,000.00 |
| Estimated cost of conversion of building for particular needs of organization | | 7,000.00 |
| Office equipment | | 5,000.00 |
| Legal and Accounting | | 6,000.00 |
| Total Capitalization | | $134,807.00 |

# FOUR BROTHERS TRUCKING COMPANY, INC.

### Statement of Income and Expenses
### for the 11½ Months Ending September 9, 1968

| | |
|---|---:|
| * Trucking Income  10/1/67–9/9/68 | $27,026.99 |
| *Expenses* | |
| Repairs | 399.98 |
| Tires | 232.88 |
| Weights and labor | 320.89 |
| Claims | 207.20 |
| Insurance | 1,109.20 |
| Permits and licenses | 547.30 |
| Towing | 525.00 |
| Travel expenses (including gas & oil) | 3,404.37 |
| Interest—International Harvest Co. | 1,160.55 |
| Depreciation | 1,909.00 |
| Total Expenses | $ 9,816.37 |
| *Net Income* for the period 10/1/67–9/9/68 | 17,210.62 |

* 1 operation only per trip      3 weeks work/month
March 1968—No activity due to repairs.

Exhibit II

## FOUR BROTHERS TRUCKING COMPANY, INC.

Statement of Operations for the period October 1, 1968 – March 31, 1969

| | | |
|---|---:|---:|
| Gross Revenues | | $22,074.52 |
| Direct Operating Costs: | | |
|   Truck Repairs and Maintenance | $ 1,349.38 | |
|   Gasoline and Oil | 2,014.68 | |
|   Tolls | 353.51 | |
|   Licenses and Registrations | 656.00 | |
|   Insurance | 601.09 | |
|   Truck Rentals | 234.03 | |
|   Labor and Labor Charges | 2,348.96 | |
|   Depreciation on Trucks and Vans | 2,794.50 | |
|   Amortization Hand Trucks, Pads and Blankets, | | |
|     Dollies,Etc. | 234.25 | |
|   Claims Paid | 1,002.61 | |
|     Total Direct Operating Costs | | 11,589.01 |
| Gross Profit on Operations | | $10,485.51 |
| Administrative Expenses: | | |
|   Bank Charges | 18.25 | |
|   Professional Fees | 250.00 | |
|   Depreciation on Office Equipment | 52.50 | |
|   Interest Expense | 1,111.80 | |
|   Payroll Taxes | 157.70 | |
|     Total Administration Expenses | | 1,590.25 |
|     Net Income Before Corporate Taxes | | 8,895.26 |
| Provision for Corporate Taxes—Estimated | | |
|   Franchise Tax | 444.38 | |
|   General Corporate Tax | 444.38 | |
|   Federal Corporate Tax | 1,229.98 | |
|     Total Corporate Taxes—Estimated | | 2,118.74 |
| Net Income | | $ 6,776.52 |

# FOUR BROTHERS TRUCKING COMPANY, INC.

## Statement of Financial Position as at March 31, 1969

### Assets

Current Assets:

| | | |
|---|---:|---:|
| Cash on Hand and in Bank | $    154.56 | |
| Accounts Receivable | 681.90 | |
| Prepaid Expenses | 761.82 | |
| **Total Current Assets** | | $  1,598.28 |

Fixed Assets:

| | | |
|---|---:|---:|
| Trucks and Vans | 22,356.00 | |
| Office Equipment | 420.00 | |
| | 22,776.00 | |
| Less: Accumulated Depreciation | 2,847.00 | |
| | 19,929.00 | |
| Unamortized Cost of Hand Trucks, Pads and Blankets, Etc. | 2,108.25 | |
| **Total Fixed Assets** | | 22,037.25 |

Other Assets:

| | | |
|---|---:|---:|
| Deposit on Van | 250.00 | |
| Deferred Interest | 2,903.28 | |
| **Total Other Assets** | | 3,153.28 |
| **Total Assets** | | **$26,788.81** |

Liabilities and Stockholders' Equity

Current Liabilities:

| | | |
|---|---|---|
| Accounts Payable | $ 506.00 | |
| Payroll Taxes Payable | 157.70 | |
| Notes Payable | 3,065.00 | |
| Notes Payable | 6,974.04 | |
| Notes Payable | 678.79 | |
| State and City Corporate Taxes | 888.76 | |
| Federal Income Tax Payable | 1,229.98 | |
| Loans and Exchanges | 25.00 | |
| Total Current Liabilities: | | $13,525.27 |

Long-Term Liabilities:

| | | |
|---|---|---|
| Notes Payable | 3,487.02 | |
| Total Long-Term Liabilities | | 3,487.02 |
| Total Liabilities | | 17,012.29 |

Stockholders' Equity:

| | | |
|---|---|---|
| Capital Stock — Common, No Par 200 Shares | 3,000.00 | |
| Retained Earnings from Current Operations | 6,776.52 | |
| Total Stockholders' Equity | | 9,776.52 |
| Total Liabilities and Stockholders' Equity | | $26,788.81 |

# Exhibit III

## August 8, 1969

### Introduction

This is a proposal to provide assistance to the Four Brothers Trucking Company, Inc. The company plans an expansion of its operations which will require approximately $147,000. The company is a small trucking firm that is interested in expanding its operation which includes adding 17 new employees from the community. It intends to locate to a large and modern garage of approximately 10,000 square feet, an amount of industrial space readily available. In order to make the move and expansion the company will need $147,168.

### Background of the Proposal

At the suggestion of their former employers, James Bonds and Richard Casey decided to form a trucking company. They resigned from their jobs in October, 1967, and purchased a 1967 International Diesel Tractor Trailer, the chattel mortgage being held by International Harvester.

Their operations proceeded with both members of the present corporation actively driving the diesel. At the end of November 1967, National Movers approached the group with an offer to provide a contract for transportation of household goods. This contract was accepted, but because of the volume of work anticipated, another driver was needed. At this time, Jim Evans and Larry Manley were asked to join the group. The firm then drove only for National through April 1968.

The company's Balance Sheet and Income Statement for the period October 1968 to March 31, 1969, indicate that it is a viable business. New financial statements as of June 30, 1969, are being prepared. Upon expansion, the business anticipates $46,870 sales per month. Based on the initial projected investment the business will require gross sales of $18,490 per month to break even.

## The Proposal

The company will locate in a larger and modern garage and intends to rent approximately 10,000 square feet. To support a breakeven sales volume estimated to be $221,880 per year, the company will need $147,168 to be used as follows:

| | |
|---|---:|
| Increase in Cash Balance | $ 10,945 |
| Increase in Accounts Receivable | 21,518 |
| Increase in Equipment | 104,170 |
| Renovation Expenses | 4,410 |
| To Decrease Current Liabilities | 6,125 |
| | $147,168 |

Exhibit IV

# FOUR BROTHERS TRUCKING COMPANY

## January 23, 1970

Circumstances that have developed require that this matter be treated in two separate phases rather than the singular originally contemplated. Consequently, we will attempt to deal with each to be followed by necessary comments and observations.

*Proposition 1*

Four Brothers is a small trucking company (our definition of this present operation is one of a leasing company not necessarily one of a trucking institute) who has applied for a loan in the area of $66,500 to be supplemental to a loan of $25,000 from the bank both of which are for the purposes of expanding the present business currently conducted.

A program such as this will require payments to the bank of approximately $560 per month which entails the monthly payment on the principal plus interest. At the end of the 48 months' period the payments to the CBDO of $1,500 would commence for the next ensuing 49 months. Considering present obligations on equipment etc., plus these loan expenses *the present operation could not prove self-sustaining, let alone make a profit.* Apparently, all are cognizant of the need for further exploration of expansion possibilities to the current business . . .

As far as this problem of the moment is concerned, applicant (Four Brothers) cannot be considered a common carrier of general freight since they hold no authority to operate from the Interstate Commerce Commission nor, in fact, from the Public Service Commission. They are what is commonly referred to as a leasing company having set aside truck equipment to two clients.

The present operation whereby Four Brothers leases some equipment . . . is an arrangement *the Public Service Commission may look upon as a device to defeat effective regulatons.* In addition, operating from Massachusetts to points in Rhode Island is interstate in effect and by its very nature which *the Interstate Commerce*

*Commission could conceivably consider to be that of an interstate common carrier operating without authority.* In any investigation the regulatory agencies would look into the nature and intent of the operation from a practical standpoint and as a result could rule it as an invasion on the common carrier field.

Four Brothers understands this fully and they are also considering filing applications for rights to operate as common carriers both in interstate and intrastate commerce. We wish to point out the pitfalls in this regard. If applicants were successful in obtaining commitments with each individual shipper being proposed, and while each operation then constituted would be a leasing arrangement, they would be closer to a contract carrier permit operation. Since the Commission would not grant any company eleven contract permits it necessarily follows the operation, as a whole, would be a common carrier operation rather than contract. If this is attempted . . . *we can name 20 of these who would protest any such applications and it would then become incumbent upon Four Brothers to prove inadequacy of present services by all of these carriers.*

## Proposition 2

In an effort to obtain garage space for any general proposed expansion contact was made with King Moving and Storage Company. It develops that King is seeking to sell, not rent, his facilities. He wants $85,000 for the building and business and offers to assist, for a limited period, the purchaser or purchasers.

As best we can determine the building is assessed for tax purposes at approximately $40,000 which is *far below* the actual sale value which he has been offered by others. It is a three-story structure and more than sufficient for the moving and storage business, storing of equipment, and storage of household effects . . . In preliminary discussions with King he has indicated a desire and willingness to have his present agency arrangements to continue, to assist purchasers in keeping his present business, requires a down payment of $20,000 with a 60-day grace period, monthly notes of about $850 per month with deferred payments when necessary during the time payment period and is willing to sell his P.S.C. certificate.

We believe that since this is an established business it should be explored more fully in three or four weeks when we receive King's financial statement for 1969. The examination of 1966, 1967, 1968 financial statements did show a reasonable profit for King. And, it should be determined what physical properties go along with the deal such as equipment, trucks, racks, etc., and spelled-out assistance.

## Observations and Conclusions

We are here concerned with four dedicated, honest, energetic people who want to make a success of their lives and they should have the opportunity. With this in mind *we cannot however permit our desires to have any effect on our beliefs as we see them.* And for their benefit and guidance, and for no other reason, the following comments, not in order of relative importance, are given.

The present leasing arrangement, as we see it, is closely aligned to that of a common or contract carrier in spite of and because of leasing equipment owned by Four Brothers, and driven by its officers. Convincing anyone such drivers are under the exclusive control of shippers would be difficult if not near impossible. Ignorance of the law would be no excuse or defense . . . One is talking about an investment of almost $200,000 and it just does not appear this situation would be sufficiently self-sustaining, but could be feasible in a long period of purchasing and leasing one or two units at a time. It just appears to us the obligations are too steep to absorb at one shot. If leasing is to be pursued then we think one step at a time should be resorted to rather than jumping headlong into a pool without swimming abilities . . .

We are very sorry to have to make this report such a complicated and dismal affair but it is involved and we conscientiously tried to unravel the facts and make it understandable.

Exhibit V

## FOUR BROTHERS TRUCKING COMPANY, INC.

Statement of Income February 1970 and September 1969 — February 1970

|  | February 1970 | Sept. 1969 – Feb. 1970 |
|---|---|---|
| Net Sales | $3,774.00 | $12,907.00 |
| Cost of Sales | 2,865.00 | 28,002.00 |
| Gross Profit (Loss) | $ 909.00 | ($15,095.00) |
| Operating Expenses: | | |
| Administrative | $544.00 | $2,833.00 |
| Total Operating Expenses | 544.00 | 2,833.00 |
| Operating Profit (Loss) | 365.00 | (17,928.00) |
| Non-Operating Income (Expenses): | | |
| Income | (26.00) | 137.00 |
| Expenses | | (207.00) |
| Total Non-Operating | (26.00) | (70.00) |
| Income (Loss) Before Taxes | 339.00 | (17,998.00) |
| Federal and State Income Taxes | –0– | –0– |
| Net Income (Loss) | $ 339.00 | ($17,998.00) |

BLACK ENTERPRISE, INC.

# FOUR BROTHERS TRUCKING COMPANY, INC.

## Balance Sheet as at February 28, 1970

### Assets

| | | |
|---|---:|---:|
| **Current Assets:** | | |
| Cash | $ 5,655 | |
| Total Current Assets | | $ 5,655 |
| **Fixed Assets:** | | |
| Machinery and Equipment | 16,775 | |
| Other Property | 1,826 | |
| | 18,601 | |
| Less: Accumulated Depreciation | 7,022 | |
| Total Fixed Assets | | 11,579 |
| **Other Assets:** | | |
| Deferred Assets | 1,861 | |
| Due from Officers | 1,612 | |
| Prepaid Expenses | 462 | |
| Security Deposits | 500 | |
| Total Other Assets | | 4,435 |
| Total Assets | | $21,669 |

## Liabilities and Stockholders' Equity

| | | |
|---|---:|---:|
| **Current Liabilities:** | | |
| Notes Payable | $10,806 | |
| Accrued Liabilities | 295 | |
| Other Current Liabilities — Non-Trade | 25 | |
| Total Current Liabilities | | $11,126 |
| **Long-Term Liabilities:** | | |
| Notes Payable | 20,000 | |
| Total Long-Term Liabilities | | 20,000 |
| **Other Liabilities** | 837 | |
| Total Other Liabilities | | 837 |
| Total Liabilities | | 31,963 |
| **Stockholders' Equity:** | | |
| Capital Stock | 3,000 | |
| Retained Earnings | (13,294) | |
| Total Stockholders' Equity | | (10,294) |
| Total Liabilities and Stockholders' Equity | | $21,669 |

## Exhibit VI

## FOUR BROTHERS TRUCKING COMPANY, INC.

### Statement of Income for period June 1 — June 30, 1970

|  | This Month |  | Year to date — 10 Months |  |
|---|---|---|---|---|
| Net Sales |  | $16,156.11 |  | $49,720.32 |
| Cost of Sales: |  |  |  |  |
| Labor | $2,018.73 |  | $15,402.88 |  |
| Overhead | 2,376.63 |  | 27,583.69 |  |
| Total Cost of Sales |  | 4,395.36 |  | 42,986.57 |
| Gross Profit (Loss) |  | $11,760.75 |  | $ 6,733.75 |
| Operating Expenses: |  |  |  |  |
| Selling | 159.45 |  | 1,328.91 |  |
| Administrative | 731.80 |  | 3,536.80 |  |
| Other | 563.82 |  | 7,494.22 |  |
| Total Operating Expenses |  | 1,455.07 |  | 12,359.93 |
| Operating Profit (Loss) |  | 10,305.68 |  | (5,626.18) |
| Non-Operating Income |  | —0— |  | 137.44 |
| Total Income (Loss) Before Taxes |  | 10,305.68 |  | (5,488.74) |
| Federal and State Income Taxes |  | —0— |  | 51.33 |
| Net Income (Loss) |  | $10,305.68 |  | ($ 5,540.07) |

# FOUR BROTHERS TRUCKING COMPANY, INC.

## Balance Sheet for period ending June 30, 1970

### Assets

| | | |
|---|---:|---:|
| **Current Assets:** | | |
| Cash | $ (733.69) | |
| Accounts Receivable | 5,870.93 | |
| Prepaid Expenses | 1,069.00 | |
| Other Current Assets | 200.00 | |
| Total Current Assets | | $ 6,406.24 |
| **Property, Plant and Equipment:** | | |
| Land and Buildings | 85,830.30 | |
| Machinery and Equipment | 79,688.92 | |
| Other Property | 1,305.15 | |
| | 166,824.37 | |
| Less: Reserve for Depreciation and Amortization | 8,641.96 | |
| Total Property, Plant and Equipment, Net | | 158,182.41 |
| **Other Assets:** | | |
| Deferred Assets | 36,731.14 | |
| Due from Officers | 6,663.60 | |
| Organization Expense | 1,605.44 | |
| Total Other Assets | | 45,000.18 |
| Total Assets | | $209,588.83 |

BLACK ENTERPRISE, INC.

## Liabilities and Net Worth

| | | |
|---|---:|---:|
| Current Liabilities: | | |
| Notes Payable — Banks | $ 2,325.66 | |
| Current Portion of Long-Term Debt | 21,612.72 | |
| Accrued Liabilities | 220.00 | |
| Accrued Federal Taxes on Income | 754.27 | |
| Other Current Liabilities | 25.00 | |
| Total Current Liabilities | | $ 24,937.65 |
| Long-Term Liabilities: | | |
| Notes Payable | 126,922.98 | |
| Total Long-Term Liabilities | | 126,922.98 |
| Other Liabilities: | | |
| CBDO | 47,548.52 | |
| Total Other Liabilities | | 47,548.52 |
| Total Liabilities | | 199,409.15 |
| Net Worth: | | |
| Common Stock | 3,000.00 | |
| Retained Earnings | 8,016.02 | |
| Earned Surplus (Deficit) | (836.34) | |
| Total Net Worth | | 10,179.68 |
| Total Liabilities and Net Worth | | $209,588.83 |

## Exhibit VII

### FOUR BROTHERS TRUCKING COMPANY, INC.

Statement of Operations for the period July 1 — July 31, 1970

| | | |
|---|---:|---:|
| Income from Trucking | | $17,731.23 |
| Direct Operating Costs: | | |
|     Truck Repairs and Maintenance | $ 150.00 | |
|     Gasoline and Oil | 847.38 | |
|     Tolls | 35.30 | |
|     Insurance | 89.00 | |
|     Truck and Trailer Rentals | ·882.88 | |
|     Labor and Labor Charges | 2,922.00 | |
|     Depreciation on Trucks | 1,335.48 | |
|     Amortization on Hand Trucks, Pads, etc. | 33.46 | |
|     Casual Labor | 2,757.72 | |
|     Tires and Equipment | 52.52 | |
|     Refunds and Claims | 64.00 | |
|         Total Direct Operating Costs | | 9,169.74 |
|         Gross Profit on Operations | | $ 8,561.49 |
| General and Administrative Expenses: | | |
|     Office Supplies | 105.59 | |
|     Payroll Taxes | 149.56 | |
|     Utilities | 3.60 | |
|     Telephone | 219.02 | |
|     Depreciation — Office Equipment | 8.75 | |
|     Bank Charges | 24.25 | |
|     Interest Expense | 745.52 | |
|     Maintenance and Repairs | 31.80 | |
|     Office Payroll | 175.00 | |
|     Burglar Alarm | 22.92 | |
|     Penalty | 52.67 | |
|         Total General and Administrative Expenses | | 1,538.68 |
| Net Profit from Operations | | $ 7,022.81 |

## Exhibit VIII

# FOUR BROTHERS TRUCKING COMPANY, INC.

## Statement of Operations August 1 – August 31, 1970

| | | |
|---|---:|---:|
| Income from Trucking | | $14,364.15 |
| Direct Operating Costs: | | |
| Commissions | $ 332.31 | |
| Truck Repairs and Maintenance | 103.41 | |
| Entertainment | 2.50 | |
| Gasoline and Oil | 1,588.41 | |
| Weights | 52.10 | |
| Tolls | 286.55 | |
| License and Registrations | 10.00 | |
| Storage and Moving Supplies | 512.55 | |
| Insurance | 100.00 | |
| Truck and Trailer Rentals | 1,038.13 | |
| Labor and Labor Charges | 7,300.76 | |
| Depreciation on Trucks and Building | 1,335.48 | |
| Amortization on Hand Trucks, Pads, etc. | 33.46 | |
| Casual Labor | 240.43 | |
| Tires and Equipment | 31.29 | |
| Refunds and Claims | 532.20 | |
| Total Direct Operating Costs | | 13,499.58 |
| Gross Profit on Operations | | $    864.57 |

General and Administrative Expenses:

| | |
|---|---:|
| Organizational Expenses | 61.73 |
| State Unemployment Insurance Fund | 95.70 |
| Office Supplies | 423.12 |
| Professional Fees — Accounting | 500.00 |
| Professional Fees — Legal | 246.00 |
| Payroll Taxes | 364.49 |
| Utilities | 113.15 |
| Miscellaneous Expenses | 3.00 |
| Telephone Company | 318.79 |
| Depreciation — Office Equipment | 8.75 |
| Bank Charges | 34.30 |
| Interest Expense | 823.82 |
| Advertisement | 53.32 |
| Taxes on Building | 306.01 |
| Maintenance and Repairs | 18.53 |
| Penalty | 15.83 |

Total General and Administrative
Expenses                                                 3,386.54

Net Profit (Loss) from Operations                ($ 2,521.97)

BLACK ENTERPRISE, INC.

Exhibit IX

# FOUR BROTHERS TRUCKING COMPANY, INC.

Statement of Operations for the period September 1 — September 30, 1970

| | | |
|---|---:|---:|
| Income from Trucking | | $12,460.87 |
| Direct Operating Costs: | | |
| Freight In | $ 5.59 | |
| Uniforms | 189.21 | |
| Truck Repairs and Maintenance | 898.87 | |
| Gasoline and Oil | 998.78 | |
| Weights | 63.60 | |
| Tolls | 339.65 | |
| License and Registration | 50.00 | |
| Storage and Moving Supplies | 1,310.04 | |
| Insurance | 121.50 | |
| Truck and Trailer Rentals | 560.66 | |
| Labor | 3,396.61 | |
| Depreciation on Trucks and Building | 1,335.48 | |
| Amortization Expense — Hand Trucks | 33.46 | |
| Casual Labor | 363.58 | |
| Refunds and Claims | 262.10 | |
| Total Direct Operating Costs | | 9,929.13 |
| Gross Profit on Operations | | $ 2,531.74 |

General and Administrative Expenses:

| | | |
|---|---|---|
| Organizational Expenses | 61.73 | |
| Office Supplies | 142.51 | |
| Professional Fees | 927.96 | |
| Miscellaneous Expenses | 33.74 | |
| Telephone Company | 600.00 | |
| Depreciation — Office Equipment | 8.75 | |
| Bank Charges | 6.60 | |
| Interest Expenses | 742.41 | |
| Advertisement | 15.00 | |
| Association — Union Dues | 80.00 | |
| Maintenance Repairs | 21.29 | |
| Penalty | 37.33 | |
| Total General and Administrative Expenses | | 2,677.32 |
| Net Profit (Loss) from Operations | | ($ 145.58) |

Exhibit X

# FOUR BROTHERS TRUCKING COMPANY, INC.

Statement of Operations for the period October 1 – October 31, 1970

| | | |
|---|---:|---:|
| Income from Trucking | | $14,900.55 |
| Direct Operating Costs: | | |
| Tires and Equipment | $1,000.00 | |
| Uniforms | 140.61 | |
| Truck Repairs and Maintenance | 715.98 | |
| Gasoline and Oil | 1,222.48 | |
| Weights | 22.00 | |
| Tolls | 217.02 | |
| Insurance | 644.33 | |
| Truck and Trailer Rentals | 1,311.47 | |
| Labor | 5,895.91 | |
| Depreciation on Trucks and Building | 1,335.48 | |
| Amortization Expense – Hand Trucks, etc. | 33.46 | |
| Casual Labor | 57.05 | |
| Refunds and Claims | 757.54 | |
| Total Direct Operating Costs | | 13,353.33 |
| Gross Profit on Operations | | $ 1,547.22 |
| General and Administrative Expenses: | | |
| Sales Taxes Expense | 27.30 | |
| Organizational Expenses | 61.73 | |
| Utilities | 99.11 | |
| Office Supplies | 41.68 | |
| Miscellaneous Expenses | 1.55 | |
| Telephone Company | 210.42 | |
| Depreciation – Office Equipment | 8.75 | |
| Bank Charges | 4.75 | |
| Interest Expenses | 749.99 | |
| Advertisement | 12.62 | |
| Maintenance and Repairs | 14.86 | |
| Real Estate Taxes | 526.01 | |
| Payroll Taxes | 245.06 | |
| Total General and Administrative Expenses | | 2,003.83 |
| Net Profit (Loss) from Operations | | ($ 456.61) |

## Exhibit XI

## FOUR BROTHERS TRUCKING COMPANY, INC.

Proposal for Additional Funding and Managerial
Assistance
January 25, 1971

### General Information

Four Brothers is a moving and storage company located at
244 Howard Avenue. The company provides the service of moving
and storage to households, the military, and commercial businesses.

In August of 1969, a proposal was made to us for funds. In
October of 1969, a final proposal was presented. The proposal
asked for funds to enable Four Brothers to relocate and expand
its operations. In January 1970, the proposal was approved authorizing a loan of $66,500. In May 1970, the corporation also
acquired a $25,000 loan from the bank.

### Purpose of the Proposal

The purpose of this proposal is to request $58,500 in additional
financial assistance and additional managerial assistance to Four
Brothers. Additional funds are required for two purposes. These
purposes are the following:

1. To reduce present short-term debt.
2. To increase the working capital position.

Additional managerial assistance is required to provide a conservative, businesslike element to the management team which already
exists.

### Nature and Background of the Business

ADDITIONAL FUNDS. Additional funds of the amount of
$58,500 are required to undo some of the wrongs of the past and
set a firm foundation for the future.

Specifically, the company was undercapitalized from the very
beginning. The original proposal to us requested a $147,168.00

BLACK ENTERPRISE, INC.

loan. Subsequently, this amount was shaved to $91,500 with $25,000 of this amount coming from the bank.

Expected sales figures were bloated and did not take into consideration the lack of the Public Service Commission license.

Insufficient working capital was provided for dealing with the long collection period of accounts receivable and the falling short of projected sales. In short, no "safety margin" was included in the original proposal. Slow accounts receivable collections for work done as an agent of Paul Van Lines has greatly aggravated the cash flow situation.

ADDITIONAL MANAGERIAL ASSISTANCE. Additional managerial assistance in the form of the power for us to approve or disapprove capital budgeting decisions is needed. It is felt that many unwise capital budgeting decisions were made by Four Brothers. At a time of prosperity when sales and net profit were high, it is a fact the company continuously plowed money back into the business in the form of additional trucks, trailers, and equipment. No provision was made to meet tax charges as well as for providing a cash cushion for the slack season or a downturn in sales. Therefore this proposal is also requesting, besides additional funds, that an agreement be drawn requiring Four Brothers to obtain written consent for any purchase above $1,000. This provision should suffice to aid the partners in developing skills in analyzing capital budgeting decisions.

## Company's Physical Facilities

The physical facilities of the company are in excellent shape. The warehouse and office are kept clean and orderly. The fifteen thousand square feet are off-limits for smoking. The exterior as well as interior are maintained very well.

## Market

The estimated sales volume for the next twelve (12) months is $145,000. For the 12 months of 1970 the company generated over $125,000 in sales.

Through the use of Paul's Interstate Commerce Commission

license rights, Four Brothers can operate on a nation-wide basis. Upon acquisiton of the Massachusetts and Boston Public Service Commission licenses, the company will be able to operate to a greater extent in the local area with larger, commercial accounts.

The large demand for trucking services means that Four Brothers has no problem in finding a market. Due to the quality of its work, the company has built a fine reputation. Unfortunately, the lack of a Public Service Commission license has hindered the company from capitalizing upon the market and its reputation. For example the company lost a very good account when IBM learned that the Public Service Commission license was lacking. Yet Four Brothers' sales figures indicate that it was able to acquire a large volume of work with smaller concerns and households.

During the slack season 90% of Four Brothers' work is military accounts done via Paul. During the trucking season, this percentage falls to 50%. An immediate goal is to reduce this percentage as much as possible due to the slowness of collection for the military accounts.

Presently the company has three main accounts and plans to increase its accounts as the season approaches. Based upon the sales performance of 1970, there is little reason to doubt that the past performance will at least be equalled in 1971.

Breakeven will require gross sales of $10,000 per month. A one-month period is estimated to reach breakeven.


*The Proposal*

CAPITAL REQUIREMENT. To support an estimated sales volume of $145,000 for a projected 12 month period, Four Brothers will need $58,500 to be used as follows:

| | | |
|---|---|---|
| Payment of Officers' back salaries | | $12,000 |
| Reduction of short-term debt | | 21,500 |
| Accounts payable | $14,500 | |
| Taxes | 7,000 | |
| Working capital | | 25,000 |
| Total funds required | | $58,500 |

Exhibit XII

# FOUR BROTHERS TRUCKING COMPANY, INC.

## Statement of Income and Retained Earnings

|  | Nine Months Ended May 31, 1971 | One Month Ended May 31, 1971 |
|---|---|---|
| Income from Trucking | $109,900.25 | $15,977.38 |
| Less: Direct Operating Costs | 63,865.61 | 5,042.95 |
| Gross Profit from Operations | $ 46,034.64 | $10,934.43 |
| Less: General and Administrative Expenses | 19,454.84 | 2,782.60 |
| Net Profit Before Depreciation | 26,579.80 | 8,151.83 |
| Less: Depreciation | 10,833.64 | 672.11 |
| Net Profit | $ 15,746.16 | $ 7,479.72 |
| Retained Earnings, September 1, 1970 | (6,601.84) | |
| Retained Earnings | $  9,144.32 | |

## FOUR BROTHERS TRUCKING COMPANY, INC.

### Balance Sheet as at May 31, 1971

#### Assets

| | | |
|---|---|---|
| **Current Assets:** | | |
| Cash | $  2,224.94 | |
| Accounts Receivable | 8,645.64 | |
| Storage Supplies Inventory | 2,500.00 | |
| Total Current Assets | | $ 13,370.58 |
| **Fixed Assets:** | | |
| Land | 15,000.00 | |
| Building | 70,830.00 | |
| Rolling Stock | 89,007.92 | |
| Office Equipment | 498.30 | |
| Miscellaneous Equipment | 4,204.01 | |
| | 179.540.23 | |
| Less: Accumulated Depreciation | 20,740.02 | |
| Total Fixed Assets | | 158,800.21 |
| **Other Assets:** | | |
| Security Deposits | 500.00 | |
| Due from Officers | 20,262.40 | |
| Prepaid Expenses | 10,871.32 | |
| Deferred Interest | 32,091.12 | |
| Organization Expense | 3,208.28 | |
| Total Other Assets | | 66,933.12 |
| Total Assets | | $239.103.91 |

Liabilities and Stockholders' Equity

Current Liabilities:

| | | |
|---|---|---|
| Accounts Payable | $29,011.03 | |
| Taxes Payable | 6,045.09 | |
| Notes Payable | 14,409.80 | |
| Mortgage Payable | 8,376.00 | |
| Total Current Liabilities | | $ 57,841.92 |

Long-Term Liabilities:

| | | |
|---|---|---|
| CBDO | 66,608.26 | |
| Notes Payable | 32,803.41 | |
| Mortgage Payable | 67,706.00 | |
| Total Long-Term Liabilities | | 167,117.67 |
| Total Liabilities | | 224,959.59 |

Stockholders' Equity:

| | | |
|---|---|---|
| Capital Stock | 5,000.00 | |
| Retained Earnings | 9,144.32 | |
| Total Stockholders' Equity | | 14,144.32 |
| Total Liabilities and Stockholders' Equity | | $239,103.91 |

# 10

# LARRY'S RADIO AND TV SERVICE

## PROLOGUE

Larry's Radio and TV Service is the story of a black television repairman who had worked twelve years for a white-owned TV and radio repair shop for $100 per week. Finally, when the white owner was forced to retire and sell the operation in 1970, Larry turned to a San Francisco CBDO for money to buy the business, as well as for money to expand its operations.

The CBDO, in this case, was a non-profit corporation organized by community residents for the total development of their neighborhood. While the concept of total development embraces many areas, this CBDO decided to concentrate on meeting the area's need for business development.

This CBDO was organized in 1968 by community leaders with experiences in politics, civil rights, and poverty programs. The board of directors was self-elected, though in a move to be representative, it numbered more than forty members. Operating authority rested with the executive director, who, in turn, supervised financial consultants charged with economic development and feasibility studies. He directed all requests for assistance to a consultant who analyzed them and developed loan packages. Once approved by a CBDO finance committee, the loan package was returned to the consultant for implementation.

Larry's Radio and TV Service represented one more in a large number of companies that the CBDO had assisted. Its other projects included a rubber-molding plant, a janitorial service, several food franchises, and an automobile dealership.

# THE CASE

## Introduction

On May 28, 1970, at the San Francisco CBDO headquarters, Larry Holmes signed a contract transferring the ownership of P.K. Radio and Television Service from Mr. and Mrs. Krescent to himself. (See Exhibit I on page 324 for a copy of the sales agreement.) Present at the ceremony were Mr. and Mrs. Holmes; Abe Mavin, the CBDO consultant; Ron Haunt, the CBDO general counsel; and the Krescents' attorney. Immediately after the signing of the papers, the group went to the TV store, where Larry removed the P.K. Radio and TV sign. At last Larry had realized his lifelong dream of owning his own business. He said: "It has been a long time coming, but at last I have done it."

A year later Larry was back at the CBDO headquarters asking Mavin for additional financing to buy two other small television repair stores available in his neighborhood. He reasoned that since his own shop had been successful, acquiring two more shops would eliminate competition and increase his income. As he put it: "Larry's numbers two and three will give me a monopoly in the neighborhood, as well as provide more good service to the community."

Mavin told Larry that he was not enthusiastic about these expansion plans since he was "not certain that the first repair shop is fully operational." He thought that Larry should continue to concentrate on the current operations instead of "spreading himself too thin." However, he could not refute Larry's argument that he had "come a long way" and that the two new stores seemed to be profitable and were available under the same terms as the first shop. However, Mavin did remember some of the initial difficulties experienced by Larry and wondered "whether the CBDO would really be doing Larry a disservice by assisting him to acquire two more stores."

## Background

In his first visit to the CBDO in August 1969, Larry described himself as a typical black man who had been "working hard all my life, but always for someone else." Born in Oakland in 1932, he spent the first nine years of his life in that city. In 1941 his father, a laborer, moved the family first to Compton, and three years later to San Francisco, as he chased employment opportunities resulting from World War II.

Larry attended junior high school in San Francisco, where he describes his grades as "fair." Later, as a student in a vocational high school, he developed an interest in electronics and began reading books on the subject. However, because he was black, he did not think the electrical engineering was a realizable goal. In fact, he was advised by his high school guidance counselor to "seek something practical" like radio repair. When he graduated from high school in 1950, he looked for a job in the newly developing field of television repair, but a few months of job hunting convinced him that he was unlikely to find a job. He said that despite his schoolwork, "employers didn't feel that a black man had the desire or the ability to be given a position as a TV repairman."

Finally, in October 1950, "out of desperation" he went to the California State Employment Office and secured a job as a shipping clerk with Apex Knitting Mills. During his seven years with that firm he never advanced beyond that entry-level job, but did not give up his dream of becoming a TV repairman. He also attended night school to further his capabilities in the TV repair field and attempted, unsuccessfully, to get a job as television repairman.

In 1957, at the age of twenty-five and married with two children, Larry indicated that he was ready "to throw in the towel." Fortunately, he had had one night school teacher who wanted to help him get a job in the TV repair field. In July of 1957, his instructor, Jack Silverstein, introduced Larry to Chuck Krescent, owner of P.K. Radio and TV Service. This introduction eventually led to Larry's getting a job with Krescent in December 1957.

In his early months at P.K. Television, Larry had several difficulties with Krescent, as the latter assumed that Larry was not efficient and would not work hard. According to Larry, "During that first year, Krescent watched me closely and allowed me to only make service calls and do light bench work." Later Krescent developed enough confidence in Larry to allow him to open and close the shop and make major repairs. However, he never allowed Larry to see the firm's books and never taught him anything about the administrative or financial end of the business. As a result,

Larry was dissatisfied with his job since he felt that he was doing most of the work. Also he was not to receive an increase above his starting salary of $80 per week for several years.

Because of his dissatisfaction with the lack of opportunity with Krescent, Larry continued to look for better jobs and took countless federal and state examinations to qualify for jobs. However, he never actually took another job because he wanted to operate his own shop. This goal was reinforced by Krescent's constant indication that he was ready for retirement and would be looking for someone to take over his business. Larry believed that Krescent's desire to retire was being hastened by an increasingly militant attitude of the black population which had translated itself into several robbery attempts at P.K. Radio and TV Service.

Despite Krescent's advancing age and his fear of changing community attitudes, he never really made an actual commitment to sell to Larry. So, after twelve years of waiting, Larry decided in 1969 to leave Krescent and take another job, even if it meant "sorting mail in the post office." He said that "a thirty-seven-year-old man had to stop dreaming and look for security." Apparently Krescent sensed this change in Larry's attitude and offered in July 1969 to sell the store to Larry or "the highest bidder." For the first time, Larry realized that he had no money to make an offer for the business and that he "had been a fool to ever think of going for myself." One last hope rested with a local CBDO which advertised that it was interested in assisting minority residents to buy businesses owned by non-residents.

### Larry and the CBDO

Larry had heard that the CBDO was interested in helping aspiring black businessmen to set up their own operations, and so, reluctantly, he went there in August 1969 and told Abe Mavin, a financial consultant, that he wanted to buy out Krescent and operate the business himself. He pointed out that he had worked for Krescent for twelve years and had learned how to operate the business in that period. In addition, he stated that the fact that he had passed many civil service examinations for radio and TV repair attested to his competence.

Mavin, who had studied accounting at UCLA and had considerable experience in assisting budding entrepreneurs, listened to

Larry's story and believed that the latter's purchase of the TV repair shop would be good for the community. Before preparing a proposal, however, Mavin checked Larry's references and secured a credit check on Larry and his wife. Both checks indicated that Larry was a good risk.

After determining that Larry was a reasonably good risk, Mavin took a detailed look at the business to determine "if the purchase made economic sense and the level of funding which would be required." Because Krescent's books were "in extremely poor shape," Mavin decided that Larry should only purchase the assets of the business at their market value. Initially, Krescent wanted an amount above the market value of the assets, but finally admitted that there were no competing buyers and that he would accept a fair market value.

Mavin prepared a proposal for Larry's Radio and TV Service, Inc., and presented it to the CBDO finance committee on September 5, 1969 (see Exhibit II on pages 325–327 for a summary of Mavin's proposal). He explained that Larry had been employed for twelve years by Krescent, who was now willing to sell the assets of the business for $2,000. He indicated that the business was viable, and that it had been in the community for thirty years with an established clientele. He pointed out that the over-all package was to cost the CBDO $3,500 with the balance to come from a commercial bank. He also mentioned that he had enrolled Larry in a business management workshop which was being held at a local community college.

From September 1969 through March 1970, Larry along with Mavin, visited several banks, attempting to raise the additional $3,500. During that same period, he contacted a lawyer to begin incorporation procedures and began becoming more involved in the operations of the TV repair store. In February Mavin sent Larry the following letter regarding enrollment in a seminar on business development:

February 6, 1970

Dear Larry:

This is to announce we are cooperating with the City in conducting a special seminar for minority-group businessmen on February 18th (7–10 P.M.) at the Brotherhood-In-Action Building.

This seminar will cover the subject of Employee Relations. Special topics to be discussed are: government-subsidized job training programs and the practical politics of hard-core labor economics.

The panelists will include: William F. Brooks, President of Ring Binders Inc.; Mary Z. Jones, Specialist in Employee Relations for AT&T; and Staff Consultants on Labor Relations from the State School of Labor and Industrial Relations.

Please complete and mail the attached self-addressed post card not later than February 12th. You may also register Mrs. Holmes if you so desire.

For additional information on registration please contact me.

Yours truly,<br>
Abraham Mavin

According to Mavin, "the objective of the seminar was to stimulate and train minority-group men with potential to open and expand growing businesses."

Also in February, Mavin had informed Larry's lawyer, Willie Williams, that it would be necessary for him to submit certain documents before a closing could be held. However, as late as March 27, Williams' secretary advised Larry that he still had not been able to begin work on Larry's papers because he was working on a time-consuming court case. Since Williams was an old family friend and the only lawyer Holmes knew, he was somewhat reluctant about changing lawyers as Mavin advised. When Williams finally found time to submit the documents, the CBDO finance committee was again raising the question as to whether Larry had sufficient funds to start a business.

The finance committee had ruled earlier that Larry would have to raise a matching $3,500 before it would release its funds. This issue became even more crucial in April when a CBDO consultant indicated that after his close examination of the business, additional funds that *were not* included in the September 1969 proposal would be needed for repairs, renovations, and rubbish removal.

Because of this growing concern for the level of funding required, the CBDO finance committee advised Mavin to secure additional funds for Larry. Over a two-week period at the end of April Mavin sent the following letter to several banks in the community where Larry's shop would be located:

Dear Sir:

Mr. Larry Holmes is a local resident who is being given financial assistance through our Business Development Program.

We are only able to offer him $3,500, though his needs are defined as approximately $7,000. Hopefully, you can be of assistance in his efforts to get the additional funds to be used as working capital. If you would let me know who Mr. Holmes could contact at your office regarding a loan, I would be most grateful.

Thank you for your cooperation in this matter.

With best regards,
Abraham Mavin


Unfortunately, in each instance the contacted banks would not assist Larry because of the neighborhood or the riskiness of the business. Fortunately for Larry, Mavin was able to convince the CBDO finance committee that there would be sufficient funds to operate the business once the place was "whipped into shape."

In order to remove part of the financial burden from Larry, Mavin convinced the finance committee to absorb some of Larry's renovation and start-up costs. The finance committee agreed to pay for Larry's sign and with the following letter contracted with a local builder to repair and renovate the store:

May 12, 1970

Acme Builders
San Francisco, California
Gentlemen:

This letter constitutes our agreement that you will provide all the materials and equipment and perform all the labor for the painting of the outside front, the iron bar rails and the interior, including the ceiling and benches, of the premises being purchased by Larry Holmes.

The work to be performed pursuant to this agreement shall be completed by June 12, 1970. It is understood that TIME is the essence of this agreement.

It is further understood that your work shall be performed in a workmanlike manner.

We will pay you the sum of $820.00 upon completion of the work contemplated in this agreement.

If you find this letter agreeable, please sign the original and return it to me, retaining the attached copy for your files. If you have any questions regarding this letter, please feel free to contact Mr. Mavin.

> Very truly yours,
> Obie Rhodes, Chairman
> CBDO Finance Committee

With these items under control the CBDO finance committee gave its final approval on the loan and the store changed hands in late May.

### Operations

Mavin told Larry that before he could begin to operate the store, he would have to make it attractive so that people would bring their radios and televisions to him for repair. Mavin felt that "people equated the way a shop looked with the kind of work it did." Larry agreed wholeheartedly with Mavin that the first order of business had to be "getting the store shipshape." Larry said, "I know if I had a television to be repaired, I certainly would not take it to a shabby-looking place."

In order to assist him in getting a presentable shop, Larry organized volunteers from his church to clean out the store, which contained a ten-year accumulation of rubbish. According to Larry, soon after the church meeting on June 6, Mavin, "nattily attired in his Edwardian suit, drove up to the front of my store, reached in the trunk of his Jaguar and pulled out a pair of green coveralls and disappeared inside the store. He donned the coveralls and began to clean out the junk." It took the group four days, working twelve hours a day, to clean out the store. The next day Acme Builders completed the renovation work.

Mavin felt that once the decorations were complete, the next step would be to set up an accounting system tailored specifically for Larry's needs. Larry stated that even though he had worked for P.K. Radio and TV twelve years, he had "never been shown the books or how they worked" and he wanted very much to learn about that operation. He said, "That is the real backbone of the business." Mavin suggested that Larry also get a federal identification number and learn how to fill out the various tax forms and how to reconcile his bank account. He set up accounting and billing systems specifically tailored for Larry, showed Larry how to operate the systems and how the information would be useful to him in running an efficient business. He also took Larry to the bank to make sure that his bank deposit slips were filled out correctly, and introduced him to the branch manager.

In the remainder of June and much of July, Mavin kept a constant check on the condition of Larry's new business. He visited the store at least once a week and counseled Larry on the techniques necessary to ensure efficiency and profitability in his operation. Of equal importance, Larry recognized the difficulties that he would encounter, and he grew to trust and welcome Mavin's suggestions. He said, "I've been trained as a repairman, and recognize that I do not know anything about the financial end of running a repair shop, but Mr. Mavin does and I can learn from him." With Mavin, Larry reviewed the financial information available from the previous owner. Larry felt that sales could be improved. Prior to his taking over the store, it was open from 9:30 A.M. to 5:30 P.M. five days a week. He decided to extend the hours of the store from 9:00 A.M. to 7:30 P.M., six days a week, reasoning that the additional hours would increase sales since most blacks did not get home until six o'clock.

Larry modified his operation so that someone would be in the shop at all times. He knew that the busiest times were in the afternoon and evenings and he had his wife handle the shop while he was away on service calls. Some days, when his wife had other things to take care of, his sons would man the store, receiving sets to be repaired and returning those that had been fixed. In this way, Larry said he "was able to keep labor cost down, thus allowing the store to become profitable almost immediately." (See Exhibit III on pages 328–330 for a summary of Larry's financial condition during his store's first year of operation.)

### The Future of Larry's Radio and TV Service

In June 1971 Larry reviewed his first year in business and noted with satisfaction that he had almost made a profit. He said, "They say the first year is the hardest and I have just come through it, and I intend to hang in and keep swinging." Later, he said that he wanted to expand his current operations to include a whole music

BLACK ENTERPRISE, INC.

section: tape recorders, phonographs, and cartridges. In addition, he indicated he wanted "to put appliances in his store since there is not one *black* place in the neighborhood selling them." While he knew that it would take some time, he wanted to "pay off my loan as soon as possible" and have his boys come in the business with him. He reasoned, that way he would not only be able to run the first store, but one or two more as well: "I could run this store and let my oldest son run the other store. All of the repair work could be done at one location and the pickup work could be done by one person. This way we could really begin a chain of TV and radio shops and young men out of high school could learn a good trade and have a future. Of course, I will need more money, since initially I will have cash flow problems, but I could go back to the CBDO and ask for additional financial assistance and of course get Mr. Mavin to come out and help us lay this thing out correctly."

On June 9, he met with Mavin to arrange the financing for the addition of the two new stores. After hearing Larry's view on expansion, Mavin began to consider whether he could take a new proposal to the CBDO finance committee.

## EPILOGUE

On June 16, 1971, Mavin stopped by to see Larry Holmes and told him that he had "decided not to recommend additional financing for the two new stores at the present time." He indicated that Larry should gain additional management experience in the running of one operation and suggested that he take courses in management "since the management of three stores is totally different from the management of one."

Mavin pointed out, for example, that Larry's inventory and accounting systems were tailored specifically to his needs at the one store and to "add two stores would mean a need for a new system which might create some difficulties since [Larry] was not fully familiar with the present system." Mavin also pointed out that Larry's operating procedures would be affected since he would be going into an unfamiliar area where he was not fully known and would have a difficult time establishing a rapport with new customers. In addition, Mavin saw a substantial increase in the need for planning, since with three stores, Larry would not be able to operate on an "as-needed basis."

Finally Mavin said that he wanted Larry to spend the "next six months to a year upgrading skills in accounting, merchandising, and management." In the meantime, Larry would also be gaining additional seasoning in the operation of his business and would be able to deal with some problems on his own. In addition, Larry would be in a position to save his own funds for investment in the new ventures.

According to Mavin:

Although Larry agreed to go along with me, I could tell by his expression that he was disappointed. But he finally said, "Knowing you, Abe, I know that you would only do what you thought best for me. It is hard to accept what you said, but I know that you are right." Later that day, he called to inform him that he had enrolled in a management course at the local technical institute.

You know, Larry is one of the hardest-working and easiest guys in the world to work with. Everything I suggested he went along with without putting up a fight even though there were times when I knew that he did not agree. Of course, the hardest time was when I suggested that he should not develop the two additional stores and he had his heart set on it.

Sometimes, though, I think he depended on me too much. For this reason I could not in good conscience recommend that he start two additional stores since I had no idea how he would function when left on his own. I was glad that he took my advice and enrolled in some management courses. But with the added courses under his belt and the experience of running the business on his own, I would feel justified in recommending his firm for additional financing—especially since in the interim months he would be able to save a few hundred dollars himself. On the other hand, had I not strongly urged him to gain some additional experience and training and he had gone into the other two shops, everything that we had accomplished together might have been wiped out. And we would have lost a good man. If I had it to do all over again, I would have no hesitation about going with Larry as a businessman.

In July 1971, after Mavin had ceased to visit Larry on a regular basis, Larry reported:

I dreamed that one day I would own a radio and TV store. In fact, I had gotten up in my thirties and it looked like I would be a TV repairman all my life. It's bad to say, but if old man Krescent hadn't gotten ill, I probably never would have attempted to start my own business.

But my problems were just beginning, for I didn't know anything about running a business. I had never been allowed to see the books; all I knew was about fixing radios and TV sets. But the local development corporation (CBDO) really helped me. They lent me the money to buy the place since no bank would and they also helped me fix the place up and learn how to operate the business.

Somebody from the CBDO was there to help me any time I had a problem but I think I depended on him too much. It was only after I had requested additional assistance to start two additional stores about a year ago and was turned down that I realized that Abe had given me some good advice when he said that I should get myself on firm ground. Had I tried to operate two additional stores when I first approached the CBDO, I would probably have had problems.

If I had it to do all over again, I would still do it, because that is the only way we are going to have anything. We must start businesses and then our children can take them over. That's what the whites do.

Exhibit I

## P.K. RADIO AND TELEVISION SERVICE
## AND
## LARRY'S RADIO AND TELEVISION SERVICE, INC.

Sales Agreement

Agreement made this 16th day of May 1970, by and between Chuck Krescent, doing business under the name of P.K. Radio and Television Service, of the City of San Francisco, State of California, to be called the Seller, and Larry's Radio and Television Service, Inc., to be called the Buyer;

### WITNESSETH

WHEREAS, the Seller agrees to sell to the Buyer, and the Buyer agrees to buy from the Seller the radio and television repair business heretofore operated by the Seller under the name and title of P.K. Radio and Television Service.

Now THEREFORE, in consideration of the sum of Two Thousand ($2,000) Dollars paid by the Buyer to the Seller, receipt of which is acknowledged hereby, the Seller agrees to convey to the Buyer, free of debt, and with all inventory, fixtures and equipment, the business heretofore operated under the name of P.K. Radio and Television Service.

The Seller acknowledges and agrees that the Buyer will not be liable or responsible for any debts incurred prior to this contract as a result of the operation of the business unless such liability or responsibility is herein specifically assumed. Seller further agrees to indemnify the Buyer, and hold him harmless from and against any debts so incurred by the Seller while doing business under the name of P.K. Radio and Television Service.

Seller: _____
                    Chuck Krescent
Buyer: _____
                    Larry Holmes

## Exhibit II

## LARRY'S RADIO AND TV SERVICE, INC.

### September 5, 1969
### Proposal B-47

This is a proposal to assist Mr. Larry Holmes, who is presently employed by the P.K. Radio and Television Service. Mr. Chuck Krescent, the owner of P.K. Radio and Television Service, is willing to sell the complete business for $2,000.00. Mr. Holmes would like to purchase this business that has been in the community for 30 years and has an established clientele. To make the purchase, Mr. Holmes will need $7,000.

P.K. Radio and Television Service has been located at its present location for the past ten years. Prior to moving to its present address, it was located across the street for 20 years. Mr. Krescent has been able to earn a comfortable living from the business over a 30-year period, indicating that his net profit for 1968 was $3,808.56. There is no reason for this business not to maintain or increase this net profit under the ownership of Mr. Holmes.

Mr. Holmes has 12 years' experience in the business, all of which have been with P.K. Radio and Television Service. Below is a brief employment record of Mr. Holmes:

Age: 39                   Marital Status: Married—two children

Work Experience:

1957 to Present     P.K. Radio and Television Service—
                            Repairman

1950 to 1957         Apex Knitting Mills—Shipping Clerk

The business employs two full-time persons. When Mr. Holmes purchases the business, he will hire one other person at a salary of $100.00 per week, his present salary.

To purchase the P.K. Radio and Television Service, Mr. Holmes will need $7,000 to be used as follows:

| | | |
|---|---|---|
| Cash Selling Price | $2,000.00 | (See attachment A) |
| Renovation and Organizational Cost | $1,500.00 | (See attachment B) |
| Working Capital | $3,500.00 | |
| | $7,000.00 | |

## Attachment A
### PK Radio & Television Service
### Assets to be Sold to Larry Holmes
### Value as of July 31, 1969

| | | |
|---|---|---:|
| 1500 | Radio & TV Tubes | $1,500.00 |
| 100 | Pilot Lamps | 10.00 |
| | Car Antennas & Staffs | 10.00 |
| | Portable TV Antennas | 15.00 |
| 20 | Rabbit Ear Antennas | 50.00 |
| 15 | Speakers & Baffles | 50.00 |
| 5 | CRT Brighteners | 7.00 |
| | Assorted Electrical Home Lamps, Fuses and Roll Wire | 60.00 |
| 150 | TV Fuses | 20.00 |
| | Extension Cords | 10.00 |
| 15 | 45 Hi-fi Adapters | 20.00 |
| 100 ft. | 300 ohm Lead-in Wire | 10.00 |
| | Assorted Wire | 15.00 |
| | Assorted Radio Batteries | 100.00 |
| | Assorted Hi-fi Stereo Carts | 150.00 |
| | Assorted Hi-fi Needles | 50.00 |
| | Assorted Resistors & Conditioners | 50.00 |
| | Assorted Crystal Mikes | 25.00 |
| | Radio & TV Knobs | 15.00 |
| | Rectifiers | 10.00 |
| 20 | Ear Plugs | 10.00 |
| | Radio & TV Schematics | 50.00 |
| 2 | TV Carriers | 25.00 |
| 2 | TV Tables | 10.00 |
| 2 | Power Amplifiers | 20.00 |
| | Willard 10 Battery Charge with 2 Batteries | 50.00 |
| | Volt ohm Meter & Caddy | 15.00 |
| | CRT Lester | 5.00 |
| | Single Generator | 25.00 |
| | Simpson V ohm Meter | 25.00 |
| | Vacuum Tube Volt Meter | 35.00 |
| | RCA Volt ohm Meter | 30.00 |
| | Dumont Scope | 100.00 |
| | Precision Tube Checker Counter | 100.00 |

$2,677.00

3    Work Tables and 1 Counter
2    Wall TV Bin Storage
1    Wall Shelves for Tubes, etc.
1    National Cash Register
     Front Iron Gates & Window Gates
2    Floor 4-door Metal Cabinets
1    Square Metal Storage Cabinet
2    Small Metal Boxes
     Phono Charger Repair Rack
     Fluorescent Fixtures
2    TV Couplers
2    Solder Guns
     Linoleum & Tools


## Attachment B
### Larry's Radio & TV Service
### Renovation and Organizational Cost

| | |
|---|---:|
| Sign | $ 250.00 |
| Telephone Deposit | 100.00 |
| Legal Fees | 300.00 |
| Accounting Fees | 100.00 |
| Painting | 200.00 |
| Carpentry | 200.00 |
| Electrical | 100.00 |
| Total | $1,250.00 |

## Exhibit III
## LARRY'S RADIO AND TELEVISION SERVICE

### Statement of Income — Twelve Months Ended May 31, 1971

| | | |
|---|---:|---:|
| Gross Income | | $16,680.50 |
| Cost of Goods Sold: | | |
|   Beginning Inventory | $2,007.52 | |
|   Purchases | 5,386.71 | |
|   Inventory Available for Sale | 7,394.23 | |
|   Less Ending Inventory | 1,962.37 | |
| Cost of Goods Sold | | 5,431.86 |
| Gross Profit | | $11,248.64 |
| General and Administrative Expenses: | | |
|   Payroll Taxes | 148.80 | |
|   Car Repairs | 128.14 | |
|   Office Supplies | 6.06 | |
|   Professional Fees | 175.00 | |
|   Labor (Officers) | 6,066.60 | |
|   Telephone | 108.61 | |
|   Postage and Stationery | 63.62 | |
|   Maintenance and Repairs | 333.24 | |
|   Deferred Interest | 285.68 | |
|   Auto Expense | 252.84 | |
|   Casual Labor | 220.00 | |
|   Utilities | 99.14 | |
|   Rent | 1,235.00 | |
|   Bank Charges | 11.14 | |
|   Sales Taxes Expenses | 936.03 | |
|   Depreciation | 648.32 | |
|   Insurance | 144.72 | |
|   Advertisement | 5.00 | |
|   Organization Expenses | 424.00 | |
|   Refunds | 2.85 | |
|   Taxes | 52.17 | |
|   Misc. Expenses | 54.47 | |
|   Total General and Administrative Expenses | | 11,401.43 |
| Net Profit (Loss) | | ($ 152.79) |

BLACK ENTERPRISE, INC.

# LARRY'S RADIO AND TELEVISION SERVICE

## Balance Sheet May 31, 1971

### Assets

| | | |
|---|---|---|
| **Current Assets:** | | |
| Cash on Hand | $ 139.21 | |
| Cash in Bank | 783.15 | |
| Inventories | 1,962.37 | |
| Total Current Assets | | $2,884.73 |
| **Fixed Assets:** | | |
| Furniture and Fixtures | 990.00 | |
| Equipment | 500.00 | |
| Automobile | 1,616.50 | |
| | 3,106.50 | |
| Less: Accumulated Depreciation | 648.32 | |
| Total Fixed Assets | | 2,458.18 |
| **Other Assets:** | | |
| Due from Officers | 620.60 | |
| Security Deposits | 270.00 | |
| Deferred Interest | 171.68 | |
| Prepaid Insurance | 279.28 | |
| Total Other Assets | | 1,341.56 |
| Total Assets | | $ 6,684.47 |

## Liabilities and Stockholders' Equity

| | | |
|---|---|---|
| **Current Liabilities:** | | |
| Payroll Taxes Payable | $ 390.90 | |
| Notes Payable — Automobile | 666.84 | |
| Notes Payable — CBDO | 720.00 | |
| Sales Taxes Payable | 264.11 | |
| Total Current Liabilities | | $ 2,041.85 |
| **Long-Term Liabilities:** | | |
| Notes Payable — Automobile | 333.42 | |
| Notes Payable — CBDO | 2,360.00 | |
| Total Long-Term Liabilities | | 2,693.42 |
| Total Liabilities | | 4,735.27 |
| **Stockholders' Equity:** | | |
| Common Stock | 2,102.00 | |
| Retained Earnings (Loss) | (152.80) | |
| Total Stockholders' Equity | | 1,949.20 |
| Total Liabilities and Stockholders' Equity | | $6,684.47 |

# 11

## ABC SHOE STORE

ABC Shoe Store is the case study of a black employee who purchased a high-fashion Harlem men's shoe store from his white employer. After using almost $3,500 of the CBDO's funds to buy the store in June 1970, he decided to invest some of his earnings in several other ventures after only two months of operation. The issue facing the Harlem CBDO in April 1971 was whether to continue to assist this entrepreneur who had misused the store's and the CBDO's funds.

The Harlem CBDO was organized in June 1968 with the purpose of "seeking to ameliorate the poor conditions of blacks living in the Harlem community." A first priority of the CBDO was to increase economic development opportunities. As a result, it raised funds in the community to provide the initial capital for blacks interested in starting business. Later, it received funds from the Model Cities Program.

The CBDO's governing body was a twenty-five-member board of directors, fifteen of whom were elected directly by community organizations. The remaining ten board positions were filled by persons with professional and technical skills selected by the fifteen elected directors. The CBDO also had an advisory board composed of persons from the business community and technical assistance organizations.

All requests for funds were reviewed by members of the business development staff who reported to an executive director. All loan packages were submitted to the board of directors for their approval. If approved, the loan was reassigned to the same staff member, who was expected to provide management assistance to the venture.

ABC Shoes was one of the first retail businesses that the CBDO had assisted. Previously it had only assisted a few manufacturers and large service businesses in an attempt to create large-scaled viable enterprises.

## THE CASE

*Introduction*

After several months of working with Tommy Mann, the owner of the ABC Shoe Store, Henry Hollas of the Harlem CBDO had decided "to take some radical action." Hollas, a young black graduate of a leading Midwestern business school, had been a local business developer for the CBDO for almost two years. Before that he had worked with Sun Oil Company in Philadelphia. He was now "tired of being jerked around" and he was going to "insist that the CBDO board give Mann an additional $18,000" for this shoe store "which was near complete collapse." As he approached the board room in April 1971 he reflected on the events of the past year and wondered if he "was doing the right thing."

*Background*

Tommy Mann was born in Miami, Florida, in 1937 and graduated from high school with a diploma in general studies in 1955. Immediately after graduation, he became a local truck driver. When he turned twenty-one, he decided to become an over-the-road truck driver, picking up trailers loaded with goods in one part of the country and delivering them to another part. While he was able to earn a good salary, he felt that the wages were about 50 per cent higher in New York City. With this in mind, Mann decided to move to Harlem in 1959, where his employer, Bolder Brothers, had an office.

In 1963 he left Bolder Brothers to work for Throws Van Lines. During this period, Mann married and soon regretted that his job kept him away from home for six and eight weeks at a time. Moreover, his wife demanded that he spend more time at home with her and their new baby. In 1966 he left Throws Van Lines to take a job with Nation Van Lines, a regional moving company. At the same time he began to look for a job that would allow him to spend more time at home.

In February 1968 he took a part-time job with a security guard service and agreed to guard the Grim Shoe Store. Robert Grim, the owner, took a liking to Mann and asked him if he "had considered going into the shoe business." Grim stated that he "would pay more money" than Mann was making as a security guard if he would work for him as a salesman. In addition, he agreed to teach Mann the shoe business. Mann agreed to Grim's proposition and went to work as a shoe salesman in September 1968.

The first four months in the store Mann "learned the business so well" that Grim turned the actual operations over to him. After that Grim only "came in on Fridays, Saturdays, and holidays." Mann stated that he "never knew that the shoe business was so lucrative, but once I found out, I liked it."

Grim had had serious problems with break-ins and holdups and felt that he could no longer stand the strain. Finally, in August 1969, he admitted to Mann that he wanted "to get out" and offered to sell the business to Mann.

Mann approached a local bank for a loan in September to purchase the business, but was turned down. Mann stated that he "was shocked by the refusal," since he "had banked there for several years and had purchased a truck through them." Disgruntled and unhappy, Mann saw a television program about an organization in Harlem interested in helping minority businessmen get started by providing financial and management assistance. Mann went to the Harlem CBDO in October where he met Henry Hollas. Hollas outlined the loan program to Mann and gave him the information to be submitted for loan consideration.

Mann took two months gathering this information, finally submitting it to the CBDO in January 1970. Hollas took Mann's data and began an analysis. First, he secured credit information on Mann which showed that there were no judgments outstanding against Mann and verified his employment history. Next, Hollas began to delve into the operations of Grim Shoe Corporation. His primary documents were Grim's 1967 and 1968 federal income tax returns and financial statements for the first eight months of 1969, which appear below:

# GRIM SHOE CORPORATION

## Federal Income Tax Information

|  | 1967 | 1968 |
|---|---|---|
| Gross Receipts or Gross Sales Less Returns and Allowances | $60,950.24 | $66,629.99 |
| Less: Cost of Goods Sold and Operations | 42,529.66 | 44,197.90 |
| Gross Profit | $18,420.58 | $22,432.09 |
| Other Income | 419.01 | 365.26 |
| Total Income | $18,839.59 | $22,797.35 |
| Compensation of Officers | 8,600.00 | 10,600.00 |
| Salaries and Wages | 2,415.00 | 2,415.00 |
| Repairs | 429.87 | 665.22 |
| Rents | 3,300.00 | 3,300.00 |
| Taxes | 1,008.00 | 739.22 |
| Interest | 68.75 | –0– |
| Depreciation | 777.07 | 807.07 |
| Advertising | 1,316.23 | 1,317.83 |
| Other Deductions | 2,731.00 | 2,461.26 |
| Total Deductions | 20,645.92 | 22,305.60 |
| Taxable Income Before Net Operating Loss | $ 1,806.33 | $ 491.75 |

# GRIM SHOE CORPORATION

### Profit and Loss Statement for the Eight Months Ended August 31, 1969

| | | |
|---|---:|---:|
| Sales | $44,780.55 | |
| Less: Sales Allowances | 91.98 | |
| Net Sales | | $44,688.57 |
| Less: Cost of Sales | | 29,415.37 |
| Gross Profit | | $15,273.20 |
| Operating Expenses: | | |
| Salaries and Wages | 7,580.00 | |
| Taxes | 223.00 | |
| Legal and Accounting | 175.00 | |
| Maintenance and Repairs | 368.09 | |
| Insurance | 1,828.41 | |
| Advertising, Stationery, Supplies and Miscellaneous | 993.03 | |
| Telephone and Telegraph | 97.44 | |
| Rent | 2,200.00 | |
| Heat, Light and Power | 359.13 | |
| Depreciation on Automobile | 295.46 | |
| Depreciation on Furniture and Fixtures | 262.57 | |
| Payroll Taxes | 377.22 | |
| Dues and Subscriptions | 15.00 | |
| Total Operating Expenses | | 14,774.35 |
| Net Profit for the Period | | $ 498.85 |

# GRIM SHOE CORPORATION

## Balance Sheet as at August 31, 1969

### Assets

| | | |
|---|---:|---:|
| **Current Assets:** | | |
| Cash in Banks | $ 5,026.82 | |
| Security Deposits | 606.00 | |
| Merchandise Inventory | 16,455.00 | |
| Total Current Assets | | $22,087.82 |
| **Fixed Assets:** | | |
| Furniture and Fixtures | 3,638.69 | |
| Automobile | 2,216.00 | |
| | 5,854.69 | |
| Less: Accumulated Depreciation | 2,722.68 | |
| Total Fixed Assets | | 3,132.01 |
| **Total Assets** | | $ 25,219.83 |

### Liabilities and Capital

| | | |
|---|---:|---:|
| **Liabilities:** | | |
| Sales Tax Payable | $ 1,046.09 | |
| Payroll Taxes Payable | 347.47 | |
| Miscellaneous Accounts Payable | 69.65 | |
| Note Payable | 8,819.70 | |
| Total Liabilities | | $10,282.91 |
| **Capital:** | | |
| Capital Stock | 15,128.82 | |
| Earned Surplus (Deficit) | (690.75) | |
| Income for Period — Eight Months Ended 8/31 | 498.85 | |
| Total Capital | | 14,936.92 |
| **Total Liabilities and Capital** | | $25,219.83 |

BLACK ENTERPRISE, INC.

From his analysis of the above financial information, Hollas saw that annual sales hovered around $60,000 and generated only a small profit, if any. However, Hollas was also aware that in federal income tax statements expenses are often overstated. This idea was confirmed when he noticed that the gross profit margin for Grim's shoes was about 30 per cent rather than the industry average of 40–50 per cent.

With this information Hollas decided to prepare the following *pro forma* income statement, which he felt was more reasonable and which showed the business making a medium-sized profit:

|  | Monthly | Yearly |
|---|---|---|
| Sales | $6,400.00 | $76,800.00 |
| Less: Sales Allowances | 128.00 | 1,536.00 |
| Gross Sales | 6,272.00 | 75,264.00 |
| Cost of Sale | 3,840.00 | 46,080.00 |
| Gross Profit | $2,432.00 | $29,184.00 |
| Operating Expenses: | | |
| Salaries — Owner | 645.00 | 7,740.00 |
| Salesman | 430.00 | 5,160.00 |
| Taxes | 28.00 | 336.00 |
| Cartage | 40.00 | 480.00 |
| Legal and Accounting | 40.00 | 480.00 |
| Insurance | 170.00 | 2,040.00 |
| Advertising, Stat., Supp. and Misc. | 115.00 | 1,380.00 |
| Telephone | 12.00 | 144.00 |
| Rent | 275.00 | 3,300.00 |
| Heat, Light and Power | 58.00 | 696.00 |
| Depreciation — Furniture and Fixtures | 30.00 | 360.00 |
| Small Business Loan Amount | 223.00 | 2,676.00 |
| Payroll Taxes | 59.40 | 712.80 |
| Total Operating Expenses | 2,125.40 | 25,504.80 |
| Net Profit | $ 306.60 | $ 3,679.20 |

With this work completed Hollas was satisfied that it would be "good for the Harlem community to have another black-owned shoe store" and he prepared a preliminary proposal for the CBDO board's consideration at its March 1970 meeting; the CBDO would lend $7,000 of the $28,500 needed. (See Exhibit I on pages 347–349 for a summary of the ABC Shoe Store proposal.) Concurrent with the CBDO board's reviewing the proposal, Hollas sent a copy to the SBA for a 90 per cent guarantee through the bank.

On March 18 the CBDO board met to discuss the funding proposals for the first quarter of the year. Hollas formally presented the Mann proposal to the board, which had received the proposal one week before. He discussed Mann's background and employment history and talked at considerable length about the necessity of "a local black resident buying out a white merchant." The board's most pressing questions concerned Grim Shoe Store's small profits over the 1967–69 period. In response to this inquiry, Hollas explained: "It seems to me that we are making a big unnecessary fuss about this simple matter. It is a well-known fact that proprietors always understate revenues and overstate expenses—especially for income tax reasons. Plus, it is a well-known fact that blacks like good shoes—like Brown shoes. Plus—it is a good opportunity for a black resident. Mr. Mann has been there and knows how much money comes in."

Though not all of the board was convinced, it did give a "tentative approval contingent on the bank and SBA lending at least $21,000." This SBA approval was forthcoming in early May and on May 13, 1970, seven months after Mann had come to the CBDO, the complete loan was approved. But before the deal could be consummated, the CBDO board required that an independent evaluation of the store's inventory be done to establish the purchase price of the inventory.

Hollas arranged to have the Grim Shoe Store's inventory valued by Mr. Al Irons, who had operated a Brown shoe store in Bedford-Stuyvesant for over fifteen years. According to Hollas:

Mr. Irons knew the shoe business well and commanded the respect of Grim and Mann. As a consultant to the CBDO he (1) conducted a detailed inventory of each item in the store; (2) passed on a few helpful suggestions to Mann on changing the arrangement of the merchandise on the shelves; and (3) pointed out that the prices should be coded on the boxes. After compiling a listing of the stock, Mr. Irons priced out the inventory and submitted a report to me on June 3, 1970. His report showed a shoe inventory value of $13,916.68, which Grim sold to Mann on June 4, 1970, along with all of the other assets of the store. Rather than pay Mr. Grim the complete purchase price, I advised Mann to hold an escrow deposit of $2,500 for one year against any contingent liabilities. Mr. Grim agreed to this arrangement and the sale was completed on June 4.


## Operations

Mann took over the ownership of the store on June 5, 1970, though he did not really start selling shoes until June 23. In the meantime, Hollas tried to become familiar with the store's operations and recognized that an information system had to be set up to ensure that Mann knew precisely what was happening on a timely basis. Using Irons' comments as a guide, Hollas had Mann rearrange the shoes and recode each for prices. He also reviewed Grim's accounting system and made minor modifications.

Hollas also saw that the store needed minor renovations and that the carpet was badly in need of cleaning. Since the store was a quality Brown shoe store, Hollas felt that the more attractive the store, the better business would be. Mann agreed and they spent the next two weeks cleaning the store.

The community residents were happy to learn that Mann had bought the Grim Shoe Store and they flowed in and out of the store buying shoes. Mann had earlier developed a knack for selling shoes and he greeted all of his customers warmly and with a smile. Sales for the month of July were $7,136.24 with the store earning a net income of $1,247.53. (See Exhibit II on pages 350–352 for ABC Shoe Store's financial statements.) Hollas attributed these sales to advertising and the grand-opening ceremonies. With so much business, Mann was forced to hire a part-time employee who came in on Fridays and Saturdays to handle the overflow. The part-time salesman had no knowledge of the shoe business, but since he was personable, Mann "felt that he could be trained."

Traditionally, August is a bad month for the shoe business and is normally the time many retailers keep their sales volume high by reducing shoe prices. According to Mann, his operation was "no exception to the rule" as he reported to Hollas in the following short note:

September 10, 1970

Mr. Henry Hollas
CBDO (Harlem)
New York, New York

Dear Henry:

All of the information that you gave me on shoe sales were correct. August is a bad month. During the month my situation was as follows:

| | |
|---|---|
| Net Sales | $5,649.18 |
| Cost of Goods Sale | 2,963.11 |
| Gross Profit | 2,686.07 |
| General and Administrative Expenses | 6,870.57 |
| Net Loss | ($3,815.50) |

Sincerely yours,
Tommy Mann

When Hollas questioned Mann about why he was submitting such an informal financial report, the latter explained that his "accountant was on vacation and had been sick" and he wanted to be sure that the CBDO got "its monthly reports on time."

Upon receiving Mann's September 1970 financial statements in early October (see Exhibit III on pages 353–355) Hollas compared it to the July statement and submitted the following report to the CBDO board:

TO: CBDO Board
FROM: Henry Hollas
SUBJECT: ABC Shoe Store
October 14, 1970

I recently received the attached September 1970 statements from the ABC Shoe Store which we funded in June. Unfortunately, we did not receive an August report from Mr. Mann because his accountant had been sick.

Upon examining the September submission and comparing it with his earlier June/July reports, I identified the following potential problem areas:

1. The Cash in Bank fell from $4,800 to $127.
2. In July there was a Due from Officer's account of $5,300 which has now grown to $8,300. Mr. Mann also shows a Subscription to Stock of $3,000, which suggests that Mr. Mann still has not put his $3,000 into the business.
3. Trade Accounts Payable have grown from $985 to $3,300.
4. Liabilities to the Bank have grown from $23,000 to $27,800.

The CBDO board received Hollas' report and instructed him to "get the facts on this operation before it is too late." Accordingly, Hollas called a meeting with Mann and his accountant, Joe Glass, on October 27. When asked about the financial state of the business, Mann "was very open" and gave the following account:

In July I saw that business was good and that I had lots of idle cash. I took $3,000 from the store and invested it in an after-hours spot, The Haven. The Haven was very close to my store.

It was quite a place to behold. It had a custom-made bar and a pool table. It was well-stocked with liquor and also had a kitchen which served waffles and fried chicken. I thought this was a good investment because it's understood in Harlem that if you keep clean—no numbers or drugs—it usually makes out okay.

Unfortunately, numbers crept into The Haven when I was not there and people stopped coming. I tried to correct this but it is too late. I can't get my customers back and bills are past due.

Also in August, another good deal came up. A buddy offered me a 1968 Cadillac for $2,500 and I couldn't pass it up. I also borrowed this from the business.

Hollas thanked Mann for his "frank explanation" and then asked Glass, the accountant, to voice his opinion. Glass estimated that "to date, about $12,000 has been taken out of the business." He thought that The Haven had "taken considerably more than $3,000" and that there were "several items which cannot be accounted for."

Hollas reported this back to the CBDO board on November 5 and one board member said: "Mann's loan should be called in default since he is obviously trying to defraud us." This recommendation led to a division in the board since several members felt that Mann "should be given a second chance." In support of the latter position, one board member said: "You know the problems that brothers [blacks] have in getting and keeping money. The man [Mann] made an honest mistake and admitted to it. I say give him another chance. The store can make money. Who are we to turn a brother out in the street?" The meeting of the CBDO board ended with the question of Mann and his status being "tabled until a later meeting."

Meanwhile, Mann was having difficulty in getting stock for his store. This was especially crucial because he was approaching the

Christmas season, when he expected the store to do over 25 per cent of its annual sales. Because of his shortage of cash and the rapid build-up of his accounts payable, his suppliers were reluctant to extend credit to the ABC Shoe Store and he was only able to buy a few shoes. The plight of the store's operations is reflected in Mann's October and November 1970 profit and loss statements (Exhibits IV and V on pages 356–357), which show sales of only about $4,000 per month and net losses in each month.

The CBDO board met again on December 10, 1970, and Hollas gave a report on the status of the ABC Shoe Store and requested that "the CBDO undertake some responsibility for helping Mr. Mann meet his obligations or close him down." He presented each board member with a November 30 financial report (see Exhibit VI on pages 358–360) which showed that after five months of operation (1) total sales of $25,300 had resulted in a net loss of $3,300; (2) the business had very little cash; (3) there was no build-up in inventories for the Christmas season; and (4) Mann still owed his company $8,600.

In response to Hollas' plea for action the board dispatched one of its members—J. C. Dunn, a local merchant—to "get the facts on the business." On December 17 Dunn sent the following memorandum to the members of the board:

TO: CBDO Board                                          December 17, 1970
FROM: J. C. Dunn
RE: ABC SHOE STORE
This memo describes my visit to ABC Shoe Store on Friday, December 11th. Mr. Mann stated:
1. He is still trying to sell his second business.
2. He still had not paid his taxes (Federal and State) which amount to $844.50.
3. He has not bought any new inventory for 2 weeks.
4. He owes three different shoe suppliers large amounts and needs $3,000 in order to pay his overdue balance and order more shoes. He stated that he owes slightly over $3,000 to Brown, $4,500 to Lee, and about $1,500 to a third supplier.
5. He plans to send these suppliers post-dated checks amounting to $3,000 and order more shoes.

I reiterated the fact to Mr. Mann that he could not expect any financial aid from us until the second business concern had been sold and the reputability of his management improved.

As of October 31st, approximately $10,000 is listed as due from officers. Approximately $4,000 can be attributed to unrecorded wages. Therefore, about $6,000 in funds have been misused. This, of course, does not include the purchase of a used Cadillac.

My recommendation is to wait and see if Mr. Mann has truly learned his lesson. If so, fine—for we all make mistakes. If not, then Mr. Mann should be replaced by someone who can do a better job of managing the business.

According to Hollas:

Christmas came and went and ABC Shoe Store's sales for December hit a low of $3,500. [See Exhibit VII on page 361 for ABC's December profit and loss statement.]

In an attempt to find out why sales had been so low I spoke with Mr. Mann, who told me that most of his funds were used in paying back bills and very little went into new merchandise. I then asked him about all of the old inventory that he had and was told "most of that stuff is either large sizes or out of style and nobody wants it." Thereupon, I asked Mr. Mann, "Would it be wise to run a sale on the shoes?" He said, "Sounds like a good idea, but I'll only get cost for the goods." I then said, "Fifty per cent of something is better than 100 per cent of nothing."

By this time Hollas was very concerned that the CBDO had not done anything to assist Mann and he "decided to take another stab at convincing the board that it should take some action." Therefore, he sent the following memorandum to the board:

TO: CBDO Board                                     January 14, 1971
FROM: H. Hollas

The purpose of this memo is to present a description of Mr. Mann as a businessman. The comments made here are exclusive of his very bad investment decision. The following comments are based upon my personal observations:

He appears to have gained a good general knowledge of the shoe business during his tenure as a shoe salesman. He seems to be very aware of the seasonal trends, style, tastes, inventory management, display techniques, price management, etc.

He is very concerned with the store's appearance and maintains its physical appearance very well. He, through his experience, is aware of the importance of an attractive physical plant.

I have personally observed Mr. Mann, on numerous occasions, during his dealings with customers. He is a good salesman and exhibits courtesy and experience in handling customers. He also instills the trait of courtesy into his salesmen.

He has been consistently up-to-date in delivering his financial statements to us. He has also been an apt pupil to my attempts to educate him in the managerial uses of his own statements. His records are orderly and up to date. All receipts are logged and all disbursements are by check. A check on the sales figures is the opening and ending inventory figures.

Mr. Mann appears to be basically responsible and highly concerned about the success of his store. As of now, the shoe store is his prime goal in life.

He is also present in the store five of the six days that it is open.

Apparently, this last appeal to the board was of sufficient persuasion because two weeks later Hollas was authorized "to commit $3,800 [the remainder of the $7,000 allocation] to ABC Shoe Store to meet its pressing obligations." Hollas argued that "$3,800 would probably not be enough, but a half loaf is better than no bread at all." As a condition of its giving this money, the board had one of its members—a lawyer—draw up a contract "designed to limit Mann's ability to squander this funding." Following are excerpts from this new agreement, which was effective February 11, 1971:

THOMAS MANN, individually and in his corporate capacity agrees to completely divest himself of all interests in said venture [The Haven] . . . not later than seven (7) days after execution of this agreement . . .

MANN further agrees and admits that he is personally liable . . . for seven thousand dollars ($7,000.00) in corporate funds which were siphoned off by him and used in other ventures . . .

MANN expressly agrees that no new or additional personnel shall be hired without the prior written consent of the CBDO . . .

MANN agrees not to purchase supplies or services in excess of the sum of twenty-five dollars ($25.00) without the CBDO's prior approval.

MANN agrees that he will pay himself . . . a salary of ninety dollars ($90.00) per week . . .

MANN agrees that fiscal and inventory controls shall be instituted as directed by the CBDO.

All stock owned by MANN shall immediately be assigned, upon the execution of this agreement, to the CBDO, to hold as escrowee, to guarantee performance of the conditions herein set forth by MANN . . .

MANN admits that because he siphoned off funds from the corporation and used same for other business ventures, it is now in need of additional finances. That in consideration of a loan from the CBDO in the sum of $3,800 it agrees and consents to all the terms and conditions aforestated in this agreement.

## Future Operations

Despite the additional $3,800 funding by the CBDO in February, ABC Shoe Store continued to operate at a loss because of the earlier financial problems. This became quite clear in April 1971 when Hollas received a quarterly statement from Mann (Exhibit VIII on pages 362–364) which showed that:

1. Sales for three months totaled only $3,056 and that the store lost $5,100.
2. Inventory was down to $6,400.
3. $1,500 in shoes was stolen from the store when Mann was unable to open it for several days because of cash shortages.
4. Accounts payable were over $7,500.

Hollas now felt that only a massive infusion of capital could save Mann's business. Therefore in late April he prepared an equity funding proposal which called for the CBDO to advance $18,000 to Mann in return for 80 per cent of the ABC Shoe Store stock. Under this proposal, which is summarized in Exhibit IX on pages 365–368, Hollas also proposed that (1) a CBDO employee monitor the store's operations while Mann became a working manager and (2) the agreement contain a "buy back" option. As Hollas prepared to go into the board meeting to defend this proposal he wondered whether the effort was justified to help someone who had misused funds in his *first months* of operation.

## EPILOGUE

Hollas entered the board room on April 29 to defend his recommendation that ABC Shoes should be provided with $18,000 in return for the CBDO's taking an 80 per cent ownership in the firm.

During the meeting the board indicated that it would not provide any additional funds to ABC Shoes, the consensus being that Mann had been given more than a fair chance. The board believed that to provide continued financial assistance to Mann, who had violated the conditions of his contract, was out of the question. The board further indicated that such action had to be dealt with in the most severe fashion, otherwise it would undermine the confidence of the groups which had funded the CBDO. Moreover, the board believed that other businessmen might believe that they could do the same thing if Mann got additional assistance. The board expressed appreciation for Hollas' strong defense of the issue, but refused even to consider any form of assistance.

In May, with the outstanding debt and no financial assistance available, Tommy Mann was forced into involuntary bankruptcy. Before the city marshal was able to serve the necessary papers and seize the assets of the company, Mann removed most of the shoes from the store and closed it.

Later Hollas talked about his experiences with ABC Shoes and the lessons that he learned:

I think the best lesson that we learned in this case is the need to monitor the early operations of any venture closely at first. It is those first couple of months and how things are handled that ultimately decide whether a man makes it or not. By the same token, we have to be able to make speedy decisions and I think in the case of Mann, much could have been avoided if we had made decisions when they were warranted, especially in the first instance when we clearly had to make a decision to either accept what Mann had done or refuse to accept it and do whatever we thought was necessary. I know the board is busy, but this is the kind of decision that should have been made by the executive director. In the long run, our indecisiveness hurt the business.

Prior to being forced into bankruptcy, Mann had indicated that while he had taken the money out of the business, "everybody else does it, so why is everybody so alarmed." Mann had felt at the time that business would pick up and that he could replace the funds out of the increased sales level of the business.

Exhibit I

ABC SHOE STORE

March 18, 1970

*Introduction*

This is a preliminary proposal to provide assistance to Mr. Tommy Mann who is presently employed by the Grim Shoe Corporation. Mr. Bob Grim, the proprietor of the store, is willing to sell the complete business for approximately $21,500.

*Purpose of the Proposal*

Mr. Mann would like to purchase this business which has been located in Harlem for approximately eleven years and has an established clientele. In order to make this purchase he will need a total of $28,500. An application in the amount of $21,500 has been filed with the Small Business Administration for a 90 per cent guarantee through one of the banking institutions participating in the SBA program. Mr. Mann is asking for $7,000 from the CBDO. The purpose of this proposal is to assist in creating a new minority-owned business.

*Nature and Background of the Proposal*

COMPANY HISTORY. The Grim Shoe Store has been located on 125th Street for the past eleven years. Mr. Grim has been able to earn a comfortable living from the business during his four years of ownership. The company sells Brown shoes and accessories for men and has an attractive and appealing window display plus a very good store layout.

FINANCIAL CONDITION. The company's financial statements for 1967, 1968 and the period January 1, 1969 to August 31, 1969 were submitted by Mr. Grim's accountant, but they are not certified. The company profit for the eight-month period of 1969 totals $498.85. The company's present operating trend indicates a very favorable outlook for the years to come. There is no reason why this business should not continue to maintain the present pace of growth under the ownership of Mr. Mann. In addition, with our assistance, a marketing plan could be formulated to increase sales appreciably.

MANAGEMENT QUALIFICATIONS. Mr. Mann is presently employed with the Grim Shoe Store as salesman and store assistant. Mr. Grim is very impressed with the performance of Mr. Mann, who is being trained in such areas as merchandising, store operations, finances, layouts and design, advertising and promotion, bookkeeping and traffic-building ideas. Mr. Mann is presently attending the Workshop on Business Opportunities, which will enhance his knowledge of the shoe trade. Also Mr. Grim intends to remain with the new owner subsequent to the sale of the business and provide the required assistance. This arrangement with Mr. Grim involves no financial outlay on the part of Mr. Mann. Mr. Grim is volunteering his time to ensure a successful transition.

## The Proposal

CAPITAL REQUIREMENTS. To purchase the Grim Shoe Store, Mr. Mann will need $28,500:

| | |
|---|---|
| Inventory | $16,500.00 |
| Furniture and Fixtures | 2,500.00 |
| Organization Expense (Legal & Accounting) | 1,725.00 |
| Working Capital | 4,300.00 |
| Rent—Deposit | 275.00 |
| Insurance | 700.00 |
| Goodwill | 2,500.00 |
| Total | $28,500.00 |

The inventory indicated on the balance sheet at a cost of $16,500 will be priced at cost, provided it is current. Proper discounts will be taken on all items not needed for the current season and Mr. Mann reserves the right to reject any merchandise in excess of current needs. Furniture and fixtures listed at $3,638.69 are being purchased for $2,500. Mr. Mann will assume no liabilities of the previous owner. A sum of $2,500 will be held in escrow for one year for any contingent liabilities as a result of unforeseen liabilities which would normally be assumed by the previous owner, Mr. Grim.

FUNDING. The *bank* is expected to approve a five-year $21,500 SBA loan. The interest rate, at this time, is not available as the bank wishes to obtain that rate prevalent at the time the loan is actually obtained.

As the company demonstrates a need for the CBDO funds it will be paid out. Repayment of the loan will commence after repayment, five years, of the bank loan.

$$61\text{--}71 \text{ months @ } \$ \quad 500.00 = \$5,500.00$$
$$72\text{--lump sum @ } \quad 1,500.00 = \quad 1,500.00$$
$$\overline{\phantom{xxxxxxxxxx}}$$
$$\$7,000.00$$

Exhibit II

## ABC SHOE STORE, INC.

Profit and Loss Statement for the Period June 23 — July 31, 1970

| | | |
|---|---:|---:|
| Gross Income | | $7,161.45 |
| Less: Sales Discount | | 25.21 |
| Net Sales | | 7,136.24 |
| Cost of Goods Sold: | | |
| Beginning Inventory | $13,916.68 | |
| Purchases | 984.70 | |
| Total Merchandise Available for Sale | 14,901.38 | |
| Less: Ending Inventory | 11,185.42 | |
| Cost of Goods Sold | | 3,715.96 |
| Gross Profit | | $3,420.28 |
| Expenditures: | | |
| Labor | 130.00 | |
| Donation | 10.00 | |
| Insurance | 46.92 | |
| Maintenance and Repairs | 387.68 | |
| Accounting Fee | 50.00 | |
| Rent | 275.00 | |
| Bank Charges | 6.95 | |
| New York Telephone | 34.67 | |
| Casual Labor | 75.00 | |
| Utilities | 279.79 | |
| Interest | 164.01 | |
| Sales Taxes | 685.66 | |
| Federal Social Security Taxes | 6.24 | |
| Total Expenditures | | 2,151.92 |
| Net Income Before Depreciation | | 1,268.36 |
| Less: Depreciation | | 20.83 |
| Net Income | | $1,247.53 |

# ABC SHOE STORE, INC.

## Balance Sheet July 31, 1970

### Assets

| | | |
|---|---|---|
| **Current Assets:** | | |
| Cash in Bank | $ 4,752.84 | |
| Cash on Hand | 200.00 | |
| Security Deposit (Rent) | 550.00 | |
| Inventory (Ending) | 11,185.42 | |
| Prepaid Insurance | 516.08 | |
| Total Current Assets | | $17,204.34 |
| **Fixed Assets:** | | |
| Furniture and Fixtures | 2,500.00 | |
| Automobile | 2,175.00 | |
| | 4,675.00 | |
| Less: Reserve for Depreciation | 20.83 | |
| Total Fixed Assets | | 4,654.17 |
| **Other Assets:** | | |
| Deferred Interest | 7,435.99 | |
| Due from Officers | 5,256.13 | |
| Organization Expenses | 3,400.00 | |
| Total Other Assets | | 16,092.12 |
| Total Assets | | $37,950.63 |

## Liabilities and Shareholders' Equity

Current Liabilities:

| | | |
|---|---|---|
| Current Portion of Long-Term Note | $5,376.00 | |
| Sales Taxes Payable | 405.16 | |
| Payroll Taxes Payable | 36.24 | |
| Accounts Payable — Insurance | 425.00 | |
| Accounts Payable — Trade | 984.70 | |
| Total Current Liabilities | | $ 7,227.10 |

Fixed Liabilities:

| | | |
|---|---|---|
| Note Payable — CBDO | 3,200.00 | |
| Note Payable — Bank | 23,276.00 | |
| Total Fixed Liabilities | | 26,476.00 |
| Total Liabilities | | 33,703.10 |

Shareholders' Equity:

| | | |
|---|---|---|
| Capital Stock | 3,000.00 | |
| Earned Surplus 7/31/70 | 1,247.53 | |
| Total Shareholders' Equity | | 4,247.53 |
| Total Liabilities and Shareholders' Equity | | $37,950.63 |

## Exhibit III
## ABC SHOE STORE, INC.

### Profit and Loss Statement for September 1970

| | | |
|---|---:|---:|
| Gross Income | | $4,423.82 |
|   Less: Sales Discount | | 14.77 |
| Net Sales | | 4,409.05 |
| Cost of Goods Sold: | | |
|   Beginning Inventory | $13,734.32 | |
|   Purchases | 534.20 | |
|   Merchandise Available for Sale | 14,268.52 | |
|   Less: Ending Inventory | 11,392.66 | |
| Cost of Goods Sold | | 2,875.86 |
| Gross Profit | | $1,533.19 |
| General and Administrative Expenses: | | |
|   Shoe Supplies | 175.00 | |
|   Donations | 10.00 | |
|   Insurance | 75.34 | |
|   Maintenance and Repairs | 72.40 | |
|   Professional Fees | 75.00 | |
|   Rent | 275.00 | |
|   Bank Charges | 1.52 | |
|   Telephone | 58.79 | |
|   Interest — Bank | 159.66 | |
|   Sales Taxes | 253.34 | |
|   Freight In | 111.43 | |
|   Depreciation | 113.44 | |
|   Office Supplies and Printing | 10.31 | |
|   Automobile Expenses | 2.22 | |
|     Total General and Administrative Expenses | | 1,393.45 |
| Net Profit | | $ 139.74 |

# ABC SHOE STORE, INC.

## Balance Sheet as at September 30, 1970

### Assets

| | | |
|---|---:|---:|
| **Current Assets:** | | |
| Cash in Bank | $   126.79 | |
| Cash on Hand | 300.00 | |
| Security Deposit | 550.00 | |
| Ending Inventory | 11,392.66 | |
| Prepaid Insurance | 1,337.65 | |
| Total Current Assets | | $13,707.10 |
| **Fixed Assets:** | | |
| Furniture and Fixtures | 2,656.22 | |
| Automobile | 2,175.00 | |
| | 4,831.22 | |
| Less: Reserve for Depreciation | 241.98 | |
| Total Fixed Assets | | 4,589.24 |
| **Other Assets:** | | |
| Subscription to Stock | 3,000.00 | |
| Deferred Rent | 275.00 | |
| Due from Officers | 8,282.36 | |
| Deferred Interest | 7,114.49 | |
| Organization Expenses | 3,400.00 | |
| Total Other Assets | | 22,071.85 |
| **Total Assets** | | $40,368.19 |

Liabilities and Shareholders' Equity

| | | |
|---|---:|---:|
| Current Liabilities: | | |
|     Current Portion of Long-Term Note | $ 5,376.00 | |
|     Sales Taxes Payable | 981.75 | |
|     Payroll Taxes Payable | 126.12 | |
|     Accounts Payable | 3,280.75 | |
|         Total Current Liabilities | | $ 9,764.62 |
| Fixed Liabilities: | | |
|     Note Payable — CBDO | 3,200.00 | |
|     Note Payable — Bank | 22,380.00 | |
|         Total Fixed Liabilities | | 25,580.00 |
|         Total Liabilities | | 35,344.62 |
| Shareholders' Equity: | | |
|     Capital Stock | 3,000.00 | |
|     Retained Earnings 9/1/70 | 1,883.83 | |
|     Earnings — September | 139.74 | |
|         Total Shareholders' Equity | | 5,023.57 |
| Total Liabilities and Shareholders' Equity | | $40,368.19 |

## Exhibit IV
## ABC SHOE STORE, INC.

### Profit and Loss Statement for October 1970

| | | |
|---|---:|---:|
| Gross Income | | $3,875.37 |
| Less: Sales Discount | | 9.85 |
| Net Sales | | 3,865.52 |
| Cost of Goods Sold: | | |
| Beginning Inventory | $11,392.66 | |
| Purchases | 413.60 | |
| Merchandise Available for Sale | 11,806.26 | |
| Less: Ending Inventory | 9,133.26 | |
| Cost of Goods Sold | | 2,673.00 |
| Gross Profit | | $1,192.52 |
| General and Administrative Expenses: | | |
| Labor | 210.00 | |
| Insurance | 75.34 | |
| Maintenance and Repairs | 34.76 | |
| Professional Fees | 75.00 | |
| Rent | 275.00 | |
| Bank Charges | 1.07 | |
| Telephone | 34.00 | |
| Interest — Bank | 157.46 | |
| Sales Taxes | 214.12 | |
| Freight In | ——— | |
| Burglar Alarm Expense | 17.28 | |
| Depreciation | 113.44 | |
| Office Supplies and Printing | 9.70 | |
| Federal Social Security Taxes | 10.08 | |
| Total General and Administrative Expenses | | 1,227.25 |
| Net Profit (Loss) | | ($ 34.73) |

BLACK ENTERPRISE, INC.

Exhibit V

## ABC SHOE STORE, INC.

Profit and Loss Statement for November 1970

| | | |
|---|---:|---:|
| Gross Income | | $4,191.95 |
| Less: Sales Discount | | 4.57 |
| Net Sales | | 4,187.38 |
| Cost of Goods Sold: | | |
| Beginning Inventory | $ 9,133.26 | |
| Purchases | 6,237.23 | |
| Merchandise Available for Sale | 15,370.49 | |
| Less: Ending Inventory | 12,445.05 | |
| Cost of Goods Sold | | 2,925.44 |
| Gross Profit | | $ 1,261.94 |
| General and Administrative Expenses: | | |
| Shoe Store Supplies | 14.49 | |
| Labor | 315.00 | |
| Insurance | 75.00 | |
| Maintenance and Repairs | 78.80 | |
| Professional Fees | 75.00 | |
| Rent | 550.00 | |
| Bank Charges | 3.00 | |
| Telephone | 76.56 | |
| Interest — Bank | 155.24 | |
| Sales Taxes | 237.28 | |
| Burglar Alarm Expense | 8.64 | |
| Depreciation | 113.44 | |
| Federal Social Security Taxes | 15.12 | |
| Total General and Administrative Expenses | | 1,717.57 |
| Net Profit (Loss) | | ($ 455.63) |

## Exhibit VI

## ABC SHOE STORE, INC.

Profit and Loss Statement for the Period June 23, 1970 — November 30, 1970

| | | |
|---|---:|---:|
| Gross Income | | $25,327.77 |
| Less: Sales Discount | | 80.40 |
| Net Sales | | 25,247.37 |
| **Cost of Goods Sold:** | | |
| Beginning Inventory | $33,835.65 | |
| Purchases | 6,237.23 | |
| Mdse. Available for Sale | 27,598.42 | |
| Less: Ending Inventory | 12,445.05 | |
| Cost of Goods Sold | | 15,153.37 |
| **Gross Profit** | | $10,094.00 |
| **General and Administrative Expenses:** | | |
| Freight In | 151.07 | |
| Utilities | 352.95 | |
| Shoe Store Supplies | 189.49 | |
| Sales Taxes | 1,713.65 | |
| Donations | 20.00 | |
| Automobile Expenditures | 90.84 | |
| Labor | 5,565.00 | |
| Burglar Alarm Expenditures | 34.56 | |
| Insurance | 347.94 | |
| Office Supplies and Printing | 102.13 | |
| Maintenance and Repairs | 848.14 | |
| Depreciation | 468.86 | |
| Miscellaneous Expenditures | 23.93 | |
| Federal Social Security Taxes | 267.12 | |
| Professional Fees | 350.00 | |
| Rent | 1,650.00 | |
| Bank Charges | 13.94 | |
| Telephone | 318.76 | |
| Casual Labor | 75.00 | |
| Interest — Bank | 798.21 | |
| Total General and Administrative Expenses | | 13,381.59 |
| Net Profit (Loss) | | ($ 3,287.59) |

## ABC SHOE STORE, INC.

### Balance Sheet as of November 30, 1970

#### Assets

Current Assets:
| | | |
|---|---|---|
| Cash in Bank | $      8.15 | |
| Cash on Hand | 300.00 | |
| Security Deposits | 550.00 | |
| Ending Inventory | 12,445.05 | |
| Prepaid Insurance | 1,296.51 | |
| Total Current Assets | | $14,599.71 |

Fixed Assets:
| | | |
|---|---|---|
| Furniture and Fixtures | 2,656.22 | |
| Automobile | 2,175.00 | |
| | 4,831.22 | |
| Reserve for Depreciation | 412.19 | |
| Total Fixed Assets | | 4,419.03 |

Other Assets:
| | | |
|---|---|---|
| Due from Officers | 8,572.11 | |
| Deferred Interest | 6,801.79 | |
| Organization Expense | 3,343.33 | |
| Leasehold Improvements | 310.00 | |
| Total Other Assets | | 19,027.23 |
| Total Assets | | $38,045.97 |

## Liabilities and Shareholders' Equity

Current Liabilities:

| | | |
|---|---|---|
| Long-Term Note — Current Portion | $ 5,376.00 | |
| Sales Taxes Payable | 1,433.15 | |
| Payroll Taxes Payable | 1,433.57 | |
| Accounts Payable | 8,406.84 | |
| Total Current Liabilities | | $16,649.56 |

Fixed Liabilities:

| | | |
|---|---|---|
| Note Payable — CBDO | 3,200.00 | |
| Note Payable — Bank | 21,484.00 | |
| Total Fixed Liabilities | | 24,684.00 |
| Total Liabilities | | 41,333.56 |

Shareholders' Equity:

| | | |
|---|---|---|
| Retained Earnings 6/23/70 — 11/30/70 | | (3,287.59) |
| Total Liabilities and Shareholders' Equity | | $38,045.97 |

Exhibit VII

## ABC SHOE STORE, INC.

### Profit and Loss Statement for December 1970

| | | |
|---|---:|---:|
| Gross Income | | $3,536.63 |
| Less: Sales Discount | | 11.55 |
| Net Sales | | 3,525.08 |
| Cost of Goods Sold: | | |
| Beginning Inventory | $12,445.05 | |
| Purchases | 466.60 | |
| Merchandise Available for Sale | 12,911.65 | |
| Less: Ending Inventory | 10,436.45 | |
| Cost of Goods Sold | | 2,475.20 |
| Gross Profit | | $1,049.88 |
| General and Administrative Expenses: . | | |
| Labor | 78.88 | |
| Casual Labor | 205.00 | |
| Insurance | 108.00 | |
| Maintenance and Repairs | 48.30 | |
| Professional Fees | 75.00 | |
| Freight In | 39.64 | |
| Rent | 275.00 | |
| Bank Charges | 5.27 | |
| Telephone | 40.00 | |
| Interest — Bank | 153.01 | |
| Sales Taxes | 199.98 | |
| Office Supplies and Printing | 7.63 | |
| Depreciation | 113.44 | |
| Total General and Administrative Expenses | | 1,349.15 |
| Net Profit (Loss) | | ($ 299.27) |

Exhibit VIII

# ABC SHOE STORE, INC.

Profit and Loss Statement for the Period January 1, 1971 — March 31, 1971

| | | |
|---|---:|---:|
| Gross Income | | $3,056.72 |
| Less: Sales Discount | | 13.13 |
| Net Sales | | 3,043.59 |
| Cost of Goods Sold: | | |
| Beginning Inventory | $10,436.45 | |
| Purchases | 185.00 | |
| Merchandise Available for Sale | 10,621.45 | |
| Ending Inventory | 6,365.90 | |
| Cost of Goods Sold | | 4,254.55 |
| Gross Profit (Loss) | | ($1,210.96) |
| General and Administrative Expenses: | | |
| Theft of Shoes from Premises | 1,454.79 | |
| Casual Labor | 94.00 | |
| Burglar Alarm | 27.28 | |
| Insurance | 324.00 | |
| Miscellaneous Expenditures | 5.00 | |
| Maintenance and Repairs | 88.63 | |
| Professional Fees | – 0 – | |
| Rent | 875.00 | |
| Bank Charges | 26.36 | |
| Interest — Bank | 445.46 | |
| Sales Taxes | 173.35 | |
| Depreciation | 340.32 | |
| Total General and Administrative Expenses | | 3,854.19 |
| Net Loss Before Gain on Sale of Auto | | (5,065.15) |
| Less: Gain on Sale of Automobile | | 6.26 |
| Net Profit (Loss) | | ($5,058.89) |

Valuation of inventory purchased at inception of business was overstated. Adjustment has been made charging this overstatement of the inventory of $2,990.15 to Goodwill on the Balance Sheet.

## ABC SHOE STORE, INC.

### Balance Sheet as at March 31, 1971

#### Assets

Current Assets:

| | | |
|---|---|---|
| Cash in Bank | $ 217.82 | |
| Security Deposits | 550.00 | |
| Ending Inventory | 6,365.90 | |
| Prepaid Insurance | 961.51 | |
| Total Current Assets | | $ 8,095.23 |

Fixed Assets:

| | | |
|---|---|---|
| Furniture and Fixtures | 2,656.22 | |
| Less: Reserve for Depreciation | 684.69 | |
| Total Fixed Assets | | 1,971.53 |

Other Assets:

| | | |
|---|---|---|
| Due from Officers | 15,019.17 | |
| Deferred Interest | 6,801.79 | |
| Organization Expense | 3,343.33 | |
| Leasehold Improvements | 310.00 | |
| Total Other Assets | | 25,474.29 |
| Total Assets | | $35,541.05 |

### Liabilities and Shareholders' Equity

Current Liabilities:

| | | |
|---|---:|---:|
| Long-Term Note — Current Portion | $ 5,376.00 | |
| Sales Taxes Payable | 1,806.48 | |
| Payroll Taxes Payable | 140.20 | |
| Accounts Payable | 7,539.00 | |
| Total Current Liabilities | | $14,861.68 |

Fixed Liabilities:

| | | |
|---|---:|---:|
| Note Payable — CBDO | 7,000.00 | |
| Note Payable — Bank | 20,290.47 | |
| Total Fixed Liabilities | | 27,290.47 |
| Total Liabilities | | 42,152.15 |

Shareholders' Equity:
Capital Stock

| | | |
|---|---:|---:|
| Retained Earnings 6/23/70 — 12/31/71 | 1,438.94 | |
| Earnings 1/1/71 — 3/31/71 | (8,050.04) | |
| Total Shareholders' Equity | | (6,611.10) |
| Total Liabilities and Shareholders' Equity | | $35,541.05 |

BLACK ENTERPRISE, INC.

Exhibit IX

## EQUITY PROPOSAL
## ABC SHOE STORE, INC.

### April 27, 1971

*Introduction*

The purpose of this proposal is to request that we assume ownership of the ABC Shoe Store, via the purchase of eighty per cent of the stock of that corporation through the contribution of $18,000 in equity capital to the corporation.

*History of the Corporation*

The shoe store is a Brown Shoe Company franchise. The store opened for business on June 23, 1970. The president of the corporation, Mr. Tommy Mann, had worked for one and a half years as a salesman in the store for the prior owner.

Funding for the new corporation came from two sources. The bank released $21,500 in loan funds, and $3,200 of our funds were released providing an initial capitalization of $24,700.

MARKETING. During the first five months of operations, the company had a net sales level of $25,247.37, and averaged slightly over $5,000 a month. Net loss for the first five months (July–November, 1970) was $3,287.59. Net sales for December 1970 were $3,535.08, and net loss for the same month was $94.27. Since December, 1970, sales and profit for the corporation have plummeted downward. Net sales for the first three months of 1971 have averaged $2,000 per month.

In February, 1971, we made an additional loan to the corporation and Mr. Mann was made personally responsible for $7,000 total.

POOR MANAGEMENT. The basic reason for the company's downturn was due to very poor management by the owner. He, during the first four months of the store's operation, siphoned funds from the corporation. The siphoning eliminated the corporation's working capital, and prevented the corporation from meeting its financial obligations. Consequently, Brown Shoe Company refused the store any further credit. All of the store's other suppliers have likewise eliminated credit purchases due to long overdue debt. The corporation was then thrown into a bad spiral which included inadequate inventory to generate sufficient income and profit to meet financial obligations, which prevented the corporation from building up an adequate inventory. Consultants in the shoe industry have estimated that a continuous inventory of approximately $12,000 is necessary for the store to meet fixed and variable costs as well as being profitable.

Mr. Mann siphoned a reported total of $8,500 from the corporation for a $3,000 night club investment, a $2,500 1968 Cadillac, and $3,000 for miscellaneous personal uses. Since October, 1970, Mr. Mann appears to have realized his errors, and has managed the funds in a businesslike manner.

In February, 1971, we imposed tight internal control upon the store and Mr. Mann claimed to have learned a hard lesson. Unfortunately, the damage has been done.

### Present Situation of the Corporation

The corporation now finds itself in a very precarious position for the following reasons:

1. The company is unable to replenish its shoe inventory via credit and it does not have the cash.
2. The store is getting deeper in debt, because sales revenue is now barely meeting even fixed costs. As of April 1, 1971, the store owed $7,921.49.
3. The reputation of the store is in danger of being badly damaged due to customers being turned away, because of inadequate inventory.

Therefore, due to lack of inventory and lack of funds, the financial situation as well as the store's reputation is taking a downward plunge. The store has proved itself to be a viable and profitable enterprise, but poor management has erased any profits. Sales are averaging around only $500 per week and the store was unable to take advantage of either the Christmas or Easter season buying due to an inadequate inventory.

*Proposed Future Direction: Equity Participation*

MANAGEMENT. It is proposed that the CBDO take complete control of the firm and by so doing it is expected that the company can become self-sustaining and profitable. This will be accomplished by placing our representative in charge of the operation. His duties will be coordination, planning, fiscal control, statement preparation and the direction of the marketing effort. It is contemplated that this will require a maximum of 25 per cent of the representative's time. Furthermore, it is contemplated that this time will steadily decrease to a monitoring function and periodic checks of the company's inventory and internal controls.

The current owner will then become a working manager and his duties will consist of purchasing, sales and record keeping.

COMPANY CONTROLS.
1. *Equity Control*
   a. The CBDO will own 80 per cent of the company's stock as a result of the investment of $18,000 with a buy-back option that cannot be exercised for one year after the contract.
   b. If our equity falls below 51%, the corporation (ABC Shoe Store, Inc.) must take over total ownership and give a personal note for the balance of the funds.
   c. ABC Shoe Store, Inc. must purchase controlling interest within three years of the equity funding, or we have the option to sell the business to new management.
2. *Other Controls*
   a. *Inventory*
      The CBDO shall have sole discretion as to when a physical inventory will be taken and it shall be taken by one of its representatives. All suppliers will be required to send us copies of all invoices for shoes delivered to the store. Daily and weekly sales records will be maintained on Brown-supplied forms.
   b. *Monetary*
      All disbursements will be paid by check which must be first approved by the CBDO.
   c. *Tax*
      A separate tax bank account will be maintained to ensure prompt payment of taxes.

## Ownership

Upon approval of this proposal, the CBDO will hold 80% equity in ABC Shoe Store, Inc. The remaining 20% will be owned by Mr. Tommy Mann, president of ABC Shoe Store, Inc. The percentage of equity held by the CBDO will decrease in proportion to the amount of equity funds repaid.

All income earned by the ABC Shoe Store, Inc. will be utilized in the following order:

1. Reduction of due from officers' balance.
2. Reduction of loan.
3. Reduction of equity.
4. Retained earnings.

USES OF FUNDS. The equity funds would be used in the following manner:

| | |
|---|---:|
| Inventory Replenishment | $ 4,300.00 |
| Reduction of Short-term Debt | 10,000.00 |
| Working Capital | 2,400.00 |
| Additional Taxes Not Yet Declared | 1,300.00 |
| Total | $18,000.00 |

MARKETING.

1. *Goals*

The annual net sales goal is $57,000 for the first year. A related goal will be implementation of efficient inventory control and management procedures to ensure that the company will realize its full income-producing potential.

2. *Strategy*

The strategy for reaching these goals includes the following:
a. Advertising.
b. Maintenance of credit standing.

Since the new ownership in June, 1970, the store has done no advertising whatsoever. It is believed that an efficient low-cost program can be very profitable.

# 12

# SOUL GUARD SERVICE

## PROLOGUE

Soul Guard Service is a case study of a black Watts detective who wanted to start a security guard service. After some false starts, Gilroy Black finally borrowed $73,000 from a local CBDO and launched his company only to overspend in the early months. After only a few months of operation he was not able to acquire a lucrative security contract without additional help from the CBDO.

The CBDO in this case was a non-profit corporation that began operations in November 1966. The founding members were twelve black men who worked in a variety of community projects and occupied high positions in some of the major social service and community agencies in Watts. This group felt that most community efforts had not concentrated on consolidating power and control in the community. Moreover, they believed that all efforts to create a power base had to begin by creating an economic base.

The founders of the CBDO became the members of a board of directors which eventually increased to twenty-six to allow for the election of additional members. The board selected an executive director, who was responsible for the implementation of its programs. The CBDO's financing came from a variety of sources, with a major portion coming from the Department of Commerce.

Operationally, all financial assistance was approved by a loan committee made up of the executive director, the manager of business assistance, the legal counsel, and four members of the board of directors. Each loan application was also sent to a commercial bank to determine if it was willing to provide some portion of the necessary funds. If the bank decided not to participate, the CBDO might still agree to the total amount required. After a loan had been approved, it was assigned to a staff monitor for follow-up.

The Watts CBDO was especially eager to finance a security agency because it had given a great deal of assistance to several firms in the area, all of which had had tremendous security problems. At one time, in fact, the CBDO had considered starting its own security service.


## THE CASE

*Introduction*

On October 2, 1971, Gilroy Black received a letter from his bank stating that it could not lend his company—Soul Guard Service— the $11,000 that it had requested. Black was surprised because the bank had led him and the Watts CBDO to believe that the loan would be made and he had agreed tentatively to take a new contract representing a billing of over $250,000 a year. Black immediately placed a call to Henry Bragg of the local CBDO to determine what he should now do.


*Background*

Gilroy Black is the founder, principal stockholder, and president of Soul Guard Service. Born in Watts, California, in 1929, he attended local schools and graduated from high school in 1947. He attended two different colleges for three and one half years, finally entering the Air Force in 1951 where he began training as a supply technician. The Korean situation, however, caused his entire class to be reassigned to the Air Force Police School. Thereupon, Black spent his five-year tour of duty as an air policeman.

In 1956, having returned from service, Black took the Los Angeles Police Force examination. He also, matter of-factly, applied to Sheriff's Detective Agency. While waiting for the results from the Police Department examination, Black received an offer from Sheriff's. He took the job, although he subsequently received notice that he had passed the Police Department examination. Black cited better salary and benefits as reasons for his remaining with Sheriff's at that time.

Black worked for Sheriff's for fourteen years, finally rising to a supervisory job. According to Black, during those years "I received numerous and various assignments which involved me increasingly in management and supervision." He also recalls that he developed a strong following among some of Sheriff's clients, to the extent that "there were times when they would wait until I had completed a current assignment and then request me specifically." This encouraged Black to begin considering a guard service of his own.

Once Black had decided to start his own company, he began in November 1969 to search for funds. He approached local banks, loan companies, and on one occasion "a loan shark," but claimed they all said the same thing, "Sounds like a good idea but we cannot help you; try the SBA." In January 1970 Black finally submitted an application to the SBA.

In the meantime, Black continued to try to seek out people who might be interested in bankrolling a black guard service for the Watts community. Black recalled that:

I stopped in a pub on a particular cold day in January and heard someone call my name. I turned around and there was Malcolm Kenneth, whom I had known previously. I had worked with Malcolm years before in Sheriff's Detective Agency. He was also searching for funds to start a guard service. In our discussions I learned that we both had submitted applications to the SBA, but had received not constructive replies. Finally, he suggested to me that we go in together; I agreed. Later, when we were discussing finances, Malcolm said that one of his white friends, Carl Vincent, was willing to invest $10,000 in the business. After numerous discussions, the three of us finally agreed to terms, and planned to organize Golden Ocean Investigation Agency. I was to be made president, since only I had an active license. When I later remarked that $12,000 would not be enough money to get the business rolling, Carl remarked, "I know where there is plenty of money. All you have to do is to submit an application form to the new Watts agency." I thought this was a great idea and finally submitted a proposal in the middle of May [1970]. [See Exhibit I on pages 386–388 for a copy of the $82,000 proposal submitted by Black.]

While my application was being processed by the CBDO, I discovered certain hidden agreements made by Malcolm and Carl involving their acquisition of additional shares of stock, once funds were granted. Realizing that these agreements might result in my losing the company and my license, I resigned from Golden Ocean in September [1970]. I also felt that the hidden agreements would have the effect of violating the provisions of the anticipated contract with the CBDO, and I could not be sure what the real intent of my two partners was—especially since I had heard of several companies in which blacks were president but whites had milked the companies and left the black officers to face the music.

The CBDO staff shared Black's views, both strategically and legally, and Henry Bragg, a monitor in the CBDO's business assistance unit, assisted Black in ending his ties with Golden Ocean. Black also credits Bragg with assisting him in rewriting his proposal to start Soul Guard Service, which was organized on October 23, 1970.

Though the CBDO loan committee had earlier approved Black's Golden Ocean proposal for a total of $71,000, it had refused to release the funds until "it knew more about Black's partners" and until a bank agreed to participate in the loan. According to a member of the committee: "We never had a moment's doubt about Mr. Black or the need for a guard service. He seemed like a very capable black businessman and we certainly need good security in Watts. Our doubts were about his partners in the venture and about the level of bank financing he should have gotten."

Once Black decided to pull out of Golden Ocean, Bragg, a former statistician with the Federal Reserve Bank, prepared the following October 26, 1970, addendum to the Golden Ocean proposal:

Soul Guard Service, Inc., is a company which will provide investigatory and security services to industry. It will offer a complete line of investigatory services, all phases of security patrols for business and industrial security purposes, armed personal escorts, industrial intelligence and missing persons investigations.

In order to begin its operation, the company will need $82,000. For details of this firm's operations see Mr. Black's earlier May 18, 1970, proposal which was written for Golden Ocean Investigation Agency, with which he is no longer associated.

The California Savings Bank has promised to grant a $11,000 three-year straight interest loan. We will provide a $71,000 loan which will be repaid after repayment of the bank loan.

Though Bragg took a great deal of time to explain to the committee that the key to the business was Gilroy Black and not the earlier Golden Ocean proposal, several committee members wanted to question Black to learn if he really knew the business and would really own it. During a subsequent interview with the committee on November 4, 1970, Black declared that he would "own 90 per cent of the business" with the "remaining 10 per cent being allocated to two black senior officers." He went on to describe his own background and to deal with the community's need for a guard service and the tremendous market potential that it offered. With respect to these points he said:

I have always been sure of the market and I have spent a great deal of time analyzing it. I've seen billions of dollars go for burglar alarms, dogs, and folding gates, with little success. Most of the people that spent money for burglar alarms have turned to guard service as the only safe way because they had found that dogs, burglar alarms, and folding gates did not do the job. As a result, several guard services have sprung up overnight and most of them are making a profit. In fact, I have followed two or three small guard services that have grown from contingents of five men to about eighty men in less than a year. Also, I remember several discussions I have had with people at Sheriff's who told me that there were no medium-priced guard services, only very expensive ones like Sheriff's and very cheap ones that did not even carry insurance on its men.

The committee was "very impressed by Black and his commitment to the community" and approved the release of the loan funds on November 5, 1970.

## Operations

Soul Guard Service had been incorporated with an initial capitalization of $1,000. Black received 90 per cent of the firm and Taylor Burns and Larry Parker received 5 per cent each. The CBDO provided $71,000 and the bank promised to lend $11,000. Thus, with $83,000 available and a booming market, Black felt that prospects were excellent.

With respect to personnel, Black recruited his key employees from Golden Ocean. Larry Parker, who had been a salesman for Golden Ocean, and whose background included owning his own business, was vice-president of Soul Guard Service. Taylor Burns, a boyhood friend of Black's who was an inspector (normally a top officer of the security contingent) at Golden Ocean, assumed the same position with Soul. Robert Vincent, a long-time friend of Black's, became the first captain at Soul. Mrs. Black, who was an assistant bookkeeper at a local film company, became the office manager, bookkeeper, and secretary of the new firm. These persons, along with local attorney George Wallace and Black, composed the board of directors of Soul Guard Service.

Once Black signed the contract with the CBDO on November 19, 1970, he went to work immediately trying to locate office space. Finally, in early December he located a loft in central Watts that had 3,000 feet of usable space. The office was in a state of disrepair and major renovations had to be done. Black requested bids for the renovation by breaking the job into small pieces and allowing subcontractors to bid for each section. In this way, Black expected to get the work done for about $17,000, twice the proposal estimate. The contractors projected that it would take several weeks to complete the work and that by February 1, 1971, the company would be able to move in.

Black also recognized that he would need time to acquire manpower and equipment. He began to advertise for guards, to solicit business, and to purchase the equipment that would be needed. At the same time he also began requesting money from the CBDO to pay for the renovations and meet salary and capital expenses. He finally received his initial CBDO funds on December 8, 1970.

As was the case with most CBDO's, a monitor was assigned the entrepreneur. In the case of Soul Guard Service, Henry Bragg was given the job. On January 7, 1971, he wrote the following progress report on Soul:

TO: File                                            January 7, 1971
FROM: Henry Bragg
RE: Soul Guard Service

It has been roughly a month since our initial disbursement to Soul, during which time we have disbursed a total of $32,345, earmarked for the following purposes:

|  |  |
|---|---|
| Furniture and Equipment | $6,600.00 |
| Uniforms and Accessories | 4,020.00 |
| Fixtures and Renovations | 3,500.00 |
| Salaries and Wages | 9,450.00 |
| Operating Expenses | 8,775.00 |
| Total | $32,345.00 |

Soul's operations during the month of December are characterized as follows:

1. Soul has a *large non-income-producing staff* approaching 50% of total employees to date. What this means is that *heavy* general and administrative expenses will lengthen by approximately three months the time at which Soul will reach breakeven. Nevertheless, it is a good staff with each individual having had sufficient prior experience in his area of operation. With respect to income-producing personnel, i.e., guards, patrolmen, and undercover personnel, the company has a backlog of prospective personnel sufficient to handle most medium-range contracts involving 12–20 people. The company is self-sufficient in this regard.

2. Sales are 90% below first month forecasts. This is due principally to slow responses from prospective clients. Sales will pick up during the second month, however, when Soul will start two contracts totalling a little over $11,000 per month.

They also expect responses from some of the prospective clients previously referred to. The company is self-sufficient along these lines.

3. Structurally, the organization is well-conceived and provides for expansion with a minimum of re-organization necessary.

With respect to accounting and record keeping, I have found Mrs. Black to be quite sufficient. After my installation of the accounting system, she commenced to handle the job with minimum assistance from me. The company also has a sound insurance package.

4. The company has the Public Relations officer who was with Mr. Black at Golden Ocean. In summary there are no needs which I can supply with respect to intensive care. Therefore, I recommend that Soul be spun off at the end of the first week in February.

By the time Soul moved into its new headquarters in mid-January, Black had hired ten guards, two secretaries, one dispatcher, three sergeants, one captain, one assistant, and one bookkeeper. His bookkeeper did not know how to set up a complete cost system so Black requested management assistance from Bragg. Bragg set up a simplified set of books and instructed the bookkeeper in proper techniques of adequately maintaining records.

Throughout December and into January, Larry had been seeing companies in the Watts and Los Angeles area who had promised to give Soul business. However, when these contracts did not materialize, Black was faced "with paying the salaries of twenty people without having any funds coming in." Because he knew that he would need more CBDO money, he told Bragg that Soul had firm contracts for over $12,000 per week, though Black later admitted that *"I fabricated a client list because I was desperate for the money."*

Bragg's initial suspicion about Soul's "clients" became evident when he "inquired about the details of some of the contracts" and was told that they were "short-term, temporary commitments." His report of January 22, 1971, said:

TO: File                                                January 22, 1971
FROM: Henry Bragg

Two weeks ago I reported that Soul was working on a contract with Coca-Cola Bottling Company involving about $5,000 per month of receivables. I also stated that during the week of January 16 Soul would begin working on a contract with the Neighborhood Clinical Society involving about $10,000 worth of receivables per month. Upon my request for copies of contracts, I learned first, that Coca-Cola had not hired Soul. With respect to the Clinic, I learned that due to organization problems and getting funded they have not been able to allow Soul to come in at this time.

The effect of this is that it will increase Soul's need for funds because it is characterized, as I had said before, by a large *non-income-producing staff.*

Bragg's further "disillusionment with Black and Soul Guard Service" becomes even more obvious in a second memorandum which he wrote three days later on January 25. This memorandum resulted from Bragg's being prodded by the Watts CBDO executive director, Dr. Carl Lindsay (a black UCLA-trained economist), to "find out what is really going on with Soul. Where are its contracts? And what is Black doing riding around in a Cadillac?" "Frustrated and hurt by Black's betrayal," Bragg sent the following report to Lindsay:

TO: Dr. Carl Lindsay                                    January 25, 1971
FROM: Henry Bragg
SUBJECT: Soul Guard Service

With respect to recent developments involving Soul contracts which proved to be *non-existent,* I am recommending that *funds be withheld* from Soul until specific conditions are met.

Being grossly misguided in my approach to dealing with our clients (that is, the presupposition that they are aware of the tremendous

376                                    BLACK ENTERPRISE, INC.

opportunities that we are providing and that this awareness would almost automatically make them deal honorably with the corporation, since jointly we are working toward the same goals; in spite of considerable evidence to the contrary, I felt that my clients were different), I have failed to take certain precautions and follow-ups which were necessary in order to assure myself that my instructions and exhortations were being executed. This notwithstanding, it has amounted to negligence.

With respect to specific conditions which Soul must meet, essentially, the company must prove itself to be self-supportive as of now. Since we have already underwritten all of the company's start-up costs, we should provide additional funds only for the taking on of large accounts whose collection period may cause working capital problem.

In order to reduce his costs, I have insisted that Mr. Black cut his non-income-producing personnel from 12 people to 4; and utilize as many of them as possible as guards. Mr. Black must also provide us with documentation (i.e., letters of agreement or contracts noted by his lawyer) of all services rendered.

Following is a schedule of expenditures by the company as of this date:

| | |
|---|---|
| Uniforms and Accessories | $ 4,423 |
| Renovation, Equipment, Furniture and Fixtures | 10,844 |
| Salaries and Wages | 8,080 |
| All other Expenses | 9,767 |
| Total | $33,114 |

Thus, according to Bragg, Black had spent $33,000 of the CBDO's $71,000 loan and *did not* have even one contract. The seriousness of this problem was confirmed when Bragg received Soul's financial statements for the month of December which showed *no sales* and a net loss of $12,800. (See Exhibit II on pages 389–391 for Soul's December statements.)

Bragg scheduled a meeting with Black on January 26 at which time he stated that "unless Soul is able to gain more of the business that it had projected, the CBDO will have to withdraw financial support." Spurred on by this statement, Black began to accept business at whatever price he could get it. He took jobs for $3 an hour, a rate which was substantially below Soul's cost. Black told Larry Parker that he "had to have more revenue coming in and requested continuous reports on the sales effort." Below is the first sales report which Parker sent to Black:

TO: Gilroy Black                                        January 30, 1971
FROM: Larry Parker

As of this date, I respectfully submit the following sales evaluation and progress report.

Many security surveys have been taken by our staff. From these many surveys, we are currently involved with the following corporations of which we feel will result into sizable contracts in the very near future. The companies in question are:

1. Coca-Cola Bottling Company—Estimated yearly gross income totals $144,000 including many surveillance details as needed throughout the year (which will be often). Our billing for surveillance will be five dollars per hour. We are anticipating this account soon.
2. Fitch and Taylor—The estimated yearly gross income totals $56,150. Due to the complexity of the budget situation which prevails at F & T, it is difficult to estimate their contractual involvement with us. However, the prospect of an early closing looks very good.
3. Earl Housing Company, Inc.—The estimated yearly gross income is $50,904. We anticipate the closing of this contract by Feburary 1. The prospects are very good.
4. Neighborhood Clinical Society, Inc.—The estimated yearly gross income is $34,272. We have been assured by the Director of this clinic that the security contract will be assigned to us within a very short period of time.

We are working on many proposals of which some may or may not result in a contract. Listed below are some of these firms:

1. Phelps Edison
2. Eastern Electric
3. First National
4. Union Gas
5. Reynolds & Company
6. Chemical Trust Company
7. Equitable Savings Bank
8. University City
9. Navy Yard
10. Dr. Greene
11. Benson Burger Drive-In
12. Super Super Markets
13. Western Airlines
14. Gertz Department Store
15. Kelly's Drive-In
16. National Airlines
17. Packers Super Market

18. Pan American Airlines
19. Roscho Super Markets
20. Sterns Department Store
21. George Hotel

This office is using all the sales techniques available to acquire accounts: telephone solicitation, mailings, physical canvassing, and all forms of advertising. It is the opinion of this office that collectors of accounts receivable will commence within the week, consequently resulting in a self-supporting firm in a much shorter period of time than anticipated by the officers of this Corporation.

Though Bragg indicated that he "thought that this and all other reports of a similar nature were written for me [Bragg] rather than for the Soul management, I decided to continue to monitor the business and dole out the funds in small doses." Apparently, Soul's sales efforts began to pay off because sales during the first six months of 1971 were: January—$1,085; February—$8,147; March—$13,755; April—$15,824; May—$17,719; and June—$24,016. Though revenues grew, Soul's expenses far outstripped the sales effort so that the company had a new operating loss of over $44,000 through June 1971. (See Exhibits III and IV on pages 392–396 for Soul's monthly operations and June 1971 statements.) Concurrently with this growth in sales, Black began to hire additional personnel so that by the end of June his staff totalled about forty persons.

At the end of July, Soul had a chance to contract with Kelly's, a major restaurant franchise, to take over the guard service of all its units in the Southern California area. Black had reviewed the proposal with Bragg and they both agreed that it was a good one. Bragg also pointed out to Black that "Kelly's offer would probably enable Soul to be operating above breakeven." At the same time Bragg noted that Soul only had $20,000 of the CBDO funds left and that if it were to survive, it must reduce its fixed expenses to a minimum and secure the bank's $11,000.

On reducing expenses, Black agreed reluctantly, as is indicated by Bragg's August 16 report to Dr. Lindsay:

TO: Dr. Lindsay                                                   August 16, 1971
FROM: H. Bragg

The following information outlines certain cost reductions made by Soul effective August 9. They were not accomplished without one helluva fight, after which we all came up bloody. Contrary to Mr.

Black's foremost fear, his key people held on, to a man, and thereby evidenced considerable company loyalty.

| | Former Weekly Salaries | Present Weekly Salaries | Savings |
|---|---|---|---|
| Vice President | $ 200 | $ 150 | $ 50 |
| Inspector | 180 | 150 | 30 |
| Captain, Night | 140 | 130 | 10 |
| Captain, Day | 140 | 130 | 10 |
| Captain, Field | 140 | 130 | 10 |
| Lieutenants (2) | 260 | 240 | 20 |
| Asst. Bookkeeper | 140 | — | 140 |
| Receptionist | 90 | — | 90 |
| Sergeants (6) | 660 | 540 | 120 |
| | $1,950 | $1,470 | $480 |

Moreover, the six sergeants are now working in the field logging a total of 240 hours per week at an average price of $3.85 per hour, or $924 in revenues per week. Finally the 1:00–9:00 graveyard shift, during which time two sergeants were on duty, has been eliminated. This move generates further savings in utilities and telephone expense. Communications are now made directly to the homes of the officers and other members of the management group during this shift.

Total impact of these salary cuts and manpower reductions, plus the additional revenue, amounts to $1,404 per week, or $5,616 per month. Not included in these figures are the savings in utilities and the preclusion of outfitting six new men at a cost of $120 each, or $720.

Black's accountant has arranged to do ledger work and create monthly statements thereafter for a fee of $200 per month. Finally, they estimate that the total tax obligation approximates $17,000.

Toward securing the bank loan, Bragg prepared a letter to the California Savings Bank in an effort to get the $11,000 which it had committed. Below are excerpts of Bragg's letter to Jim Gong of the bank:

Mr. James Gong                                          August 18, 1971
California Savings Bank
Los Angeles, California

Dear Jim:
    Attached please find operating statistics relative to the activity of Soul Guard Service . . .

To date we have disbursed to Soul a total of $51,370 of a $71,000 allocation, with $19,630 remaining. Their payment to us begins January 1, 1973, by which time you will have been repaid . . .

I had hoped that you would have long since received this material; however, numerous incidents have prohibited its submission.

I shall be happy to provide whatever additional information is necessary for your deliberations, as we move toward finalizing the request for the $11,000 loan.

Sincerely,
Henry Bragg

While Black continued to add to his accounts and negotiate the Kelly's contract, he received the following notice from the Internal Revenue Service stating that unless he paid the tax liability owed, the government would be forced to seize the assets of the corporation:

| | |
|---|---|
| Date of This Notice: | September 24, 1971 |
| Your Identifying No.: | XX-3296872 |
| Tax Form: | 941 |
| Period Ended: | June 30, 1971 |
| Tax Balance: | $10,422.65 |
| Interest Accrued: | $23.78 |
| Amount Due: | $10,446.43 |

FINAL NOTICE BEFORE SEIZURE

Although notice and demands have been made for payment of your Federal tax liability shown above, our records indicate that you have not paid the amount due.

To avoid seizure action, full payment of the amount due shown above must reach this office within ten days from the date of this letter. Your check or money order should be made payable to the "Internal Revenue Service" and forwarded *with this notice* in the enclosed envelope.

Otherwise, *ten days* after the date of this letter, and *with no further notice to you,* we will have no alternative but to enforce collection as provided by law. Seizure will be made of wages, salaries, commissions or other income due you. Bank accounts, receivables or other property or rights to property belonging to you may also be seized.

If you have already made recent payment which has not been

credited to your account, please get in touch with the office at the address shown below so your account will be corrected.

Upon questioning Black, Bragg found that this was not the first time Soul had received a notice from the IRS. Black explained that he had used the withholding taxes as a source of funds when his business volume did not reach projections in the first months of operation. Black felt that if he landed the Kelly's contract, he would pay off the tax liability from its profits.

Impressed with Mr. Black's candor and attitude, Bragg visited the Internal Revenue Service office on October 4 and got them to agree to give Black a thirty-day grace period on the tax situation. Bragg then attempted to get the CBDO management to release some of its committed funds to pay off the tax liability. However, Dr. Lindsay refused this request with the following explanation:

The [CBDO's] contract with the Commerce Department expressly forbids our using federal funds to pay off an obligation owed to a federal office. In other words, since Black owes $10,000 he must pay off that liability *before we can release any further funds to him.*

Bragg's next avenue for rescuing Black was through some large advance payment on a contract or through using the pending $11,000 bank loan to pay off the IRS. While Gong of the bank had assured Bragg since August that "the bank was completing the necessary paper work," the latter was still concerned that the money was not forthcoming.

Meanwhile, on October 21, Black received a call from Kelly's requesting that he, his lawyer, and Bragg meet with the operations manager to discuss the terms of the contract. At that meeting, the Kelly's operations manager said his company would sign the contract with Soul if it was assured that Soul's pending tax liability was satisfied. He explained that "the company doesn't want to do business with a firm which might not be around." Four days later, with the tentative contract and the tax notice, Black went to the bank to request the $11,000. Jim Gong told Black that "it would take a couple of days to get an answer and that he would be in touch by October 28. On October 28, Black received the following letter notifying him that the bank *would not* be granting the $11,000 loan:

Dear Mr. Black:

Please be advised that since our October 25th conversation, the situation has changed here at the bank. We find that it is no longer feasible for us to make the $11,000 loan we tentatively committed to you last year.

With best regards for your continued success, I remain

Yours sincerely,
James Gong

Black immediately placed a call to Bragg, hoping the CBDO would help him get the bank's money, get Kelly's to sign a contract, or release the CBDO funds.

## EPILOGUE

Henry Bragg talked to Gilroy Black on October 28, 1971, and learned that the bank had reneged on its agreement to lend Soul Guard Service $11,000. Bragg was furious since he had counted on the bank's $11,000 being used to pay Soul's tax liability, and without it, Soul would lose the Kelly's contract. Bragg felt that his hands were tied since the CBDO was not allowed to release its funds to meet the tax liability.

Bragg, however, remembered that one member of the CBDO board, Spencer Pompey, was also a member of the bank's board and that he might be able to get the bank to change its position. Bragg called Dr. Lindsay and explained the situation to him. Lindsay took the matter into his hands and informed Pompey of the situation with Soul Guard Service. In requesting Pompey's assistance, he indicated that the CBDO could help Black sue the bank for breach of contract, but that that could not accomplish the aims; moreover, it would not help the bank's already poor reputation in the black community. Pompey agreed to assist the CBDO and promised to get back to Lindsay as soon as he heard something positive. In the meantime, Lindsay, Bragg, and Gil Black attempted to locate another source of financing.

On October 30 Lindsay received a call from James Gong of the bank indicating that a mistake had been made and it would abide by any agreement that it had made to lend to Soul Guard Service. Gong also called Black and informed him that the loan funds could be picked up the next day.

On November 2 Gilroy Black picked up the money and immediately went to the offices of the Internal Revenue Service, where he gave the agent in charge a check for $10,450. Later that day, Black presented proof of his payment of back taxes and signed an agreement with Kelly's to provide guard service to their restaurants in the area. After returning to his office Black informed Bragg that he had signed the agreement with Kelly's and would be needing the remaining $20,000 from the CBDO in the near future. One week later Black picked up a check at the CBDO headquarters.

In a subsequent conversation, Lindsay said:

If we had it to do all over again we would still make a loan to Gilroy Black. Black was one of the few blacks in the country who had been able to get a license to operate a guard agency and the possibility for profit is unlimited. For too long—in an industry where we made up a goodly percentage of the employees—we have not been able to get any of the profits. I was glad to see Gil Black come along. And I believe that we will be able to provide better assistance to the next man that comes along.

In the beginning we did not provide close enough follow-up to Black. As a result, he told us one thing and we could not evaluate it. We had seen no documentation. We were just going on hearsay. Fortunately, Black had enough money so that even though he ran into problems, he was able to survive and go on to do all right. I don't think we will ever allow an entrepreneur to invest as much money as Black invested in furniture and renovations. If Bragg had known better at the time he would only have invested a minimal amount in furniture and fixtures and trimmings and used his money for working capital. But this is the kind of thing that a staff learns.

Before Bragg had a lot of theoretical notions about how things should work. We are now pretty sure that the theoretical sounds good, but we are concerned about the pragmatic if it works. The only other lesson that we are going to remember is that you have to let the man solve some of his own problems. We went to the tax people for Black, when he should have done it. Next time around, we will be a lot smarter and on top of these things from the word go.

BLACK ENTERPRISE, INC.

In another meeting Black shared his experiences. He said:

I made several mistakes and had it not been for the CBDO coming in when it did I would have been wiped out. I started off putting a lot of money in renovations and furniture. Later, when I needed money, I realized that I would have been much better off to put one third of the (same) money into the renovations and furniture and fixtures. I would never do that again and if anybody asked me how to start off I would suggest that they get the bare necessities as far as furniture and fixtures are concerned and save their money for more important things.

Another mistake I made was in staffing up too soon. Here again I could have saved a lot of money that might have allowed us to take on additional work if I had hired people on an as-needed basis. Some of these employees were administrative and I really did not need that many. In fact, after Henry twisted my arm to force me to get rid of some of the administrative people and make them income-producing, I realized the net impact. In the beginning I did not control many of the expenses and as a result, when things got to where breakeven should be, we still were operating at a loss.

And the biggest lesson of all was not to mess around with those taxes. They can get you in trouble. Currently I pay my taxes on a weekly basis—that way I am assured of not having any tax problems. Those Internal Revenue boys will put you in jail for messing with Uncle Sam's money. But if I had it to do all over again, I would certainly do it, because the impact of this business on the community and the city for that matter is tremendous.

## Exhibit I

## FUNDING PROPOSAL
### Golden Ocean Investigation Agency


This is a proposal to request assistance for the Golden Ocean Investigation Agency. We plan to sustain and expand our recently initiated operation and will require approximately $82,000.

This company is potentially a medium-size operation providing security services to industry. Although at the time this proposal was initially presented to you [early April], the company was not operational, it has recently recruited, partially staffed its operation, and negotiated some sizable contracts. Our current plan includes a total staff of 71 employees recruited almost entirely from the Watts community. Based upon recently negotiated contracts, the company's rolls might easily exceed 125 employees.

The Golden Ocean Investigation Agency was organized by me on January 30, 1970 while I was still employed by Sheriff's Detective Agency, a company I was employed by for fourteen years. During these years, I was assigned in various undercover and investigative roles and it was during these assignments that I made several contacts which have provided me with the nucleus of a clientele for this operation.

The company offers a complete line of security patrols, for business and industrial security purposes, armed personal escorts, industrial intelligence and missing persons investigations. Our uniformed security guard service will include armed and unarmed uni-formed guard patrols, motor patrol security and a complete line of polygraph service.

With the steadily increasing rise in business losses through pilferage, vandalism and organized hi-jacking, the ever-increasing need for an operation such as ours is clearly evident.

I am a licensed detective in the State of California and my agency is certified to do business in Los Angeles. I am presently in the process of incorporating this operation.

Because the Golden Ocean Agency only commenced its operations in April, we have no financial statements available. Anticipated clients and revenues are conditionally estimated to be in excess of $42,000 a month. Upon expansion the company expects sales of $54,395 per month.

We feel that my military and employment experiences give a good indication of my management potential. Also we feel that my personal appearance, ability to communicate well, and ease with which I handle interviews are also indicative of my managerial potential.

The company intends to remain within Watts and is currently pursuing leads on office space. We intend to rent approximately 2,000 square feet of space.

To reach breakeven the company will need $84,508. I have a personal cash investment of $2,300 available which leaves $82,208 to be financed. These monies will be used as follows:

| | |
|---|---:|
| Initial Operating Cash Balance | $18,180.00 |
| Accounts Receivable | 54,540.00 |
| Machinery, Equipment and Furniture | 10,558.00 |
| Fixtures, Renovation and Organizational Costs | 8,100.00 |
| Uniforms and Accessories | 5,250.00 |
| Total | $96,628.00 |
| Accounts Payable, Accrued Expenses | 12,120.00 |
| Grand Total | $84,508.00 |

Please see the following attachments:
                    Weekly Payroll Expenses
                    Monthly Operating Expenses

Weekly Payroll Expenses:

| | |
|---|---:|
| President | $ 200.00 |
| Vice President | 140.00 |
| Treasurer-Secretary | 125.00 |
| Chief Inspector | 120.00 |
| Lieutenant | 100.00 |
| Motor Patrol Sgts. | 74.00 |
| Squad Sgts. (2 @ $74.00 ea.) | 148.00 |
| Typist | 75.00 |
| Secretary | 125.00 |
| Switchboard Operator | 75.00 |
| Investigators (10 @ $15 per wk.)* | 150.00 |
| Uniform Guards (50 @ $70 per wk.) | 3,500.00 |
| | $4,832.00 |
| Fringe Benefits (15%) | 725.00 |
| Total Weekly Payroll | $5,557.00 |

Total Monthly Payroll: $5,557×4.3=$23,895
Total number of Employees=71

\* Undercover agents receive a minimum of $100.00 per week from the client as an employee on client's payroll. In addition, the agency pays him $15.00 per week.

Monthly Operating Expenses:

| | |
|---|---:|
| Rent | $ 300.00 |
| Telephone and Telegraph | 150.00 |
| Heat, Light, Power and Water | 100.00 |
| Insurance and Bonding | 1,800.00 |
| Stationery and Supplies | 600.00 |
| Advertising | 500.00 |
| Repairs | 100.00 |
| Accounting fees | 200.00 |
| Sanitation and Carting | 50.00 |
| Payroll Taxes | 105.00 |
| Business Taxes | 50.00 |
| Machine Rentals | 100.00 |
| Uniform Maintenance and Equipment | 150.00 |
| Legal Fees | 250.00 |
| Total Monthly Expenses | $4,455.00 |

Total Weekly Operating Expenses $4,455÷4.3=$1,035

## Exhibit II
## SOUL GUARD SERVICE

Operating Statement — December 1, 1970 — December 31, 1970

| | | |
|---|---:|---:|
| Sales | | — 0 — |
| Total Sales | | — 0 — |
| Gross Profit | | — 0 — |
| Expenses: | | |
| Salaries and Wages | $2,229.00 | |
| Officers' Salaries | 1,665.00 | |
| Rent | 75.00 | |
| Equipment Rental | 53.00 | |
| Repairs and Maintenance | 50.00 | |
| Auto and Travel | 540.46 | |
| Stationery and Postage | 29.40 | |
| Office Supplies | 809.57 | |
| Telephone | 430.00 | |
| Tolls and Packing | 35.00 | |
| Insurance | 4,200.00 | |
| Advertising | 230.00 | |
| Professional Service | 1,825.00 | |
| Licenses and Permits | 100.00 | |
| Payroll Taxes | 295.94 | |
| Miscellaneous Expenses | 243.56 | |
| Total Expenses | | $12,810.93 |
| Operating Net (Loss) | | ($12,810.93) |

# SOUL GUARD SERVICE

## Balance Sheet as at December 31, 1970

### Assets

| | | |
|---|---:|---:|
| **Current Assets:** | | |
| Cash in Bank | $ 2,792.51 | |
| Cash in Bank | 25.00 | |
| Uniforms | 2,896.35 | |
| Uniform Accessories | 1,526.37 | |
| Total Current Assets | | $ 7,240.23 |
| **Fixed Assets:** | | |
| Furniture and Fixtures | 6,356.04 | |
| Equipment and Machinery | 2,269.34 | |
| Vehicles | 700.00 | |
| Total Fixed Assets | | 9,325.30 |
| **Other Assets:** | | |
| Organization Costs | 375.00 | |
| Deposits | 730.00 | |
| Total Other Assets | | 1,105.00 |
| Total Assets | | $17,670.61 |

BLACK ENTERPRISE, INC.

Liabilities and Net Worth

Current Liabilities:
| | | |
|---|---:|---:|
| Payroll Taxes Payable | $   931.54 | |
| Loan Payable | 705.00 | |
| Loan Payable | 205.00 | |
| Total Current Liabilities | | $ 1,841.54 |

Fixed Liabilities:
| | | |
|---|---:|---:|
| Note Payable — CBDO | 27,620.00 | |
| Total Fixed Liabilities | | 27,620.00 |
| Total Liabilities | | 29,461.54 |

Net Worth:
| | | |
|---|---:|---:|
| Capital Stock Outstanding | 1,020.00 | |
| Retained Earnings — Begin | — 0 — | |
| Profit (Loss) | (12,810.93) | |
| Total Net Worth | | (11,790.93) |
| Total Liabilities and Net Worth | | $17,670.61 |

Exhibit III

## SOUL GUARD SERVICE

Monthly Operating Statements January-June 1971

|  | January | February |
|---|---|---|
| Total Sales | $1,085.00 | $ 8,147.30 |
| Expenses: | | |
|   Salaries and Wages | 4,967.00 | 4,093.46 |
|   Officers Salaries | 2,220.00 | 1,955.00 |
|   Guard Payroll | 322.10 | 2,352.00 |
|   Rent | 150.00 | 150.00 |
|   Equipment Rental | 30.66 | 42.40 |
|   Repairs and Maintenance | 21.20 | 150.25 |
|   Auto Loss | | |
|   Auto and Travel | 82.87 | |
|   Stationary and Postage | 60.00 | |
|   Office Supplies | 291.98 | 116.06 |
|   Telephone | | 531.76 |
|   Uniform Maintenance | | |
|   Light, Heat, Power | 8.31 | 8.31 |
|   Insurance | 189.00 | 733.50 |
|   Advertising | 22.73 | 550.63 |
|   Miscellaneous Expenses | 157.13 | 143.00 |
|   Licenses and Permits | 225.00 | |
|   Payroll Taxes | 464.53 | 568.54 |
|   Bank Charges | | |
|   Depreciation | | |
|   Dog Expenses | | 46.94 |
|   Total Expenses | $9,212.51 | $11,441.95 |
|   Operating Profit (Loss) | ($8,127.51) | ($3,294.65) |

BLACK ENTERPRISE, INC.

| March | April | May | June |
|---|---|---|---|
| $13,754.57 | $15,823.74 | $17,719.38 | $24,016.42 |
| 4,003.75 | 5,039.07 | 5,697.28 | 7,260.51 |
| 2,204.25 | 2,070.00 | 2,230.00 | 2,865.00 |
| 2,997.38 | 7,902.21 | 8,762.04 | 11,959.93 |
| 150.00 | 150.00 | 150.00 | 150.00 |
| 114.56 | 21.20 | 237.44 | |
| 118.22 | 189.14 | 326.81 | 79.24 |
| | | 700.00 | |
| 80.33 | 159.50 | 50.00 | 1,082.71 |
| 246.50 | 165.00 | 263.85 | 433.43 |
| 741.96 | 390.96 | 901.18 | 567.66 |
| | 5.00 | 12.20 | |
| 8.31 | | 170.44 | 124.14 |
| 1,988.64 | 395.80 | 670.00 | 466.00 |
| 1,502.73 | 152.10 | 3,381.07 | 988.35 |
| 548.10 | 997.18 | 584.32 | 990.98 |
| | | 540.00 | 22.50 |
| 616.75 | 1,140.01 | 1,275.13 | 1,733.09 |
| 113.70 | 41.27 | 407.30 | 441.47 |
| 400.00 | 410.00 | | |
| 731.05 | 73.90 | 36.98 | 313.00 |
| $16,566.23 | $19,302.34 | $26,396.04 | $29,478.01 |
| ($2,811.65) | ($3,478.60) | ($8,676.66) | ($5,461.59) |

Exhibit IV

## SOUL GUARD SERVICE

Operating Statement December 1, 1970 — June 30, 1971

| | | |
|---|---:|---:|
| Total Sales | | $80,546.41 |
| Expenses: | | |
| Salaries and Wages | $33,290.07 | |
| Officers' Salaries | 15,209.25 | |
| Guard Payroll | 39,495.76 | |
| Rent | 975.00 | |
| Equipment Rental | 499.26 | |
| Repairs and Maintenance | 983.60 | |
| Auto Loss | 700.00 | |
| Auto and Travel | 1,995.87 | |
| Stationery and Postage | 89.40 | |
| Office Supplies | 2,094.27 | |
| Telephone | 3,563.52 | |
| Tolls and Parking | 35.00 | |
| Uniform Maintenance | 17.20 | |
| Light, Heat, Power | 302.89 | |
| Insurance | 3,142.66 | |
| Advertising | 6,827.61 | |
| Professional Services | 1,825.00 | |
| Miscellaneous Expenses | 3,664.27 | |
| License and Permits | 887.50 | |
| Payroll Taxes | 6,593.99 | |
| Bank Charges | 1,004.02 | |
| Depreciation | 810.00 | |
| Dog Expenses | 1,201.87 | |
| Total Expenses | | 125,208.01 |
| Operating Profit (Loss) | | ($44,661.60) |

BLACK ENTERPRISE, INC.

# SOUL GUARD SERVICE

## Balance Sheet as at June 30, 1971

### Assets

**Current Assets:**

| | | |
|---|---:|---:|
| Cash in Bank | $ 270.27 | |
| Cash in Bank | 11.14 | |
| Accounts Receivable Trade | 6,026.23 | |
| Uniforms | 7,090.29 | |
| Uniform Accessories | 3,586.69 | |
| Advances Employees | 994.45 | |
| Exchange | —0— | |
| Police Dogs | 1,590.00 | |
| Exchange | —0— | |
| Payroll Exchange | 606.64 | |
| Total Current Assets | | $19,635.17 |

**Fixed Assets:**

| | | |
|---|---:|---:|
| Furniture and Fixtures | 10,871.62 | |
| Equipment and Machinery | 2,429.74 | |
| Vehicles | 662.50 | |
| Less: Accumulated Depreciation | 1,570.00 | |
| Total Fixed Assets | | 12,393.86 |

**Other Assets:**

| | | |
|---|---:|---:|
| Prepaid Insurance | 3,514.74 | |
| Organization Costs | 375.00 | |
| Security Deposits | 1,480.00 | |
| Total Other Assets | | 5,369.74 |
| Total Assets | | $37,398.77 |

## Liabilities and Net Worth

| | | |
|---|---:|---:|
| **Current Liabilities:** | | |
| Accounts Payable | $ 8,749.99 | |
| Payroll Taxes Payable | 18,511.33 | |
| Salaries Payable | 1,730.00 | |
| Loan Payable | 550.00 | |
| Loan Payable | 129.05 | |
| Total Current Liabilities | | $ 29,670.37 |
| **Fixed Liabilities:** | | |
| Note Payable — CBDO | 51,370.00 | |
| Total Fixed Liabilities | | 51,370.00 |
| Total Liabilities | | 81,040.37 |
| **Net Worth:** | | |
| Capital Stock Outstanding | 1,020.00 | |
| Retained Earnings — Begin | —0— | |
| Profit or Loss | (44,661.60) | |
| Total Net Worth | | (43,641.60) |
| Total Liabilities and Net Worth | | $37,398.77 |

BLACK ENTERPRISE, INC.

# V

# Looking Back
# and Looking Forward

Part V contains the concluding chapter of this examination of black-owned businesses assisted by CBDOs. This last part discusses the major problems which are plaguing these new entrepreneurs, as well as the problems confronting CBDOs. This final chapter also begins an examination of possible methods of strengthening CBDOs and lays the framework for further study in the area of black business development.

# 13

# PROBLEMS AND SOLUTIONS

## INTRODUCTION

With the aid of CBDOs blacks have made incremental strides in becoming businessmen. Several black communities have had, in essence, access to organizations able to provide financial as well as managerial and technical assistance. In the nine cases CBDOs provided numerous kinds of assistance, often being the *only* agencies willing and able to provide assistance to black businessmen. These nine cases not only related the experiences of businesses and CBDOs, but also began to document the problems encountered by both groups that must be resolved if the blacks are to continue to make appreciable gains in the development of business enterprises.

This final chapter will first assess the continuing problems encountered by black businessmen and CBDOs, and then outline briefly initial approaches for dealing with these problems.

## THE PROBLEMS

### Deficiencies of Black-Owned Businesses

One can probably argue that the problems facing small black businesses are no different than those facing small non-black businesses. While this may be true, it is essential to remember that the black community has had so few business successes that it can afford to have practically no failures. Some of the more obvious problem areas can be summarized as follows: *capital, management, technical experience, fiscal control, marketing, and profit motivation.*

CAPITAL. During a CBDO-sponsored tour of a black ghetto in New York City, a seven-year-old boy remarked: "Ain't nothing wrong with black folks that money can't buy." While this statement reflects a simplistic solution to the problems of black businessmen, implicit is the assertion that proper capitalization guarantees success. While this is not necessarily true, the absence of proper capitalization is certainly a sure path to failure. And capital is certainly one of the ingredients that is always in short supply. As Berkeley Burrell and John Seder said: "Traditionally, if the would-be entrepreneur doesn't know somebody who has money, he will probably never start a business and will spend his life working for somebody else . . . For there is no established mechanism in the American private-enterprise system that provides risk capital to would-be businessmen who do not have collateral or co-signers. The banks do not provide it, Wall Street does not provide it, nobody provides it in the private sector."[1]

Unquestionably, there is an absence of capital in the black community. The nine cases illustrate dramatically this fact as the entrepreneurs were able to provide very few equity funds. Moreover, in several cases, in addition to providing start-up financial assistance, CBDOs also provided working capital to help firms through particularly difficult situations. A Los Angeles CBDO official seemed to articulate the attitude of many CBDOs when he said:

As a group we recognize that there might be, and more often than not, there is, a need for additional funds, since any method used to project the financial needs of a company is based on various assumptions that are in a constant state of flux. Once these assumptions change, then obviously the need for funds also changes; normally the need increases. This is one of the reasons that community agencies can be effective; they have a flexibility at the community level in dealing with various financial situations coupled with an intimate knowledge of each situation.

[1] Burrel, Berkeley, and John Seder, *Getting It Together.* New York: Harcourt Brace Jovanovich, Inc., 1971, p. 225.

Despite the CBDO's willingness and ability to provide start-up capital and working capital, it was apparent that in several of the cases, the question of sufficient funds was paramount. For example, while *Bailey's ARC Transmissions* had a number of problems, certainly one of the most crucial was insufficient start-up money as Bob Bailey was back at the CBDO requesting additional assistance after only a few months of operation. The proposal used to request his funds was based on the optimistic projections submitted by the franchisor, without any contingency provisions. Thus, as a Detroit CBDO official stated: "When the assumptions change, so do the needs for funds—and that usually means up." Similarly, cash shortages were encountered by *Merritt Plastics* and *Clark's Creations*. Ken Alston attempted starting a plastics manufacturing operation with only $95,000, most of which was to go into machinery. Cal Clark likewise was given only $45,000 to launch a dress manufacturing operation and he had to go back to the CBDO later for an equal amount of money.

Despite the failure of some CBDOs to provide sufficient funds, two of the entrepreneurs were able to get their insufficient funds supplemented soon enough to turn their businesses around. Larry Holmes, the owner of *Larry's Radio and TV Service,* received a loan of only $3,500 but was able to survive with the subsidies—painting and renovation—provided by the CBDO. *Four Brothers Trucking Company* agreed to a total loan of less than $100,000 when the firm needed about $150,000. Moreover, the Roxbury CBDO allowed the firm to purchase a building, thereby weakening its position even more. However, it was able to stave off the creditors until the CBDO arranged additional funds. These two, and similar cases where the businessmen started off with insufficient funds and were able to effect a turnaround, represent the exception rather than the rule since at any point these businesses could have gone under. Thus with the odds heavily weighed against black businessmen making a go of it, it seems clear that they must at least start off with sufficient funds.

MANAGEMENT. Management in any business is an ingredient essential to success since it charts the course and coordinates the systems to accomplish its goals. In the absence of good management, there is no direction and coordination and the business flounders helplessly. All nine cases illustrated problems with management, though some were more severe than others. And whereas in some cases the owners were willing to supplement their management inadequacies with assistance from CBDOs, in others the owners had neither the necessary management skills nor the desire to accept management assistance from the CBDOs. Cal Clark of *Clark's Creations* was advised not to attempt to manufacture but to design and contract out the production. When he refused to do so, he was unable to coordinate all of the manufacturing activities and consequently was never successful. In contrast the owners of *Larry's Radio and TV Service* and *Albert's Originals* had limited management skills, but were willing to let their respective CBDOs assist them and consequently were able to achieve some measure of success.

Although the CBDOs' management assistance was not always the best, it was there on a continuous basis, and as their staffs grew in experience, the CBDOs were able either to render good assistance or to find it from outside sources. *Jeff's All-Star Ribs* is an excellent example of the kind of unique technical assistance that CBDOs have provided to save a business. When Jefferson Davis was faced with territorial infringement from All-Star Ribs, Inc., the Baltimore CBDO staff immediately went to work to protect his interest. Its lawyers and financial analysts all joined in to effect a favorable solution to the problem.

TECHNICAL EXPERIENCE. Businessmen will be able better to minimize their problems if they have a working knowledge of the "delivery" operations of a business. Four factors support this rationale: 1) the entrepreneur will know how to provide the products or services; 2) he will have a working knowledge of the industry's problems and practices; 3) he will know the sources of supply for raw materials and methods of distribution; and 4) he will be able to solve start-up problems in a shorter period of time.

In several of the cases, the owners' inexperience contributed greatly to the demise of the businesses since it forced them to make numerous costly mistakes that might have otherwise been avoided. From the outset Ken Alston (*Merritt Plastics*) had no understanding of the plastics business and was totally unable to deal with marketing, costing, or machinery requirements. Instead, he had to spend most of his time learning the business while incurring expenses for labor, overhead, and materials. Similarly, Cal Clark (*Clark's Crea-*

*tions*) was a designer and did not really understand the nature of dress manufacturing and the need to plan for his market. Even though trained by the franchisor, Bob Bailey (*Bailey's ARC Transmissions*) had no working knowledge of the transmission repair business and consequently was unable to supervise his employees or check their work to ensure that he was getting optimal productivity. This raises the question of whether franchisees can be trained in all technical areas, regardless of the skill requirements.

FISCAL CONTROL. Another crucial area where black businessmen are often found lacking is in fiscal control—an adequate record-keeping system which ensures that management is always informed of the status of the business' various components. Moreover, such a system ensures that management has the information necessary to make good business decisions. Examples of inadequate fiscal control were found in several cases. For example, the Atlanta CBDO found that *Albert's Originals'* record keeping was especially poor in inventory control, purchasing, and accounts receivable. The lack of fiscal control was especially crucial in accounts receivable, where the absence of sufficient records made it difficult for Albert to determine what bills were scheduled to be collected. Similarly, he was unable to price his goods properly and to determine his cash flow position so that it was only at the last minute that he learned he did not have sufficient funds.

Another case that illustrated the problems caused by poor fiscal control was *Soul Guard Service*. Gilroy Black never was able to determine adequately his overhead costs. As a result, he continued to carry an expensive core staff that jeopardized his cash position. As a result of deficiencies like these, many of the black businessmen were unable to make sound decisions, a condition which contributed to their complete failures or, at best, weakened positions.

MARKETING. Another recurring problem for many of the businessmen was the absence of effective marketing, a critical area for any firm since it affects the ability of the firm to sell its goods or services. Many of the entrepreneurs assumed that just because they could produce a product or a service, they could sell it without any thought to competition or to reaching the market. Ken Alston of *Merritt Plastics* never clearly defined or attacked his market because he believed that an "interest" in his products amounted to a desire to buy them. For example, he believed that he had $400,000 in "orders" when actually the firm only sold about 10 per cent of that amount.

Just as Alston "sold for the sake of selling" so did Cal Clark of *Clark's Creations* design for the sake of designing. As one CBDO report said:

> . . . he has not shown that he is capable of modifying his creative designs so that they can be directed toward a specific "hole" in the market . . . Many of his silk-screen designs have already been knocked off by machine silk-screeners who achieve a remarkably similar effect for much less money. They make many of Clark's things non-competitive . . .
> This kind of information seems to have no effect on the direction of Clark's creativity. The problem is that he is creating in a vacuum.

Thus, instead of creating with an eye toward selling his creations, Clark created only to satisfy his own need to create. Thus, businessmen should make sure that they have a market and some plan of action to reach it.

PROFIT MOTIVATION. In business, motivation is an intangible quality which makes an individual want to succeed, no matter what the cost. One might view it as a "creative insecurity" which forces a man not to accept his lot. Consequently, he is forever seeking new levels of achievement. It is clear from the nine case studies that motivation is a key ingredient to ensuring success in a business. Seemingly always unanswered is how motivation is translated into successful business operations. "Wanting to succeed," or "wanting to go into business" does not ensure success. The evidence in the cases suggests that if the entrepreneur is to be successful, his motivation must be directed toward the basic business goal of profitability. Therefore, essential for the successful development of a business development program are entrepreneurs who are characterized by a high degree of *profit motivation*.

In our nine cases, several of the owners seemed to lack this essential ingredient, with *Soul Guard Service* and *ABC Shoe Store* being good examples. In his first six months of operations, Gil Black exhibited this lack of profit motivation by unwisely investing over 25 per cent of his total appropriation in renovations that made his offices look like "a brokerage house." Black also maintained a large staff, even when the business had no sales. On top of that he paid them substantially more than the going wages in the industry, a practice which contributed greatly to his high monthly outlays. As a Watts CBDO official observed: "Gil was like a man intent on giving away money instead of making a profit."

Perhaps the most complicated instance of a lack of profit motivation was that of Tommy Mann of *ABC Shoe Store*. Initially Mann had a profitable operation, but in his foolish quest for an even greater return he made poor investments with funds which his shoe store needed. The criticism here is that Mann was imprudent in his use of funds, a serious violation of any guidelines if one is really interested in making his business a going concern. Since the objective of any business—old or new—is to make profits, it is absolutely necessary for the Gil Blacks and Tommy Manns to have a high degree of profit motivation. This profit motivation should force them to incur only the most necessary costs and to watch every dollar as though it were their last. New firms, especially, cannot afford to spend large sums of money for non-essentials, but must wait until the business has developed profits *and* a positive cash flow before even considering "luxury" expenditures. For, as we saw, if funds are expended injudiciously this can spell the end of the firm, a condition the black community can ill afford.

## The CBDO and Its Problems

As one can surmise from the case studies, CBDOs across the country have been and will probably continue to be one major difference between the success and failure of many black-owned ventures. It is not simply a matter of financial and management assistance, but of the presence of an entity whose primary function is to promote business development in the black community. The importance of the CBDO was seen in a number of ways; although because the CBDO is *also* a new business, it too has its problems.

Follow-up discussions with many black businessmen assisted by CBDOs elicited a variety of responses about the value of CBDOs. Some entrepreneurs were noticeably hostile because of the dictates laid down by the CBDO staff; some felt that they should have gotten more financial support; and others felt that CBDO management assistance specialists left them too early or were too demanding on them to assess problem situations. Almost all, however, admitted that the faults they found with CBDOs were relatively minor and in sharp contrast to the many strengths of CBDOs. Moreover none believed that they would have gotten the chance to be businessmen without the aid of the CBDOs. Regardless of the faults that they found, the businessmen spoke highly of the major services provided by CBDO staffs: financial and managerial assistance.

Despite CBDOs' achievements it is clear that CBDOs have not solved *all* their operational problems. Foremost among these problems are: *funding, follow-up, and staff inexperience.*

FUNDING. For CBDOs to be successful in assisting black businesses, they must have sufficient funds to be able to provide adequate support to firms. Adequate support means not only financial support for investment purposes, but for adequate staff and facilities. While none of the cases dealt specifically with the financial resources of CBDOs, it is clear that some CBDOs did not have sufficient financial resources to offer comprehensive programs.

An official for the Detroit CBDO that sponsored *Bailey's ARC Transmissions,* for example, admits that his CBDO was unable to provide Bailey with a "good business consultant" because its staff had to handle other matters. He said: "Once Bailey had opened and things seemed to be starting off right, we assigned our limited staff to other cases. Although our man saw Bailey at intervals, during the interim, the business continued to get worse. This also meant that our man was operating on a crisis basis rather than being able to plan for the firm. The harm done in the interim was irreparable and ultimately contributed to the loss of the business." Thus while Bailey made many mistakes, a contributing cause of his failure was the inability of the CBDO to master the resources to monitor his progress.

In addition to having funds to provide CBDO support, CBDOs must also have funds to hire external consultant services on an as-needed basis. While these same services might be gotten through volunteers, this might not be adequate for a number of reasons (see Chapter 4). For example, the needs of the business might be as urgent as *Clark's Creations,* which needed production and marketing consultants to ensure that its operations would be able to achieve optimal productivity. Fortunately, the Atlanta CBDO had the resources to get the consulting services needed by Clark. This is not true for a majority of the nation's CBDOs. Thus it is not enough for CBDOs to provide entrepreneurs with sufficient funds. CBDOs must have sufficient resources to provide the managerial, technical, and consulting assistance needed by the firms. Otherwise, chances for success are severely limited.

FOLLOW-UP. Together with adequate support funds, CBDOs must have adequate follow-up systems which, in many instances, can minimize problems faced by businessmen. Follow-up starts with the disbursement of funds and continues periodically to ensure that the owner's administrative controls are operational, that taxes are paid, that problems are dealt with on a timely basis, etc.

Most of the nine cases indirectly showed the value of good CBDO follow-up, though one can certainly see the problems which can result, in part, from inadequate follow-up. And the absence of good follow-up procedures does not necessarily imply an incompetent staff. As in the case of *ABC Shoe Store,* Henry Hollas of the CBDO made only the "small" mistake of not delving into Mann's August operations. Therefore, it was in October, after receipt of ABC Shoe Store's September financial statements, that he realized that Mann had taken money from the business. Moreover, by the time Hollas brought the matter to the attention of the CBDO board of directors, it was November and too late for the business to purchase fall inventory, thus starting it on its fall downward.

It seems fair to say that adequate follow-up is indispensable if CBDOs are to give black businessmen every possible chance to succeed. This follow-up allows CBDOs to pinpoint problems quickly and to act before they become irreversible ones. One case which illustrates the use of CBDO follow-up to assist an entrepreneur in solving a problem was found in the *Soul Guard Service* case. Gilroy Black had insisted on several occasions to his CBDO representative, Henry Bragg, that he had several contracts. It was only after the CBDO executive director insisted that Bragg demand the whereabouts of the contracts that he found that Soul Guard had no contracts. Bragg was then able to force Black to begin to contract for services so that at least a portion of his costs was covered. Though Gil Black did eventually encounter problems because of operating indiscretions, the situation could have been disastrous if the CBDO had not remained close to Black's business operations.

STAFF INEXPERIENCE. In the final analysis, no CBDO can really be stronger than its weakest staff member since, like any management consulting firm, CBDOs are selling people. A weak link in the staff chain can lead to the quick death of a business. In CBDOs across the country, inexperience on the parts of staffs has contributed in various degrees to the problems of black entrepreneurs. While most businessmen possess some technical skills, capital, and profit motivation, many are usually lacking in management and technical skills and they look to CBDOs for guidance. It is difficult indeed for a CBDO to assist when its staff does not possess sufficient experience itself.

In the *Merritt Plastics* case, Vince Edwards of the Chicago CBDO indicated that "Merritt Plastics is one of our most promising businesses," without having taken one look at the operating statements. In another instance Edwards indicated that "the company is doing quite well since it has a full line of products, a complete insurance package, and a market that it can handle." As we now know this was simply overoptimism brought on by inexperience.

*Albert's Originals* is a case which is indicative of CBDOs which supply too much assistance because of their inexperience. In this case, the CBDO management assistance specialist took it upon himself to handle many problems that Albert should have been capable of handling: speaking to the landlord about keeping the stairwells clean and asking Albert's customers to pay money due him. The issue here is not whether Albert needed these things, but whether they were more properly his responsibility or the CBDO's. Or as one CBDO executive director said: "Our staff's inexperience sometimes perpetuates the man's [businessman's] problems since we do too much for him so *we* can learn."

Concomitant with the lack of experience on the part of CBDO staffs is their corresponding lack of training in the various technical specialties of the businesses. The result is obvious: it is difficult to help someone else if you do not have the requisite skills. In such a case the staff member is liable to make the same mistakes that the entrepreneur himself might make. The cases of *Merritt Plastics* and *Bailey's ARC Transmissions* illustrate the problems caused by the absence of adequately trained CBDO personnel. Vince Edwards' background and training were in economics and insurance, neither of which prepared him to analyze Merritt's operations. Consequently, all he did was report on events at Merritt without being able to make a thorough analysis of the significance of those events. Similarly, none of the CBDO staff persons assigned to *Bailey's ARC Transmissions* had any experience with auto mechanics. MBA degrees are good for business management, but they do not generate transmission profits. While these cases do not suggest that every CBDO should hire a plastics expert or auto mechanic, they do point the way to having specialized consultants on call to the CBDO.

OTHER PROBLEMS. Two other problems which are common to CBDOs' operations are the (1) assigning of risk and (2) uncoordinated economic activities. Before moving into the final section of the book, we will touch upon these briefly.

*Personal risk or personal responsibility* can be a crucial variable in determining the success of a business. One could argue that it is important that funds not be given too freely, lest they defeat their purpose—to generate profits. For in the absence of risk, one may no longer be concerned with profitability and funds may be used injudiciously for non-economic goals. This point is certainly brought home in several of the cases in which the owners incurred little, if any, risk.

Cal Clark (*Clark's Creations*) had little concern with whether his business was profitable, so long as he was pleased with his designs. Ken Alston (*Merritt Plastics*) spent the CBDO's $250,000 as if "the well would never run dry." And in the only case of obvious outright mismanagement of funds, Tommy Mann used *ABC Shoe Store's* profits for personal gains. Certainly if an entrepreneur is to be successful, he must feel some responsibility for the funds invested in his venture; therefore, CBDOs must determine how they are going to pass on enough risk to ensure a higher degree of entrepreneurial performance.

A final problem that CBDOs must begin to face squarely is that of their *uncoordinated business development activities*. The development of businesses should be part of a larger economic pattern so that the black community is not overrun with competing businesses. As former director of the OEO's Economic Development Division, Geoffrey Faux states: "One of the reasons that ghettos do not attract capital . . . is the absence of organized and integrated economic activity . . . the CDC . . . must organize and nurture the environment for business investment rather than simply act as a venture capitalist."[2]

In reviewing the nine cases, one invariably finds that CBDOs were able to provide financial, managerial, and technical assistance to black entrepreneurs. As a result, the CBDOs' staffs were able to limit the probability of failure, a strategy which does not necessarily guarantee success. However, still to be answered is the issue of how the efforts started over the past few years can be improved to eliminate the problems of both the businessmen and the CBDOs.

## STRENGTHENING COMMUNITY
## BUSINESS DEVELOPMENT

### The Black Entrepreneurial Gap

Even with the aid of CBDOs, the strides that blacks are making in becoming capitalists—when measured in terms of how far they have to go—are taking place slowly. Admittedly, not as slowly as before, but slower than necessary, given the needs of the black community. Part of the reasons may lie in American racial attitudes. In addition, several other conditions contribute to the black entrepreneurial gap. Among these are:

1. The relative scarcity of CBDOs in the country (about one hundred in 1972), the majority of which are concentrated in urban areas. Yet the problems of becoming a businessman are not confined to the city nor do they necessarily fit the resources of the relatively few CBDOs. Given the tremendous tasks that CBDOs must accomplish, they need tremendous amounts of support—especially financial. Because the financial and other resources of CBDOs have been limited, the gap among black businessmen continues to exist and is

[2] Faux, Geoffrey, *CDCs: New Hope for the Inner City*. New York: Twentieth Century Fund, 1971, p. 90.

BLACK ENTERPRISE, INC.

growing as few blacks have been able to get into business, let alone gain experience.

2. The inability of blacks to avail themselves of advanced training which goes beyond simple profit and loss and involves the optimal utilization of resources.

3. The exclusion of blacks from skilled trades and administrative positions, resulting in their always having to progress faster to catch up with whites in the development of business skills. Blacks are just beginning to go into manufacturing, banking, wholesaling, and other major industries on any appreciable level and it will be years before they will gain sufficient experience and understanding of such areas to be able to progress into more complex ventures.

4. The refusal of the public sector to provide the broad base support needed to encourage black business development. For example, the Small Business Administration (SBA), which was created to perpetuate small business, until the latter part of the 1960s made few loans to minorities.

5. The refusal of corporate America until the mid-1960s to purchase goods and services from black firms. Most purchasing agents would categorically exclude black firms from doing business with their firms. The closing of this valuable avenue of business became a negative influence in the hopes of black businessmen. Thus, while many black businessmen would have preferred to do business with the larger industrial community and gain valuable exposure and experience, they were usually prevented from doing so and had to relegate themselves to a smaller segregated market for their goods and services.

If the entrepreneurial gap is to be closed and blacks are to develop management talent and an entrepreneurial tradition—the hallmarks of successful capitalism—then the evolutionary process whereby blacks have slowly begun to develop skills and experience and marshal capital must be accelerated. In the first instance this means that the CBDOs themselves must start strengthening their own operations. In addition and to accelerate CBDOs' development, a coalition of resources—the black community, schools, business, and government—is called for. All must provide increased guidance and assistance to CBDOs as they strengthen themselves to continue solving the problems of black businessmen. Let us now examine briefly the future roles of the CBDOs and their supporters.

## Continued Self-Development of the CBDO

Though other institutions must become increasingly involved in supporting CBDOs, the CBDO must also contribute to its own development. Three areas which are relevant to this strengthening are financial, communication, and coordination.

First, CBDOs must begin to become financially independent, for only by becoming so can they begin to exert more control over their operations. There are a number of ways that they can approach independence, each depending on the circumstances of the particular community. In some areas, it will be feasible for CBDOs to take greater equity portions in the businesses they assist and as these businesses grow, the value of the CBDOs' investments will also increase. Or CBDOs might acquire and operate businesses themselves with the profits being used as investment seed money for black entrepreneurs. Regardless of how some degree of financial independence is achieved, CBDOs could then be more responsive to the needs of community residents instead of to government and other funding sources.

A second major problem is an absence of good inter-CBDO communication. As this book went into production, no effective network existed so that CBDOs could share experiences with each other. In the absence of a clearinghouse, CBDOs often duplicate the ineffective work of each other. For example, a southern CBDO developed a portable fruit-processing plant and encountered several problems inherent in the start-up of the operation. Unfortunately, there was no formalized way for another CBDO to know of the work of the southern CBDO and more importantly, that that CBDO scrapped the project because it was unprofitable. Thus a West Coast CBDO later went through the same process before finally realizing that its operation was equally unprofitable. This represented a loss of valuable funds and a poor utilization of staff resources. A formalized national CBDO clearinghouse with a communication organ would certainly be an invaluable asset to all CBDOs, since one of their strengths must be an ability to transfer their learning experiences to one another.

Finally the many CBDOs in large urban areas like New York, Chicago, and Los Angeles must begin to cooperate. Since in each city CBDOs are funded separately, there is always a tendency for them to compete with each other. This overzealousness can sometimes do serious injury to the community since one CBDO can be played off against another by government, businesses, and foundations in terms of the funds to be allocated.

Where more than one CBDO exists in an area, they should make an effort to communicate on a periodic basis to reduce duplication of effort. One clear advantage of the proximity of such CBDOs is their ability to exchange information on projects. CBDOs might also agree to various categories of ventures being divided among themselves. Similarly, the presence of more than one CBDO in an area could be utilized to joint-venture projects, thus reducing the financial commitment of each CBDO.

## Improved Outside Support for the CBDO

THE INFLUENCE OF THE BLACK COMMUNITY. Any non-CBDO effort to strengthen black business development must necessarily start with the black community itself. Thus concerned citizens in every black community interested in developing indigenous businesses should seriously consider CBDOs as vehicles for achieving their objectives. These citizens should exert whatever influence they can in influencing the exact role of their community's CBDO since history shows that CBDOs can go in a variety of directions. In one city, a CBDO funded a shopping center, an electronics plant, and a chain of supermarkets. In another, a CBDO assisted in the development of a public housing project. In a third, a CBDO-sponsored electronics plant made a sizable profit in its second year of operation, while in still another, a CBDO made investments of over $4 million in fifty small businesses and created a $100 million mortgage pool for ghetto residents. Thus, while there is little question that CBDOs can and do contribute to community economic development, it is important that the affected community residents be involved, insofar as possible, in influencing how these community agencies attack economic problems.

A NEW AND INCREASED ROLE FOR THE COLLEGES. One of the most crucial problems facing the black community is the development of persons who understand the processes involved in starting businesses, leveraging money, and assessing risky situations. These persons must also be able to diagnose business problems and find solutions. Granted that the number of blacks with managerial talent is on the increase as more blacks avail themselves of the opportunity to study business administration in colleges and graduate schools. Yet this group represents only a small part of the black population. Moreover, there is the question of how to help those who are unable to pursue the traditional business academic career. Thus the colleges of the country must turn their attention to providing specialized programs to foster business development in the black community.

For example, one significant contribution to the growth of the black business community would be through colleges assisting in the training of black businessmen. While several schools now have programs to help black entrepreneurs, the ingredient we suggest adding is that these programs should be operated in *conjunction* with CBDOs. The colleges could join with CBDOs which recognize, because of their direct involvement, the specialized skills necessary for black businessmen to be successful, and together they could develop a program tailored specifically to their needs. Utilizing the experiences of CBDOs, colleges could develop basic as well as advanced management training programs. The basic management training program would impart an understanding of the functional areas of business and would be designed for businessmen who have minor, if any, involvement in business. The advanced management training program would seek to provide additional training for minority entrepreneurs who have been reasonably successful, but who still need additional knowledge in specialized areas. Such courses could be designed so that they met at hours convenient for working people and would offer theory as well as applications of proper business techniques with emphasis on making profits and surviving in the world of business.

Just as colleges can assist black businessmen directly, they can help them *indirectly* through assisting CBDOs in areas where the latters' short histories leave them in relatively weakened positions. Colleges have utilized their research facilities to solve problems of health, science, etc. and now they should explore the possibility of providing research for CBDOs. This business research component would then permit CBDOs to utilize their manpower more efficiently, since CBDO staffs would then be able to spend more time at direct financial, management, and technical assistance.

BUSINESS AND THE CBDO. Without a doubt, American business—industrial and financial institutions—can contribute to the CBDOs' effort to increase the number of *successful* black businessmen. First, businesses could lend senior executives to CBDOs on an intermediate or short-term basis. The CBDOs would utilize the talents of these executives in assisting them in planning, designing, and developing new programs. Some executives could run training programs for employees of the business firms; others could help with the layout of new projects; and others could counsel on how to obtain financing.

Second, business with its multiplicity of needs for goods and services could establish an arrangement with the CBDOs to encourage blacks to supply more of these goods and services. Most black businessmen have had bad experiences with large industrial firms, or they have heard stories of the difficulties of doing business with white firms. Consequently, many no longer approach firms outside of the black community. By teaming up with the CBDO to provide opportunities for minorities to sell their goods, business could fulfill its commitment to help minority groups. For example, in conjunction with the CBDOs, business might arrange meetings between purchasing agents and black entrepreneurs. In this way, the purchasing agents would get a chance to do away with some of their biases and hopefully learn that each has a business need to be fulfilled.

Finally, the business community might explore the advisability of providing direct financial support to CBDOs and/or utilizing their skills to marshal financial support from other sources. Many corporations make gifts to worthwhile institutions and certainly CBDOs can be put in this category. Similarly, other corporations sponsor foundations that provide financial support for worthwhile projects. Through either mechanism corporations could make financial contributions to CBDOs and thereby perpetuate the ideals of American business. Where corporations were unable to provide direct financial support to CBDOs, they might provide some other useful services. These could range from use of their facilities and services to giving favorable long-term leases on property and machinery. In this way the same end is achieved as though some direct financial support were given.

Banks and financial institutions can also provide unique services to CBDOs. In addition to providing increased amounts of capital, they could use their skills in raising funds for CBDOs. Financial institutions have long undertaken the raising of funds and by bringing this kind of expertise to the black community, they could provide badly needed capital to the minority businesses assisted by the CBDO. While more than the usual amount of risk would probably be entailed, financial institutions have the genius to sell other high-risk situations and CBDO-sponsored businesses should be no exception.

THE GOVERNMENT AND THE CBDO. The government—federal, state, and local—must expand its role to provide the leadership necessary for CBDOs to accomplish their goals. To date it has come up with a number of creative programs to assist minorities in business, but the impact of these programs must be accelerated if there are to be positive results.

First, the government must serve as an example to be followed. It should take the lead in pioneering new programs and providing increased assistance to CBDOs. Where CBDOs need help in developing new kinds of businesses or new management and technical assistance methods, the government should reverse the trend of being last and become first in endorsing new methodologies. Otherwise, other institutions might stand off and view the attempts of CBDOs with dismay and skepticism. But given the government taking a position of leadership, the others are more likely to view these attempts in a positive sense.

Second, the government must begin to appreciate that it will take time for CBDOs to realize their full potential since most do not have enough trained personnel and sufficient contact with other CBDOs. Clearly, the nation lacks a systematic approach for utilizing the potential of CBDOs. Thus, what the government must sponsor is an institute concerned with the training of CBDO personnel; the carrying out of expanded research for CBDOs; the development of new ideas and approaches for CBDOs; the providing of a formal means of communication between CBDOs; and the preparation of a publication devoted exclusively to CBDOs and their perpetuation.

Finally, it is a foregone conclusion that if CBDOs are to become more successful in helping blacks become businessmen, the government must provide a major portion of their funds. To increase aid to CBDOs in the short run will not be inexpensive, but in the long run will probably be a lot cheaper than non-utilization of the country's most valuable resources—its human capital. Given adequate financial support, there can be little doubt that CBDOs could greatly increase the number of black businesses in this country. This in itself could repay the funds invested in CBDOs by increased tax receipts from these businesses, as well as the expanded job and business opportunities in the black community.

But the government should be forewarned that as CBDOs grow in size and sophistication, their financial needs will be substantially greater as they attempt to develop larger and more complex ventures. Given the outlook for the CBDOs in the next few years, the amount of financial support provided by the government must be substantially increased; otherwise the learning experiences of the CBDOs will be wasted.


## CONCLUSION

Most of this volume has traced the development of a concept and presented cases which relate the progress of the black community's business development activities. In this last chapter we have discussed some of the problems of black businessmen and the community organizations assisting them, as well as outlined the assistance to be provided by various institutions. *This is not the end of the story, however. It is the beginning.* For the black community is still decades behind the American capitalist system. The CBDOs have been and are doing a good job on a short-term basis. But the black community still needs a long-term economic development program. It is with the next twenty-five years that one should now be concerned if there is to be true black business development in this country. The authors' current effort should provide the springboard for this forward look into this complex subject.

# APPENDIX A

## THE BEDFORD-STUYVESANT
## RESTORATION CORPORATION

The Bedford-Stuyvesant section of Brooklyn, New York, is often referred to as the country's second largest ghetto after Chicago's South Side. It is an area of 650 blocks which stretches over nine square miles and contains about 425,000 persons, of whom 80 per cent are black and another 10 to 15 per cent Puerto Rican. In terms of problems, it has an infant mortality rate which is twice the national average, a juvenile delinquency rate which is double New York City's, only one high school, a high school drop-out rate of 70 per cent, a combined under- and unemployment rate which normally exceeds 35 per cent, one third of its families live on annual incomes of less than $3,000, and many streets are characterized by abandoned cars and dilapidated housing.[1]

On February 4, 1966, Senator Robert Kennedy took a walking tour of Bedford-Stuyvesant. At the end of the tour he visited a meeting of community people where he was told:

We've had enough speeches, Senator. The facts are in. Your brother talked about it better than any black radical. We need action—no more surveys or picture-taking sessions.[2]

[1] Bedford-Stuyvesant Restoration Corporation, *Annual Report*, 1968, p. 4.
[2] Goldman, R. L., *Performance in Black and White*. New York: The Ford Foundation, 1969, pp. 3-4.

After Kennedy's tour of Bedford-Stuyvesant, he decided that he wanted a total program—total in terms of attacking all the ills of Bedford-Stuyvesant and in terms of harnessing all sources of power to the task: the community, the government, foundations, and private business. A key feature was to be maximum funding *and* involvement from the private sector to reduce bureaucratic delays and inflexibility in getting and using money. Under this approach the most important principle was to involve the white power structure and the black community together on specific programs.

Kennedy promised action and on returning to Bedford-Stuyvesant in December 1966, he announced that the area was to become the testing ground for a new experiment in community rejuvenation. The people of Bedford-Stuyvesant, in concert with political and business leaders, would guide and control a massive attack on their own economic, social, and environmental ills.

The method for the implementation of the task was in itself unique. Directing this urban redevelopment effort were two non-profit corporations: the Bedford-Stuyvesant Restoration Corporation and the Bedford-Stuyvesant Development and Services (D & S) Corporation. Restoration's twenty-six board members were local residents who were to set priorities and direct programs. D & S's twelve-man board, whose membership was drawn from the nation's business establishment, was to be responsible for providing supportive services to the Restoration Corporation.

Though Kennedy did not expect it, persuading white businessmen to join his effort was not an arduous task. First he approached Andre Meyer, the powerful chairman of Lazard Freres, a large investment house. He believed if Meyer would enroll, others might more easily fall into line. According to Robert Goldman:

The argument to Meyer was that the existing anti-poverty and welfare programs were not adequate to the needs of the ghetto . . . and that what was needed was an ingredient hitherto missing from ghetto development programs: the influence and problem solving capabilities of America's business leaders. Here was the opportunity to put this capability to use in . . . the urban crisis.[8]

[8] Goldman, *op. cit.*, p. 22.

After Meyer had agreed to join the D & S board, Kennedy then called on each of the other men he had in mind and got their agreement to join the D & S board.[4] Having formed the white board, he turned his attention to forming the black partner, a task which proved to be more difficult than his previous recruiting effort.

Kennedy's consultations with the community began in the spring of 1966 and were, at best, sporadic since his main concern was the identification of funds and the formation of the white board. Through the assistance of a local civic leader, Kennedy was successful in getting the Bedford-Stuyvesant Renewal and Rehabilitation (R & R) Corporation started in the winter of 1966. However, by the end of the year a power struggle between factions of the R & R Corporation developed over the choice of the executive director. This dispute was the culmination of a series of disputes which convinced part of the R & R board leadership and Kennedy that his objectives could only be accomplished by changing the make-up of the community board. The result of this struggle was the formation of a new community corporation— the Restoration Corporation—which was announced on March 31, 1967.

In June 1967 the Bedford-Stuyvesant partners submitted a two-year funding proposal to the United States Department of Labor under Title I, Part D of the Economic Opportunity Act of 1964, a section commonly referred to as the Special Impact Program. In part, the proposal said:

. . . D & S and Restoration, as joint sponsors, hereby apply for a two-year grant pursuant to Title I, Part D of EOA, in the amount of $7,000,000, to be matched by a non-federal contribution of at

[4] The twelve original members of the D & S board were Meyer; William Paley, chairman of CBS; C. Douglas Dillon, former Secretary of the Treasury; David E. Lilienthal, chairman of Development and Resources Corporation; George S. Moore, chairman of the First National City Bank; James F. Oates, Jr., chairman of the Equitable Life Assurance Society; Thomas J. Watson, chairman of IBM; J. M. Kaplan of the Kaplan Fund; Benno Schmidt, managing partner of J. H. Whitney and Company; Roswell Gilpatric, senior partner in Cravath, Swaine & Moore; Senator Jacob Javits; and Kennedy himself.

least $778,000 in cash or kind, for the conduct of the following programs.[5]

The partners' second important source of funds was the Ford Foundation. The Foundation decided to set aside $750,000 for general administrative support to be dispensed in two stages: $350,000 at the outset, and the remaining $400,000 to match additional privately raised funds. In addition to these grants, the partners received approximately $2,000,000 more from other foundations and private sources during their first two years of operation.

Under the Special Impact (SIP) grant, the partners agreed to operate the following programs in the initial two years:

- *Economic Development*—to develop locally owned businesses through the operation of a loan program; to attract plants into the community; and induce national companies to locate franchises in the community.
- *Community Facility*—to build an office building for the partners and other community organizations with the renovation work being done by local contractors, using local unskilled labor where possible.
- *Community Planning*—to train local residents to participate in and direct their own community planning. It involved training a survey team and the establishment of two neighborhood centers which would develop programs.
- *Home Improvement Program*—to recruit local unemployed men and train them in basic exterior renovation skills so that they could repair the exterior fronts of brownstone houses in selected blocks.
- *Manpower*—subcontracted by the partners to Opportunities Industrialization Center (OIC), this effort was to provide job training.

The Ford Foundation and other private funds were to be used by the following programs:

- *Mortgage Pool*—a fund to be used to finance FHA-insured mortgages for local residents.
- *Scattered Housing Program*—a revolving fund to renovate abandoned property and resell it to community residents.
- *Superblock*—a new construction effort designed to create a parklike area for use by community residents.

[5] Bedford-Stuyvesant Restoration and D & S Corporations' joint application to the U. S. Department of Labor, June 23, 1967, p. 8.

- *"Inside Bedford-Stuyvesant"*—a local television show focusing on the community and Restoration programs.

Of all of Restoration's programs during its formative years, the most crucial was local business development. This program emphasized the establishment and expansion of business enterprises owned and operated largely by local residents. The philosophy supporting this approach was that any move at improving a community's economic base must include the development of the residents' undernourished pride of ownership. While non-residents occasionally received aid under local business development, such aid clearly had to benefit the residents of Bedford-Stuyvesant.

Restoration began hiring staff for its business development component in July 1968, and by the end of the year, the staff had assisted twenty-five businesses in various aspects of their operations. Of the twenty-five, twelve could be classified as manufacturing, seven as retail, and six as service establishments. With respect to financial aid, Restoration provided loans of approximately $1 million to these businesses; of great importance, its contributions stimulated banks and private investors to provide a nearly equal amount of capital.

An important aspect of Restoration's program was that in almost all of its ventures it encouraged the participation of the private sector, particularly commercial banks. While Restoration desired to stretch its financial resources, this consideration was not as important as the local businessman establishing a continuous relationship with banks. To this end, Restoration aggressively tried to convince banks to make their resources available to clients whom both Restoration and the bank saw as reasonably good risks.

Restoration felt that an important task was to provide the means for ensuring that local businesses would maintain their existence and grow into financially sound firms able to pump dollars and job opportunities into the community. It was to this end that Restoration directed its management assistance effort. It adopted a "contact man" system in which each client (businessman) was assigned to a Restoration representative who was given full responsibility for helping that client until a successful business operation was established.

The contact man was expected to provide a wide range of services to the client. These usually started with assisting the client in preparing a request for funds from Restoration and other lending institutions. Typically, the contact man then assisted the client in coordinating Restoration's and the client's activities with a bank, obtaining a business location, and selecting equipment and machinery. In effect, he provided any service which might help a businessman starting or expanding an operation. Once the doors of the business were open, it was his responsibility to ensure that this enterprise would be a success and add to the economic development of the community. The contact man, regardless of his skills, could be a Jack-of-all-trades and often went outside of Restoration to seek specialized skills. However, under this approach, even outside assistance, whether from volunteers or paid consultants, was secured under the direction of the contact man.

# APPENDIX B

## SELECTED COMMUNITY BUSINESS
## DEVELOPMENT ORGANIZATIONS

| Name, City, Year Started | Funding Sources | Activities |
|---|---|---|
| Action Industries, Inc.<br>Venice, Calif.<br>1964 | Financial support has come from the Department of Labor, sale of stock, and Commonwealth United. | Invests in business opportunities that are needed by the community, with an emphasis on retail operations. |
| Albina Corporation<br>Portland, Ore.<br>1968 | Supported by grants from the OEO and the Department of Labor. | Seeks to increase the income of ghetto residents through stock ownership in the corporation. |
| Baltimore Association of Organized Contractors<br>Baltimore, Md.<br>1968 | Sponsored by the Council for Equal Business Opportunity and funded by membership dues. | Provides informational and technical assistance to minority contractors in Baltimore. The program extends free training programs on contractor procedures and techniques to all minority contractors who are members of the dues-paying association. |
| Baltimore Council for Equal Business Opportunity, Inc.<br>Baltimore, Md.<br>1967 | Partially funded by a two-year Ford Foundation grant; local business community provides the remainder of the financial support. | Provides professional counseling to new and established minority businessmen in the metropolitan Baltimore area. The program extends free technical assistance and program information to minority-group applicants who possess some basic managerial and technical knowledge. |

| *Name, City, Year Started* | *Funding Sources* | *Activities* |
|---|---|---|
| Bedford-Stuyvesant Restoration Corporation Brooklyn, N.Y. 1967 | Supported by private contributions, grants from the Ford Foundation, and grants from government agencies such as the U. S. Office of Economic Opportunity (Special Impact Program). | Assists potential entrepreneurs in the area through loans, equity capital, and management assistance where needed. Applies normal business criteria to applicants for loans or equity capital, with the exception that the required amount of owner's equity may be reduced in special cases. |
| Black Businessmen's League Buffalo, N.Y. 1969 | Funded by monthly assessments on its members. | Furnishes informational assistance to new and established minority businessmen in Buffalo. Acts as a broker in providing business technical assistance and expects to develop an investment/financing capability of its own through member assessments and other means. |
| Black Economic Union Cleveland, Ohio 1967 | Funded by the Ford Foundation, the EDA, local corporations, and the city of Cleveland. | Provides financing and free business counseling to new and established minority businessmen in the Cleveland area. |
| Black Economic Union Kansas City, Mo. 1968 | Sponsored by the BEU National Office and is funded by the National Office, the OEO, and private donations. | Provides financial and free technical and management assistance to new and established minority businesses in the Kansas City area. |
| Black Economic Union Los Angeles, Calif. 1966 | Funded by the Economic Development Administration of the U. S. Department of Commerce and the Ford Foundation. | Provides management, technical, and financial assistance to minority businessmen in Los Angeles. Any feasible business is eligible for assistance, with emphasis placed on manufacturing and housing. Funds are available to provide seed money needed to meet SBA loan requirements. |
| Black Peoples Unity Movement Camden, N.J. 1967 | Supported by funds from local industry and the New Jersey Department of Community Affairs. | Provides professional counseling and technical assistance to new and established businesses. Also provides financial assistance. |

| *Name, City, Year Started* | *Funding Sources* | *Activities* |
|---|---|---|
| Brooklyn Local Economic Development Corporation Brooklyn, N.Y. 1968 | A New York membership corporation composed of thirty-one black businessmen from Brooklyn who provided the initial funding. | Provides technical assistance, business counseling, and financial assistance to all Brooklyn minority groups or individuals who desire to organize a new business or revitalize an existing business enterprise. It makes unsecured loans to businessmen for the purpose of supplying the necessary ten per cent equity capital needed to obtain loans from other sources. |
| Buffalo Equity Foundation Buffalo, N.Y. 1969 | Supported by private donations. | Provides equity financing to businessmen who have proof of need and social disadvantage. |
| Business and Job Development Corporation Pittsburgh, Pa. 1964 | An autonomous organization which receives funds for operation from the U. S. Department of Commerce EDA. | Provides technical assistance to prospective minority businessmen in the Pittsburgh area. |
| Businessmen's Development Corporation (BDC) Philadelphia, Pa. 1967 | Funded by sale of stock to its members. | Seeks to establish business for its ownership or which will be owned by independent minority entrepreneurs. |
| Business Opportunities, Incorporated Louisville, Ky. 1970 | Business Opportunities has a twelve-member board of directors, all of whom have purchased shares in the corporation and thus have provided initial funding. | Created by interested citizens through the assistance of the Urban League of Louisville, offers technical assistance and business counseling to local minority groups and individuals desiring to organize a new business or improve an ongoing enterprise. |
| Business Opportunities Program Action for Boston Community Development Boston, Mass. 1968 | Funded by the OEO and is the designated community action agency in Boston. | Provides brokerage services, bringing together businessmen or aspiring businessmen and business opportunities. The program also sponsors an extensive business education program. Services are provided free to interested minority residents of Boston's ghetto neighborhoods. |

| Name, City, Year Started | Funding Sources | Activities |
|---|---|---|
| Chicago Economic Development Corporation (CEDC) Chicago, Ill. 1965 | Funded by private sources, the OEO, the Department of Commerce, and the SBA. | Provides technical assistance to new and established minority businesses in Chicago. It extends information on sources of funds and management counseling to any minority individual or company that needs help and cannot afford to pay for the type of services CEDC renders. |
| Cincinnati Business Assistance Project (CBAP)—Determined Young Men Cincinnati, Ohio 1968 | Administrative costs covered by the EDA. The Guarantee Fund of CBAP, used to guarantee financing from local financing institutions and the SBA, consists of over $300,000 from the Ford Foundation, the Episcopal Church National Foundation, and local corporations and individuals. | Provides free business counseling and financing guarantees to new and established minority businessmen in Cincinnati whose character and business proposal meet with the standards of the evaluating committee. |
| The Circle, Inc. Roxbury, Mass. 1968 | Largely self-financed but receives foundation and government support (the OEO and the EDA) for certain component activities. | Provides financial, technical, and informational assistance in the establishment of new businesses in Boston. Extends both equity and loan capital and provides broad technical assistance to entrepreneurs whose business ventures contribute to broad economic development and offer ownership opportunities to the Boston minority community. |
| Cleveland Business and Economic Development Corp. Cleveland, Ohio 1965 | Funded by the EDA and private sources. | Provides free business counseling, training, and loan packaging services to new and established minority businessmen in the Cleveland area. |
| Colorado Economic Development Association Denver, Colo. 1969 | Funded by several participating banks, a foundation, and the SBA. | Provides access to loans for debt financing from banks in the Denver area. All members of disadvantaged minority groups in metropolitan Denver who are in business or are prospective businessmen are eligible. |

| *Name, City, Year Started* | *Funding Sources* | *Activities* |
|---|---|---|
| Community Economic Development Corporation of People's Development Corporation Washington, D.C. 1969 | Funded by Special Impact Grant from the OEO. | Provides financial, technical, and informational assistance to new minority businesses in Washington, D.C. The program extends equity and loan capital and provides a broad range of technical assistance to entrepreneurs with a viable business proposal who are inclined to sell an equity position to CEDC. |
| Community Industrial Development Corporation Columbus, Ohio 1968 | Funded by the SBA. | Provides financial, technical, and informational assistance to new and established minority businessmen in the city of Columbus. The program extends direct loan and equity financing and free manpower, sales, and legal counseling to assist in establishing inner-city-owned and -operated businesses and industrial facilities. |
| Community Resources for Encouragement of Economic Development Columbus, Ohio 1969 | Financed by its membership through the sale of stock. | Provides managerial and technical assistance and extends equity financing to Columbus area minority entrepreneurs who are unable to obtain financial assistance through traditional channels. |
| Denver Community Development Corporation Denver, Colo. 1970 | Funded by Special Impact Grant from the OEO. | Provides technical assistance to economic development activities; develops community organizations for community investment; generates manpower training and local transportation. |
| East Boston Community Development Corporation East Boston, Mass. 1970 | Funded by Special Impact Grant from the OEO and the Archdiocese of Boston. | Provides a planning staff and financial assistance for the development of needed community projects. |

| Name, City, Year Started | Funding Sources | Activities |
|---|---|---|
| East Central Citizens Organization Development Corporation Columbus, Ohio 1965 | Funded by the OEO, Model Cities, and private donations. | Operates community-owned businesses and provides free technical and informational assistance to new and existing businesses in East Central Columbus. Business counseling and assistance with loan applications are provided on the criteria of profit potential with preference given to small entrepreneurs who cannot get assistance through normal channels. |
| Ebony Development Corporation Baltimore, Md. 1968 | Funding assistance from a Ford Foundation grant, five Baltimore banks, and the SBA. | Provides financial and technical assistance to minority businessmen in Baltimore. The program is a Local Development Corporation under Section 502 of the 1958 Small Business Act which extends direct loans to applicants who are clients of the Baltimore Council for Equal Business Opportunity. |
| Economic Development Corporation of Greater Detroit Detroit, Mich. 1969 | Funded and sponsored by the business community of Detroit and operates as a non-profit corporation. | Acts as a funding source and liaison with the business establishment to minority groups in Detroit which are identified by Inner City Business Improvement Forum. The program also assists in arranging for technical assistance to minority enterprises. |
| Economic Development and Employment Program of the Atlanta Urban League Atlanta, Ga. 1969 | Funding support is derived chiefly from the Atlanta Community Chest. | Provides informational and technical assistance to new minority businessmen in the Atlanta area. The program specializes in acting as a broker between business buyers and sellers and in coordinating assistance to new businessmen. |

| Name, City, Year Started | Funding Sources | Activities |
|---|---|---|
| Economic Resources Corporation Los Angeles, Calif. 1968 | Funded by the OEO and EDA. | Provides financial, technical, and informational assistance to minority-owned businesses in the OEO Special Impact Area of Los Angeles. Extends equity and loan capital and free technical assistance to all minority individuals in the Special Impact Area who have an economic need for capital in starting a business. |
| Fighton Rochester, N.Y. 1968 | Funded by the Department of Labor under its manpower training program. | Concerned with developing an economic base through capital ownership. |
| Gary Economic Development Corporation Gary, Ind. 1969 | Funded by the U. S. Department of Labor's Concentrated Employment Program and the Model Cities Program. | Provides direct management and technical assistance to minority group members interested in managerial advice or financial aid for existing or proposed businesses. The program also refers inquiries to nine other cooperating business assistance organizations of Gary. |
| Greater Memphis Urban Development Corporation Memphis, Tenn. 1969 | Funded by the Memphis Chamber of Commerce and the OEO. | Secures equity in ventures in exchange for capital investments and loans to new and existing businesses. |
| Greater Philadelphia Community Development Corporation Philadelphia, Pa. 1968 | Funded through private contributions and a grant from Philadelphia business enterprises. | Provides financial, technical, and management assistance to encourage expansion of existing businesses and creation of new businesses in the low-income areas of Philadelphia. Special emphasis is placed on local ownership and management in choosing assistance recipients. |
| Greater Philadelphia Enterprises Development Corporation Philadelphia, Pa. 1966 | Funded by the SBA, Job Loan Corporation, and several Philadelphia banks. | Provides technical and indirect financial assistance to minority businessmen in the Philadelphia area. The program provides assistance in obtaining equity and loan capital and counsels owner-managers in sound business procedures. |

| Name, City, Year Started | Funding Sources | Activities |
|---|---|---|
| Harlem Commonwealth Council New York, N.Y. 1968 | Funded by the OEO and foundations. | Stimulates economic development in Harlem and the South Bronx areas of New York. Sponsors a local development corporation which will capitalize new minority-owned businesses in the Harlem-East Harlem community. |
| Hough Development Corporation Cleveland, Ohio 1967 | Funded by Special Impact grant from the OEO and private contributions. | Promotes community ownership and entrepreneurship as a means of strengthening new and established businesses. |
| Inner City Business Improvement Forum Detroit, Mich. 1968 | Sponsored by funds from industry, foundations, the OEO, and local groups. | Provides financial, managerial, and technical assistance to minority entrepreneurs in the Detroit area. |
| Kenwood Oakland Community Organization Chicago, Ill. 1965 | Funded through the Community Renewal Society "Toward Responsible Freedom" Project. | Provides free technical, management training, and referral assistance to new and established minority businessmen who are residents of the Kenwood Oakland Community in Chicago. |
| L.I.F.T. Incorporated Kansas City, Kan. 1969 | Has established working relationships with the SBA and the Black Economic Union as well as with funding sources in Kansas City. | Provides financial and technical assistance in the establishment of minority businesses in Kansas City. The program extends loan guarantees and technical assistance to applicants who cannot obtain funding through conventional lending sources. |
| Massive Economic Neighborhood Development, Inc. New York, N.Y. 1969 | Supported through a grant from the New York City Economic Development Administration. | Offers referral services to businessmen of East Harlem and provides business counseling and workshop programs. Some workshops conducted in Spanish. |
| MEDIC Enterprises, Inc. Newark, N.J. 1969 | Funded by the Greater Newark Urban Coalition, the Center for Community Change, the New Jersey Department of Community Affairs, and the EDA. | Provides free management and technical assistance to minority entrepreneurs whose business proposal is feasible and potentially beneficial to the Newark community. |

| *Name, City, Year Started* | *Funding Sources* | *Activities* |
|---|---|---|
| Minority Contractors Association Dallas, Tex. 1969 | Sponsored by the Urban League of Greater Dallas in association with the U. S. Department of Urban Development and the OEO. | Provides management assistance to minority contractors in Dallas. Management, marketing, and manpower assistance are provided free to enable minority-group members to meet the standard qualifications of the contract construction industry to compete effectively for construction contracts offered by the public and private sectors. |
| North Lawndale Economic Development Corporation Chicago, Ill. 1968 | Funds have come from the local community, Ford, Sears Roebuck and Wiebolt Foundations, and the city of Chicago. | Chief activity is the assembling of sixteen parcels of land for a shopping center, low- and middle-income housing, and educational facilities. |
| Operation Bootstrap Los Angeles, Calif. 1965 | Supported by funds and equipment donated by local corporations. | Develops businesses that will provide meaningful benefits to the community. |
| PACT, Inc. San Francisco, Calif. 1965 | Funded by grants from local and federal government agencies. | Provides direct technical assistance and referrals to financing sources for the formation or improvement of businesses by disadvantaged minority-group residents of the San Francisco area. |
| Progress Enterprises, Inc. Philadelphia, Pa. 1962 | Supported by equity investment from the parishioners of Zion Baptist Church. | Develops viable businesses that will provide benefits to the surrounding community. |
| Reconstruction and Development Corporation Washington, D.C. 1968 | Funded primarily by the Ford Foundation. | Provides financial, technical, and informational assistance to new and established minority businesses in the disturbance-damaged corridors of Seventh and Fourteenth Streets, N.W., and H Street, N.E., Washington, D.C. |

| Name, City, Year Started | Funding Sources | Activities |
|---|---|---|
| San Francisco Local Development Corporation<br>San Francisco, Calif.<br>1968 | Funded with grants from private foundations and the U. S. Department of Commerce, EDA. | Provides a broad range of business services and financial assistance to minority businesses which are economically feasible and of benefit to the poverty community of San Francisco. |
| South Central Improvement Action Council, Inc. (IMPAC)<br>Los Angeles, Calif.<br>1970 | Funded by a grant from the EDA of the Department of Commerce. | Provides technical and informational assistance to new and established businesses within the minority community of Los Angeles. The program extends free technical information to all minority-group applicants in the South Central Los Angeles area. |
| Southern Regional Council, Inc.<br>Atlanta, Ga.<br>1965 | Supported by grants from government agencies. | Provides assistance to minority individuals and groups in finding financial assistance and other resources needed to open or expand an enterprise. |
| Southside Revitalization Corporation<br>Racine, Wis.<br>1971 | Supported by funds from S. C. Johnson & Son, the OEO, and the Racine City Council. | Mobilizes available capital and provides technical assistance for housing rehabilitation, new home construction, and small business development. |
| Southwest Virginia Community Development Fund<br>Roanoke, Va.<br>1969 | Funding support has come from a Special Impact Grant from the OEO. | Activities have been confined to building houses in rural areas and in developing labor-intensive businesses. |
| Talent Assistance Program<br>Chicago, Ill.<br>1969 | Funds provided by the Department of Labor. | Provides free technical assistance to new and established businessmen in Chicago. Extends technical assistance in such areas as planning, marketing, and accounting, through its pool of volunteers. It also helps minority businessmen obtain direct loans and equity financing from banks and the SBA. |

| Name, City, Year Started | Funding Sources | Activities |
|---|---|---|
| Union Sarah Economic Development Corporation St. Louis, Mo. 1969 | Funded by a Special Impact Grant from the OEO. | Provides technical assistance and short-term working capital to minority contractors. Also provides technical and financial assistance. |
| United Durham, Inc. Durham, N.C. 1969 | Funds have come from the sale of various classes of stock to community and non-community residents. | Pursues a broad-based economic growth policy of investing in viable businesses. The profits from these ventures are earmarked for community services. |
| United Inner City Development Foundation Seattle, Wash. 1969 | Supported by funds from the OEO, the National Business League, Model Cities, and the state of Washington. | Provides financial and technical assistance and counseling to minority entrepreneurs. |
| United Minority Economic Council Oakland, Calif. 1970 | Funded by a grant from the U. S. Department of Commerce, EDA. | Serves to bring together various segments of the community to develop businesses which improve the economic health of Oakland minority communities. Provides business referral services to minority members. |

# BIBLIOGRAPHY

Abend, J., "U.S. Negroes Gain Ground in Business," *International Management,* March 1968, Vol. 23.

Adams, Sherman, "Banks and the Urban Crisis," *Banking Magazine,* June 1968.

"Aiding Black Capitalism," *Business Week,* August 17, 1968.

Allen, Louis L., "Making Capitalism Work in the Ghettos," *Harvard Business Review,* May–June 1969.

Allen, Robert L., *Black Awakening in Capitalist America,* New York: Doubleday, 1970.

Allvine, Fred C., "Black Business Development," *Journal of Marketing,* Vol. 34.

Alonso, William, "What Are New Towns For?," *Urban Studies,* February 1970.

Alperovitz, Gar, "Are Community Corporations the Answer?" *Boston* (June 1968), 60:49–52.

————, "The Ghetto & Co., Inc.," *VISTA Volunteer* (January 1969), 4–7.

America, Richard F., "What Do You People Want?," *Harvard Business Review* (March–April 1969), 103–12.

American Assembly, *Black Economic Development,* edited by W. F. Haddad and G. Douglas Pugh, Englewood Cliffs, New Jersey: Prentice-Hall, 1969.

Anderson, Martin, *The Federal Bulldozer,* Cambridge, Massachusetts: M.I.T. Press, 1964.

Ashbury, Edith Evans, "Negro Businesses to Receive Advice and Financial Aid," New York *Times,* June 18, 1964.

Bailey, Ronald (ed.), *Black Business Enterprise,* New York: Basic Books, 1971.

Beard, Charles A., and Mary R. Beard, *The Rise of American Civilization,* New York: Macmillan, 1930.

Bergsman, Joel, "Alternatives to the Non-Guilded Ghetto: Notes on Different Goals and Strategies," Urban Institute Working Paper, 1970.

Bernstein, Louis M., "Does Franchising Create a Secure Outlet for the Small Aspiring Entrepreneur?," *Journal of Retailing,* Vol. 44, No. 4, Winter 1968–69.

"Black Capitalism," *The Economist* (December 14, 1968), 39.

"Black Capitalism: Problems and Prospects," *Saturday Review,* Vol. LII, August 23, 1969. Special Issue.

"Black Cities: Colonies or City States?," *Black Scholar,* April 1970.

Bloom, Gordon F., "Black Capitalism in Ghetto Supermarkets: Problems and Prospects," *Industrial Management Review,* Vol. 11 (Spring 1970), 37–48.

Bluestone, Barry, "Black Capitalism: The Path to Black Liberation?," *The Review of Radical Political Economics,* Vol. 1 (May 1969), 36–55.

Boggs, James, "Black Capitalism: A Dead End Street," *Renewal* (November 1969), 5–10.

Boggs, James, Charles Johnson, and John Williams, "The Myth and Irrationality of Black Capitalism," *Proceedings of the National Black Economic Conference,* Detroit, April 25–27, 1969, 2–9.

Booms, Bernard H., and James G. Ward, Jr., "The Cons of Black Capitalism —Will This Policy Cure Urban Ills?," *Business Horizons,* Vol. 12 (October 1969), 17–26.

Brazer, Marjorie Cain, "Economic and Social Disparities Between Central Cities and Their Suburbs," *Land Economics,* August 1967.

Brazier, Arthur M., *Black Self-Determination: The Woodlawn Organization,* Grand Rapids, Michigan: Eerdmans, 1969.

Brimmer, Andrew F., *Black Capitalism: An Assessment,* Birmingham, Alabama, 54th Annual Meeting of the Association for the Study of Negro Life and History, October 1969.

———, "The Trouble with Black Capitalism," *Nation's Business,* Vol. 57 (May 1969), 78–79.

Brimmer, Andrew F., and Henry S. Terrell, *The Economic Potential of Black Capitalism,* speech given before the 82nd Annual Meeting of the American Economic Association, December 29, 1969.

Burlage, Charles L., *The Small Businessman and His Problems,* New York: Vantage Press, 1958.

Burrell, Berkeley, and John Seder, *Getting It Together,* New York: Harcourt Brace Jovanovich, 1971

*Business Enterprises of Negroes in Tennessee,* Nashville: Department of Economics, Tennessee A & I State University, 1961.

Caplovitz, David, "How the Poor Get Bilked," in Miller, *Poverty American Style,* Belmont, California: Wadsworth, 1966.

———, *The Poor Pay More,* New York: The Free Press, 1963.

Carmichael, Stokely, *Black Power: The Politics of Liberation,* New York: Random House, 1967.

Carroll, James D., and Joel B. Hinks, "The Proposed Community Self-Determination Act of 1968: Summary and Analysis," Washington, D.C.: Legislative Reference Service, Library of Congress, September 27, 1968.

Cervantes, Alfonso J., "To Prevent a Chain of Super-Watts," *Harvard Business Review*, Vol. 45 (September–October 1967), 45, 55–65.

"Cities, Ghettos, and the Call for Community Control," *New Generation* (Summer 1969), 51. (Available from the National Committee on Employment of Youth, N.Y.)

Cole, Arthur H., *Business Enterprise in Its Social Setting*, Cambridge, Massachusetts: Harvard University Press, 1959.

"Community Development," *City*, July–August 1968. (Available from Urban America, Inc., Washington, D.C.)

"Community Development Corporations: A New Approach to the Poverty Problem," *Harvard Law Review*, January 1969.

"Community Self-Determination: The Bill and the Debate," *New Generation* (Fall 1968), 50.

Community Self-Determination Symposium. December 12, 1968, Washington, D.C., 53pp. (Available from the U. S. Senate Subcommittee on Employment, Manpower, and Poverty.)

Cross, Theodore L., *Black Capitalism: Strategy for Business in the Ghetto*, New York: Atheneum, 1969, 258pp.

Desiderio, Robert J., and Raymond G. Sanchez, "The Community Development Corporation," *Boston College Industrial and Commercial Law Review* (Winter 1969) 10:217–64.

Diggs, Charles C., Jr., "The Constructive Rise of Black Business Development in Detroit," Congressional Record, Washington, D.C.: U. S. Government Printing Office, April 3, 1969, 1p.

Downs, Anthony, "Alternative Futures for the American Ghetto," *Daedalus*, Fall 1968.

Du Bois, William Edward Burghardt, *Black Folk, Then and Now: An Essay in the History and Sociology of the Negro Race*, New York: H. Holt and Company, 1939.

Durham, Laird, *Black Capitalism: Critical Issues in Urban Management*, Washington, D.C.: published and distributed by Communication Service Corp., for Arthur D. Little, Inc., 1970.

*East Harlem Business Survey*, New York: Massive Economic Neighborhood Development, September–October 1966, 30pp.

"Economic Development of the Ghetto: Corporate Aid vs. Community Control," *New Generation* (Spring 1968), 50.

Editors of *Wall Street Journal, Business and Blacks: Efforts to Increase Minority Employees and Entrepreneurs*, Princeton, New Jersey: Dow Jones Books, 1968, 1969, 1970.

Edel, Matthew, "Community Development Corporations," paper prepared for The Center for Community Economic Development, Cambridge, Massachusetts, January 1970. (Xeroxed.)

———, "Development or Dispersal: Approaches to Ghetto Poverty," in Jerome Rothenberg and Matthew Edel, *Urban Economics: Text and Readings*, Macmillan, 1971.

Elliot, A. Wright, "Black Capitalism and the Business Community," in William F. Haddad and G. Douglas Pugh (eds.), *Black Economic Development*, Englewood Cliffs, New Jersey: Prentice-Hall, 1969, pp. 74–84.

Epps, Richard W., "The Appeal of Black Capitalism," in Federal Reserve Bank of Philadelphia, *Business Review* (May 1969), 9–15.

Epstein, Edwin M., and David P. Hampton (eds.), *Black Americans and White Business*, Encino and Belmont, California: Dickenson Publishing Company, 1971.

Executive Study Conference, *The Selection and Training of Negroes for Managerial Positions*, Princeton, New Jersey: Educational Testing Service, 1965.

*Experiment in Economic Self-Determination*, Cleveland, Ohio: Hough Area Development Corp., October 1968, 7pp.

Farmer, Richard N., "Black Businessmen in Indiana," *Indiana Business Review*, Vol. 43 (November–December 1968), 11–16.

———, "The Dilemma of the Black Businessman: Clarification of the Current Situation," *Indiana Business Review*, Vol. 44 (March–April 1969), 13, 27–28.

———, "The Pros of Black Capitalism: A Modest Program Can Pay Dividends," *Business Horizons*, Vol. 13 (February 1970), 37–40.

Farnsworth, Clyde H., "U.S. Links Deficit in Payments to Black Unrest," New York *Times*, November 18, 1969.

Faux, Geoffrey, *CDCs: New Hope for the Inner City*, New York: Twentieth Century Fund, 1971.

Fields, Charles L., "Industry's Response to the Black MBA," *The MBA* (April–May 1969), 60–70.

Fitch, Lyle C., "Eight Goals for an Urbanizing America," *Daedalus*, Fall 1968.

Fitzhugh, H. Naylor (ed.), *Problems and Opportunities Confronting Negroes in the Field of Business*, Washington, D.C.: National Conference on Small Business, December 1961. (U. S. Department of Commerce.)

Foley, Eugene P., *The Achieving Ghetto*, Washington, D.C.: The National Press, 1969.

———, "The Negro Businessman: In Search of a Tradition," in Talcott Parsons and Kenneth B. Clark (eds.), *The Negro American*, Boston: Beacon Press, 1965, pp. 555–92.

Forman, James, "Total Control as the Only Solution to the Economic Problems of Black People: The Black Manifesto," in *Renewal* (June 1969), 9–1.

Frazier, E. Franklin, "Negro Business: A Social Myth," in *Black Bourgeoisie,* New York: The Free Press, 1957, pp. 153–73.

Fried, Marc, "The History of Negro Migration to Cities," in Daniel P. Moynihan (ed.), *On Understanding Poverty,* American Academy of Arts and Sciences Library, New York: Basic Books, 1969.

Galbraith, John, *The New Industrial State,* Boston: Houghton Mifflin, 1967.

Gardner, Thomas J., "Problems in the Development of Financial Institutions Among Negroes," unpublished doctoral dissertation, The Graduate School of Business Administration, New York University, New York, New York, 1958.

Garrity, J. T., "Red Ink for Ghetto Industries?," *Harvard Business Review,* Vol. 46 (May–June 1968), 4 et seq.

Gaston, A. G., *Green Power,* Birmingham: A. G. Gaston Boy's Club, 1969.

Gibson, D. Parks, *The $30 Billion Negro,* London: Macmillan, 1969, 300pp.

Ginzberg, Eli (ed.), *Business and the Negro Crises,* New York: McGraw-Hill, 1968.

——— (ed.), *The Negro Challenge to the Business Community,* New York: McGraw-Hill, 1964.

Gloster, Jesse E., *Minority Business Enterprise in Houston, Texas,* Houston: Department of Economics, Texas Southern University, 1969.

Goodpaster, Gary S., "An Introduction to the Community Development Corporation," *Journal of Urban Law* (1969), 46:603–65.

Green, Gerson, and Geoffrey Faux, "The Social Utility of Black Enterprise," in William F. Haddad and G. Douglas Pugh (eds.), *Black Economic Development,* Englewood Cliffs, New Jersey: Prentice-Hall, 1969, pp. 21–37.

Haddad, William F., and G. Douglas Pugh (eds.), *Black Economic Development,* Englewood Cliffs, New Jersey: Prentice-Hall, 1969.

Hallman, Howard, *Community Control,* Washington Center for Metropolitan Studies, 1969 (pamphlet).

———, *Neighborhood Control of Public Programs: Community Corporations and Neighborhood Boards,* New York: Praeger, 1970.

Harmon, J. H., *Negro As Businessman,* College Park, Maryland: McGrath Publishing Company, 1969 (reprint of 1929 edition).

Harris, Abram L., *The Negro As Capitalist: A Study of Banking and Business Among American Negroes,* Philadelphia: American Academy of Political and Social Science, 1936.

Harris, Britton, "The City of the Future: The Problem of Optimal Design," *Regional Science Association: Papers and Proceedings, European Congress,* 1966.

Harrison, Bennett, "A Pilot Project in Economic Development Planning for American Urban Slums," *International Development Review,* March 1968.

Hazard, Leland, "Business Must Put Up," *Harvard Business Review,* Vol. 46 (January–February 1968), 2–12, 168–70.

Heistand, D. L., *Economic Growth and Employment Opportunities for Minorities,* New York: Columbia University Press, 1964.

Henderson, William L., and Larry Ladebur, "Government Incentives and Black Economic Development," *Review of Social Economy,* September 1969.

Hertz, David B., "Is Partnership Possible?," in William F. Haddad and G. Douglas Pugh (eds.), *Black Economic Development,* Englewood Cliffs, New Jersey: Prentice-Hall, 1969.

Hirschman, Albert, *The Strategy of Economic Development,* New Haven, Connecticut: Yale University Press, 1958.

Inniss, Roy, "Separatist Economics: A New Social Contract," pp. 50–59 in William F. Haddad and G. Douglas Pugh (eds.), *Black Economic Development,* Englewood Cliffs, New Jersey: Prentice-Hall, 1969.

Irons, Edward D., "A Positive View of Black Capitalism," *Bankers Magazine,* Vol. 153 (Spring 1970), 43–47.

"Is Black Capitalism the Answer?," *Business Week* (August 3, 1968), 60–61.

Jacobs, Jane, *The Economy of Cities,* New York: Ghettonomics, Inc., 1970.

Johnson, Lawrence, and Wendell Smith, "Black Managers," in William F. Haddad and G. Douglas Pugh (eds.), *Black Economic Development,* Englewood Cliffs, New Jersey: Prentice-Hall, 1969, pp. 112–25.

Jones, Edward, *Black Businessman in America: His Beginning, His Problems, His Future,* New York: Grosset & Dunlap, 1971.

Jones, Thomas B., *How the Negro Can Start His Own Business,* New York: Pilot Books, Inc., 1968.

Josephson, Matthew, *The Robber Barons,* New York: Harcourt, Brace, 1934.

Kain, John F., *Race and Poverty: The Economics of Discrimination,* Englewood Cliffs, New Jersey: Prentice-Hall, 1969.

Kain, John F., and Joseph J. Persky, "Alternatives to the Gilded Ghetto," *The Public Interest* (Winter 1969), 14:74–87.

Kinzer, Robert H., and Edward Sagarin, *The Negro in American Business: The Conflict Between Separation and Integration,* New York: Greenberg, 1950.

Kotler, Milton, *Neighborhood Government*, New York: Bobbs-Merrill, 1969.

Krentzman, H. C., and J. N. Samaras, "Can Small Business Use Consultants?," *Harvard Business Review*, Vol. 38, No. 3, May–June 1960.

Lee, Roy, "The Black Businessman: Career Patterns and Occupational Mobility," unpublished doctoral dissertation, The Graduate School of Business Administration, New York University, New York, New York, 1968.

Levine, Charles H., "The Dilemma of the Black Businessman: A New Approach?," *Indiana Business Review*, Vol. 44 (March–April 1969), 12, 22–26.

Levitan, Sar A., "Community Self-Determination and Entrepreneurship: Their Problems and Limitations," *Poverty and Human Resources Abstracts* (January–February 1969), 4:16–24.

Levitan, Sar A., and Robert Taggart III, "Developing Business in the Ghetto," *The Conference Board Record*, Vol. VI (July 1969), 13–21.

Levitan, Sar A., Garth L. Mangum, and Robert Taggart III, *Economic Opportunity in the Ghetto: The Partnership of Government and Business*, Baltimore: The Johns Hopkins Press, 1970. Policy Studies in Employment and Welfare Number 3.

Lewis, Gordon F., "A Comparison of Some Aspects of the Backgrounds and Careers of Small Businessmen and American Business Leaders," *American Journal of Sociology*, January 1960.

"The Limits of Black Capitalism," *Harvard Business Review*, Vol. 47, No. 1, January–February 1969.

Little, Robert W., and Thaddeus H. Spratlen, "Ownership Alternatives for Inner-City Businesses," *Improving Marketing in the Inner City*, New York: Random House (in press, 1971).

McClaughry, John, "Black Ownership and National Politics," in William F. Haddad and G. Douglas Pugh (eds.), *Black Economic Development*, Englewood Cliffs, New Jersey: Prentice-Hall, 1969, pp. 38–49.

———, "The Community Self-Determination Act, *Ripon Forum* (September 1968) 4:13–14.

McClelland, David C., "Black Capitalism: Making It Work," *Think* (International Business Machines Corp.), Armonk, New York, Vol. 35 (July–August 1969), 6–11.

McEvoy, James, *Black Power and Student Rebellion*, Belmont, California: Wadsworth, 1969.

McKersie, Robert B., "Vitalize Black Enterprise," *Harvard Business Review*, Vol. 46, No. 5, September–October 1968.

McKissick, Floyd, *Three-Fifths of a Man*, New York: Macmillan, 1969.

McLaurin, Dunbar, *The Ghediplan*, New York: Ghettonomics, Inc., 1968.

McNeish, Peter F., "Where Does the Money Come From?," in William F. Haddad and G. Douglas Pugh (eds.), *Black Economic Development,* Englewood Cliffs, New Jersey: Prentice-Hall, 1969, pp. 85–97.

Miller, Kenneth H., "Community Capitalism and the Community Self-Determination Act," *Harvard Journal of Legislation* (1969), 2:413–69.

"Minority Enterprise," *Journal of Small Business,* Vol. 7, April–July 1969, Special Issue.

Morrill, Richard, "The Negro Ghetto: Problems and Alternatives," *Geographical Review,* July 1965.

Moskowitz, Milton, "Black Capitalism—Where It's At," *Business and Society,* a biweekly report on business and social responsibility, Vol. I, December 17, 1968.

*National Black Economic Development Conference on Urban Capital,* Detroit: NBEDC, April 1969, 1p.

Nevins, Raphael F., "Search for Black Management," *The MBA* (April–May 1969), 8–18.

*New Minority Enterprises,* Washington, D.C.: Community Relations Services, U. S. Department of Justice, 1969, 166pp.

Nyhart, J. D., "Urban Development Banking in the United States: An Initial Feasibility Study Based on Simulated Financial Statement Projections," Cambridge: Massachusetts Institute of Technology, 1969, 68pp.

Oak, Vishnu V., *The Negro's Adventure in General Business,* Yellow Springs, Ohio: The Antioch Press, 1949. (Vol. II of the series—The Negro Entrepreneur.)

Ofari, Earl, *The Myth of Black Capitalism,* New York: Monthly Review, 1970.

Osofsky, Gilbert, *Harlem: The Making of a Ghetto,* New York: Harper & Row, 1966.

Panschon, William, "Businessmen, Educators Move to Enlist Black Grads," *Indiana Business Review,* Vol. 44 (March–April 1969), 12–16.

Perry, Stewart E., "Black Institutions, Black Separatism, and Ghetto Economic Development," paper prepared for the annual meeting of the Society for Applied Anthropology, Mexico City, April 1969.

Pierce, Joseph A., *Negro Business and Business Education—Their Present and Prospective Development,* New York: Harper & Brothers, Publishers, 1947.

Piven, Frances Fox, and Richard A. Cloward, "Black Control of Cities," *The New Republic,* September 30, 1967, and October 7, 1967.

Poinsett, Alex, "The Economics of Liberation," *Ebony* (August 1969).

*Proceedings of the Conference on the Role of Black Managers in Society,* Nashville, Tennessee: Fisk University, Department of Business Administration, and Vanderbilt University, Graduate School of Management, February 2–4, 1970.

Pugh, G. Douglas, "Bonding Minority Contractors," in William F. Haddad and G. Douglas Pugh (eds.), *Black Economic Development,* Englewood Cliffs, New Jersey: Prentice-Hall, 1969, pp. 138–50.

Puryear, Alvin N., "Financial and Managerial Assistance for the Black Ghetto Businessman," *Urban Problems and Techniques,* Trenton, New Jersey: Chandler-Davis Publishing Company, 1970.

————, "The Importance of Profit Motivation and Management Assistance in the Development of Small Businesses," *Journal of Small Business Management,* Vol. 8 (October 1970).

————, "Restoration: A Profile of Economic Development," Neil Chamberlain, *Business and the Cities,* New York: Basic Books, 1970.

Puryear, Alvin N., and John Oxendine, "Profit Motivation and Management Assistance in Community Development Corporations," *Law and Contemporary Problems* (Winter 1971).

Ray, Genevieve, "Cleveland: The Hough Area Development Corporation," *VISTA Volunteer,* OEO, October 1969.

*The Review of Black Political Economy,* New York: The Black Economic Research Center (112 West 120th Street, New York City), 1970.

*The Review of Black Political Economy,* Vol. 1, No. 1, Spring/Summer, 1970 includes:
Glenn Dixon, "Outputs of Minority Entrepreneurship Programs," 3–17.
Robert S. Browne, "Toward an Overall Assessment of Our Alternatives," 18–27.
Daniel Fusfeld, "The Basic Economics of the Urban and Racial Crisis," 58–83.
Charles Tate, "Brimmer and Black Capitalism," 84–90.

Ridgeway, James, "Community Development," *New Republic* (August 24, 1969) 159:7–8.

Rosen, Summer M., "Better Mousetraps: Reflections on Economic Development in the Ghetto," Social Policy Papers (July 1968) No. 1, 19pp., New Careers Department Center, New York University.

Rosenbloom, Richard S., and Robin Marris (eds.), *Social Innovation in the City: A Collection of Working Papers,* Cambridge: Harvard University Press, 1969.

Samuels, Howard J., "Compensatory Capitalism," in William F. Haddad and G. Douglas Pugh (eds.), *Black Economic Development,* Englewood Cliffs, New Jersey: Prentice-Hall, 1969, pp. 60–73.

Schoen, S. H., "Qualifying Negroes for Business," *Office*, Vol. 67, February 1968.

Schucter, Arnold, "Beyond Black Capitalism," *Bankers Magazine*, Vol. 152 (Summer 1969), 28–39.

Seligman, Ben, *The Potentates*, New York: Dial Press, 1970.

Sethi, S. Prakash, *Business Corporations and the Black Man*, Scranton, Pennsylvania: Chandler Publishing Company, 1970.

Skala, Martin, "Inner-City Enterprises: Current Experience," in William F. Haddad and G. Douglas Pugh (eds.), *Black Economic Development*, Englewood Cliffs, New Jersey: Prentice-Hall, 1969, pp. 151–71.

Smalley, Orange, "Variations in Entrepreneurship," *Explorations in Entrepreneurial History*, 1964, Vol. 1, No. 3, Series II.

Smith, Howard R., "A Model of Entrepreneurial Evolution," *Explorations in Entrepreneurial History*, Winter 1968, Vol. 5, No. 2, Series II.

Smolensky, Eugene, et al., "The Prisoner's Dilemma and Ghetto Expansion," *Land Economics*, November 1968.

Sorenson, Gary W., "Black Economic Independence—Some Preliminary Thoughts," *Western Economic Journal*, Vol. 7 (September 1969), 287 (abstract).

Spain, James S., "Black Executives: The Darkies at the Bottom of the Stairs," *The MBA* (April–May 1969), 34–44.

Spratlen, Thaddeus H., "A Black Perspective on 'Black Business Development,'" *Journal of Marketing*, Vol. 34 (October 1970), 72–73.

Sturdivant, Frederick D., "The Limits of Black Capitalism," *Harvard Business Review*, Vol. 47 (January–February 1969), 122–28.

"Symposium on Black Capitalism," *Bankers Magazine*, Vol. 152 (Spring 1969), 10–19.

Tabb, William, *The Political Economy of the Black Ghetto*, New York: Norton, 1970.

Triandis, Harry and Pola, "The Building of Nations," *Psychology Today*, March 1969, Vol. 2, No. 10.

Tucker, Sterling, *Beyond the Burning: Life and Death of the Ghetto*, New York: Association Press, 1968.

U. S. Congress, Congressional Record, "The Domestic Development Bank and the Economic Opportunity Corporation," 90th Congress, 1st sess., 1967, Vol. 133, No. 170, October 23, 1967, S113.

Venable, Abraham S., "Mobilizing Dormant Resources: Negro Entrepreneurs," *The MBA*, Vol. 1, May 1967.

Vernon, Raymond, "The Changing Economic Function of the Central City," Committee for Economic Development, Supplementary Paper, No. 6, January 1959.

Vietorisz, Thomas, and Bennett Harrison, "The Uncertain Prospects for Ghetto Development," *The Economic Development of Harlem*, New York: Praeger, 1970.

"Walter E. Washington on Black Capitalism," *Bankers Magazine*, Vol. 152 (Summer 1969), 40.

Walton, C. C., "Speculations on the 'Soulful' Corporation," *Review of Social Economy*, March 1968.

Washington, Booker T., *The Negro in Business*, Boston: Hertel, Jenkins & Company, 1907.

"What Business Can Do for the Negro," *Nation's Business*, Vol. 55, No. 2, October 1967.

"Whose Black Capitalism?," *The Economist* (March 1, 1969), 39–40.

Wilcox, Preston, *The Black Manifesto and the Black Masses*, New York: AAI, July 9, 1969, 6pp. and bibliography and footnotes. (Mimeo.)

————, *Economic Potential in a Ghetto: Credit Unions and Security Deposits in East Harlem*, New York: Afram Associates, Inc., December 7, 1966, 16pp. (Mimeo.)

————, "Education for Liberation," in *New Generation* (Winter 1968), 17–21.

Williams, John, *An Abridged Analysis of the Labor Question*, Detroit: NBEDC, League of Revolutionary Black Workers, April 1969, 14pp.

Williamson, Harold F., and John A. Buttrick (eds.), *Economic Development*, Englewood Cliffs, New Jersey: Prentice-Hall, 1954.

Wilmore, Gayraud, Jr., *The Churches' Response to the Black Manifesto*, Board of National Missions, June 30, 1969, 18pp. and bibliography.

Wilson, James Q., "The War on Cities," *The Public Interest*, Spring 1966.

Wright, Nathan, Jr., *Black Power and Urban Unrest*, New York: Hawthorn, 1967.

Young, Harding B., "The Negro's Participation in American Business," *Journal of Negro Education*, Vol. 32, No. 4, Fall 1963.

# INDEX

Assembly-selected board of directors, 33
Atlanta, Ga., 6
  CBDOs in, 430, 434. *See also* Clark's Creations
  Citizen's Trust Company, 25
Atlanta Life Insurance Company, 28
Atlanta University, 25

Bailey, Robert (Bob), 51–84, 401, 403, 406
Bailey, Ronald, 437
Bailey's ARC Transmissions, 9, 51–84, 401, 403, 406, 408–9
  balance sheets,
    October 1970, 79
    December 1970, 82
  income statements,
    to October 31, 1970, 77
    to December 31, 1970, 80–81
  proposal, 74–76
  statement of financial position, May 1971, 83–84
  statement of operations, January 1971–May 1971, 83
Baltimore, Md., 6
  CBDOs in, 425, 430. *See also* Jeff's All-Star Ribs
Baltimore *Afro-American,* 26
Baltimore Association of Organized Contractors, 425
Baltimore Council for Equal Business Opportunity, Incorporated, 425
*Banking Magazine,* 437, 442, 446, 447
Banks, 42, 415–16
  black, 7, 19, 21–22, 24, 28
Beard, Charles A., 437
Beard, Mary R., 437
Bedford-Stuyvesant, 5–6, 419–24
Bedford-Stuyvesant Development and Services Corporation, 420–21
Bedford-Stuyvesant Renewal and Rehabilitation Corporation, 421

Bedford-Stuyvesant Restoration Corporation, 5–6, 419–24, 426
Bell, James, 224
Benevolent associations, 18–19
Bergsman, Joel, 437
Bernstein, Louis M., 437
*Beyond the Burning,* 446
Bibliography, 437–47
Birmingham, Ala., bank, 22
Black, Gilroy, 3–4, 369–96, 403, 404–5, 407–8
Black, Mrs. Gilroy, 374
*Black Americans and White Business,* 440
*Black Awakening in Capitalist America,* 437
*Black Bourgeoisie,* 441
*Black Business Enterprise,* 437
*Black Businessman in America,* 442
Black Businessmen's League, 426
*Black Capitalism: An Assessment,* 438
*Black Capitalism: Critical Issues in Urban Management,* 439
*Black Capitalism: Strategy for Business in the Ghetto,* 439
*Black Economic Development,* 437, 440ff.
Black Economic Union, 28, 426
*Black Folk, Then and Now,* 439
*Black Manifesto and the Black Masses, The,* 447
Black Peoples Unity Movement, 426
*Black Power: The Politics of Liberation,* 438
*Black Power and the Student Rebellion,* 443
*Black Power and Urban Unrest,* 447
*Black Scholar,* 438
*Black Self-Determination,* 438
Bloom, Gordon F., 438
Blount, Art, 224–25
Bluestone, Barry, 438

income statements,
   November 1970–February 1971,
     107–8
   November 1970–June 1971, 111–
     12
   proposal, 105–6
Johnson, Charles, 438
Johnson, John H., 26
Johnson, Lawrence, 442
Johnson, Van, 67, 71
Johnson, Wyman, 175, 182
Johnson Motor Lines, 282
Johnson Products, 28
Johnson Publications, 26, 28
Jones, Edward, 442
Jones, Mary Z., 317
Jones, Thomas B., 442
Josephson, Matthew, 442
*Journal of Marketing,* 437, 446
*Journal of Negro Education,* 447
*Journal of Retailing,* 437
*Journal of Small Business,* 444, 445
*Journal of Urban Law,* 441
Joyner, William, 52, 68, 71–72

Kain, John F., 442
Kaneel, Ron, 65–66
Kansas City, Kan., CBDO, 432
Kansas City, Mo.,
  All-Star Ribs, 92
  CBDO, 426
Kelly's (restaurants), 379, 381, 382
Kenance Fibres Corporation, 211, 219,
   224ff., 233
Kennedy, John, 27
Kennedy, Robert F., 5, 419–21
Kenneth, Malcolm, 371
Kenwood Oakland Community Organ-
   ization, 432
Kerkoort, Ken, 211, 212
King, John, 263ff., 268, 271, 292
King, Martin Luther, Jr., 26–27
King Moving and Storage building,
   263–65, 268–71, 292–93

Kinney Shoes, 181
Kinzer, Robert H., 442
Knights of Pythias, 22
Kotler, Milton, 443
Krentzman, H. C., 443
Krescent, Chuck, 313ff., 323

Labor, Department of, and Bedford-
   Stuyvesant, 421
Ladebur, Larry, 442
*Land Economics,* 438, 446
Lane, Lunsford, 20
Larry's Radio and TV Service, 10,
   312–30, 401, 402
  balance sheet, May 1971, 329–30
  proposal, 325–27
  statement of income, May 1971, 328
*Law and Contemporary Problems,*
   445
Lazard Freres, 420
Lee, Ralph, 57
Lee, Roy, 443
Levine, Charles H., 443
Levitan, Sar A., 443
Lewis, Barry, 262–65, 268, 270, 271
Lewis, Gordon F., 443
L.I.F.T. Incorporated, 432
Lindsay, Carl, 376, 379, 382ff.
Lineman, Cary, 211–12
Little, Robert W., 443
Loans. *See* Funding
Locke, Sonny, 90–91, 93ff., 99–100,
   101
Lopez, Pedro, 121, 122, 125
Los Angeles, Calif., 6
  All-Star Ribs, 92
  CBDOs, 426, 431, 433, 434. *See
    also* Soul Guard Service
Lynch, Saul, 269
Lynn, Mass., 258, 264

McClaughry, John, 443
McClelland, David C., 443
McEvoy, James, 443